CRITICAL RESTORATIVE JUSTICE

Theories and practices of justice do not meet the socio-political challenges of our times. For those theorists attempting to develop an alternative to the criminal justice system, restorative justice has provided an alternative horizon. The restorative justice approach involves meeting people, and understanding and recognising their vulnerability through participatory and deliberative forums and practices. The aim of this collection is to bridge the distance between restorative justice and the critical theory tradition. It, on the one hand, takes into account the limits of restorative justice as they have been articulated, or can be articulated through critical social theory, and, on the other hand, emphasises the ground-breaking potential that restorative justice can bring to this tradition as a way to address crimes, conflicts and injustices, and to pursue justice.

Critical Restorative Justice

Edited by
Ivo Aertsen and Brunilda Pali

• HART •
PUBLISHING
OXFORD AND PORTLAND, OREGON
2017

Hart Publishing
An imprint of Bloomsbury Publishing Plc

Hart Publishing Ltd
Kemp House
Chawley Park
Cumnor Hill
Oxford OX2 9PH
UK

Bloomsbury Publishing Plc
50 Bedford Square
London
WC1B 3DP
UK

www.hartpub.co.uk
www.bloomsbury.com

Published in North America (US and Canada) by
Hart Publishing
c/o International Specialized Book Services
920 NE 58th Avenue, Suite 300
Portland, OR 97213-3786
USA

www.isbs.com

First published 2017

British Library Cataloguing-in-Publication Data
A catalogue record for this book is available from the British Library.

ISBN: HB: 978-1-50990-664-2
ePDF: 978-1-50990-662-8
ePub: 978-1-50990-663-5

Library of Congress Cataloging-in-Publication Data

Names: Aertsen, Ivo, editor. | Pali, Brunilda, editor.

Title: Critical restorative justice / edited by Ivo Aertsen and Brunilda Pali.

Description: Oxford [UK] ; Portland, Oregon : Hart Publishing, 2017. | Includes bibliographical references and index.

Identifiers: LCCN 2017029130 (print) | LCCN 2017031523 (ebook) | ISBN 9781509906635 (Epub) | ISBN 9781509906642 (hardback : alk. paper)

Subjects: LCSH: Restorative justice. | Reparation (Criminal justice)

Classification: LCC K970 (ebook) | LCC K970 .C79 2017 (print) | DDC 364.6/8—dc23

LC record available at https://lccn.loc.gov/2017029130

Typeset by Compuscript Ltd, Shannon
Printed and bound in Great Britain by TJ International Ltd, Padstow, Cornwall

Contents

List of Contributors

Editors

Ivo Aertsen is Full Professor of Criminology at the University of Leuven (Belgium). He holds degrees in Psychology, Law and Criminology from the same university. At the Leuven Institute of Criminology (LINC) he is leading the Research Line on 'Restorative Justice and Victimology'. His main fields of research and teaching are victimology, penology and restorative justice. Ivo Aertsen has been chair of the European Forum for Restorative Justice (EFRJ) from 2000–2004, and has coordinated COST Action A21 on Restorative Justice research in Europe from 2002–2006. He has been an expert for the United Nations, the Council of Europe, the OSCE and the European Union. Furthermore, he was appointed as expert to the Belgian Parliamentary Commission on sexual abuse in the church (2010–2011), followed by membership of the Permanent Arbitration Chamber on sexual abuse (2012–2016). Ivo Aertsen was also the academic coordinator of the European FP7 project ALTERNATIVE (2012–2016) on developing alternative understandings of justice and security. He also acts as Editor-in-Chief of *Restorative Justice, An International Journal.*

Brunilda Pali is currently a post-doc researcher in the Leuven Institute of Criminology. She obtained her PhD in 2016 at the KU Leuven Institute of Criminology on 'Doing Restorative Justice in Intercultural Contexts: An Alternative Discourse of Justice and Security'. In the Leuven Institute of Criminology, Brunilda has also worked as a researcher on several EU-funded projects, besides the FP7 project ALTERNATIVE. She is also co-editor of the book *Restoring Justice and Security in Intercultural Europe.* Besides criminology, Brunilda has a background in Psychology (Bosphorus University, Istanbul), Gender Studies (Central European University, Budapest), and Cultural Studies (Bilgi University, Istanbul). She is also currently the Secretary of the European Forum for Restorative Justice Board. She publishes on multiple themes, such as restorative justice, critical criminology, security, social movements, gender and arts.

Contributors

Pauline GM Aarten is Assistant Professor of Criminology and Victimology and research coordinator of INTERVICT, the International Victimology Institute Tilburg. She obtained her PhD on suspended sentencing in the Netherlands in 2014. Her research falls mainly under the broader theme of 'Victims and Society', and includes life narratives, victim-offender overlap, the criminal justice system, terrorism and international crimes. She is currently working on a large international project assessing the impact of international reparative justice procedures for victims in Cambodia, Congo, Suriname and Cyprus.

Daniel Achutti has a PhD degree in Criminal Sciences obtained at Pontifical Catholic University of Rio Grande do Sul (PUCRS/Brazil), where he also obtained his Master degree in Criminal Sciences. He is Assistant Professor, researcher and head of the School of Law at the Universidade La Salle (Unilasalle—Brazil), criminal lawyer, and member of the Brazilian Bar Association, section of Rio Grande do Sul state.

Ida Helene Asmussen holds a BA degree in Nordic Studies and Linguistics and a BA, LLM and PhD degree in law from the University of Copenhagen. Her PhD thesis is titled 'From Rule of Law to Rule of Love: A Confessional Practice in Restorative Justice'. She is currently doing a post-doc within the framework of the UCPH excellence programme for Interdisciplinary Research 2016, headed by Prof Eske Willerslev, Centre of Geogenetics, UCPH. Ida has previously worked as a deputy judge.

Gabriella Benedek is a social development practitioner in Hungary. She is trained in the Development School, postgraduate diploma in London Metropolitan University, and has developed and led several of Foresee Research Group's strategic projects in the field of community development, research, extra-curricular education and programme evaluation. Gabriella's main fields of interests are civil society and active citizenship, community conflicts, network development and local philanthropy, hence her career and work have been grounded on empowerment and participatory approaches to conflict resolution, dialogue, research and management, and evaluation.

Harry Blagg is Professor of Criminology and Associate Dean of Research at the University of Western Australia's Law School having previously been a Senior Research Fellow at the Crime Research Centre (UWA) and Professor of Criminology and Criminal Justice (Plymouth University, UK). He has published and researched extensively in the field of Indigenous justice issues, restorative justice, and justice reform and innovation. He is currently involved in research initiatives on young people with cognitive impairment and the justice system and family violence in Indigenous communities.

Daniela Bolivar is a Professor of Psychology at the University of Chile. She holds degrees in Community Psychology (Pontificia Universidad Católica de Chile) and a PhD in Criminology (Leuven Institute of Criminology, KU Leuven, Belgium). Daniela is the author of a number of publications in the field of victimology and restorative justice, and has worked as a researcher at the European Forum for Restorative Justice, University of Leuven (KU Leuven, Belgium) and National Institute of Criminalistics and Criminology (NICC, Belgium).

Erik Claes lectures in Philosophy and Law at Odisee (Brussels), School of Social Work. He obtained his PhD degree in Law on 'Legality and Adjudication in the Criminal Law' (rewarded with the Fernand Collin Prize for Law in 2002). He has published several articles on restorative justice and criminal law theory. He co-edited (with R Foqué) *Punishment, Restorative Justice and the Morality of Law* (2005); (with A Duff) *Privacy and the Criminal Law* (2006); (with B Keirsbilck) *Limits of the Law* (2009). His recent research focuses on restorative justice and citizenship. He coordinates an action research project on Restorative Justice and Urban Citizenship in Brussels.

Borbala Fellegi, PhD, is a researcher, mediator, conference and peace-making circle facilitator as well as a trainer and lecturer. She is a faculty member of the International Institute for Restorative Practices Graduate School (US). Her PhD thesis was about the implementation of restorative justice in Hungary. From 2008 on, as founder and Executive Director of the Foresee Research Group, she is in charge of Hungarian and EU programmes researching the potential application of mediation and peace-making circles in community conflicts and in prison settings, as well as being involved in different community building, researching and training projects in Hungary related to conflict resolution. She has been working as consultant for the Council of Europe, the UNODC, the National Crime Prevention Board and the Office of Justice in Hungary. She gives training and lectures at five universities. Besides numerous articles and book chapters, she is the author of *Towards Restoration and Peace* (2009), one of the first comprehensive studies on the implementation of restorative justice in Hungary.

Nele Gulinck lectures at Odisee, School of Social Work (Brussels). She studied social work and is trained in Digital Storytelling (supervised by Outti Vellacott, Digitales Londen). She has a large experience as a coach in digital story projects (in close collaboration with Museum M Leuven). She is a practice-based researcher in the project on Restorative Justice and Urban Citizenship in Brussels.

Gabor Hera is a sociologist working as a researcher at the Foresee Research Group in Hungary. He studies manifestations of social exclusion, prejudices and hate crimes toward different minority groups, especially towards the Roma. He has conducted over 40 significant research programmes in the last 20 years, in close cooperation with Hungarian and international organisations, such as the European Monitoring Center for Racism and Xenophobia, the Council of Europe and the Decade of Roma Inclusion Secretariat. He has taught 'Research Methodology' at four universities since 1999. He graduated and earned his PhD in Sociology of Science.

Minne Huysmans lectures at Odisee (Brussels). He obtained a Master in Social Work at the VUB (2009) and was victim-offender mediator in juvenile cases until 2012. He is a practice-based researcher in the project on Restorative Justice and Urban Citizenship in Brussels.

Katrin Kremmel is a PhD candidate at the Social and Cultural Anthropology department of the University of Vienna, where she works on asylum practices, statehood and citizenship in a rural Austrian town. Prior to her PhD studies, she worked as a researcher at the Institute for the Sociology of Law and Criminology (IRKS) in Vienna, where she pursued her research interests in migration and legal sociology within the European FP7 project ALTERNATIVE.

Iman Lechkar lectures at Odisee (Brussels), School of Social Work. She obtained a PhD degree in Cultural Anthropology on Islam-related conversions in a Belgian, secular context (2012). She coordinated a research project on superdiversity and higher education in Brussels. She is a practice-based researcher in the project on Restorative Justice and Urban Citizenship in Brussels.

Ronnie Lippens is Professor of Criminology at Keele University. His research interests include critical criminology and organisational criminology, but latterly they have focused also on the imaginary of justice, law and order, as expressed in eg novels, paintings and public art. He has published numerous contributions (in Dutch as well as in English) on those topics in a wide variety of venues. He is currently working on a closer analysis of the emergence of forms of governance in what could be called prophetic art, painting and sculpture, in particular.

Giuseppe Maglione is a Lecturer in Criminology at Edinburgh Napier University, School of Life, Sport and Social Sciences. Giuseppe received a PhD in Legal Theory from the University of Florence and carried out research on mediation and restorative justice at the Humboldt-Universität of Berlin, University of Oslo, Max Planck Institute in Freiburg, Leuven Institute of Criminology and Oñati International Institute of Sociology of Law. In addition to his research activity, he has extensively worked as victim-offender mediator and trainer in mediation for police forces and NGOs in Italy and Norway. He is currently member of the Scottish Restorative Justice Forum.

Claudia Mazzucato is Associate Professor of Criminal Law in the Faculty of Political and Social Sciences of the Università Cattolica del Sacro Cuore. She is senior researcher at the Centro Studi 'Federico Stella' sulla Giustizia penale e la Politica criminale of the same university, where she coordinates the research units on restorative justice, and law and humanities. She is a victim-offender mediator and restorative justice facilitator, with an extensive experience especially regarding severe crimes. Her primary scholarly interests are in the fields of theory of punishment, criminal law reform, restorative justice, law and humanities, and juvenile justice. She has written books, book chapters and articles on these topics.

Raffaella Pallamolla is Assistant Professor of Criminal Law at Centro Universitário Ritter dos Reis—UniRitter, Brazil; PhD candidate in Public Law at Universidad Autónoma de Barcelona (UAB), Spain and in Social Science at Pontifícia Universidade Católica do Rio Grande do Sul (PUCRS), Brazil. She has a Master's degree in Criminal Sciences at PUCRS, Brazil and in Criminology and Penal Execution at UAB, Spain. She is Vice-President of the Special Commission of Restorative Practices and Mediation of OAB/RS (Bar Association, Brazil), and a criminal lawyer.

George Pavlich holds a Canada Research Chair in Social Theory, Culture and Law and is Professor of Law and Sociology at the University of Alberta. He is the author of numerous journal articles, including recent work on sovereignty and criminal law at the Cape of Good Hope around 1795. He has written *Justice Fragmented: Mediating Community Disputes under Postmodern Conditions* (1996); *Critique and Radical Discourses on Crime* (2000); *Governing Paradoxes of Restorative Justice* (2005); and *Law and Society Redefined* (2011). He is a co-editor (with Myra Hird) of *Sociology for the Asking: Questioning Sociology* (3rd edn, forthcoming); (with Charles Barbour) *After Sovereignty*; (with A Brannigan) *Governance and Regulation in Social Life*; (with Gary Wickham) *Rethinking Law and Society: Foucault's Bequest*, and is currently working on the topic of criminal accusation.

Christa Pelikan is a researcher at the Institute for the Sociology of Law and Criminology in Vienna. She has been working in the field of criminal law, especially juvenile justice and in the field of family law. Starting in 1985, she has been doing accompanying research on the large Austrian pilot project on 'Victim-Offender Mediation in Juvenile Justice' and later on a pilot project 'Victim-Offender Mediation in General Criminal Law'. She has chaired the Committee of Experts on Mediation in Penal Matters within the European Committee on Crime Problems (CDPC) and has been a member of the Criminological Scientific Council to the CDPC of the Council of Europe. She is a founding member of the European Forum for Restorative Justice and has been the chair of its Communication Committee, participating in various GROTIUS, AGIS and COST projects at EU level. She was actively involved in the European FP7 project ALTERNATIVE about conflict resolution in intercultural settings taking place in Austria, Belgium, Hungary, Northern Ireland, Norway and Serbia.

Antony Pemberton is Professor of Victimology and Director of INTERVICT, the International Victimology Institute Tilburg at Tilburg University in the Netherlands. He is a political scientist and a criminologist. His research interests concern the broad topic of 'Victims and Society', including victims' perspectives on justice, societal reactions to victims and processes of victimisation, cultural victimology, narrative victimology and the ethics of victimology. He has published over 80 articles, book chapters and books on the subject of victimology. Most of his current ideas are reflected in his inaugural address in Tilburg, 'Victimology with a Hammer: The Challenge of Victimology' (2015).

Federico Reggio has a PhD in Philosophy of Law, Methodology and Legal Traditions at the University of Padua, where he has been working as Research Fellow since 2007. In 2014/2015 he taught a Law and Literature tandem-type course at the University of Verona. In February 2015, he was habilitated as Associate Professor in Philosophy of Law at the National Selection 'Abilitazione Scientifica Nazionale 2013'. He is a lawyer and a professional mediator and trainer of mediators in Italy, where he collaborates with mediation and training centres officially recognised by the Italian Ministry of Justice. He is co-founder of an association for the assistance to crime victims in Verona (ASAV).

Josep Tamarit Sumalla, Doctor in Law (University of Barcelona, 1988) is Full Professor of Criminal Law at the University of Lleida and at the Universitat Oberta de Catalunya. He is Director of the Criminology Programme at the Universitat Oberta de Catalunya, Principal Investigator of the Consolidated Group Research 'Criminal Justice System' (Catalan Government), and Principal Investigator of the research project 'Sexual Child Victimisation and Penal Protection' in the Spanish Department of Science and Competitivity. He has written numerous book and articles both in English and Spanish on restorative and criminal justice. He is President of the Catalan Society of Victimology.

Leo Van Garsse holds a degree of Master in Pedagogy (Catholic University of Leuven, 1981). He first worked as a social worker in prison aftercare and as director of a half-way house for young offenders. From 1987 onwards, he became actively involved in the practice and the implementation of several applications of victim-offender mediation in Flanders (Belgium). From 1998 on, he was employed by Suggnomè, Forum for Mediation and Restorative Justice, an umbrella organisation for the promotion of restorative justice in Flanders. As a representative of Suggnomè, Leo Van Garsse was closely involved in the preparation of the law on victim-offender mediation, approved by the Belgian Parliament on 22 June 2005. In the past few years, Leo Van Garsse was connected to Ghent University, Department of Social Welfare Studies, where he was studying the developments in the field of forensic social work in Flanders. In April 2015, he obtained a PhD in Pedagogy at Ghent University. Since 2007, Leo Van Garsse has also been connected to the University of Leuven as fellow-researcher within the Leuven Institute of Criminology (LINC). He has written several articles on victim-offender mediation and on social work in the field of criminal justice.

Lode Walgrave is Emeritus Professor in Criminology at the KU Leuven (Belgium), where he taught Youth Criminology and Theoretical Criminology, and directed the Research Group on Youth Criminology, doing research on youth crime, prevention and youth justice. He served as a member of the KU Leuven Research Council. Lode Walgrave chaired the International Network for Research on Restorative Justice. He received the European Criminology Award in 2008. He was guest professor or a fellow at the Université de Montréal, the Australian National University Canberra and at the University of Pennsylvania, Philadelphia. He has given key note speeches and guest lectures to congresses and conferences in almost all parts of the world, and in most European countries. He has published more than 350 titles in Dutch, which is his mother tongue, in English and in French. Translations are published in Chinese, German, Korean, Portuguese, Russian and Spanish.

Introduction: Restorative Justice and Critical Social Theory

BRUNILDA PALI AND IVO AERTSEN

BACKGROUND

THIS PUBLICATION IS a collection of 18 papers initially presented and discussed at an Exploratory Workshop funded by the European Science Foundation, and organised by the Leuven Institute of Criminology on 15 to 17 October 2014. The aim of the Workshop was mainly to bridge restorative justice (RJ) and the critical social theory tradition, thus on the one hand to take into account the limits of RJ as they have been articulated, or can be articulated through critical social theory, and on the other hand to emphasise the ground breaking potential that RJ can offer to this tradition, mainly as a way to address crimes, conflicts and injustices, and to pursue justice in intercultural Europe and beyond.

Current theories and practices of justice do not adequately meet the socio-political challenges of our times. For those theorists attempting to develop an alternative to the criminal justice system, RJ has provided a new horizon. Doing justice in a RJ perspective means defying the abstract and alienating notions of criminal law, encountering concrete others, understanding and recognising both their capabilities and vulnerabilities through participatory and deliberative forums and practices. Once the complex lifeworld and the vulnerability of the concrete other are recognised, taking active responsibility is a central aspect of most RJ practices, be it victim-offender mediation, conferencing, peace-making circles or still (always) evolving models. When offered an appropriate space, people are able to proceed into this participatory endeavour much further than we assumed in our classical way of thinking about doing justice. Moreover, RJ's major strength lies in its discursive potential, because it can turn into a participatory forum for explicating values, norm clarification and development, and finding lived and sustainable solutions to problems, especially important in an intercultural and diverse Europe. In a more general way, RJ can promote active citizenship and create an approach where people are more at ease in dealing with matters that are important to them, like crime, conflict and (in)justice. A RJ experience helps and prepares participants, and their surroundings, to look at others and otherness in a different way.

But, at the same time, RJ has raised a number of criticisms. The well known criticisms relate first to the restricted reach of RJ programmes, limiting its field of application to minor or mainly property offences or to juvenile offenders, hence merely functioning as a diversion strategy vis-à-vis the criminal justice process, leaving the operation and the logic of an ever-expanding criminal justice system unaffected. Many times, the pre-dominant offender focus of RJ programmes and the weak position of the victim have been criticised—a one-sided orientation that becomes obvious looking at the mainly offender related criteria for selection and referral of 'appropriate' cases to be dealt with by mediation or conferencing programmes. The lack of legal safeguards and legal protection has been another, recurrent concern toward RJ processes, usually considering and applying safeguards as they are defined within criminal justice proceedings. Furthermore and most importantly, many critics have argued that RJ, as the criminal justice system, only responds to the immediacy of the conflict or harm without situating it in a broader framework addressing social and structural issues. The fact that RJ (again in the extension of criminal justice proceedings) strongly individualises crime phenomena and prioritises individual responsibility, leads to what has been called 'governing at a distance' through the newly created community oriented sanctions and types of control. Thus, while on the one hand, RJ has been presented as a new paradigm of justice, on the other hand, it has remained quite a legalistically oriented and system-confirming approach to crime and conflict, replicating to a high degree criminal justice's legal concepts, categories and principles. As the field of RJ develops further, it needs to take seriously the criticisms and to develop self-reflexivity. We think that engaging with critical social theory can enable RJ to reach a breakthrough of its true potential, both theoretically and practically.

These are mainly the reasons why we deemed it necessary to bring together a group of people in a workshop to 'work' at the intersections of critical social theory and RJ in order to provoke the critical pulse of the RJ field, and support its becoming truly a praxis of justice, able to answer many challenges in current intercultural and heterogeneous Europe. The label critical theory has been applied to various established and emergent theoretical perspectives that differ in significant ways and that have diverse origins and political allegiances. While generally the term is historically associated and used synonymously with the work of the 'Frankfurt School', using the term exclusively in relation to their work is misleading, as it was especially the founders of that school who insisted on a conception of critical theory as always embedded in processes of historical change. Critical scholars commonly draw on social theory to analyse social structures and processes in a historical context. Some of the other points that characterise the critical theory and research field are a critical examination of knowledge itself which is seen as structured by existing sets of social relations, revealing and uncovering the 'reification' of the present into an inevitable social and natural order, and a critical engagement with society and social change. Critical researchers also commonly focus: on issues of oppression, exclusion, domination, exploitation and injustice based on social categories like class, race, ethnicity or gender and their intersections; on other forms of social relations like patriarchy, heterosexism, disability discrimination, religious oppression; and on questions related to imperialism, colonisation, and globalisation.

The papers that were presented at the seminar were targeted although diverse contributions under the common frame of 'restorative justice and critical social theory: addressing crimes, conflicts, and injustices in intercultural Europe', but many papers went beyond the European borders. The project was highly ambitious and aimed at offering a critical and meaningful contribution to the restorative justice field. The purpose was to push the boundaries of the field both towards envisioning the eventual development of its practices towards new areas, and towards theoretical expansion and imagination for the academic sector. At the same time, the idea was to open the 'gates' of RJ radically to a variety of disciplines, including sociologists, philosophers, psychologists, anthropologists and social theorists, in order to promote their future engagement with developments, ideas and proposals from the field, which has remained too much self-protecting and self-affirming.

STRUCTURE OF THE BOOK

The book is conceived and organised in three sections. Part I 'Bridging the Theoretical Gap and Sharpening the Critical Edge' brings together seven chapters which attempt, on the one hand, to expand the theoretical and critical scope of RJ, by looking at different theoretical trends and schools of thought that have a relevance for the field, and on the other hand, to offer counter-criticism towards the existing critique, either by delineating narrower boundaries or by bringing into the picture empirical evidence.

In chapter 1, 'Is a Critical Model of Restorative Justice Possible? A Penal Abolitionist Approach', Daniel Achutti explores the main propositions of critical criminology, especially those of penal abolitionists such as Louk Hulsman and Nils Christie to assess whether such approaches are able to offer tools for critical analysis that can support RJ programmes to resist becoming another tool for the enhancement of penal control and net widening. From this theoretical background, the analysis contends that restorative justice, once supported by the criticism of the penal abolitionists, is a possible way to avoid net widening while simultaneously offering the stakeholders a qualified mechanism of conflict resolution.

Chapter 2, 'Deconstructing Empowerment in Restorative Justice' by Daniela Bolívar argues that although empowerment is one of the central notions within RJ, it remains one of the less defined concepts. The author argues that RJ advocates have been unable to construct a framework that seriously engages with the transformative aspect that the notion of empowerment is supposed to embrace. She argues that it is not possible to claim to offer empowerment without having first a clear understanding of power relations and dynamics within a society, and secondly without offering resources that are necessary to deal with this in an adequate way. The author analyses the concept of empowerment through the lens of community psychology, deconstructing the notion of empowerment at individual, organisational and community level, and drawing important lessons for RJ.

Chapter 3, 'Restorative Justice and the Decision-making Process: Beyond Deliberative Democracy?' by Raffaella Pallamolla, based on the idea that restorative justice is a bottom-up way of doing justice, aims at bringing together restorative justice and theories of deliberative and communicative democracy. Her main objective is to assess whether restorative justice can be understood as a form of deliberative democracy or as a form of communicative democracy. Basing her field work on the current restorative justice programmes in Brazil, she also assesses if restorative justice is able to modify the standard (or the logic) of the decision-making processes of the criminal justice system and to change, consequently, the quality of such democratic processes.

Chapter 4, 'Doing Restorative Justice "Otherwise": Decolonising Practices in the Global South' by Harry Blagg is concerned with the relationship between RJ and the emerging sphere of Indigenous justice, particularly in Australia, arguing that the two projects rarely intersect. The author suggests that current forms of restorative practice, most notably those developed by the white justice system and imposed from above onto Indigenous society, do not meet the justice demands of Indigenous people, who rarely recognise their own conflict resolution methods within these mainstream practices. Drawing on Elizabeth Povinelli's (2002) notion of 'cunning recognition', the author argues that state initiated RJ reflects a Eurocentric imaginary of its Indigenous Other, assuming that a few concessions to Indigenous 'culture' can 'sugar the bitter pill of Indigenous dispossession'. However, the author argues, despite all the cunning concessions, it is land that remains at the centre of Indigenous cosmology, and which marks a radical and incommensurable difference between the Indigenous and the non-Indigenous.

Chapter 5, 'Outlining a Historical and Critical Ontology of Restorative Justice' by Giuseppe Maglione aims to outline a historico-philosophical investigation into the conditions of possibility of RJ, from a Foucauldian perspective. Through Foucauldian lenses, RJ appears as a cultural formation constituted by three different but interlinked dimensions: 'a game of truth, relations of power, and forms of relation to oneself and to others'. Therefore, the focus of his contribution is posited on historically reconstructing and critically problematising the 'true' discourses, power relationships and ethical 'potential' of RJ. His perspective serves not only the purpose of diagnosing and de-familiarising what we take for granted in RJ but also of imagining specific forms of resistance to it, developing in this way a critical tension which might make RJ a challenge to the 'conventional' criminal justice.

Chapter 6, 'Restorative Justice is Not a Panacea Against All Social Evils" by Lode Walgrave argues that as many scholars evaluate all social institutions and social movements through their potential to diminish social inequalities, RJ is also criticised for not embedding in its discursive practices strategies to eliminate deprivation, inequality and discrimination. The author argues against this criticism as being based on a misconception of RJ and on the complex of social institutions. According to Walgrave, RJ must not be conceptualised as a movement for social change in the way we live, but as a movement that aims to change the way we respond to crime. However, this 'fundamentalist' position—as he calls his own position—does not mean that the RJ movement can remain blind to the structural social problems.

In chapter 7, 'Restorative Justice, Procedural Justice and Care', Josep Tamarit Sumalla argues, in a counter-critique fashion, that the criticism on RJ fails to take into account empirical research. As a result, the author presents extensive data that confirm that RJ is able to satisfy participants and communities, particularly victims' needs, by improving their wellbeing and reducing the emotional distress produced by crime. Based on these data, the author argues that, theoretically, justice in a restorative practice can be valued both from a theraupetic justice perspective and particularly from the procedural perspective, as far as victims can feel that they have been heard and treated fairly, experiencing a secondary effect besides the reparation obtained (outcome). Therefore, he argues that RJ can be a bridge between the care needs and the demands for justice.

Part II 'Applying Analytical Tools and Frameworks to Research and Practice' brings together six chapters which attempt to apply different analytical tools—genealogical, sociological, theoretical—to concrete developments within the RJ field, research or practice.

Chapter 8, 'Restorative Justice and Democratic Citizenship: A New Social Pedagogy or Back to "Social Defence"?' by Leo Van Garsse argues that to maintain its critical potential, RJ is in need of finding an adequate language and moving away from offering a merely instrumental approach. The crafting of that language can be supported by focusing upon the social-pedagogical potential of RJ and promoting RJ as a learning process in democratic and participatory citizenship. The author nevertheless reflects on the 'social defence' doctrine in Belgium, to show that questions and contexts of today only seem new, but have many parallels in history. He therefore draws attention to certain lessons that could be learned from history in situating the pedagogical RJ agenda in a defendable balance between private concerns and the collective interest, or between pragmatism and legality.

Chapter 9, 'Old Goffman as a New Research Strategy in Restorative Justice' by Ida Helene Asmussen argues that during the last 20 years the social constructivist approach to truth has seriously challenged the way in which we experience science and reality, something that applies inevitably also to the RJ theory and research. Turning to one of the most recognised thinkers in face-to-face communication, Erving Goffman, the author argues that he offers a vision of how the new approach to truth can be incorporated into and complement the RJ research. The chapter provides analytical tools and concepts to qualitative, micro-sociological research in RJ that can respond to the social constructivist notion of truth.

In chapter 10, 'Lifeworld, Law and Justice', Katrin Kremmel and Christa Pelikan explicate the potential of two important concepts of Habermasian theory for a critical theory of restorative justice: the concept of the lifeworld and the discourse free from domination. Making obvious that these concepts share the focus on questions of communication and questions of freedom, the authors emphasise this connection and its bearing on law by referring further to German sociologist of law Detlev Frehsee and his delineation of the different levels of law's function and law's potential efficacy: the level of norm-setting, the level of the procedure and the level of execution. For both the lifeworld approach and the discourse free from domination, the authors illustrate with empirical material from research and from practical involvement in law-making processes.

In chapter 11, '"Cultural" Problematisations in the Restorative Justice Discourse' Brunilda Pali examines discursively the way 'culture' is thematised and problematised in RJ, both by a critical literature review and through analysing empirical data. She argues that there are many forces that push a field or a discourse in a certain direction, like political debates, policy reforms and requirements, socio-economic conditions, concrete cases and events, and sometimes global or supranational forces, and depending on these forces, and the ways the discourse bends to or resists to them, matters start to be problematised in certain manners, and not in others. The chapter has two main objectives. The first objective is to trace in the RJ literature its 'cultural' problematisations. The second objective is to argue for prioritising certain forms of problematisations rather than others through presenting some findings from her empirical data gathered through interviews conducted within mediation programmes in Europe.

Chapter 12, 'To Talk or Not to Talk? The Limits and Potential of Restorative Justice in Addressing Social Inequalities' by Borbala Fellegi, Gabor Hera and Gabriella Benedek addresses the question whether RJ can challenge existing class and power structures. Their data show that being influenced by social deprivation and discrimination can lead to criminal offences, referring to the main historical and sociological processes that have led to the current state of social inequalities in Hungarian society, with special emphasis on the situation of the Roma population, and to emerging discourses that link poverty, ethnicity and criminality. Based on their empirical research conducted in a small town in Hungary, the authors tackle the following questions: what is considered as conflict by the local inhabitants; to what extent are the local Roma and other marginalised populations linked to criminal activities as victims and/or offenders; who is considered locally as socially disadvantaged; and what is their position within the local power structures. The authors discuss the potential and the limitations of the RJ approach in this context.

Chapter 13, 'Digital Stories and Restorative Justice in Brussels' by Erik Claes, Iman Lechkar, Minne Huysmans and Nele Gulinck, explores the potentials of digital storytelling for RJ, grounded in action research on RJ in the very heart of Brussels: the Anneessens quarter (a highly dense, superdiverse transit-zone for migrants with high unemployment rates). The authors' main argument is that digital storytelling as a participatory project, combined with other urban interventions, has the potential to 'reinvent' RJ concepts. In order to do so, RJ must be integrated into a set of urban interventions that connect social networks, transform conflict zones in public spaces and aim at making civic aspirations visible in concrete environmental projects. The authors passionately argue that digital storytelling has the power to transform classic RJ programmes into innovative, restorative practices that meet urban challenges in a digital era.

Part III 'Philosophical Explorations for Restorative Justice' brings together five original contributions which propose creative philosophical explorations in the field of RJ.

Chapter 14, 'Restorative Justice and the Potential of "Exemplarity": In Search of a "Persuasive" Coherence Within Criminal Justice' by Claudia Mazzucato highlights the difference between a criminal justice system which focuses on punishment, coercion, deterrence, incapacitation, enforcement and negative sanctions, and restorative justice and responsive regulation which focuses on rule of conduct, compliance, persuasion, participation, positive sanctions and reparation. The author argues that restorative justice can show criminal law how to 'work' in a different way and to rethink its aims, drafting an idea in which the law and the justice system have the primary task to protect, not to control or punish. The author puts forward a new theory of criminal law in which norms of conduct are more important than mere sanctions. Basing her arguments on the philosophy of Alessandro Ferrara, the author argues that restorative justice oriented norms talk about the experience of injustices through the 'force of example', where *is* and *ought* merge. Just as norms address the citizens as examples do, and stimulate their reflective judgement, persuading them, and asking them to comply, sanctions should also address citizens as examples do, stimulating their reflective judgement, persuading them, and asking them to comply.

Chapter 15, 'The Broken Tablets of Moses and the Exodus from (Post-) Modernity: On Rethinking the Role and the Rule of Law in a Dialogical Way' by Federico Reggio argues that RJ makes a deep provoking question about the possibility and the necessity of rethinking law and justice in light of different conceptual premises and underlying values. Nevertheless, the author argues that the possibility of rooting RJ's proposals in solid philosophical and ethical grounds is challenged by the contemporary 'postmodern' Western culture, characterised by a highly secularised and sceptical tendency and by a widespread lack of systemic thinking. The author argues on the possibility of consolidating the restorative paradigm in light of the idea of a 'dialogical justice'—which is relational—with the aim of offering both some critical arguments and hopefully innovative philosophical proposals to the current debate.

Chapter 16, 'Control Society, Sovereign Victim Culture and Restorative Justice' by Ronnie Lippens questions the image of victimhood underpinning the text of EU Directive 2012/29/EU of 25 October 2012 establishing minimum standards on the rights, support and protection of victims of crime, an image which projects victims as atomically separate entities. The author situates this image within a 'sovereign victim culture' that flourishes at the heart of the 'control society'. He argues that it is the form of life and the sense of ambivalence that the 'control society' generates, which has contributed to the emergence and subsequent development of the restorative justice movement. However, he argues that while once they might have formed the conditions of possibility for restorative justice to emerge, perhaps today in their 'sovereign victim culture' guise, they have become its own conditions of impossibility.

In chapter 17, 'Promised Communities and Unrestored Justice', George Pavlich takes issue with the notion of community in RJ, proposing an alternative way of envisioning community that relies on Roberto Esposito's conception of community/immunity and on a 'dissociative' critique of the community justice measures. According to the author, RJ should be seen as a transformative endeavour always located in processes of 'being with', mobilised when relations are problematised in context, around the name of crime or destructive conflict, while focusing on changing the relations that bring people to wrongdoing. Pavlich argues that RJ has to be cognisant of the obligations that its specific practices require, paying attention to the kinds of subjects its truth-telling demands, and putting the focus on changing rather than fixing identities, but without denying responsibility for provisional wrongdoing, conceived as democratic promise. Both law and RJ could be articulated to a transformative politics that emerges where everyday life is arrested through harms and permanently struggles to project a promise of justice that (heterogeneously) is always of the future, to come.

In chapter 18, 'A Radical in Disguise: Judith Shklar's Victimology and Restorative Justice', Antony Pemberton and Pauline Aarten consider the possibility that the experience of victimisation is fundamentally at odds with features of criminal justice systems. Likewise, the authors also challenge the assumption that RJ fully represent the victimological perspective, returning to Judith Shklar, one of the most important thinkers about the subject and experience of victimology. The authors argue that her views are radical, not only about the way we shape our institutions in response to crime, but also about the way we should try to understand the subject of injustice and the manner in which we go about increasing our knowledge of this experience and the effects of our responses to it.

Part I

Bridging the Theoretical Gap and Sharpening the Critical Edge

1

Is a Critical Model of Restorative Justice Possible?

A Penal Abolitionist Approach*

DANIEL ACHUTTI

I. INTRODUCTION

ACCORDING TO COHEN (1986), penal abolitionism—a criminal policy movement whose intentions are clearly stated by its own denomination—emerged out of the countercultural policies of the 1960s, which gave rise to the labelling approach and the new criminology, or critical criminology. It focuses on building up a radical critique that is able to challenge the prison system and its punitive mechanism (Anitua, 2008: 697), towards designing a different way to deal with situations officially regarded as criminal (Cohen, 1986: 3; Elbert, 2003: 105).

The abolitionists criticise the use of punishment to restrain a person accused and convicted of committing a crime, questioning the centrality of penal law as a mean of social control. Moreover, they claim that the criminal justice system does more harm than good to society and, therefore, does not deserve to remain in operation (Cohen, 1988: 25).

According to these authors, punishment is not an adequate way to react to torts, for no matter how well it is employed, it will not produce the desired effects, given that beyond its most latent objective (punishing the

* This article presents part of the results of the doctoral thesis developed at the Pontifical Catholic University of Rio Grande do Sul (PUCRS/Brazil) and at the University of Leuven (KU Leuven/Belgium), with financial support from PUCRS and from Coordination for the Improvement of Higher Education Personnel (CAPES), Ministry of Education of Brazil (process no. 3770-10-9), between 2009–2012. Currently the research project is developed with the support of Unilasalle (Brazil) and the National Council for Research and Development (CNPq/Brazil). English translation by Simone Hailliot.

criminal), the whole system was created to perpetuate an unfair, selective and stigmatising social order, in such a way that even systems whose functioning is considered satisfactory will be somehow violent.

These and other criticisms, resulting from the insightful way abolitionists see the criminal justice system, are not new in the context of critical criminology: since the 1970s, when Thomas Mathiesen, Herman Bianchi, Nils Christie and Louk Hulsman presented their perspectives denying modern penal control, they gained notoriety in academic circles and became known as the leading critics of the existence of the criminal justice system itself, therefore proposing its abolition.

However, the issue of penal abolitionism often causes different interlocutors to react in a similar way: 'it would be excellent if it were not utopian'. Traditionally characterised as such, criminal abolitionism has become unattainable, especially in a period marked by the state's increased attempts to control crime. Its virtues (strong and accurate criticism of the criminal justice system) are shyly pointed out, whereas the unworkable nature of its ultimate goal is magnified.

It is not intended, at this moment, to discuss the possibility or impossibility of abolishing the penal system. The idea is to check if it is possible to analyse penal abolitionism considering only its negative aspects, ie would it be possible to identify, at the very heart of the abolitionist argument, propositional-constructive aspects in relation to the criminal system? Would abolitionists be so naive as to be concerned only with the deconstruction of the penal system, without trying to find a new way of managing criminal conflicts?

This is precisely the point I want to develop: it is indeed possible to identify clear propositional-constructive aspects in the abolitionist criticism. With their criticism, the authors proposed a new way to approach and understand conflicts, which later gained strong impetus in North America and Europe under the label of *restorative justice*.

The intention here is to address the close relationship between penal abolitionism and restorative justice, with special emphasis on Nils Christie's and Louk Hulsman's works. It is hoped, in the end, to demonstrate that penal abolitionism has not only posed negative criticisms to the penal system; it has also presented itself as one of the most important *alternatives to punishment*, and not a mere *alternative punishment*.

II. PENAL ABOLITIONISM: A BRIEF HISTORICAL REVIEW

Penal abolitionism can be seen both as a social movement, encompassing the Scandinavian movement for the abolition of prisons in 1960, as well as the activities of the group Radical Alternatives to Prison (RAP) in England in the 1970s, and the groups of Michel Foucault in France, and KRAK in

West Germany, and as a theoretical perspective that seeks to challenge the validity of the penal model of guilt and punishment and to present new approaches to social conflict officially regarded as criminal (Scheerer, 1986; Zaffaroni, 1991; Sim, 1994; Passetti and Silva, 1997; Andrade, 2006; Batista, 2011).

The first time criminologists presented themselves as abolitionists was in 1983, during the IX World Congress of Criminology in Vienna. At that time, supporters of an early abolitionist *movement* could be found only in Norway, among a few members of KROM (Nórsk Forening for Kriminal Reform), and in North America, in the Quaker Committee on Prisons and Justice, organised in May of the same year during the First International Conference on Prison Abolition in Toronto, Canada (Van Swaaningen, 1986).

Academically speaking, one could not think of an organised abolitionist movement, but since the 1960s Nils Christie and Thomas Mathiesen in Norway, and Herman Bianchi and Louk Hulsman in the Netherlands, have published works that addressed penal abolitionism.

As Van Swaaningen (1986: 10) puts it:

> [Academic] abolitionism gradually developed from critical criminological theories like the labeling-approach of Goffman and Lemert, the ethnomethodology of Garfinkel and Cicourel, and the 'New Criminology' of Taylor, Walton and Young. Ever since the new criminologists, united in the 'European Group for the Study of Deviance and Social Control', initiated alternative conferences to the governmental criminology-conferences, criminology could no longer be considered as an auxiliary science of criminal law. As a more or less logical extension of this, criminologists themselves began to present ways of conflict-settlement, as alternatives to the criminal justice approach.

To Marie-Andrée Bertrand (2007), penal abolitionism can be seen as 'an ideal and a program that seeks to put a stop to imprisonment, to even empty prisons, but it can also mean the will to replace the criminal justice system by civil arrangements' (Bertrand, 2007: 4). On the other hand, Vicenzo Ruggiero (2010) states that 'abolitionism is not merely a programme, but also an approach, a perspective, a methodology, and most of all a way of seeing' (Ruggiero, 2010: 1).

According to Scheerer (1986), it is an essentially negative perspective, totally sceptical of the criminal justice system and its promises. The many abolitionists briefly note that the criminal justice system operates within illegality; it acts from the selection of its customers, giving them stigmatising labels hardly disposable after the first contact with the system; it alienates the parties involved in the conflict, substituting them for legal technicians who seek a legal response to the problem; it produces more problems than solutions; it spreads a (punitive) culture that propagates the idea that justice can be done via punishment (incarceration) in events officially considered as a *crime*.

Although it is not possible to consider penal abolitionism as a science or a system of ideas with a method, an object and unmistakable concepts (Scheerer, 1986; Elbert, 2003), nor state that it is a theoretical construct that is not concerned with such issues, abolitionists have undoubtedly framed an important 'field of discussion and of pragmatic, simple and creative work. Its openness and unconcern for methodical care is a result of an anti-reductionism that aims not to confuse method with ideas ... It can be said that abolitionism "made it simple" (as opposed to what occurs discursively within the realm of criminal law and criminology), proposing "another logic" to the theme of crime' (Elbert, 2003: 108).

In 1986, US magazine Contemporary Crisis (later replaced by Crime, Law and Social Change magazine) dedicated its first issue to the theme of penal abolitionism, thus becoming a reference on the subject.

In line with Vera Andrade (2006), it is important to highlight that it is not possible to speak of abolitionism, but of abolitionisms: 'as a theoretical perspective, there are different types of abolitionisms, with different methodological foundations for abolition' (Andrade, 2006: 463–65). This idea is also supported by Eugenio Raúl Zaffaroni (1991), who distinguishes four abolitionist variants: (a) the Marxist tendency of Thomas Mathiesen; (b) the structural line of Michel Foucault; (c) the phenomenological-historicist view of Nils Christie; and (d) the phenomenological orientation of Louk Hulsman.

Due to the fact that a deep analysis of the abolitionist proposals of these authors would be an unfeasible task at this moment, the criterion adopted for the analysis of such variants is to work with those who exert the greatest influence on the topic discussed here, namely the ones advocated by Louk Hulsman and Nils Christie. That does not mean we do not recognise the importance and significance of the works of Michel Foucault, Thomas Mathiesen and Thomas Bianchi; however, given the focus of this study, priority will be given to Hulsman's and Christie's contributions.

A. Penal Abolitionism According to Louk Hulsman

Considered the most important theorist of penal abolitionism, Louk Hulsman (1920–2009) aimed at deconstructing the conventional language of criminal justice so as to find a new way to understand criminal events. Hulsman's concern was not to abolish all systems of social control; instead, his idea was to substitute the centralised state system for decentralised mechanisms to manage conflicts which do not have a conciliator or an arbitrator to impose a decision on the parties, but 'people who try to help stakeholders understand their situation and find, themselves, the solution' (Hulsman and Celis, 2005: 267).

To this end, it was fundamental that the beginning of the construction of an alternative mechanism to solve conflicts challenged the concept of *crime*: considered by the author as the 'cornerstone' of the penal system, challenging this concept would lead to a 'complete renovation of the entire discourse surrounding the so-called criminal phenomenon and the social reaction it raises' (Hulsman and Celis, 1997: 95) and the search for support in a flexible notion that can be applied to any type of interpersonal conflict that demands solutions: we refer to the notion of 'problematic situations' (Hulsman and Celis, 2005: 264).

Stemming from this notion, new perspectives about conflicts would be created, allowing the parties to perceive that any conduct is only labelled as crime when it is classified as such by criminal law: when the criminal phenomenon is viewed from different standpoints, it is detached from the label of *crime* and regarded as a *problematic situation*, an open concept that, as mentioned by Hulsman and Bernat de Celis (2005), attempts to leave 'in the hands of the parties the possibility to choose the framework of interpretation of the event as well as the orientation that should lead to a possible answer' (Hulsman and Celis, 2005: 264).

By explicitly giving the conflict back to the parties (Hulsman and Celis, 1997), the author wishes to achieve two objectives: (a) the elimination of social problems caused by the penal system, such as the mass production of guilty individuals, the stigmatisation of convicts and the marginalization of many social groups, among others; and (b) the revitalisation of social interaction: the absence of the centralised structure of criminal justice will allow society to seek other mechanisms, preferably decentralised and integrated to the local community, to solve their problems (De Folter, 1986).

Moreover, the decentralised mechanisms mentioned above should necessarily abandon the social and cultural organisation of criminal justice: considered by Hulsman as an organisation culturally dedicated to the *reconstruction of reality* whose focus is a past incident, precisely defined in time and space, that freezes a certain action (crime) and aims to examine the suspect's intention, to whom *criminal guilt* can be attributed—such organisation 'isolates the individual from his environment, his friends, his family, the material substratum of his world. He is also separated from those people who feel victimised in a situation which can be attributed to his action' (Hulsman, 1991: 683). In this sense, the author states that 'the cultural organisation of criminal justice creates "fictitious individuals", and a "fictitious interaction" between them' (Hulsman, 1991: 684).

Decentralised mechanisms, in turn, would provide the parties the opportunity to engage in real interaction, in which the actual problems arising from the problematic situation could be discussed without restrictions and, most importantly, not only to meet the requirements and legal determinations. Therefore, the aim is to create opportunities for the parties to understand everyone's situation and, thereafter, to try and reach a group conclusion about what to do to solve the problem.

Another point to be avoided is the passive position occupied by victims in the criminal justice system: instead of being mere tools (means) for the successful implementation of legal proceedings, they should take an active role in the process and freely express their views on the episode, resuming the important position now occupied by the state-prosecutor (Hulsman, 1991: 685).

For Ruggiero (2011), in order to effectively abandon the cultural and social organisation of criminal justice, the abolitionist approach should be oriented (a) to the parties directly involved; and (b) to the criticism of the idea that different criminalised situations can be classified as *equivalent*, as if the fact of being *criminalised* could make them be equal: each problem or event should be 'characterised by its own contours and features, and information about these is a precondition for different understandings of the acts observed and the practical responses to them' (Ruggiero, 2011: 101).

In other words, as Ruggiero (2011) suggests, the highly formal context of criminal justice should be substituted for decentralised mechanisms of conflict management that concede greater flexibility to understand the problem, thus creating a supportive environment for a *participatory dispute* between those directly involved in the situation.

For Hulsman and Bernat de Celis (2005), the adoption of new mechanisms requires each situation to be considered 'in its multiple dimensions, and not as an *act* and *its immediate actor*' (Hulsman and Celis, 2005: 266); that means the authors intend to eliminate the idea that the only possible solution lies in the intervention operated by the criminal justice system. The authors are not unaware that decriminalising an act will not make it less problematic, but the option for not considering it a *crime* will open doors for it to be addressed in other ways, beyond the binomial *crime-punishment* (Hulsman and Celis, 2005).

Having said that, it is possible to summarise Hulsman's proposals in three fundamental postulates: (a) the abolition of the current criminal justice system, replacing it by decentralised mechanisms of conflict management; (b) in such mechanisms, the active participation of both victim and offender in the conduction and resolution of the cases is of paramount importance, with special attention to the satisfaction of their interests through a *participatory dispute* in which the particularities of each case may be fully discussed; and (c) to prevent the colonisation of new mechanisms by the practices, routines and habits of the penal system, the adoption of a new *language*, or a new *grammar*, as De Folter (1986) puts it, is a key issue, and the term 'crime' must be replaced by 'problematic situation', 'conflict', 'undesired behaviours', etc.

With these criticisms, Hulsman seeks to demonstrate that, contrary to what it may seem, the rationality of the criminal justice system has inconsistencies and, for this reason, it does not allow events to be effectively resolved, but only receive a criminal legal response that is totally detached from the perception that the main stakeholders have of what happened. The legal response, in turn, besides not including the parties' considerations, determines that the person found guilty should be removed from his environment and sent to another place—prison—so that, isolated from the rest of society, he can learn, paradoxically, how to live in society. New ways of perceiving, interpreting and dealing with conflicts: that is Hulsman's proposal.

B. Nils Christie's Minimalist Abolitionism

Nils Christie, Professor of the Institute of Criminology, Faculty of Law at the University of Oslo, stands since the 1970s as an obstinate critic of the way social control is exerted by the penal system. Unable to reconcile the structure of the traditional criminal justice model with its social consequences, the author vehemently challenges what he calls 'intentional infliction of pain' (or, in legal and criminal terms, implementation and execution of a prison sentence), the power of professionals and state centralisation in conflict management. However, he does not advocate the complete abolition of the penal system, for he understands that, in very exceptional cases, nothing can be done but keep the offender away from the social environment. It is noteworthy that, within this perspective, the author's opinion is clear: when in doubt, do not punish; when punishing, do it as painlessly as possible (Christie, 1981).

As a proposal for conflict management, Christie (1981) starts from the idea that it is necessary to 'look for alternatives to punishment, not only alternative punishments' (Christie, 1981: 11), and suggests a decentralised community system of justice in which the parties take active participation in solving their problems, rather than having their conflicts taken away by the state and by the court professionals (Cohen, 1988; Christie, 1977 and 1986a).

Despite not advocating the complete abolition of the penal system, due to the belief that absolutely exceptional cases may require a repressive response by the state, Christie may still be considered a moderate abolitionist. His abolitionist propositions are less comprehensive than those of Hulsman, but his criticism of the criminal justice system is also sharp, defending its reduction to a maximum limit, as well as the establishment of a decentralised mechanism for conflict resolution that allows the parties not to resort to the criminal justice system.

Initially, it is worth mentioning again that when Christie (1981) thinks of alternative mechanisms to the criminal justice system, he is looking for *alternatives to punishment*, and not *alternative punishments*. Based on this assumption, in 1977 the author begins, in the well-known article 'Conflicts as Property', to advocate an anti-criminological approach (for criminology, at that time, was directly identified with positivist criminology), marking its role as a critic of the official (positivist) criminology, the criminal justice system and the way it operates and applies sanctions.

Three of Christie's criticisms can be identified as the most important: the first one refers to the appropriation of conflicts by the state; the second, to the professionalisation of the main legal actors and the implications of this fact for criminal justice; and the third, to the simplistic way criminal justice views criminal facts and the parties involved.

(1) By proposing a mechanism that returns the conflict to the parties, Christie (1977) envisions a system consisting of neighbourhood courts, located as close as possible to the communities, so that local values can always be taken into consideration. This model of justice would be victim-oriented, follow its own hierarchical procedures and take into account the interests of both victims and offenders, without neglecting the community. Local courts 'would represent a blend of elements from civil and criminal courts, but with a strong emphasis on the civil side' (Christie, 1977: 10–11), previously analysed by legal professionals to avoid undue punishments.

(2) Considering the broad participation of professionals in conflict management as something harmful, Christie (1977) is incisive in dealing with the issue: the participation of laymen in conflict management is of paramount importance to prevent the bureaucratisation of criminal justice and the division of labour from interfering with the way cases are handled. Therefore, mediators could not be professionals—only in exceptional cases, to allow the system to last and not to run the risk of disappearing due to lack of volunteers. The power of the specialised professionals is very strong and tends to set the parties increasingly apart from each other when there is no need for involvement.

According to Ruggiero (2011), the knowledge held by professionals differs from the knowledge acquired in the everyday life of communities, and it would be plausible to assume that 'the quantity and nature of information held by members of a group will make sweeping concepts such as "crime" needless to that group' (Ruggiero, 2011: 104).

Consequently, an individual approach to conflicts in criminal justice remains unfeasible: bureaucratisation and division of labour do not allow agents to realise the magnitude of the consequences of their work in offices and registries; for this reason, the responsibility of handling each case is always diluted, or dissolved. On the other hand, in the neighbourhood courts members of the community participate in the deliberations, which prevents that lack of knowledge about the case eventually justifies exemptions from responsibility.

(3) Finally, Christie's criticism (1986a, 1986b) of the simplistic way criminal law sees and deals with the human being is ultimate: when working on

the basis of binary systems (yes/no, good/bad, guilty/innocent) criminal law reflects a simplistic image of human beings and their actions. As a consequence, little information is required by the courts, so that the simpler the case, the easier will be the dynamics of its classification within penal law:

> The more we look at the act as a point in time and not as a process the more easy is made the task of classifying the act in a penal law perspective. The less we know of the total situation, the simpler becomes our classificatory task. (Christie, 1986b: 96)

Obviously, by avoiding the perception of the social interaction that contributed to the occurrence of a criminal event and by seeking to blame only the *immediate actor*, such a system will fail to work with a *collective* perspective of responsibility: responsibility will always be *individual* rather than attributed to the group or community in which the offender lives. By doing this, criminal justice achieves the goal of classifying both the author of the delict and the facts, and believes that it is possible, because of their classification, to consider different cases as equal. For Christie (1998b; 2007; 2010), there are no similar cases: they are *made* equal by the artificial mechanisms of penal law, and this undermines the possibility of each case being treated according to their peculiarities.

The author states that courts and courtrooms are not to be searched when one wants to unveil *all* the case history and the characteristics that differentiate it from others. Criminal justice accepts only the information considered relevant by the law: 'what the parties might feel to be of central importance might be seen as irrelevant and therefore cut off in court' (Christie, 2007: 373).

Thus, it can be observed that Christie proposes (a) a model of communitarian conflict management focused on the local resolution of cases, without (b) the intervention of legal professionals and, most importantly, that (c) allows the parties to be fully known as complex beings that are in constant interaction with their environment and the people around them, thus allowing the details (considered irrelevant by penal courts) to be taken into consideration before any decision-making.

A balanced and active involvement of both victim and offender, together with other members of the community, is a core issue in Christie's framework, which can be delineated from the *proximity* between the involved parties and the local court, by the knowledge of the social interactions of the victim and the offender and by the balanced *dialogue* between the parties (Ruggiero, 2011).

III. PENAL ABOLITIONISM AND RESTORATIVE JUSTICE: THEORETICAL APPROACHES

It can be said that restorative justice has gained new impetus since (a) specific practical experiences of victim-offender mediation in Canada in 1974, and in other countries in the following years; and (b) the fragmentation (or crisis) of critical criminology, with the emergence of penal abolitionism as one of its major theoretical perspectives, from the second half of the 1970s on (Braithwaite, 2002; Anitua, 2008; Walgrave, 2008; Van Ness and Strong, 2010; Hoyle, 2010; Ruggiero, 2010 and 2011).

The dissatisfaction with the traditional criminal justice system (Hoyle, 2010; Wright, 1996) found, in the 1970s and 1980s, widespread cultural support for the development of (a) models of justice aimed at meeting the needs of victims of crimes (Albrecht, 2010); and (b) critical criminology and, within this context, the abolitionist approach.

Penal abolitionism, in turn, has internal variations (Andrade, 2006; Hjemdal and Mathiesen, 2011); but these, instead of weakening its arguments, foster its expansion: the different critical analyses allow a single problem to be seen and thought in different ways.

In this sense, the critical framework of abolitionists can be considered as the most consistent and accurate among current criminological approaches considered *critical*: by reaching the backbone that underpins the criminal justice system—the concept of crime and the appropriation of conflicts by the state—penal abolitionism provides enough theoretical basis to expose the impairing structural limitations (Rubio, 2012) that prevent this system from offering, in each case, an adequate solution. There are *legal responses*, but never *solutions*. The abolitionist considerations highlight the need to pursue an alternative to this inefficient structure, without, however, neglecting the pitfalls that many reformisms, under the same argument, bring along.

Analyses of Hulsman's and Christie's penal abolitionist discourses make it possible to notice a direct connection with the restorative justice movement: as Ruggiero (2011) asserts, 'there is clearly an abolitionist element in the proposition that the state centralised administration of penal justice should be replaced by decentralised forms of autonomous conflict regulation' (Ruggiero, 2011: 100). In general, the author suggests that penal abolitionists 'advocate new ways of dealing with undesirable behaviour, and in doing so they situate themselves in an original position within the debate around restorative justice' (Ruggiero, 2011: 100). By positing the adoption of decentralised mechanisms that approximate the parties and grant them the option to dialogue and try to find the best solution to their cases, penal abolitionists, since Christie's *Conflict as Property* (1977), present a way to handle conflicts that is different from the one employed by the traditional criminal justice system.

As pointed out by Van Ness and Strong (2010), the various topics covered by Christie throughout his work make him a reference in the literature on restorative justice. The same, however, cannot be said about Hulsman's work, but as we can see, both authors provide important criticisms which, taken together, suggest the creation of a model for conflict management that is very close to what today is called restorative justice.

For Ruggiero (2011), however, it is not an easy task to identify to what extent abolitionist proposals have influenced the growing interest in non-criminal measures. Nonetheless, beyond the simple negative criticism that it is a utopian proposal, Christie's and Hulsman's abolitionist criticism can give us a glimpse of concrete possibilities for structuring a conflict resolution mechanism. Once disconnected from abolitionism's ultimate proposal—the abolition of incarceration or of the penal system as a whole—the criticism built by Hulsman and Christie takes an innovative character, with many possible interpretations. It is possible to say, therefore, that the authors outline important approaches to be followed for the structuring of a system for conflict resolution that is detached from modern penal rationality.

Under the abolitionist perspective, restorative justice (a) cannot fall prey to the criminal justice system, so as to avoid being relegated to the role of a mere expansionist supplement of punitive power; (b) requires the adoption of a new language for its operation, so that it is not colonised by the practices and traditional notions of criminal justice; (c) does not make a distinction between *tort* and *offence*, in order to allow the stakeholders to decide how they will manage the situation; (d) must not be dominated by professionals, under penalty of being dragged into the crime control industry and the modern bureaucratic logic; (e) must reject any stereotypes about the parties, avoiding revictimisation of victims and stigmatisation of offenders; (f) should focus on meeting the needs of victims, offenders and their communities of care, through the collective involvement in the attribution of responsibilities to meet the conditions stipulated in any agreement reached; and (g) should, fundamentally, encourage the active participation of the parties in solving their cases, so that the decision arising from the meeting is a product of their own proposals.

Finally, in line with Ruggiero (2011), it is possible to affirm that restorative justice creates no winners or losers; rather, it aims at meeting the parties' basic needs, so as to reach a decision in everyone's best interests. The reduction of the use of the criminal justice system to manage conflicts is, therefore, the expected result of the implementation of restorative justice under an abolitionist perspective.

IV. FINAL CONSIDERATIONS: TOWARDS AN ABOLITIONIST MODEL OF RESTORATIVE JUSTICE

As stated by Salo de Carvalho (2002), it is not reasonable to accept the *demonisation* of abolitionist proposals. According to the author, there are at least three positive aspects derived from this perspective: (a) its usefulness to the phenomenological assessment of the (in)efficacy of the criminal justice system; (b) the academic irreversibility of its technical and doctrinal foundations in relation to criminological science; and (c) the viability of some of its proposals as criminal policy, in particular those relating to the abolition of incarceration, the criminalisation processes and the denial of the ideology of treatment.

With this, the author (Carvalho, 2002) concludes that penal abolitionism can be considered as a *guiding utopia*, in the sense proposed by Alessandro Baratta (1999), when it comes to taking it as a *guide* for the development of criminal policies that reduce the incidence of the penal system.

However, we also agree with Elena Larrauri (2005), for whom it is not possible to say that abolitionism proposes that 'nothing be done' and that no other way of solving conflicts can exist just because it does not accept the punitive logic. Accordingly, in addition to the well-known negative criticism and the positive aspects pointed out by Carvalho, Hulsman's and Christie's penal abolitionism have yet a third possible reading: by outlining important steps to be considered for the *creation* and the *structuring* of an alternative justice system, it can be concluded that the works of both authors have, due to their criticism, an important *propositional-constructive* character, sensitive to criminalising interferences of the traditional criminal justice system.

Even though this has not been the authors' intention, the open and creative way their works were built allows a broader reading: besides presenting the most important criticisms to the criminal justice system among critical criminological (or anticriminological) schools, they also suggest the first steps towards the characterisation of an informal conflict management model detached from the traditional crime-punishment paradigm.

The abolitionist criticism can therefore be taken into consideration for the construction of a critical and qualified mechanism of restorative justice in Brazil, basically because it will not allow this system to be structured according to the criminalising language of the traditional criminal justice system.

In this respect, Luiz Antônio Chies Bogo (2002) is right when he mentions that abolitionist theories and criticisms are in 'opposition to the perversities offered by the bureaucratic "rationality" of the modern criminal legal system' (Bogo, 2002: 187), either as critical guidance and reflection about the paradoxes of the penal system or as 'propositions of alternative and extra-penal forms for conflict resolution' (Chies, 2002: 187).

Although Carvalho (2010) had, at first, adopted a different position in relation to the risk of violation of fundamental rights and guarantees through more informal legal proceedings (Carvalho, 2002 and 2004), after conducting some research on the role of criminal justice actors he went on to point out that a democratic model of Justice cannot assume 'that the only legitimate voice in the process is the one of the legal authority, as if the whole rite had the State representative as its sole interested party' (Carvalho, 2010: 50). And this, according to the author, should not be attributed to the fact that the concentration of power in the hands of the judge tends to overestimate its role and reinforce the idea that the magistrate is, in fact, the main character in the procedural ritual, but to the idea that:

> [the] conflict belongs to the people; the suit should be the mechanism focused on trying to solve the case, and it should involve both the offender(s) and the victim(s). Otherwise, the lawsuit becomes mere bureaucracy, an end in itself, a form just for the sake of form. (Carvalho, 2010: 51)

Thus, Carvalho (2010) states that restorative justice proceedings can be used to promote the active participation of the parties, concluding that 'the intervention and the classification of the conflict as "penal" usually produces more problems than solutions' (Carvalho, 2010: 252).

Furthermore, for cases that remain in the traditional criminal justice system, the author argues that the parties should be provided with opportunities to be heard, so that they can effectively intervene in the resolution of the conflict: 'the openness of the procedure, with emphasis on non-technocratic speeches, can contribute positively to the rupture, change and, who knows, the overcoming of the inquisitorial mind-set that sets up the criminal justice system logic' (Carvalho, 2010: 252).

It is possible to conclude, therefore, that the abolitionists' critics, once read from a propositional perspective, point directly towards a similar model of conflict administration to restorative justice. Such model, if well-structured and if those responsible for its implementation are aware of the challenges and obstacles they will face, might be an important tool to decrease, not to increase, the harmful action of penal system.

REFERENCES

Achutti, D and Pallamolla, R (2011) 'Brazil' in E Zinsstag, M Teunkens and B Pali (eds), *Conferencing: A Way Forward for Restorative Justice in Europe* (Leuven, European Forum for Restorative Justice).

—— (2012) 'Restorative Justice in Juvenile Courts in Brazil: A Brief Review of Porto Alegre and São Caetano Pilot Projects' 11 *Universitas Psychologica* 1093.

Albrecht, B (2010) 'Multicultural Challenges for Restorative Justice: Mediators' Experience from Norway and Finland' 11 *Journal of Scandinavian Studies in Criminology and Crime Prevention* 3.

Andrade, VRPD (2006) 'Minimalismos e Abolicionismos: a crise do sistema penal entre a deslegitimação e a expansão' 13 *Revista da ESMESC* 1093.

Anitua, GI (2008) *Histórias dos Pensamentos Criminológicos* (Rio de Janeiro, Revan).

Baratta, A (1999) *Criminologia Crítica e Crítica do Direito Penal. Introdução à sociologia do Direito Penal*, 2nd edn (Rio de Janeiro, Freitas Bastos/ICC).
Batista, V (2011) *Introdução Crítica à Criminologia Brasileira* (Rio de Janeiro, Revan).
Bertrand, M-A (2007) 'Comments by Marie-Andrée Bertrand' in J Feest and B Paul (eds), '*Does Abolitionism Have a Future? Documentation of an Email Exchange Among Abolitionists* (University of Hamburgo), available at www.sozialwiss.uni-hamburg.de/publish/IKS/KrimInstituteVereinigungenZs/Zusatzmaterial.html.
Braithwaite, J (2002) *Restorative Justice and Responsive Regulation* (Oxford, Oxford University Press).
Carvalho, SD (2002) 'Considerações sobre as Incongruências da Justiça Penal Consensual: retórica garantista, prática abolicionista' in A Wunderlich and SD Carvalho (eds), *Diálogos Sobre a Justiça Dialogal: teses e antíteses sobre os processos de informalização e privatização da justiça penal* (Rio de Janeiro, Lumen Juris).
—— (2004) 'Cinco Teses para Entender a Desjudicialização Material do Processo Penal Brasileiro' in A. Wunderlich and SD Carvalho (eds), *Novos Diálogos Sobre os Juizados Especiais Criminais* (Rio de Janeiro, Lumen Juris).
—— (2010) *O Papel dos Atores do Sistema Penal na Era do Punitivismo (o exemplo privilegiado da aplicação da pena)* (Rio de Janeiro, Lumen Juris).
Chies, LAB (2002) 'É Possível se Ter o Abolicionismo como Meta, Admitindo-se o Garantismo como Estratégia?' in A Wunderlich and SD Carvalho (eds), *Diálogos Sobre a Justiça Dialogal: teses e antíteses sobre os processos de informalização e privatização da justiça penal* (Rio de Janeiro, Lumen Juris).
Christie, N (1977) 'Conflicts as Property' 17 *British Journal of Criminology* 1.
—— (1981) *Limits to Pain: The Role of Punishment in Penal Policy* (Eugene, Wipf and Stock Publishers).
—— (1986a) 'Crime Control as Drama' 13 *Journal of Law and Society* 1.
—— (1986b) 'Images of Man in Modern Penal Law' 10 *Contemporary Crises (Crime, Law and Social Change)* 95.
—— (1998a) 'Roots of a Perspective' in S Holdaway and P Rock (eds), *Thinking about Criminology* (London, University College London Press).
—— (1998b) 'Between Civility and State' in V Ruggiero, N South and I Taylor (eds), *The New European Criminology: Crime and Social Order in Europe* (London and New York, Routledge).
—— (2007) 'Restorative Justice: Answers to Deficits in Modernity?' in D Downes, P Rock, C Chinkin and C Gearty (eds), *Crime, Social Control and Human Rights: From Moral Panics to States of Denial, Essays in Honour of Stanley Cohen* (London, Willan Publishing).
—— (2010) 'Victim Movements at a Crossroad' 12 *Punishment and Society* 115.
—— (2011) *Uma Razoável Quantidade de Crime* (Rio de Janeiro, Revan).
Cohen, S (1986) 'Editorial' 10 *Contemporary Crises (Crime, Law and Social Change)* 335.
—— (1988) *Against Criminology* (New Jersey, Transaction Publishers).
Elbert, C (2003) *Manual Básico de Criminologia* (Porto Alegre, Ricardo Lenz).
Folter, de, RS (1986) 'On the Methodological Foundation of the Abolitionist Approach to the Criminal Justice System: A Comparison of the Ideas of Hulsman, Mathiesen and Foucault' 10 *Contemporary Crises (Crime, Law and Social Change)* 39.

Hjemdal, OK and Mathiesen, M (2011) 'A New Look at Victim and Offender: An Abolitionist Approach' in M Bosworth and C Hoyle (eds), *What is Criminology?* (Oxford, Oxford University Press).
Hoyle, C (2010) 'The Case for Restorative Justice' in C Hoyle and C Cunneen (eds), *Debating Restorative Justice* (Oxford and Portland, Hart Publishing).
Hulsman, L (1986) 'Critical Criminology and the Concept of Crime' 10 *Contemporary Crises (Crime, Law and Social Change)* 63.
—— (1991) 'The Abolitionist Case: Alternative Crime Policies' 25 *Israel Law Review* 681.
Hulsman, L and Celis, JBD (1997) *Penas Perdidas: o sistema penal em questão*, 2nd edn (Niterói, Luam).
—— (2005) 'A Aposta por uma Teoria da Abolição do Sistema Penal' 8 *Revista Verve* 246.
Johnstone, G and Van Ness, DW (2007) 'The Meaning of Restorative Justice' in G Johnstone and DW Van Ness (eds), *Handbook of Restorative Justice* (Cullompton and Portland, OR, Willan Publishing).
Larrauri, E (1991) *La Herencia de la Criminología Crítica* (Madrid, Siglo Veintiuno de España).
—— (2005) 'Abolicionismo y Garantismo' 20 *Revista de Estudos Criminais* 11.
Pallamolla, RDP (2009) *Justiça Restaurativa: da teoria à prática* (São Paulo, IBCCRIM).
Passetti, E (2006) 'Um Ensaio sobre um Abolicionismo Penal' 9 *Revista Verve* 83.
Passetti, E and Silva, RBD (1997) 'Prefácio' in E Passetti and RBD Silva (eds), *Conversações Abolicionistas. Uma crítica do sistema penal e da sociedade punitiva* (São Paulo, IBCCRIM).
Ruggiero, V (2010) *Penal Abolitionism: A Celebration* (Oxford, Oxford University Press).
—— (2011) 'An Abolitionist View of Restorative Justice' 39 *International Journal of Law, Crime and Justice* 100.
Rubio, OS (2012) 'Inversión Ideológica y Derecho Penal Mínimo, Decolonial, Intercultural y Antihegemónico' in PCC Borges (ed), *Leituras de um Realismo Jurídico-Penal Marginal: homenagem a Alessandro Baratta* (São Paulo, Cultura Acadêmica) 137–62.
Scheerer, S (1986) 'Towards Abolitionism' 10 *Contemporary Crises (Crime, Law and Social Change)* 5.
Sim, J (1994) 'The Abolitionist Approach: a British Perspective' in A Duff, S Marshall, RE Dobash and P Russell (eds), *Penal Theory and Practice: Tradition and Innovation in Criminal Justice* (Manchester, Manchester University Press).
Van Ness, D and Strong, KH (2010) *Restoring Justice: An Introduction to Restorative Justice*, 4th edn (New Providence, Anderson Publishing).
Van Swaaningen, R (1986) 'What is Abolitionism? An Introduction' in H Bianchi and R Van Swaaningen (eds), *Abolitionism: Towards a Non-repressive Approach to Crime* (Amsterdam, Free University Press).
—— (1999) 'Reclaiming Critical Criminology: Social Justice and the European Tradition' 3 *Theoretical Criminology* 5.
Walgrave, L (2008) *Restorative Justice, Self-interest and Responsible Citizenship* (Cullompton and Portland, OR, Willan Publishing).

Wright, M (1996) *Justice for Victims and Offenders: A Restorative Response to Crime*, 2nd edn (Winchester, Waterside Press).
Zaffaroni, ER (1991) *Em Busca das Penas Perdidas. A perda de legitimidade do sistema penal* (Rio de Janeiro, Revan).
—— (2005) 'La Criminología como Curso' in ER Zaffaroni (ed), *En Torno a la Cuestión Penal* (Montevideo-Buenos Aires, B de F Editorial).

2

Deconstructing Empowerment in Restorative Justice

DANIELA BOLÍVAR

I. EMPOWERMENT AND RESTORATIVE JUSTICE

RESTORATIVE JUSTICE (RJ) is expected to be an empowering experience, because victims and offenders can identify their needs and actively participate in identifying, defining and actually constructing the way they want to meet their needs. RJ searches for a participative and integrating model of justice in which victims, offenders and community members may engage in the detection, analysis, and solution of social and crime-related conflicts.

In Braithwaite's sense (2002), empowerment means inclusion, participation, voice and non-dominion. RJ should promote the attendance of every stakeholder that has a say in the conflict, as well as prevent power imbalances within RJ meetings. Non-domination, inclusivity and a spirit of collaboration between victims and offenders will help parties to resolve the conflict by themselves (Pranis, 2007).

Underlying the notion of empowerment, as used in RJ texts and writings, there are two central assumptions: (a) the idea that the mere experience of crime disempowers victims, offenders and communities; and (b) Christie's notion of crime as owned by the stakeholders, and, together with that, the idea that criminal justice, while appropriating conflicts, disempowers parties in their capacities to respond to it (Aertsen *et al.*, 2011; Barton, 2000; Christie, 1977).

Therefore, it is believed that *victims need to be empowered* (Larson and Zehr, 2007; McCold and Wachtel, 2002; Zehr, 2005). 'At minimum, this means they must be key in determining what their needs are, how they should be met, and when they should be met' (Zehr, 2005: 194). Two ideas feed such a belief. One the one hand, victimological research has established that one of the effects of victimisation is to feel powerless (Van Ness and Strong, 2006; Zehr, 2005). Victims may lose their sense of control and experience damage in their sense of self-efficacy. So, if harm is a form of disempowerment, restoration can only be achieved through a participatory process that makes victims actively involved in the search for answers (Bolívar, 2010; McCold and Wachtel, 2002; Larson and Zehr, 2007; Van Ness and Strong, 2006; Zehr, 2005). In victimological language, a person who can regain a sense of control is someone who overcomes the label of 'victim' and becomes a 'survivor' (see, eg Thompson, 2000). In other words, someone who makes the transition between being 'in need', requiring help and services from society, to become 'an equal' who, instead, can offer/do something to/for others. On the other hand, we assume that victims want more than having a witness role. Besides, receiving information may not even be enough. Some victims may want to be heard (Zehr, 2005), tell their own story (Toews and Zehr, 2003; Barton, 2000), and have a say in the decision-making, having the opportunity to define and meet their own needs (Barton, 2000; Toews and Zehr, 2003; Zehr, 2005).

Offenders would also need to be empowered. When the criminal justice system appropriates the conflict, offenders become alienated not only from the decision-making process but also from the harm they have caused and the way to repair it. RJ may consequently offer two main things to offenders: As any stakeholder, offenders are empowered when they tell their stories in their own way to 'reveal whatever sense of injustice they wish to see repaired' (Braithwaite, 2002: 569). When taking responsibility, the offender is also able to move the external locus of control to an internal one. By assuming their actions, offenders understand they can control their actions and therefore their fate, being able to engage in their own rehabilitation (Zehr, 2005). In this sense, offender's empowerment is linked to acknowledgment, and with this, to the possibility of constructing changes for oneself and for others. On the other hand, by condemning the facts and not the person, RJ represents a process in which offender's subjectivity is valued, respected and heard. By solely offering to the offender the opportunity to make amends, RJ builds room for social integration, and for reconstructing a new social identity. By being acquainted with the facts and recognising the harm caused, offenders may demonstrate that behind their labels of 'offenders' they can understand other's suffering, and erase the gap created between them and 'their' victims.

Finally, *communities also need to be empowered*. 'Communities' need to exercise their own responsibilities and therefore become empowered when they can both experience crime in an active way and regain the social control that has been ceded to the state (Dzur and Olson, 2004). Communities should also be able to receive and integrate their members that have suffered the consequences of crime (either as victims or offenders). Therefore, an empowered community is one able to offer social support (Barton, 2003) and to construct mechanisms of social reintegration.

As a consequence, we may conclude that RJ is expected to fulfil two needs at the same time: it offers empowerment in terms of a participatory procedure (in opposition to what the criminal justice system does) and offers empowerment in terms of the harm caused, engaging victims, offenders and their communities in their own restoration/rehabilitation processes.

A. Problematic Nature?

Despite the popularity of the notion, dissident voices have been raised to warn academics and practitioners about the problematic nature of the notion of empowerment within RJ literature. One of these voices is Richards' (2011). She has argued that in RJ 'empowerment' has been taken for granted and therefore never challenged. Instead, the discourse of empowerment has remained 'invisible' and unproblematic, even by critical criminologists. This invisibility, argues this author, exists because the word itself is apolitical: independently if one is conservative or liberal, one will always agree that all stakeholders need to be empowered.

This criticism stresses two relevant problems. On the one hand, it emphasises the 'mechanical' adoption of the concept within the RJ discourse, because participation, and in particular the participating mechanisms offered by RJ, are assumed to lead automatically to empowerment. On the other hand, Richards stresses the indisputable positive nature of the concept, which is able to go beyond political ideologies, and to install a common discourse of good intentions for all stakeholders.

I believe Richards' criticism (2011) requires to be complemented with developments from other disciplines in which 'empowerment' plays a central role. One of them is community psychology (CP). Aertsen *et al.* (2011) have already done this exercise, focusing on the victim perspective. As result they have argued that the concept, as conceived in RJ, has been unable to address a wider dimension than the individual victim and offender, which is contrary to what the notion of 'empowerment' in PC suggests. In addition, they stress how empowerment in the field of justice can only be achieved when *offered*, putting into discussion the bottom-up ideology behind empowerment in PC. In this chapter, I will develop these ideas further and argue that what has been considered the problematic nature of empowerment comes from a deficient understanding of what empowerment is. Instead, I will argue that the difficult aspects of empowerment come from other sources, all of them linked to paradoxes involved in the theory and practice of RJ.

II. DECONSTRUCTING THE NOTION OF EMPOWERMENT

A. Community Psychology's Concept of Empowerment

As already announced, empowerment is not an exclusive notion of RJ. Other disciplines of social sciences have adopted it as well, and in certain cases, in a very central position. That is the case of community psychology (CP). The theoretical developments on empowerment may be well linked to RJ (see also Aertsen *et al.*, 2011).

CP has been defined as a field of research and intervention that works on the prevention of psychosocial problems and the promotion of the integral development of people (Sánchez Vidal, 1996). As a response to the medical model applied in psychology (in which health is delivered by expert professional to sick patients), CP adopts, among other things, the assumption that psychological problems may have a social origin. The intervention should be focused, therefore, on the environment and not just on the individual. Secondly, the individual-perspective is not enough to explain and to intervene in mental health problems. For this reason, CP needs not only an ecological and systemic model as a theoretical framework but also a multidisciplinary approach to the field. Finally, the community as a whole is the target of the intervention. This intervention, by definition, is a bottom-up one, since the individual is a participant and no longer a passive patient. The professional leaves his/her role as an expert to become a facilitator. The individual, on the other hand, becomes a protagonist of his wellbeing, creating an equal relationship between professional and individual (Kloos *et al.*, 2012).

According to Kofkin (2003), CP is guided by the following principles: (a) research, theory and practice necessarily are developed within a value system; (b) it is impossible to understand the individual without taking into account his social context; (c) the improvement of people's lives often requires social change; and (d) the diversity and strengths models (in contrast to the deficit model) are important guide values for research, theory and practice.

Within the field of CP, empowerment is both a value orientation and a theoretical model for understanding the efforts to exert control over decisions that affect one's life, organisational functioning and the quality of the community (Zimmerman, 2000). It is the way that people, organisations and communities gain mastery over their lives; it involves both a psychological sense of personal control and a concern with actual social influence, political power and legal rights (Rappaport, 1987).

As a *theory* (Zimmerman, 2000), two dimensions should be distinguished: empowerment as a process and as an outcome. Both dimensions can be operationalised within the three levels of analysis in the study of empowerment: individual, organisational and community levels. As a process, empowerment at the individual level means learning decision-making skills and managing resources. It may also mean to learn to work with others in order to achieve common goals. Naturally, empowerment may be studied at the individual level but is not a mere individual phenomenon. The notion cannot ignore the person-environment fit: it involves skill development and cultural awareness. For example, an empowered person may not have real power (to vote) but awareness of the alternatives in different contexts (Zimmerman, 1990).

At the organisational level, the process of empowerment means opportunities to participate in decision-making, sharing responsibilities and leadership. At this level, empowerment implies access to resources, open government structure and tolerance for diversity. As an outcome, empowerment can be observed in indicators such as sense of control, existence of critical awareness and participatory behaviours in the individuals, networking and policy influence in the organisation, and organisational coalitions, pluralistic leadership and resident's participatory skills in the community.

Empowerment can also be understood as *value orientation* (Zimmerman, 2000). In this sense, social problems exist because of unequal distribution of and access to resources. The language itself suggests alternative ways to understand the role of the professionals; which means to transform experts into collaborators. Finally, the notion of empowerment involves social identity, emphasises the role of the environment and the value of diversity and social integration. Community participation is not merely about having one's own voice heard; it is about setting the agenda.

Consequently, empowering interventions should then approach the underpowered. These interventions are concerned 'with many who are excluded by the majority society on the basis of their demographic characteristics or of their physical or emotional difficulties, experienced either in the past or in the present' (Rappaport, 1990).

B. Some Useful Distinctions

(i) Empowerment Versus Participation

Are empowerment and participation synonymous? RJ literature seems to suggest that they are, or, at least, that both notions are automatically linked. Morris, Maxwell and Robertson (1993: 77) argue, for example, that (victim) participation is what empowers. Participation then has been assumed as an idea that will benefit all to the same level (Richards, 2011).

For authors from other areas of social sciences, however, these notions certainly differ, or at least, they have niceties relevant to highlight. One of the most well-known definitions of participation is the one proposed by Arnstein in 1969. In his article 'A Ladder of Citizen Participation', he describes how participation 'is a categorical term for citizen power. It is the redistribution of power that enables the have-not citizens, presently excluded from the political and economic processes, to be deliberately included in the future' (Arnstein, 1969: 216). For him, participation is the strategy that defines how information is shared, how goals and policies are set and how benefits are parcelled out. Participation implies having the real power to influence outcomes and therefore actual redistribution of power. When this does not happen, then participation is an empty ritual that allows the power-holders 'to claim that all sides were considered, but makes it possible for only some of those sides to benefit' (Arnstein, 1969: 216). Arnstein then proposes a scale of different degrees of participation with increasing levels of power. The first two levels, which he calls 'Manipulation' and 'Therapy', are actually considered manifestations of non-participation. At these levels the power-holder aims to 'cure' or 'educate' participants. The following three levels are manifestations of tokenism: 'Informing', 'Consultation' and 'Placation'. In the first two, participants can be heard but they will not necessarily be heeded by the power-holder. In 'Placation' participants can advise, but the power-holders are in the end those who decide. At a higher degree of decision-making, Arnstein locates 'Parternship' which allows participants to negotiate with power-holders, and 'Delegated Power' and 'Citizen Control' which give participants the majority or full managerial power.

Participation thus means a process in which individuals take part in the decision-making in the environments that affect them (Heller *et al.*, 1984), in which they are able to freely make choices and control opportunities.

Arnstein's definition implies that participation is only possible when the power-holder redistributes power. In other words, this is necessarily a top-down strategy. Empowerment, on the contrary, implies going in exactly the opposite direction. Even though one could argue that participation is the means to achieve empowerment, the latter is a more complex phenomenon that may lead to increased feelings of competence, but also contribute to development of what has been called critical awareness, and consciousness of the social and historical context (Freire, 2005). Empowerment means that the individual is able not only to act, but also to influence and actively transform his environment (Zimmerman, 1995; 2000). In other words, while participation implies involvement and decision-making, empowerment is necessarily linked to the idea of social change. Empowerment thus goes beyond participation, it means bottom-up movement, questioning the status quo, the current power relations, and other intersecting oppressions (see also Aertsen *et al.*, 2011).

I argue that RJ should promote both participation and empowerment, as they are both mechanisms needed to promote democracy and wellbeing; while offering room for participation indicates authorities' willingness to consider civil society, empowerment will allow people to identify and initiate needed changes.

(ii) Empowerment Versus Power

As a corollary of our discussion on participation, we may conclude that empowerment is not synonymous with power. Zimmerman (1995), when discussing the results of Gruber and Trickett (1987) in the educational field, refers to the distinction between these two terms. Empowerment, he says, is not to have the power of making decision, but to have the confidence that one can (could) influence those decisions. Zimmerman stresses, therefore, that the importance of the concept of empowerment resides in its interactional component which is, in concrete, the capacity of understanding the context in which people live. This could imply, then, that what is empowering in a mediation process is not just the fact that one could influence the final outcome or be part of a decision-making process, but also the secondary benefit of understanding the conflict, to have access to the resources needed to resolve it and to capture the role that such outcome could have in a wider context.

From a victim perspective, this would give an answer to the debate in terms of how much involvement victims want. In 2004, Wemmers and Cyr reported interviews with 59 victims. In their study, the authors concluded:

> Like those who oppose victim participation, the majority of victims are well aware of the risk of introducing arbitrariness into sentencing should victims be granted decision-making power. Most victims are quite clear that while they seek input, they are content to leave decision control in the hands of authorities. (Wemmers and Cyr, 2004: 270)

According to the distinctions we are making here, Wemmers and Cyr's victims would not want to exercise full power but to achieve a certain degree of participation. However, in Wemmer and Cyr's study, victims' power was defined as having a role in sentencing, which may definitely differ from empowerment, as we understand this concept here.

(iii) Empowerment Versus Responsibility

For Richards (2011) one of the problems of the narrative of empowerment in RJ is that it is linked to its targets' activity, in opposition to the passivity of the criminal justice system, where offenders and victims are passive or absent. So, to be empowered 'is to act' (Richards, 2011: 97), that is, to create active bodies. This emphasis on action increases offenders', victims' and communities' sense of responsibilisation, which becomes, in Richards' view, a secondary and negative effect of its intervention. For example, offenders' parents may feel pushed to apologise on behalf of their children and offer restitution to the victims. Richards concludes that RJ may increase this sense of responsibility in disempowered or marginalised individuals. What Richards is pointing out seems to be related to two main factors: (a) the fact that responsibility may become guilt at a certain point of the intervention; (b) that feelings of guilt can go beyond the individual offender and be experienced by other participants in the meeting.

Hoyle and Palmer (2014) make a similar point. Even though they are not specifically referring to RJ interventions, I believe we can perfectly translate their conclusions to our field. They argue that in cases of intimate partner violence, to promote empowerment may carry two important risks: (a) to transform one form of control into another (from offender to agency staff member); and (b) responsibilisation for future victimisation (McDermott and Garofalo, 2004 in Hoyle and Palmer, 2014). They also argue that victims who are in real danger of further victimisation 'but do not yet feel ready for change may be left vulnerable to further, and perhaps fatal, violence if they are left to choose how the system should respond to their victimization' (Hoyle and Palmer, 2014: 205). This risk could occur if RJ facilitators do not carry out proper risk assessments and allow the RJ encounter to become one element more within the cycle of violence.

I believe that what underlies these apprehensions is the idea that empowerment refers exclusively to self-awareness and that such awareness merely means consciousness of one's own role in the offence. Empowerment certainly is about developing an internal locus of control, however, this does not merely refer to awareness of one's own deficits but also of one's own *competences*. It is about identifying one's needs but at the same time identifying internal and external resources to meet them. Secondly, empowerment is mainly possible in the context of social interaction. It is not about a lonely process in which one is confronted with one's own limitations. Empowerment means a social-construction and conscious process of critical awareness of one's social environment. The individual is able to see himself *in context* and to identify personal and structural aspects in need of change in order to promote individual and social development.

C. Features from the RJ Practice

Having defined empowerment in CP's terms, now we have a second problem to solve: reflecting on the extent to which the practice of RJ is actually in line with the theoretical assumptions of empowerment. In concrete, whether RJ is actually addressing the powerless and whether RJ practice is able to facilitate both top-down (from the criminal policy to stakeholders) and bottom-up (from stakeholders to criminal policy) methods of communication. In the next paragraphs, this issue will be considered, based on victim-oriented research.

(i) Who is RJ Addressing?

I believe that RJ practices are 'empowering the empowered'. This statement is based on recent evidence indicating that (a) RJ seems to be a practice in which mainly 'resilient victims' participate; and (b) perhaps more concerning, that social agents are 'choosing' to whom RJ can be offered.

(a) The 'RJ Client'

In a previous work I shared the results of interviews that took place before mediation with victims participating and non-participating in RJ in Belgium and Spain. What I found were relevant differences between the two groups. Victims participating in RJ had less long-lasting emotional effects as a consequence of the crime. In other words, their emotional damage was less pronounced than that of non-participants (Bolívar, 2013). Laxminarayan, Lens and Pemberton (2013) arrived at the same conclusion when comparing victims participating in RJ with victims who took part in a victim impact statement programme (VIS). They compared traumatic stress symptoms in both groups and concluded that RJ victims were presenting less symptoms than VIS victims.

Maybe not coincidently, I could also observe in my own research that some victims who went to direct mediation and evaluated their experiences as very successful were involved in community participation. They were participating in different types of civic organisations and have different degrees of social leadership. Perhaps for the same reason, all these victims considered mediation as a means not only to help the offender and themselves, but also society. This social dimension was relevant in order to make sense of the experience, beyond their individual case.

These pieces of evidence would indicate that victims who decide to participate in RJ might present not only some degree of 'resilience' but perhaps also of 'empowerment'.

(b) 'Choosing' the RJ Client

At this point, the question arises whether this feature is only the result of the voluntary nature of RJ. If that is the case, voluntariness would act as a filter that would ensure that those who take part in RJ are those who have a 'restorative' way of thinking or are already on their way to recovery. This explanation may be a logical one, but it is based on the premise that all individuals (victims and offenders) have equal information and access to RJ.

I believe this is not the case. Individuals are not only unequally informed; individuals are *selectively* informed. According to some European evaluations (APAV and INTERVICT, 2009; Matrix and Felix, 2010), professionals, jurists, lawyers, and social agents are the ones actively (nevertheless perhaps unconsciously) selecting who are the appropriate individuals for taking part in victim-offender mediation or family group conferencing. Putting it another way, perhaps the 'resilient' profile of the clients of RJ (at least in terms of victims of crime) that we have found in research is mirroring the selective way we offer mediation or conferencing.

There seem to be different 'filters' of such selection. The first one corresponds to the scope of RJ. We know that, at least in most of Europe, either because of legislation or mere practice, RJ has mainly been applied to minor crimes. Prosecutors and judges remain the gatekeepers of the offer. Cases are usually referred to RJ, which in practice means that the level of self-referral remains low (Bolívar, 2015).

At this point Hart's (1995 cited in Shier, 2001) adaptation of Arnstein's ladder (1969) in the field of child participation could help us to reflect on this issue further. This author locates in the top three levels of participation, children-initiated activities, in which they have the idea, set the agenda and involve adults to collaborate. This model makes sense to RJ theory and practice. In order to promote genuine participation and to become a manifestation of redistribution of power, victim- and offender-initiated processes of RJ should, in the first place, be the way to implement RJ. If this does not happen, it means that, despite our goodwill, we are still appropriating the conflict from the parties. In addition to collaborating with social injustice, the main consequence of offering RJ to the 'good people' is that we are not only ensuring a positive result for the practice (which might be logical from a public policy perspective), we are also avoiding that RJ enriches its methodology by receiving a wider clientele in terms of motivations, emotions and expectations.

(ii) How is RJ Taking Place?

(a) Shaping People's Experiences

In addition to selecting the 'RJ client' we are also shaping their experiences. In recent European comparative research, we observed that victims of crime tended to be satisfied and to agree upon the way that mediation was implemented in their country, regardless of the institutional context, for example, whether this was a diversionary programme or not. Perhaps more importantly, this research also showed that the topics discussed in the encounters differed depending on the institutional context: in the two diversionary schemes studied, economic compensation was discussed more frequently than the emotional consequences of the crime. However, the opposite occurred in the non-diversionary scheme included in the sample (Bolívar et al., 2015). These findings brought back a conversation I had, some time ago, with a mediator who was working on a diversionary scheme. Referring to a case, the mediator commented 'the whole conversation went around money, because that is what parties wanted'. This might have been true. Parties are entitled to be interested only in material methods of reparation. No moral judgement should be raised regarding this fact. However, from a critical perspective, we have the obligation to wonder whether the extent to which parties only discuss financial issues is because of the way the conversation is settled and established. Is the format of the meeting (the way the invitation is done, the way that parties arrive at the meeting, the way in which the mediator stimulates the conversation and so on) impeding the appearance of other concerns or topics? RJ's institutional contexts and the manner that facilitators guide the dialogue may certainly create discourses and narratives that will shape the way that individuals experience RJ.

(b) Paradoxical Relationship with the Criminal Justice System

If participation is redistribution of power and empowerment is about social awareness of means and resources, it is the turn to think what we mean by redistribution of power and awareness. Earlier in this chapter, I argued that power is not equivalent to people (victim)'s power of sentencing. So, if this is not power, then what is it?

Aertsen has argued (2006) that the RJ process expects to have an impact on the criminal justice system, because it allows a vertical communication between stakeholders and the criminal procedure. From this point of view, and in the line of procedural justice theorists, power would not be about having influence on the outcome (sentencing in this case) but power in the decision-making. As observed by Van Camp and Wemmers in victims of crime's discourses (2013) '[t]he restorative procedure and outcome were not seen in terms of decision making and formal decisions, but in terms of empowerment and validation through dialogue and process control' (Van Camp and Wemmers, 2013: 127). This means that, while having a perception of process control (instead of decision control) individuals may develop a feeling of fairness regardless of the outcome of the process. As a consequence, these authors argue, justice for victims is about recognition and not about punishment. According to their findings, Van Camp and Wemmers (2013) define empowerment as a way 'to take back control and shift the burden [to the offenders] of shame and responsibility' (2013: 123). Empowerment in RJ would be, therefore, to understand one's own and the other's role in the offence, promoting an atmosphere of recognition and, perhaps more importantly, self-recognition (Bolívar, 2012).

While I fully agree with Van Camp and Wemmers' arguments, I do consider we still require to remain alert about RJ developments in practice and wonder about the consequences of diversional schemes for victims and offenders. In most of Europe, it seems clear that the 'shadow of the criminal procedure' is present throughout the whole RJ process. Not only are judges and prosecutors deciding who attends mediation, they are also defining what role RJ has in it. It has been observed, for example, that victims perceive, and become confused by, the contradictory logic between the adversarial and polarised traditional system and the participatory and neutral atmosphere in mediation. They realise mediation offers an 'alternative' discourse but that remains subordinated to the dominant and traditional view (Bolívar, 2014; Bachinger and Pelikan, 2015). The potential benefits that an offender could obtain as a result of his participation in restorative justice may play a role in it. Honkatukia (2015) observed how Finnish victims' discourses about their experiences in RJ were full of contradictions, even when they openly confirmed to be satisfied with the process. In other words, even when victims recognise the benefits of an RJ process such as mediation, the offender's judicial benefits linked to RJ may create a context in which parties' subjective experience may have an ambiguous connotation. Indeed, we should we aware that Van Camp and Wemmers' findings were obtained in the context of programmes dealing with cases of serious crimes in two scenarios: at post-sentence level (Canada) and at different stages of the criminal proceedings by an organisation that aims to work independently (but in coordination) with the criminal justice system (Belgium). The question arises if the need for process control (instead of decision control) would also be observed in less serious offences dealt with by diversionary models of RJ.

My hypothesis is it would not. Interviews by Bachinger and Pelikan (2015) revealed that, despite possible contradictions and ambiguities, it made sense to victims to have an influence in the final decision. The same was registered and observed in Bolívar (2012) in which parties were content that authorities could accept their agreement as a solution for their case.

In sum, I would argue we have two different contexts in which awareness and redistribution of power may mean different things. In diversionary schemes, it may imply a direct communication between the parties and the authorities, as the parties' decision 'replaces' the authority's decision; in non-diversionary schemes that aspire to work independently of the criminal justice system, it would imply promoting process control over decision control. However, if the 'RJ client' is not the disempowered, but the 'selective client' of RJ, we need to wonder whether these issues really represent a re-distribution of power, or whether they merely represent an auto-regulating mechanism through which we only give control to those whose voice we are willing to hear.

(c) Difficult Principle of Non-domination

RJ should promote the involvement of victims, offenders and those connected to them in the decision-making process (Johnstone and Van Ness, 2007) avoiding any type of domination (Braithwaite, 2002). In practice, this means promoting the attendance of every stakeholder who has a say in the conflict, as well as preventing power imbalances within RJ meetings. Non-domination, inclusivity and a spirit of collaboration between victim and offender will help parties to resolve the conflict by themselves (Pranis, 2007). Inclusivity, collaboration and non-domination will ensure that the victim can finally be heard and taken into account in the definition and solution of the conflict (see, e.g. Strang, 2002; Zehr, 2005).

Non-domination and inclusivity can also be applied to the programme itself. The programme should be inclusive by focusing on both victims' and offenders' needs. 'Programmes where victims are exploited as props for programmes that are oriented only to the rehabilitation of offenders are morally unacceptable ... the key principle here is equal concern for all stakeholders' (Braithwaite, 2002: 567). The programme should also be inclusive by aiming to meet, hear and address different types of needs, people and conflicts. In other words, to improve its capacity to respond, the programme should not impose its own agenda or planning onto its participants, offering instead flexibility in terms of processes and outcomes (see, e.g. Daly, 2006; Dignan and Cavadino, 1998; Strang, 2002).

Despite the general recognition of the fundamental role of this principle in RJ's philosophy, practice has proved that this principle is not easy to fulfil. Rosenblatt (2012) researched youth offender panels in the United Kingdom and concluded that, when communities take the floor, victims' involvement is limited. Not only did victims rarely attend these meetings, also panel members did not succeed in bringing to the panel the 'victim perspective'. In my own research, I could also observe that diversionary schemes, by being closer to the criminal justice system, are automatically closer to offenders, leaving victims' voice relegated to a second place (Bolívar, 2015).

III. CONCLUDING THOUGHTS

Translating CP's notion of empowerment into the RJ language, empowerment may be understood in different ways at individual, organisational and community levels.

(a) At the individual level, victims and offenders should not only have the opportunity to participate but *learn to participate* through a reflective process created in dialogue with others. As a result, victims and offenders should develop a sense of control of their own lives, but also a sense of critical awareness of both the context in which the offence took place and the nature/characteristics of the social reaction to it. This means that the themes of RJ encounters, especially when the community is involved, could not be limited only to the consequences of the crime, but extend also to the structural factors behind the commission of the crime, defining different levels of responsibilisation.

(b) At the organisational level, I would adopt the term 'empowered RJ programmes'. These are the ones, that, despite the institutional context in which they are implemented (offender-oriented or victim-oriented, for example), are able, on the one hand, to guarantee equal voice to all participants and, on the other hand, to have a political effect in terms of influencing the public/state response to crime. This influence could be visualised at different levels. At the level of the case, the programme could influence the response of the court; at the level of the criminal policy, the programme could generate inputs for crime prevention; at the level of specific territories, the programme could collaborate with local networks in order to develop new ways of dealing with local conflicts.

(c) In turn, RJ may become an empowering process for communities, when they have access to RJ's spaces of deliberation and democracy. The community then becomes aware of the available social, judicial and community resources and it would know how to have access to them. Tolerance to diversity is expressed in accepting and promoting social reintegration of victims and offenders. The community will then achieve the development of participatory skills and a stronger sense of community identity.

These definitions may make sense: however, structural changes are an impossible mission when participation is in fact taking place, following Arnstein's ladder, at the 'tokenism' level: we could then be informing and consulting, but the final structure is finally the one deciding.

From that point of view, there are serious challenges that the practice of RJ needs to face in order to become in reality an 'empowering' and 'participative' experience.

At the individual level, RJ should be available for all victims and offenders, ensuring not only equal access to information but also to concrete practices. This means not only guaranteeing national coverage of RJ services. It also means critically discussing concepts such as eligibility, suitability and safeguards, allowing, alongside institutional referrals, victim- and offender-initiated RJ processes.

At the organisational level, RJ services should also be themselves empowered. They should be able to communicate to the system (the criminal justice system, politicians, etc) the feedback given by victims and offenders through their practice, challenging general structures and proposing changes in the ways to deal with crime. RJ services should also be able to deal with diversity and allow individuals with all types of motivations, emotions and needs to participate. In turn, RJ practitioners should also be aware of their own biases and of the limitations that their own practice is constantly imposing to the principle of non-domination.

At the community level, we need an RJ programme that is able to include the community and promote social reintegration at different levels, in addition to being committed to the ideal of social change. This implies the tasks of creating social support for RJ, rising awareness about the needs of victims and offenders, and adopting in their daily practice a community perspective of the offence.

REFERENCES

Aertsen, I (2006) 'The Intermediate Position of Restorative Justice: The Case of Belgium' in I Aertsen, T Daems, and L Robert (eds), *Institutionalizing Restorative Justice* (Cullompton, Willan Publishing).

Aertsen, I, Bolívar, D, De Mesmaecker, V and Lauwers, N (2011) 'Restorative Justice and the Active Victim: Exploring Empowerment' 14 *Temida* 5.

Aertsen, I, Vanfraechem, I and Bolívar, D (eds) (2015) *Victims and Restorative Justice* (London, Routledge).
APAV and INTERVICT (2009) *Victims in Europe: Implementation of the EU Framework Decision on the Standing of Victims in the Criminal Proceedings in the Member States of the European Union* (Lisboa, Victim Support Europe).
Arnstein, SR (1969) 'A Ladder of Citizen Participation' 35 *Journal of the American Institute of Planners* 216.
Bachinger, L and Pelikan, C (2015) 'Victims and Restorative Justice in Austria' in D Bolivar, I Aertsen and I Vanfraechem (eds), *Victims and Restorative Justice: An Empirical Study on the Needs, Experiences and Position of the Victim Within Restorative Justice Practices*, Country Report (Leuven, European Forum for Restorative Justice), available at www.euforumrj.org/wp-content/uploads/2015/05/report_victimsandRJ-2.pdf.
Barton, C (2000) 'Empowerment and Retribution in Criminal Justice' in H Strang and J Braithwaite (eds), *Restorative Justice: Philosophy to Practice* (Aldershot, Ashgate/ Dartmouth).
—— (2003) *Restorative Justice, the Empowerment Model* (Annandale, VA, Hawkins Press).
Bolívar, D (2010) 'Conceptualizing "Victim's Restoration" in Restorative Justice' 17 *International Review of Victimology* 237.
—— (2012) *Victim-Offender Mediation and Victim's Restoration: A Victimological Study in the Context of Restorative Justice*, PhD dissertation (Leuven, KU Leuven).
—— (2013) 'For Whom is Restorative Justice? A Mixed-Method Study on Victims and (Non-) Participation' 1 *Restorative Justice: An International Journal* 190.
—— (2014) 'La Mediación Víctima-Ofensor como Alternativa al Sistema Penal: La Perspectiva de las Víctimas' 6 *Sistema Penal and Violência* 13.
—— (2015) 'The Local Practice of Restorative Justice: Are Victims Sufficiently Involved?' in I Aertsen, I Vanfraechem and D Bolivar (eds), *Victims and Restorative Justice* (London, Routledge).
Bolívar, D, Pelikan, C and Lemonne, A (2015) 'Victims and Restorative Justice: Towards a Comparison' in I Aertsen, I Vanfraechem and D Bolivar (eds), *Victims and Restorative Justice* (London, Routledge).
Braithwaite, J (2002) 'Setting Standards for Restorative Justice' 42 *British Journal of Criminology* 563.
Christie, N (1977) 'Conflicts as Property' 17 *British Journal of Criminology* 1.
Daly, K (2006) 'Justice for Victims of Sexual Assault: Court or Conference?' in K Heimer and C Kruttschnitt (eds), *Gender and Crime: Patterns of Victimization and Offending* (New York, New York University Press).
Dignan, J and Cavadino, M (1998) 'Which Model of Criminal Justice Offers the Best Scope for Assisting Victims of Crime?' in E Fattah and T Peters (eds), *Support for Crime Victims in a Comparative Perspective, a Collection of Essays Dedicated to the Memory of Prof Frederic Mcclintock* (Leuven, Leuven University Press).
Dzur, A and Olson, S (2004) 'The Value of Community Participation in Restorative Justice' 35 *Journal of Social Philosophy* 91.
Freire, P (2005) *Pedagogía del Oprimido* (Siglo xxi).
Gruber, J and Trickett, E (1987) 'Empowerment in the Governing of an Alternative Public School' 15 *American Journal of Community Psychology* 353.

Heller, K, Price, R, Reinharz, S, Riger, S and Wandersman, A (1984) *Psychology and Community Change: Challenges of the Future* (Homewood, IL, Dorsey).

Honkatukia, P. (2015) 'Victims and Restorative Justice in Finland' in D Bolivar, I Aertsen and I Vanfraechem (eds), *Victims and Restorative Justice: An Empirical Study on the Needs, Experiences and Position of the Victim Within Restorative Justice Practices*, Country Report (Leuven, European Forum for Restorative Justice), available at www.euforumrj.org/wp-content/uploads/2015/05/report_victimsandRJ-2.pdf.

Hoyle, C and Palmer, N (2014) 'Family Justice Centres: A Model for Empowerment?' 20 *International Review of Victimology* 191.

Johnstone, G and Van Ness, D (2007) 'The Meaning of Restorative Justice' in G Johnstone and D Van Ness (eds), *Handbook of Restorative Justice* (Cullompton, Willan Publishing).

Kloos, B, Hill, J, Thomas, E, Wandersman, A, Elias, M and Dalton, J (2012) *Community Psychology: Linking Individuals and Communities*, 3rd edn (Belmont, Wadsworth, orig pub 2007).

Kofkin, J (2003) *Community Psychology: Guiding Principles and Orienting Concepts* (New Jersey, Prentice Hall).

Larson, J and Zehr, H (2007) 'The Ideas of Engagement and Empowerment' in G Johnstone and R Van Ness (eds), *Handbook of Restorative Justice* (Cullompton, Willian Publishing).

Laxminarayan, M, Lens, K and Pemberton, A (2013) 'Victim-Offender Encounters in the Netherlands' in D Bolívar, I Aertsen and I Vanfraechem (eds), *Victims and Restorative Justice: An Empirical Study on the Needs, Experiences and Position of the Victim Within Restorative Justice Practices*, Country Report (Leuven, European Forum for Restorative Justice), available at www.euforumrj.org/wp-content/uploads/2015/05/report_victimsandRJ-2.pdf.

Matrix Insight and Felix, AE (2010) *A Study for an Impact Assessment on Ways of Improving the Support, Protection and Rights of Victims Across Europe* (Matrix Insight and Andersson Elffers Felix), available at http://ec.europa.eu/justice/criminal/files/matrix_2010_ia_final_report_en.pdf.

McCold, P and Wachtel, B (2002) 'Restorative Justice and Theory Validation' in E Weitekamp and H-J Kerner (eds), *Restorative Justice: Theoretical Foundations* (Cullompton, Willan Publishing).

Morris, A, Maxwell, G and Robertson, J (1993) 'Giving Victims a Voice: A New Zealand Experiment' 32(4) *Howard Journal* 304.

Pranis, K (2007) 'Restorative Values' in G Johnstone and D Van Ness (eds), *Handbook of Restorative Justice* (Cullompton, Willan Publishing).

Rappaport, J (1987) 'Terms of Empowerment/Exemplars of Prevention: Toward a Theory for Community Psychology' 15 *American Journal of Community Psychology* 121.

—— (1990) 'Research Methods and the Empowerment Social Agenda in Researching Community Psychology' in P Tolan, C Keys, C Fern and J Leonard (eds), *Researching Community Psychology: Issues of Theory and Methods* (Washington, DC, American Psychological Association).

Richards, K (2011) 'Restorative Justice and "Empowerment": Producing and Governing Active Subjects through "Empowering" Practices' 19 *Critical Criminology* 91.

Rosenblatt, F (2012) 'Restorative Justice and the Blurring Between Victims and Community Members', paper presented at the 14th International Symposium of the World Society of Victimology, The Hague, the Netherlands.
Sánchez Vidal, A (1996) *Psicología Comunitaria: Bases Conceptuales y Métodos de Intervención* (Barcelona, EUB).
Shier, H (2001) 'Pathways to Participation: Openings, Opportunities and Obligations' 15 *Children and Society* 107.
Strang, H (2002) *Repair or Revenge: Victims and Restorative Justice* (Oxford, Clarendon Press).
Thompson, M (2000) 'Life After Rape: A Chance to Speak?' 15(4) *Sexual and Relationship Therapy* 325.
Toews, B and Zehr, H (2003) 'Ways of Knowing for a Restorative Worldview' in E Weitekamp and H-J Kerner (eds), *Restorative Justice in Context: International Practice and Directions* (Cullompton, Willan Publishing).
Van Camp, T and Wemmers, J-A (2013) 'Victim Satisfaction with Restorative Justice: More than Simply Procedural Justice' 19 *International Review of Victimology* 117.
Van Ness, D and Strong, K (2006) *Restoring Justice: An Introduction to Restorative Justice*, 3rd edn (Anderson Publishing).
Wemmers, J-A and Cyr, K (2004) 'Victims' Perspectives on Restorative Justice: How Much Involvement are Victims Looking For?' 11 *International Review of Victimology* 259.
Zehr, H (2005) *Changing Lenses: A New Focus for Crime* (Waterloo, Herald Press, orig pub 1990).
Zimmerman, M (1990) 'Taking Aim on Empowerment Research: On the Distinction Between Individual and Psychological Conceptions' 18 *American Journal of Community Psychology* 169.
—— (1995) 'Psychological Empowerment: Issues and Illustrations' 23 *American Journal of Community Psychology* 581.
—— (2000) 'Empowerment Theory: Psychological, Organizational and Community Levels of Analysis' in J Rappaport and E Seidman (eds), *Handbook of Community Psychology* (New York, Kluwer Academic).

3

Restorative Justice and the Decision-making Process: Beyond Deliberative Democracy?

RAFFAELLA DA PORCIUNCULA PALLAMOLLA

I. INTRODUCTION

THE INTENTION OF this chapter is to develop the subject of restorative justice articulated with the theories of the deliberative and communicative democracy. The aim is to initiate an approximation between restorative justice and the theories of democracy mentioned in order to identify whether restorative justice can be understood as a form of deliberative democracy or, more than that, as a form of communicative democracy.

For this purpose, the theoretical assumptions of the deliberative democracy will be exposed especially from the work of Seyla Benhabib. Then, some criticisms to this model, formulated by Iris Young, will be addressed, as well as brief notions of the theory of communicative democracy proposed by this author. At the end, presenting some characteristics of restorative justice, points of contact between this and the theories of democracy mentioned above will be discussed.

II. DELIBERATIVE DEMOCRACY AND COMMUNICATIVE DEMOCRACY: BRIEF NOTIONS

According to Benhabib (1996), in complex modern democratic societies, the challenge of ensuring three public goods—legitimacy, economic welfare, and a viable sense of collective identity—is present. These three aspects relate to each other in a very complex way. Due to this interdependence, the excessive achievement of one good can put at risk and stop the realisation of the others. In a well-functioning democracy, there is balance between these goods. Yet, according to the same author, in analysing the model of deliberative democracy, particular attention must be paid to the good of legitimacy. That is because:

> [The] legitimacy in complex democratic societies must be thought to result from the free and unconstrained public deliberation of all about matters of common concern. Thus a public sphere of deliberation about matters of mutual concern is essential to the legitimacy of democratic institutions. (Benhabib, 1996: 68)

For Benhabib (1996), the normative basis of democracy, understood as a form of organisation of collective life, lies not in achieving economic well-being or a collective sense of collective identity, but in a deliberative model:

> Democracy, in my view, is best understood as a model for organizing the collective and public exercise of power in the major institutions of a society on the basis of the principle that decisions affecting the well-being of a collectivity can be viewed as the outcome of a procedure of free and reasoned deliberation among individuals considered as moral and political equals. (Benhabib, 1996: 68)

In a deliberative democracy model, in order to guarantee the legitimacy and the rationality of the collective decision-making processes, it is necessary that political institutions are organised in such a way 'that what is considered the common interest of all results from processes of collective deliberation conducted rationally and fairly among free and equal individuals' (Benhabib, 1996: 69).

The greater the approximation of processes for the collective decision-making model of deliberative democracy, that is, the more the decisions of the institutions are opened to public processes of appropriate deliberation and led by free and equal citizens, the greater the presumption of legitimacy and rationality of such processes. This is because the legitimacy of democratic institutions, which claim obligatory power for themselves, is based on the assumption that decisions arising from them represent, in an impartial manner, the interests of all (Benhabib, 1996).

Yet, in line with Benhabib (1996), it is the discourse model of ethics which provides the most general principles and moral institutions to claim the validity of the deliberative model. This model is based on the idea that the validity of the rules follows an agreement reached through a deliberative process made among all those who are affected by its consequences. This deliberation process has the following characteristics (Benhabib, 1996: 70):

(1) participation in such deliberation is governed by the norms of equality and symmetry; all have the same chances to initiate speech acts, to question, to interrogate, and to open debate;
(2) all have the right to question the assigned topics of conversation; and
(3) all have the right to initiate reflexive arguments about the very rules of the discourse procedure and the way in which they are applied or carried out. There are no prima facie rules limiting the agenda of the conversation, or the identity of the participants, as long as each excluded

person or group can justifiably show that they are relevantly affected by the proposed norm under question.

As regards the procedure described above (called the practical discourse), despite it serving 'for critically evaluating the criteria of membership and the rules for agenda setting, and for the structuring of public discussions within and among institutions' (Benhabib, 1996: 70), it is not enough just simply to transpose it to a macro institutional level in order to have a democracy theory: it is also necessary to pay attention to the specificities of the institutions and the practical viability of adopting such a model (Benhabib, 1996: 70).

According to what has been previously stated, in the deliberative democracy model, deliberative procedures confer legitimacy and a certain degree of practical rationality to the collective decision-making processes. In line with Benhabib (1996), the deliberative processes are essential to the rationality of the collective decision-making process for three reasons:

(i) The deliberative processes transmit information. The new information is transmitted because no participant can anticipate and predict how issues on ethics and politics will be perceived by others nor is he able to hold all necessary information relating to a decision that will affect everyone. Besides that, when dealing with complex social and political issues, individuals often have visions and desires, but not a pre-established list of preferences. In fact, it is the deliberative process itself which will enable the individual's critical reflection in order to clarify their own choices and preferences. During this process, some conflicts between desires, visions and opinions of a particular individual may also come up, leading him to seek a more conscious ordering. In order to sustain one's point of view to others, the individual will be led to present good reasons: 'nobody can convince others in public of her point of view without being able to state why what appears good, plausible, just, and expedient from the standpoint of all involved' (Benhabib, 1996: 72).

In addition, the deliberative democracy model, although guided by practical rationality, is not immune to misinterpretation and wrong uses or abuses. That is because the procedural models of rationality are not able to 'dictate outcomes nor define the quality of the reasons advanced in argumentation nor control the quality of the reasoning and rules of logic and inference used by participants' (Benhabib, 1996: 72). However, the discourse model has means to avoid such problems by ensuring that no result is fixed, that everything can be reviewed and re-examined, to the extent that all affected individuals are able to initiate such deliberative discourse.

Finally, the author considers that 'proceduralism is a rational answer to persisting value conflicts at the substantive level' (Benhabib, 1996: 73) that mark modernity. It is assumed that there is a pluralism of values, however, the challenge of democratic rationality 'is to arrive at acceptable formulations of the common good despite this inevitable value-pluralism' (Benhabib, 1996: 73), with the intention of seeking agreements not in terms of substantive beliefs, but on the level 'of procedures, processes, and practices for attaining and revising beliefs' (Benhabib, 1996: 73).

(ii) The model of deliberative democracy assumes that there is a conflict of values and interests in social life. However, social life needs conflicts of interest as well as cooperation. The task of democratic procedures is to convince—even that individual or group whose interests were negatively affected—that the conditions of mutual cooperation are still legitimate:

> [The] more conflicts of interests there are the more it is important to have procedural solutions of conflict adjudication through which parties whose interests are negatively affected can find recourse to other methods of the articulation and representation of their grievances. (Benhabib, 1996: 73)

(iii) The proceduralist model of democracy as well as the deliberative model are aware that no modern society is able to address their subjects through an assembly of mass that deliberates in public and collectively. There is a limit to the size of the deliberative body and overcoming this limit affects the nature of the reasoning process. In any case, Benhabib states that the deliberative model and the proceduralist model of democracy do not have to work with the idea of a deliberative general assembly because it is a model in which procedural specifications privilege a plurality of modes of association in which all affected can have the right to articulate their point of view. It is through the interlocking net of these multiple forms of associations, networks and organisations that an anonymous 'public conversation' results (Benhabib, 1996: 72–74).

Iris Young was responsible for formulating various criticisms of the deliberative democracy model and for drawing attention to the fact that today's societies are not 'ideal societies' as in the sense addressed by the theory. According to the author, this means that 'our democratic policy discussions do not occur under conditions free of coercion and threat, and free of the distorting influence of unequal power and control over resources' (Young, 2000: 17).

Yet, according to Young (2000), the tendency is that democratic processes are formally used by the powerful in order to perpetuate injustice and preserve privileges, which result from a vicious circle between social, economic and political inequalities. Increasing democratic inclusion in decision-making processes is one of the ways to break this circle, aiming at promoting fairer results, in line with what theorists of deliberative democracy propose, which would be, despite criticism, the model responsible for providing important ideals about inclusion practices.

In this direction, according to Young (2000), the model of decision-making processes of deliberative democracy 'entails several normative ideals for the relationships and dispositions of deliberating parties, among them inclusion, equality, reasonableness, and publicity' (Young, 2000: 23). Such normative ideals, according to the author, can be understood as follows (Young, 2000):

(a) *Inclusion*: the inclusion (participation) of all who are affected by a decision in the process of discussion and decision-making is what gives normative legitimacy to a democratic decision. The inclusion, as an ideal, involves a norm of moral respect. Including those who will be affected by the decision means: do not treat them as a means to an end and do not disregard their voices, interests and perspectives that will help in the search for the solution of a problem.
(b) *Political equality*: this is the normative ideal of democracy. All of those affected by the decision should not only be included, but also must be on an equal footing, so that everyone has an equal right and opportunity to express their interests and concerns, as well as to question the arguments and proposals of others. However, this is only possible if another condition for equality is present: non-domination, which means that nobody can make use of coercion or threats in order to make others agree with a particular proposal or outcome.
(c) *Reasonableness*: when the ideals described above are observed, participants can be confident that the result achieved is the result of good reasons and not of fear, force or of false consensus. However, in order to keep confidence in the process, the participants must be willing to be reasonable. That doesn't always mean having reasonable ideas, but being willing to listen to others about their reasons and why their ideas may be incorrect or inappropriate, as well as entering into a discussion to solve problems and reach a collective agreement (even though, in the end, this may not seem possible, you must want to reach it). Rushing the debate and judging a particular idea as irrational too rashly, without hearing the opinions of others, is a symptom of a lack of reasonableness. In short, it is essential that the participants are actually open to a democratic debate, that is, avoiding, not only unquestionable beliefs or strict ideas, but also putting their interests above the interests of others.
(d) *Publicity*: from the ideals described above follows the idea that the interaction among the participants in a process of democratic decision-making is something public (or collective) where people appear as accountable to each other. This *public* 'consists of a plurality of different individual and collective experiences, histories, commitments, ideals, interests, and goals that face one another to discuss collective problems under a common set of procedures' (Young, 2000: 25). This plurality requires from the participants a responsible approach when expressing their ideas in relation to all the other participants. In order to make content public, it is necessary that the manifestations seek, in their form and content, to be understandable and

acceptable, but this does not necessarily guarantee their immediate understanding and acceptance. Expressions of bewilderment, divergence, questions and answers, are part of the deliberative dialogue.

Regarding the criticism of Young of the deliberative democracy model, it can be said that they were basically directed to the privileged discourse model by the deliberative democracy, which would be responsible for silencing other kinds of discourse. On deliberative democracy, the hegemonic discourse would be the 'rationalist, male, univocal, hegemonic discourse of a transparent polity that disregards the emotions, polyvocity, multiplicity, and differences in the articulation of the voice of the public' (Benhabib, 1996: 74).

In this sense, although Young agrees with the criticisms of the democracy model based on the arguments of the theorists of deliberative democracy, and therefore considers that it is preferable to devise a 'conception of democracy that understands politics as the meeting of people to decide public ends and policies in a rational way' (Young, 1996: 121) rather than one that considers democracy 'primarily as a process of expressing one's preferences and demands, and registering them in a vote' (Young, 1996: 120), the author makes two important criticisms of the model of deliberative democracy (Young, 1996: 122):

(1) that the model tends to restrict democratic debate to argumentation and that it can, in practice, lead to the exclusion of certain people who do not dominate this kind of process of reasoning methodically; and
(2) the assumption that unity is a point of departure or arrival of democratic debate, which could also have the effect of exclusion.

For the purposes of this chapter, it is important to briefly analyse the first criticism formulated by Young.

In an ideal deliberative democracy, all participants are on an equal footing to the extent that economic and political powers were left out of the deliberative process. However, Young (1996) argues that:

> the social power that can prevent people from being equal speakers derives not only from economic dependence or political domination but also from an internalized sense of the right one has to speak or not to speak, and from the devaluation of some people's style of speech and the elevation of others. (Young, 1996: 122)

This means that there will only be discussion and equal understanding among people if, in addition to cultural differences and unequal social positions, political and economic power are eliminated. Nevertheless, the model of deliberative democracy does not consider these other differences, because it 'tends to assume that deliberation is both culturally neutral and universal' (Young, 1996: 122).

Yet, the theory proposed by Young (1996), of a communicative democracy, establishes an even more inclusive communication model by taking into consideration (1) social differences; (2) that power very often permeates the discourse itself; besides recognising (3) that deliberative practices have cultural specificities. In this direction, Young proposes that a democratic theory that is based on discussion must admit different forms and styles of speech and not only that kind of discourse normally considered by the deliberative democracy theorists: one which is given by a white man, well-educated, middle-class, in a formal and generic way, dispassionate, incorporeal, etc. Finally, it is worth mentioning that the author proposes three forms of communication that add up to critical reasoning and which are required for a broad conception of communicative democracy: (1) greeting; (2) rhetoric; and (3) narratives or the act of telling stories (storytelling) (Young, 1996: 128–31). According to Young (1996), these forms of communication:

> Help establish and maintain the plurality that I have argued, following Arendt, is necessary to the meaning and existence of publicity. Where such a public contains group-based cultural, social perspectival, and valuative differences, moreover, these communicative forms supplement argument by providing ways of speaking across difference in the absence of significant shared understandings. (Young, 1996: 129)

III. RESTORATIVE JUSTICE: BRIEF NOTIONS

Although restorative justice has been applied in several countries for three decades, there is not a complete consensus on the concept of such justice. However, there is a certain consensus around the definition presented by Tony Marshall. According to him, 'restorative justice is a process whereby all the parties with a stake in a particular offense come together to resolve collectively how to deal with the aftermath of the offence and its implications for the future' (Marshall, 1996: 37).

Due to the extent of Marshall's definition, the authors Johnstone and Van Ness (2007) work with three conceptions of restorative justice, which are of great value for understanding this model of justice: reparative, transformative, and encounter conceptions. The first one conceives restorative justice as a form of justice focused on the *repair* of the harm (material or symbolic) caused by the crime (conflict). Supporters of this conception, besides turning their attention to repair of the victim, seek to (re)integrate the offender into his or her community and restore the community itself, in which it participates, as part of the restorative process, in order to contribute to the formulation and accomplishment of the restorative agreement, as well as develop its capacity to solve its own conflicts. The meeting of those involved is sought, but it is not essential, to the extent that the state can repair the victim in another way, for example, by imposing a penalty on the offender other than a fine or prison.

The second conception turns to *transformation*, this being understood in a broader sense. The intent of restorative justice, in this conception, is to transform people's understanding of themselves and how they relate to others.

It seeks to transform people's way of life, based on the assumption that we are all connected to each other and to the world. Finally, it aims to introduce a change in the language itself, abolishing distinctions between crime and other harmful behaviours (as the abolitionist Louk Hulsman has proposed), substituting the word 'crime' by the term 'problematic situations'. Although targeting profound transformations, this conception does not neglect the repair of the damage, since it considers it essential to identify the needs of those involved in the conflict (victim, offender and community) so you can try to meet them as far as possible. The third and final conception is that of the *encounter* or *dialogue*. In it, restorative justice is seen as a form of conflict resolution that enables the victim, offender and other interested parties to meet in an environment that is not so formal (such as forums and courts) so that (mainly) the victim and offender are able to abandon the passivity that is imposed on them by the criminal proceedings and take active positions in discussions and decision-making about their conflicts.

From this last conception, which favours dialogue among those involved in the conflict, that is, among those who were affected directly or indirectly by the crime, it is possible to bring restorative justice closer to a democratic experience, to the extent that all speak and listen respectfully, and in balanced conditions of power, provided by the formatting process, performance of the facilitator or mediator and values of restorative justice. Thus, instead of a penalty imposed by the judge, dialogue is used so that those involved seek to reach an agreement (Larrauri, 2004) on what can be done for the benefit of the victim, of the offender and of the community itself.

Through this process, the victim has room to express his or her grief and say what damage has been caused; the offender can become aware of the consequences of his or her actions and choose to do something to repair the damage; and, together, they will arrive at an agreement which, of course, must be reasonable and not disregard human rights.

IV. FINAL CONSIDERATIONS: POSSIBLE APPROACHES OF RESTORATIVE JUSTICE TO MODELS OF DELIBERATIVE AND COMMUNICATIVE DEMOCRACY

Although the decisions of the criminal justice system and the democratic quality of its processes of decision-making have not received much attention from modern political scientists, who preferred to turn their attention to parliaments, parties, bureaucracy, etc, Parkinson and Roche (2004) state that this picture has changed from the development of deliberative democracy theories. From them, theorists of democracy began to analyse with great interest small scale decision-making processes, such as those that were beginning to be applied by the criminal justice system from the mid-1980s, and which later came to be identified as *restorative justice*.

That is because, as explained in the previous section, the model of justice proposed by restorative justice makes use of different methods for solving conflicts from those traditionally used by the criminal justice system. Instead of criminal proceedings in which a criminal justice instrument attributes guilt to someone accused of having committed a crime, restorative justice uses mechanisms that favour dialogue among those who are directly or indirectly involved in the conflict (crime) to try to reach an agreement on what should be done about it. Among these mechanisms are, for example, mediation, restorative circles and conferences.

In addition to these considerations with regard to restorative justice, it is interesting to observe that the values of this model of justice bear significant resemblance to the normative ideal of deliberative democracy.

The values listed by Braithwaite, one of the most respected restorative justice theorists, are quite enlightening, to the extent that they focus, above all, on the deliberative procedure carried out by restorative justice, seeking to preserve the aims of such justice, among them, reducing the violence of the criminal justice system's performance itself.

Braithwaite (2003) divides restorative values into three groups. In order to formulate them, he used as a source the values expressed by international treaties to justify human rights, and the values that appear repeatedly in empirical evaluations of the experience of victims and offenders, in which they say what they want (and expect) from a restorative process in criminal justice.

The first group of values proposed by the author is one that covers the mandatory values of the restorative process, which must inevitably be respected and even imposed (constraining values) to prevent the process from becoming oppressive. For the purpose of this chapter, the analysis of such values suffices, since they are the priority and act as tools to ensure the restorative procedure.

(a) *Non-domination*: domination appears in the restorative processes as in any other event of social interaction. Therefore, restorative justice must be structured to minimise the differences in existing power.

However, the process will not be restorative if the mediator takes an active posture, trying to avoid domination. The attempt to dominate the other must be circumvented, with the responsibility lying, in the first place, on the participants, who are expected to identify the domination and give a voice to whoever is being dominated. If this attempt fails or does not occur, the mediator might interfere and give a voice to the person who is dominated.

Parkinson and Roche (2004), while highlighting the role of the mediator in ensuring the balance of power in the deliberative process, point out that, on many occasions, it can come from those involved:

> As with other deliberative processes, the mediator has a key role to play in ensuring that meetings are not dominated by the assertive and opinionated. Sometimes, support can come from unexpected sources: the dynamics of face-to-face deliberations mean that people on one side can come to new understandings of those on the other, so that people in the victim's group have been known to leap to the defense of the offender, and vice versa. (Parkinson and Roche, 2004: 512)

This changing process of understandings and perspectives that occurs in the deliberative processes of restorative justice, in particular during mediation, is made possible by the meeting between victim and offender, whose goal is to overcome the dichotomy that exists between them, dispelling the myths (stereotypes) related to one and to the other:

> when they meet face to face, victim and offender can overcome the myths and mutual stereotypes, since this meeting occurs with the guidance of a *facilitateur.* The primary aim is the resumption of the dialogue, the secondary is deterrence. (Azevedo, 2005: 124)

Yet, in terms of the balance of power, the problems faced by the deliberative processes of restorative justice are quite significant and are not often overcome by the participants, especially in cases involving juvenile offenders (in the position of offenders) and women (in the position of victims or offenders) (Braithwaite 2003).

(b) *Empowerment*: non-domination implies empowerment. From such principle comes the 'power' of the participants to tell their stories in their own way, in order to reveal their impressions about the injustice they suffered and how they would like it to be repaired. It is about giving voice to those involved and understanding their point of view.

With respect to the empowerment of the victims, Zehr (2008) notes that they 'need to feel needed and heard throughout the entire process. At least, this means that they must be the centerpiece in determining what their needs are, and how and when they must be met' (Zehr, 2008: 183). This empowerment, thus, helps the victims to actively participate in the justice process and feel treated more fairly.

With regard to the existing empowerment in these collective decision-making processes, it might be useful to recall the idea of empowerment developed by Young (1997) in 'Punishment, Treatment, Empowerment: Three Approaches to Policy for Pregnant Addicts', a chapter in her book *Intersecting Voices: Dilemmas of Gender, Political Philosophy and Policy*. The notion of empowerment that is developed by the author in this chapter goes beyond the dimension of individual empowerment and reaches the *social dimension*. In the work mentioned, Young (1997) deals with two approaches used by social services providers and therapists who use the idea of empowerment in their treatment. However, according to the author, only one of them abandons the individualist approach, focused on the development of individual autonomy, self-control and confidence, to focus on the development of social solidarity through the awareness and the possibility of collective action. In this perspective, empowerment is related to the development of a sense of collective influence on the social conditions of a person's life. Empowerment takes place at both levels, personal and collective, and, for this reason, according to Young (1997), this perspective involves the ideals of participatory democracy, critical self-reflection and collective action:

> I define this meaning of empowerment as a process in which individual, relatively powerless persons engage in dialogue with each other and thereby come to understand the social sources of their powerlessness and see the possibility of acting collectively to change their social environment. In this process, each participant is personally empowered, undergoes some personal transformation, but in the context of a reciprocal aiding of others in doing so, in order that together they might be empowered to engage in effective collective action. (Young, 1997: 91)

In this form of treatment, the confessional model of therapeutic conversation is abandoned and gives way to a speech termed by the political movements as 'consciousness raising'. Instead of being monological, a characteristic of the confessional model, in which the individual tells his own story alone, even in the presence of others, the speech of consciousness raising is dialogical and empowering because it 'develops in people the ability to be reflective and critical about the social base where individual action is situated' (Young, 1997: 91). In this type of speech, where everyone has the same right to speak, criticise others and be criticised, participants discuss and build 'an understanding of their personal lives as socially conditioned, limited in a manner similar to that of other institutional structures, power relations, cultural assumptions, or economic forces' (Young, 1997: 91). It is also noted that the speech model developed by the author becomes closer to her communicative democracy model, at least with regard to the speech strategy used in the debate, that is, the act of telling stories (storytelling). Telling stories, listening to other people's interpretations of them without ever losing the analysis of the social dimension, also integrates the restorative process, which aims to empower all those involved in the conflict and overcome the individual dimensions of the conflicts.

In addition to this ritual of speech, the other rites discussed by Young in her communicative democracy model (rhetoric and greeting) are also easily found in restorative processes, especially because those involved in the processes normally do not resemble those who speak the 'ideal' discourse thought by theorists supporting deliberative democracy.

In this regard, Parkinson and Roche (2004) point out that, in line with the criticism of Young, in order to measure how inclusive a process is, it is necessary not only to check who is present but also to examine which rules guide their participation, because the 'citizens may be physically present, but for all intents and purposes, effectively excluded by the norms and rules governing the way people should deliberate' (Parkinson and Roche, 2004: 511).

(c) *Obeying (or honouring) the maximum sanctions established by law*: although restorative justice works through the notion of reintregative shaming,[1] even admitting the idea of a non-destructive stigmatisation, any degrading or humiliating outcome must be forbidden.

(d) *Respectful listening*: in addition to the sanctions established by law being the limit to empowerment, the citizens must not disrespect or oppress others. Listening to each other respectfully is a condition of participation and, if it is not met, the participant is asked to leave, because his excessive empowerment obstructs the empowerment of others.

(e) *Equal concern for all participants*: restorative justice needs to be concerned with the needs and empowerment of the offender, the victim and the community affected by the offence. Somehow, all must win. That doesn't mean, however, that everyone will have the same help, since this will vary according to each other's need.

(f) *Accountability, appealability*: this is the principle most strongly defended by Braithwaite. Any person involved in a criminal case or in another sphere of law should have the right to opt for a restorative process rather than the traditional legal process; the opposite option must also be admitted.

(g) *Respect for human rights*: that is, those contained in the Universal Declaration of Human Rights and in the Declaration of Basic Principles of Justice for Victims of Crime and Abuse of Power, as well as in other international instruments.

In this chapter, there is no space to collate individually each of the values of restorative justice. However, considering the content of the listed values, it is believed to be possible to sustain that restorative justice is a practice of deliberative democracy and that, perhaps because of the particularities involved in the conflicts (crimes), it is necessary to seek for support, not only

[1] The idea of a reintegrative shaming was exhaustively developed by John Brathwaite in his work. According to him, reintegrative shaming 'is shaming which is followed by efforts to reintegrate the offender back into the community of law-abiding or respectable citizens through words or gestures of forgiveness or ceremonies to decertify the offender as deviant. Shaming and reintegration do not occur simultaneously but sequentially, with reintegration occurring before deviance becomes a master status ... It is not distinguished from stigmatization by its potency, but by (a) a finite rather than open duration which is terminated by forgiveness; and by (b) efforts to maintain bonds of love or respect throughout the finite period of suffering shame' (Braithwaite, 1989: 100–1).

in the model of deliberative democracy, but also on the basis of the communicative democracy model proposed by Young.

REFERENCES

Azevedo, RG (2005) 'O paradigma emergente em seu labirinto: notas para o aperfeiçoamento dos Juizados Especiais Criminais' in A Wunderlich and SD Carvalho (eds), *Novos diálogos sobre os Juizados Especiais Criminais* (Rio de Janeiro, Lumen Júris).

Benhabib, S (1996) 'Toward a Deliberative Model of Democratic Legitimacy' in S Benhabib (ed), *Democracy and Difference* (Princeton, NJ, Princeton University Press).

Braithwaite, J (1989) *Crime, Shame and Reintegration* (Cambridge, Cambridge University Press).

—— (2003) 'Principles of Restorative Justice' in AV Hirsch, J Roberts, A Bottoms, K Roach and M Schiff (eds), *Restorative Justice and Criminal Justice: Competing or Reconcilable Paradigms?* (Oxford and Portland, OR, Hart Publishing).

Johnstone, G and Van Ness, DW (2007) 'The Meaning of Restorative Justice' in G Johnstone and DW Van Ness (eds), *Handbook of Restorative Justice* (Cullompton, Willan Publishing).

Larrauri, E (2004) 'Tendencias actuales en la justicia restauradora' in FP Álvares (ed), *SERTA in memoriam Alexandri Baratta* (Salamanca, Universidad de Salamanca–Aquilafuente).

Marshall, T (1996) *The Evolution of Restorative Justice in Britain: European Journal on Criminal Policy Research* (Heidelberg, Springer).

Parkinson, J and Roche, D (2004) 'Restorative Justice: Deliberative Democracy in Action?' *Australian Journal of Political Science* 39.

Young, IM (1996) 'Communication and the Other: Beyond Deliberative Democracy' in S Benhabib (ed), *Democracy and Difference* (Princeton, NJ, Princeton University Press).

—— (1997) *Intersecting Voices: Dilemmas of Gender, Political Philosophy and Policy* (Princeton, NJ, Princeton University Press).

—— (2000) *Inclusion and Democracy* (Oxford, Oxford University Press).

Zehr, H (2008) *Trocando as lentes: um novo foco sobre o crime e a justiça* (São Paulo, Palas Athena).

4

Doing Restorative Justice 'Otherwise': Decolonising Practices in the Global South

HARRY BLAGG

I. INTRODUCTION

THIS CHAPTER IS concerned with the relationship between restorative justice (RJ) and the emerging sphere of Indigenous justice, particularly in Australia. These two projects, restorative justice and Indigenous justice, are fundamentally different projects. Restorative justice, despite claims to the contrary, is a modernist, Euro-American concept concerned with reforming what remains an essentially Western approach to justice reform; whereas Indigenous justice adopts a decolonising stance and is concerned with transforming relationships between settler colonialism and Indigenous peoples. Restorative justice processes may have utility for Indigenous communities provided they are not viewed as ends in themselves but, instead, act as points of cultural interface with Indigenous owned processes.

I want to suggest that current forms of restorative practice, most notably those developed by the white justice system and imposed from above onto Indigenous society, do not meet the justice demands of Indigenous people, who rarely see their interests and experiences reflected in these mainstream practices. Restorative justice generally presents itself as an alternative to the mainstream system, but from an Indigenous perspective it looks more like a simple variation on a familiar theme.

State initiated restorative justice reflects a Eurocentric imaginary of its Indigenous Other, assuming that a few concessions to Indigenous 'culture' (such as having Indigenous elders present at diversionary conferences) can sugar the bitter pill of Indigenous dispossession. Elizabeth Povinelli (2002) refers to such strategies as 'cunning' recognition: accepting a degree of cultural difference as long as it does not constitute a *radical alterity* that threatens white supremacy, particularly where this includes claims to land.

However, it is place (or 'country' for Australia's Aboriginal people) that remains at the centre of Indigenous knowledge; as Aileen Moreton-Robinson (2003: 45) suggests, 'the inalienable nature of our (Aboriginal people's) relationship to land, marks a radical, indeed incommensurable, difference between us and the non-Indigenous'.

A number of Australian criminologists have been critical of a founding myth of restorative justice, that it is rooted in Indigenous practice (Cunneen, 1997; Blagg, 1997). Furthermore, in Australia the introduction of programmes claiming to be grounded in restorative philosophies, such as diversionary programmes for Indigenous youth, has not halted, let alone reversed, the slide towards mass incarceration. It is possible to envisage a situation in the very near future in a number of Australian States (notably Western Australia, the Northern Territory and Queensland) where there will be more Indigenous children involved in the care and protection and justice systems than free in the community. One problem is that calls for alternative forms of dispute resolution based on Aboriginal law, rather than Orientalised[1] versions of Aboriginal law popularised by white commentators, have met with obstinate silence from governments, who can point to a few initiatives, largely dominated by the police and other mainstream agencies, as demonstrating their commitment to Indigenous justice reform. The early promise of restorative justice lay in its commitment to collective problem solving and faith in the capacity of lay peoples to resolve conflict (Roach, 2003) rather than in any one particular institutionalised practice or method (Clamp, 2013). I want to suggest that a critical restorative justice, relevant to the needs of Indigenous and other colonised subjects, should be informed by the interconnected processes of what Walter Mignolo (2007; 2011) calls *decoloniality* and *inter-culturality* (as I discuss in more detail later). First, restorative justice must acknowledge its place as an ideology of the Global North rather than something emerging organically from the Global South.

II. NORTH AND SOUTH

The constructs, Global North and Global South, are metaphors rather than firm geographical terrains: the South being a metaphor for the world colonised in violence and suffering most acutely from the forces of neo-liberal global capitalism and imperialism (Sousa Santos, 2008). For centuries epistemologies of the Global North have dominated the world. However, there

[1] This term originates in the work of Edward Said (2004) to denote the way the 'West' constructs its colonised Other through various stereotypes (lazy, timeless, emotional, sensual, exotic, etc). The realities of their lives are distorted to fit in with these stereotypes.

are signs that this has begun to change. Comaroff and Comaroff (2011) assert that Euro-American modernity is 'drifting southwards', as it is the South that is now, 'tracking at the front end of history' (Commaroff and Comaroff, 2011: 44). As neo-liberalism continues to erode the foundations of the northern welfare state and its hegemonic consensus, resulting in the increased casualisation of the labour market, massive disparities between rich and poor, and destruction of the living wage, it is creating the kinds of total destitution, insecurity and instability of life once characteristic of the non-Western, 'developing' world. The cities of the North now play host to beggars and vagrants, the homeless and unwaged, the sick and mentally ill and, most despised of all, the undocumented alien. Such processes have also seen the emergence of forms of protest and resistance germinated in the South. The rise of popular, anti-austerity movements in Europe and citizens coalitions against state violence (such as Momentum in the United Kingdom, Black Lives Matter in the United States) testify to the emergence of forms of grass-roots activist politics once synonymous with movements in the Global South (Commaroff and Comaroff, 2011: 44).

In recent years, issues raised by counter-migration, the presence of the Global South in the geographic north, has seen 'colonial hysteria' (Galeano, 1997) about mixedness, boundaries and cultural miscegenation migrate from the periphery to the metropolitan centre itself: reflected in the emergence of anti-immigrant and anti-Muslim movements, such as UKIP in England and Pegida in Germany; the resurgence of anti-Semitism, widespread Islamophobia and systemic discrimination against Roma peoples, who remain subject to a form of internal colonisation (Ponzanesi and Blaagaard, 2012). Europe, it seems, is not being spared its own 'postcolonial moment' (Gilroy, 2011). Critics ominously observe 'new forms of inclusion and exclusion based on linguistic, racial, ethnic and religious divisions' (Ponzanesi and Blaagaard, 2012: 3), where the instruments of criminal justice are being used punitively to manage unwanted populations who have committed no crimes (other than that of being Other), as much as to punish 'offenders'. In so far as they are fulfilling this role, they are marking a return to colonial forms of control, only this time they are doing so in the metropolitan centre rather than in the imperial periphery: an eventuality long foretold in the works of Franz Fanon (1990) and Hannah Arendt (1973). Etienne Balibar (2004), for example, speaks of 'European apartheid' where a multiplicity of invisible borders are being constructed within, as well as on the boundaries of, nation-states, that are ideological, racialised and politicised.

What role is there for a critical restorative practice in an era where the resources of the criminal justice system in Europe are becoming steadily more concerned with warehousing the undocumented and unwanted than with adjudicating guilt or innocence? There is a real danger that restorative practices will be bifurcated to reflect this 'apartheid' and reserved for those of 'us' who can claim citizen status, and deemed redeemable, while the retributive apparatuses of the justice system are employed to manage those with 'weak claims of membership' (Aliverti, 2015). Zygmunt Bauman employed the term 'adiaphorization' to describe the processes via which people are de-humanised and pushed beyond the circle of moral calculus (Bauman and Lyon, 2012). Once expunged from society, their lives become worthless, what Agamben called *homo sacer*, the one who can be killed without consequences (Agamben, 1998).

Should restorative justice break free from its place on the margins of the criminal justice system and re-connect with the stream of peace-making and neighbourhood-based justice movements? Most compellingly: what role is there for restorative justice in re-humanising our relationships with the de-humanised Other?

Most contributors to this collection would argue that restorative justice has had a largely energising impact on debates about justice in late modernity. For many, it has offered a compelling alternative to the narrative of punitive populism, and has equipped scholars, researchers and practitioners with a set of counter-arguments to the negative mantra of 'tough on crime' correctional policies. For many activists engaged within or on the margins of the justice system, it has provided a language and context within which to imagine an alternative justice model: person centred and de-bureaucratised.

Restorative thinking assisted many to demystify justice, transforming it from a static, rule-bound, opaque and highly bureaucratised system that 'does things' to people, into a highly interactive sphere of encounters and transformative experiences that enable people to 'do things' for each Other. I do not intend to dispute the 'success' of restorative justice in shifting at least some 'lenses' (Zehr, 2005), rather that its global ambitions and claims reflect a continuity with an essentially modernist and Eurocentric *Weltanschauung* at a time when the world, even the European world, is being radically transformed.

III. EPISTEMOLOGIES OF THE SOUTH

Critical Indigenous scholarship stresses the extent to which seemingly progressive ideas emanating from the Global North are nonetheless embedded in a body of modernist knowledge that has supported and legitimated colonial social relations and justified the dispossession of Indigenous people. Restorative justice has not emerged organically from within Indigenous communities, it arrives on the back of a wagon train of top-down government policies, statutes and laws that also include mandatory sentencing laws, assimilationist child removal policies, insensitive and inappropriate forms of policing, and the destruction of native flora and fauna. There is what we might call, after the ideas of Robert Michels, the 'iron law of white intervention' into the Aboriginal domain: a 'concern' about social issues in

Indigenous communities ineluctably leads to a significant deployment of the repressive state apparatuses, followed by mass incarceration. For example, research (Anthony and Blagg, 2013) in remote communities in the Northern Territory of Australia in the wake of a national moral panic about an epidemic of child abuse, found a surge in police numbers resulting in a 250 per cent increase in arrests for driving related matters, and no increase at all in rates of arrest for child abuse. Data I present later demonstrates that: a decade of politicalised 'concern' with the victimisation of Indigenous women on remote Indigenous communities has seen a massive leap in the imprisonment of these very women.

In relation to Indigenous peoples globally, a *relevant* restorative justice would take into account what Boaventura de Sousa Santos (Sousa Santos, 2014) describes as *epistemologies of the south*; meaning that it would be willing to take into account the alternative beliefs and values of Indigenous societies, which are often dismissed as 'folklore' by non-Indigenous structures. In recent years there has been a global renaissance of Indigenous cultural politics. In South America, to take a topical example, it energised the *gira izquierda* ('left turn') (known also as a 'second independence' or the 'South American spring') in political life: the election of Movimiento al Socialismo (MAS) in Bolivia, for example, has seen control of the state wrested from the hands of a Washington-connected neo-liberal clique (Postero, 2006). Bolivia's 'Pluri-National Government' has initiated wide-ranging measures to recognise the rights of what the 2009 Constitution calls 'nation and rural native indigenous people', consisting of 'every human collective that shares a cultural identity, language, historic tradition, institutions, territory and world view, whose existence predates the Spanish colonial invasion'.[2] More broadly in Latin America there has been a shift towards a greater emphasis on 'the interconnectedness of economics with the political, socio-cultural, and environmental spheres' (Walsh, 2010). For example, in the Andes Region and Ecuador there is a pronounced emphasis on the notion of *buen vivir*, 'living well' as an alternative to just material progress and self-enrichment (Walsh, 2010).

Indigenous epistemologies form the bedrock of resistance to attempts by the Global North to 'standardise and homogenise' (Meyer and Maldonado Alvarado, 2010) the Indigenous world. The world's 340 million or so Indigenous peoples vary considerably across the globe, yet they share common experiences of 'loss of land and subsistence, abrogation of treaties, and the imposition of psychologically and socially destructive assimilation policies' (Niezen, 2003); historical injustices acknowledged in the UN Declaration on the Rights of Indigenous Peoples (2008) which establishes 'that

[2] Political Constitution of Plurinational State of Bolivia 2009 (Constitución Política del Estado) (BOL) (Max Planck Institute (trans), 2014).

indigenous peoples are equal to all other peoples, while recognizing the right of all peoples to be different, to consider themselves different, and to be respected as such' (61/295). The settler colonial state has been a poor custodian of Indigenous rights; the settler state has persecuted rather than protected Indigenous people. Indigenous people globally seek *restitution* and *reparation* for a host of crimes committed by settler colonists, and their demands include: native title and land rights; the end to impunity from prosecution for human rights abuses (including genocide); a focus on state (rather than just individual) violence; a leading role for strategies of self-determination; the recognition of Indigenous sovereignty, and a willingness to acknowledge Aboriginal law as a fact of life for Indigenous peoples.

This kind of engagement would, inevitably, commit restorative practitioners to become involved in the labour of *decoloniality*; that is, actively working with Indigenous peoples to decolonise a range of structures, mentalities and organisations that have perpetuated Indigenous dispossession, rather than simply offering a discrete service on the margins of the mainstream justice system. Restorative justice is often viewed by Indigenous activists as just another globalised and de-territorialised 'method' circulating in the reified ether of international policy transfer through the medium of Western NGOs. Embedded in a northern epistemology and philosophy, restorative justice is focused on individual as opposed to collective rights, and individual 'victims' and 'offenders' as autonomous agents, each with responsibility for his/her own actions: notions at odds with Indigenous ontology. A more 'critical' form of restorative justice might be capable of moving beyond these Eurocentric constructs of 'responsibilisation' and forge alliances with Indigenous peoples in a non-colonising way, in what is often called the 'in-between' or 'liminal' space between the mainstream and Indigenous cultures (Blagg, 2008).

IV. A CRITICAL RESTORATIVE JUSTICE?

Critical thinking in relation to restorative justice might begin by questioning the extent to which, in relation to the Global South, it represents a genuinely emancipatory practice, or simply a part of contemporary 'coloniality of power' (Quijano, 2000); meaning the perpetuation in contemporary post-colonial societies of social discrimination originating under colonialism that has survived colonial administration and became integrated in succeeding social orders (Wallerstein, 1995). Does restorative justice simply legitimate Western style solutions, while posing as a practice sympathetic to Indigenous goals and cultures? Looking across the social sciences (criminology, sociology, psychology, anthropology and victimology, for example) the term 'critical' implies a commitment to what today would be called a 'reflexive' practice, implying a capacity to reflect on our work in a way that allows us to be constructively critical of our endeavours. It involves a willingness to be self-critical, but it also assumes a preparedness to look at the bigger picture and critique the structures and processes that determine the parameters of our work. Critical victimology, for example, is concerned with de-mystifying the way social systems authorise and accredit certain subjects (ideally, white, elderly, socially and culturally integrated) as 'victims' while others (the ethnic/gendered/racial/religious Other) are denied victim status, and are, indeed, deemed responsible for any harm that befalls them. In criminology, a critical stance has been associated with challenging taken for granted assumptions about the neutrality of our laws and systems of justice, recognising in them profoundly embedded cultural beliefs and values and a tendency to reinforce the status quo (DeKeseredy, 2011). Rather than viewing the justice system as built upon shared value consensus, a critical approach takes account of social inequalities and cultural conflict, which are played out within the arena of the justice system. It tends to see the criminal justice system as a site of social, cultural, economic and racial contestation rather than a neutral and impartial set of mechanisms. Working as a criminologist within a *decolonising* framework of ideas requires a degree of 'disciplinary disobedience' (Mignolo, 2011); listening, for example, to the voices of critical anthropologists and historians of the colonial encounter.

Critical thinking in relation to restorative justice should question its own place within this homogenising and standardising process. Through an engagement with southern epistemologies, enunciated in the works of writers as diverse as Maori critic Linda Tuhiuai Smith (1999), John and Jean Comaroff (2011) in South Africa and a number of writers with a base in South America, particularly concerned with Amerindian issues (Cathy Walsh, Walter Mignolo, Boaventura de Sousa Santos, Antonio Escobar, Walter Mignolo and Nelson Maldonado-Torres) we might begin to map out a radical and critical restorative justice committed to healing the harms created by colonialism.

V. THE POSTCOLONIAL TURN AND THE NORTH IN THE SOUTH

Boaventura de Sousa Santos (2014) employs the term 'epistemicide' to describe how Western domination has systemically denied the knowledge systems and epistemologies indigenous to the Global South, a process he describes as a form of 'cognitive injustice'—a massive failure to respect the knowledge rights and interests of groups who live differently. Theorists from the South also stress the extent to which colonisation takes place in the head, the heart and the imagination, embrocating itself into the realms of culture and knowledge production. Spivak (Landry and Maclean, 1996) talks, for example, of the 'epistemological violence' of colonisation. Postcolonial theories seek to rescue the colonised subject's society and validate subaltern voices drowned out by colonial discourses. Research on Indigenous people and justice has been hindered by the fixation amongst criminologists of the Global North on the nation-state as its primary unit of analysis. Because Indigenous people do not form recognisable nation-states and are largely subsumed within the settler state's systems of national representation, they are neglected by criminological research founded on forms of methodological nationalism that ignore struggles 'above and below' nation-state (Clarke *et al*, 2015).

There is, increasingly, a Global South in the geographic north, and a Global North in the geographic south. Settler colonist societies, such as Canada, New Zealand and Australia, are globally northern societies transplanted into the geographic south. A steep north/south divide runs between settler colonists and the Indigenous Other. Indigenous resistance does not seek to topple colonial power, but reconfigure relationships and create plural forms of sovereignty. It encourages mutual understanding, but on terms radically different from prevailing forms of 'multiculturalism' which accepts a degree of cultural difference, but only as a transitional moment on the way to eventual assimilation into the hegemonic mainstream.

Viewed from the perspective of the Global South, there is nothing inherently radical or progressive about restorative justice. Evidence also suggests that the countries that have done most to resist punitive populism, have done so pretty much on the basis of adherence to pre-existing values associated with social democracy, rather than by reference to restorative practices as such (Pratt and Erikson, 2013), while the society that produces the most literature on contemporary 'RJ' (the United States) is the brand leader in punitive excess and institutionalised and racialised state violence. Chris Cunneen (2011) insightfully argues that there is no reason why RJ could not be deployed alongside repressive crime control measures and, in the case of Australia at least, it cheerfully co-exists with extreme forms of punitive excess directed at Australia's Indigenous people. The fact is that in many societies restorative justice has been *enclaved* into the justice system, where it exists in a non-threatening symbiosis with punitive sanctions as part of a punishment continuum. In Western Australia, the objectives of the 1994 Young Offenders Act (YOA) include (in section 6(ii)) '*punishing* and managing young persons who have committed offences' (emphasis added),[3] yet the Act also includes reference to reintegration and the protection of legal rights. This is important because it conflicts with beliefs that, over time, restorative justice would change the way the system as a whole treats young people. Instead, the reverse occurred; instead of restorative justice humanising the system, it has been co-opted onto its margins and its radical edge

[3] The focus on punishment as an aim of youth justice is in breach of the principles (and the spirit) of the UN Convention on the Rights of the Child.

blunted. It is quite possible to have policy commitment to restorative justice and have mass incarceration. The major factor driving punitive excess in Australia is race, as Baldry and Cunneen (2014: 4) maintain:

> [P]unishment in Australia is highly racialised. The two jurisdictions in Australia, which have the highest imprisonment rates (the Northern Territory and Western Australia), are also the jurisdictions with the largest proportion of Indigenous people living within their boundaries. Indeed in Western Australia, Indigenous imprisonment rates are well beyond any meaningful comparison to other rates in Australia.

The fact that these jurisdictions employ the justice system to manage the fruits of indigenous dispossession is, naturally, not emblazoned on their websites. The webpage of the WA Department for Corrections Youth Justice Services is a floral tribute to its adherence to the kinds of goals of modern youth justice policy, 'evidence led', 'multi-agency', 'what works', etc, describing itself thus:

> Youth Justice Services is a multi-disciplinary team working to provide an evidenced based responsive service to young people and their families when they come into contact with the youth justice system. It aims to reduce antisocial behaviour, strengthen interagency partnerships and prevent likelihood of further escalation through the youth justice system.

While reference is made to detention only being a 'sanction of last resort', it neglects to mention that for many Indigenous youth incarceration is an inevitable and normalised aspect of life.

The incarceration of Indigenous people in Australia has risen exponentially as part of a new strategy of 'governing through crime' that masks a new assimilationist strategy by the settler state (Anthony, 2010) since the mid-1990s. Recent data (ABS, 2012–2013) indicates that the difference between Indigenous and non-Indigenous imprisonment has steadily increased since the early 2000s. Indigenous people constitute around 28 per cent of prisoners (sentenced and remand) in Australia generally, while they constitute roughly 2 per cent of the population. In 'frontier' States such as Western Australia, the Northern Territory and Queensland, they make up a significant proportion of the prisoner population. In Western Australia, for example, where they are 3.6 per cent of the population they represent 40 per cent of the adult prison population generally, over 50 per cent of the women's prison population, and a staggering 78 per cent of the juvenile detention regime (ABS, 2012–2013). The Northern Territory (NT) has shown the highest increase in the rate of imprisonment of Indigenous people in the last decade. Indigenous people make up 86 per cent of the prisoner population (ABS, 2012–2013) and approximately 30 per cent of the total NT population. Between 2002 and 2012, Aboriginal women's imprisonment increased by 72 per cent. Queensland has experienced a surge in imprisonment rates in the last few years, even by Australian standards:

Indigenous people comprise 32 per cent (2,243 prisoners) of the adult prisoner population.

In Western Australia, a suite of 'front end' diversionary options was established under the YOA 1994 including formal and informal police cautioning and a system of multi-agency Juvenile Justice Teams (JJTs) tasked with increasing the rate of diversion for youths at risk of enmeshment in the justice system through family conferencing. The 'teams' were Western Australia's contribution to the restorative 'turn' which saw many Australian States introduce diversionary schemes loosely based on the New Zealand model established under the 1989 Children, Young Persons and their Families Act. Police in Western Australia have discretion to refer the matter to a Juvenile Justice Team, conditional on the offence not falling within one of the Scheduled Offences of the YOA, which include crimes of violence, some traffic and drug-related offences. The diversionary initiatives were successful in halving the numbers of young people being taken to the Perth Children's Court by police. Unfortunately, most of those diverted were non-Aboriginal. The Aboriginal over-representation *rate* actually increased after the reforms. Aboriginal representative bodies in WA pointed to a lack of commitment by government to fully implement those recommendations that might have increased the rate of diversion.[4] Since 2000, there has been a steady *decrease* in the number of cautions issued, noticeably for non-Indigenous persons, along with police referrals to JJTs. In 2007, around 80 per cent of Non-Aboriginal young people were being diverted from court, while only 55 per cent of young Aboriginal people were diverted (Blagg, 2008: 34). The familiar repertoire of strategies and schemes established as part of the diversionary turn in the 1990s are clearly irrelevant in contexts increasingly shaped by the mass imprisonment of those who are deemed beyond 'integration'. For their part, Indigenous youth and their families are not 'marginalised' by the justice system. They are oppressed by it.

Mainstream criminology, by which I mean those criminological perspectives and methods developed on the basis of Western paradigms of knowledge, produces an array of explanations for Indigenous over-representation in terms that resonate with mainstream values and interests; generally pathologising Indigenous culture and/or identifying various manifest symptoms such as alcohol abuse and 'poor parenting' as causing Indigenous over-representation (see Weatherburn, 2014, as a particularly decontextualised account). I would hesitate to call these perspectives 'theories' as they are in a real sense abandoning theoretical explanations altogether, in favour of a bloodless empiricism and a crude 'realism' that eschews the kinds of grounded approach required to make sense of historically structured inequality.

[4] See Aboriginal Justice Council (1999).

The decline in interest in theoretical inquiry is reflected in the emergence of what I call RJ and flat-pack justice.

VI. FROM RESTORATIVE JUSTICE TO 'RJ INC' AND FLAT-PACK JUSTICE

'RJ' refers to the product we are sold at conferences and seminars, particularly in the United States, where world's 'best practice' is defined and the 'what works?' 'evidence base' assembled. It is being packaged and exported globally, through numerous supranational bodies and institutions concerned with 'policy transfer', 'policy diffusion' and 'policy convergence'. RJ has become a standardised, homogenised commodity—a brand, rather like McDonalds or Starbucks—much the same everywhere one travels (generally bland and indigestible). For example, US 'Loss Prevention' company CEC offers a 'mobile-based platform ... to identify, qualify and divert your low risk offenders from the traditional legal process by enrolling them in CEC's accredited educational programme all within minutes'.[5] RJ is part of this package. We find ourselves increasingly having to 'sell' restorative solutions in neo-liberal terms: it is a cheap alternative; it saves 'time'; it upholds the status quo; it does not challenge the fundamental injustice of a justice system or threaten power. This homogenised and standardised package arrives rather like a flat-packed bookshelf to be assembled at the local level with a few local cultural adornments. It complements other flat-pack justice commodities with neat acronyms, TJ (therapeutic jurisprudence), POCs (problem oriented courts). Whatever the strengths and weaknesses of these models in the domestic context, once transported overseas they can easily reinforce a 'developmental' paradigm where it is assumed that these societies are inevitably developing towards 'us', and that their own models of conflict resolution are defunct. Walter Mignolo (2011) asserts that 'development' 'embodied a re-organization of the logic of coloniality', not an end to it. Indigenous peoples, in particular, rarely buy in to the ideology of 'development' as an ideal, desirable and necessary process, as Walsh maintains: '[t]he very idea of development itself is a concept and word that does not exist in the cosmovisions, conceptual categories, and languages of indigenous communities' (Walsh, 2007).

VII. TRAVELLING JUSTICE

There is now a burgeoning literature on 'policy convergence' (convergence around standardised neo-liberal values, of course). 'What is common to all

[5] See www.correctiveeducation.com/home/whatiscec#What-is-CEC?.

this literature', Clarke et al (2015) suggest, 'is the rather linear notion of movement being described. Policy ideas or models are rendered as "objects" to be loaded up on a truck at point A and unloaded at point B'. The non-Western world does appear in the production process, for what meditation on the merits of RJ would be complete without reference to native peace-keeping? However, there is always the sense that this is a highly selective process, where 'we' cherry-pick those elements of Indigenous knowledge that suit our predilections while ignoring those that conflict with them. Comaroff and Comaroff (2011) sum this up perfectly when they describe the ways the Global South is viewed from the perspective of the North, as simply a repository of 'unprocessed data' to be processed in the North:

> [The South is] treated less as sources of refined knowledge than as reservoirs of raw fact: of the historical, natural, and ethnographic minutiae from which Euro-modernity might fashion its testable theories and transcendent truths, its axioms and certitudes, its premises, postulates and principles.

The Comaroffs correctly point out that Southern epistemology is insinuated into the Western knowledge production process as a kind of 'raw material', to be refined in the academies, NGOs and think tanks of the West. I am not arguing that policy transfer is an inevitably negative practice: it can be energising and productive. However, policy exchange should involve a process of dialogue and negotiation. As Edward Said (1984) observes in *The World, the Text, and the Critic*:

> Like people and schools of criticism ideas and theories travel–from person to person, from situation to situation, from one period to another. Cultural and intellectual life are usually nourished and often sustained by the circulation of ideas.

Said (1984: 4) offers the caveat that such movements 'are never unimpeded', they undergo processes of 'representation and institutionalisation different from those at the point of origin', arguing that travelling ideas tend to dissipate as they traverse time and space, they become domesticated and assimilated, losing their radical meaning, particularly so when they move from the South to the North. Restorative justice has travelled globally and been translated in the process. Take, for example, the New Zealand family conferencing approach, embedded in legislation that empowers Maori society and lays down strict limits on the role of the police in the justice process. As it has 'travelled' northwards, the ideas have been de-radicalised and assimilated into mainstream justice. Restorative justice, it could be argued, has been 'represented and institutionalised'. The unfortunate coupling of restorative processes with 'shaming' as it travelled across the Tasman Sea to Australia, for example, de-radicalised the idea, leaving it the property of an unreformed and ill-informed justice and policing system.

Restorative justice has emerged in societies where criminal events occur against a backdrop of (relative) normality, while transitional justice usually operates in contexts shaped by massive human rights violations, war and genocide. Participants in restorative justice ceremonies (the family conference, the face to face meeting between victim and offender) may return to a world normalised by the encounter—they may look forward to getting on with their lives. Post-conflict societies are often typified by large-scale destruction, social upheaval and anomie: a world 'out of joint', unlikely to be set right without significant investment. Transitional justice recognises the profound trauma created by state crimes, ethnic cleansing and state-sanctioned rape. Recent critical writing on transitional justice (Green and Ward, 2004; Stanley and McCulloch, 2013) suggests that transitioning towards stable democracy demands long-term nation building, complemented by a vibrant civil society, and may require bringing powerful state actors to account, and might involve significant elements of retributive justice (Uprimny and Saffon, 2007).

VIII. AN 'INTERCULTURAL' RESTORATIVE JUSTICE?

'Intercultural' dialogue attempts to construct engagement spaces in-between cultures and respects a 'pluriverse' of epistemologies and worldviews. It aims to create greater mutual understanding between the margins and the mainstream, North and South (Merlan, 1998; Escobar, 2011). There are concerns, however, that intercultural spaces can themselves become sites of assimilation, at least for Indigenous peoples, as Morphy and Morphy argue, '[t]he intercultural, once articulated as a conceptual space, has the potential to become the space where Aboriginal people gradually merge with the mainstream' (Morphy and Morphy, 2013). Helpfully, Cathy Walsh (2007) distinguishes between what she calls 'functional' and 'critical' interculturality: whereas 'functional' inter-culturality does not address underlying inequalities that seek to maintain the system, the latter 'seeks its major transformation in social, political, epistemic, and existential terms. That is, a new ordering of structures, institutions, and relations'.

Walsh identifies characteristics necessary for a critical praxis: transformative ideas and practices that seek to build new social structures and institutions respectful of difference. Similarly, Mignolo (2007) draws the distinction between 'multiculturalism', which 'concede[s] "culture" while maintaining "epistemology"', and 'inter-culturality' which was devised by 'Indigenous intellectuals to claim epistemic rights'. The question is: how can restorative justice assist in promoting the epistemic rights of the Other? Validate the worldview of the Other and create this major transformation of social structures and institutions? Of course, as an isolated practice restorative justice cannot. It has to build alliances with those groups the mainstream choses to ignore, and often oppresses, such as immigrants, Roma, the undocumented.

IX. SITES OF RESURGENCE

Building such alliances with Indigenous peoples has to begin by acknowledging long-standing claims to land. In my introduction, I noted the importance of land for Indigenous peoples. Land is becoming what Caulthord (2014) calls a 'site of resurgence' for Indigenous culture. In the Kimberley region of Western Australia, Kimberley Aboriginal Law and Culture (KALACC), an influential community controlled body representing the interests of Kimberley Aboriginal people in relation to cultural issues, is engaged in developing justice alternatives based around 'community owned' justice mechanisms on Aboriginal country, in particular the *Yiriman* Project, which provides an intensive cultural immersion and 'healing' experience on traditional lands for at risk young people run by Elders (Blagg, 2012). *Yiriman* is breaking with the traditional model of *community based* approaches to work with young people, that simply move the front door of the agency into the community without changing the way it works, by building the interventions around law, land and culture. The project has an uneasy relationship with the mainstream youth justice system which wants to 'use' the project but apply only its own management and control systems, effectively becoming the 'boss' on the camps, something the Elders will not accede to (Blagg, 2012). What is interesting about the *Yiriman* is that it has captured the imagination of the local judiciary and the police; in the latter case it has re-energised the otherwise moribund Juvenile Justice Teams, which are in decline elsewhere.

In other parts of the Kimberley, traditional owners are attempting to create similar projects, leveraging off their (limited) ownership of land under Australia's Native Title regime, to create on-country projects that build a 'hybrid moral economy' somewhere in-between the mainstream world of work and Indigenous cultural practices. These practices involve working with, rather than exploiting, the land by nurturing native fruits and medicines. Traditional Owner groups, such as the *Yawuru* people in the Kimberley, aim to build partnerships with mainstream agencies that will see on-country engagement in the hybrid economy replacing involvement in the white justice system for many *Yawuru* people, who are routinely rotated through the prison system because they are dispossessed of country, the victims of failed white policies of social engineering or survivors of inter-generational trauma. This kind of engagement is truly 'restorative' as it restores the land, and restores the people to the land, while building the capacities of Indigenous communities to create peaceful futures for the children.

X. CONCLUDING COMMENTS

Theories from the South are forthright in debunking the belief in the inherent superiority of Western forms of knowledge. Critical restorative practices would begin by questioning not just the shortcomings of our adversarial system as a solution to individual crime-related problems, but be willing to challenge the extent to which it is deliberately criminogenic in nature. Simply promoting tolerance and dialogue as ends in themselves, without exploring the systemic causes of inequality that drive people into crime, simply turns restorative justice into RJ—a slave to the system it purports to challenge. A critical restorative justice would question the semi-mystical faith in the 'conference' as the cornerstone of restorative practice and the insistence on 'epiphany' as its desired outcome, rather than mutual understanding and problem solving. It would remain sceptical about the role of powerful agencies such as the police as the custodians of restorative processes. It would move on from the unfortunate focus on shaming, especially for young offenders (naturally, it should be reserved for fat cats and dictators who do have a public status to lose). In relation to the world's Indigenous people, restorative justice practitioners have to accept that our belief that the practices we have adopted accord with Indigenous worldviews is an Orientalist fiction, intended not so much to assist *them* as to make *us* feel better by warming up the cold leftovers of Western justice with some Orientalist spice. Instead, restorative justice needs to engage with the historical demands of Indigenous people for their land and their way of life; though constantly imperilled by forces of neo-liberalism and colonialism, they remain resilient and provide a vision of an alternative to Euro-modernity.

REFERENCES

Aboriginal Justice Council (1999) *Getting Stronger on Justice* (Perth, Department of Indigenous Affairs).

Agambon, G (1998) *Homo Sacer: Sovereign Power and Bare Life* (D Heller-Roazen (trans), Stanford, CA, Stanford University Press).

Aliverti, A (2015) 'Doing Away with Decency? Foreigners, Punishment and the Liberal State' in A Erikson (ed), *Punishing the Other: The Social Production of Immorality Revisited* (London, Routledge).

Anthony, T (2010) 'Governing Through Crime in the Intervention' 27(2) *Law in Context* 90.

Anthony, T and Blagg, H (2013) 'STOP in the Name of Who's Law? Driving and the Regulation of Contested Space in Central Australia' 22(1) *Social and Legal Studies* 43.

Arendt, H (1973) *The Origins of Totalitarianism* (New York, Harvest Books).

Australian Bureau of Statistics (ABS) *Prisoners in Australia, 2011*, Cat No 4517.0 (Canberra, 2012–2013).

Baldry, E and Cunneen, C (2014) 'Imprisoned Indigenous Women and the Shadow of Colonial Patriarchy' 47(2) *Australian and New Zealand Journal of Criminology* 1.

Balibar, E (2004) *We, the People of Europe? Reflections on Transnational Citizenship* (J. Swenson (trans), Princeton, NJ and Oxford, Princeton University Press).

Bauman, Z and Lyon, D (2012) *Liquid Surveillance: A Conversation* (Oxford, Polity).
Blagg, H (1997) 'A Just Measure of Shame? Aboriginal Youth and Conferencing in Australia' 37(4) *British Journal of Criminology* 481.
—— (1998) 'Restorative Visions and Restorative Justice Practices: Conferencing, Ceremony and Reconciliation in Australia' 10(1) *Current Issues in Criminal Justice* 5.
—— (2008) *Crime, Aboriginality and the Decolonisation of Justice* (Sydney, Hawkins Press).
—— (2012) 'Re-Imagining Youth Justice: Cultural Contestation in the Kimberley Region of Australia Since the 1991 Royal Commission into Aboriginal Deaths in Custody' 16(4) *Theoretical Criminology* 481.
—— (2016) 'From Terra Nullius to Terra Liquidus? Liquid Modernity and the Indigenous Other' in A Erikson (ed), *Punishing the Other: The Social Production of Immorality Revisited* (London, Routledge).
Caulthord, G (2014) *Red Skin, White Masks: Rejecting the Colonial Politics of Recognition* (Minneapolis, MN, University of Minnesota Press).
Clamp, K (2013) *Restorative Justice in Transition* (London, Routledge).
Clarke, J, Bainton, D, Lendvai, N and Stubbs, P (2015) *Making Policy Move: Towards a Politics of Translation and Assemblage* (Bristol, Policy Press).
Comaroff, J and Comaroff, JL (2011) *Theory from the South: Or, How Euro-America is Evolving Toward Africa* (Stellenbosch, SUN Media Stellenbosch).
Connell, R (2007) *Southern Theory: The Global Dynamics of Knowledge in Social Science* (London, Allen and Unwin).
Cunneen, C (1997) 'Community Conferencing and the Fiction of Indigenous Control' 30(3) *Australian and New Zealand Journal of Criminology* 292.
—— (2005) 'Racism, Discrimination and the Over-Representation of Indigenous People in the Criminal Justice System: Some Conceptual and Explanatory Issues' 17(2) *Current Issues in Criminal Justice* 329.
—— (2011) 'Indigeneity, Sovereignty and the Law: Challenging the Process of Criminalisation' 110(2) *South Atlantic Quarterly* 309.
DeKeseredy, W (2011) *Contemporary Critical Criminology* (Oxford, Routledge).
Escobar, A (2011) *Encountering Development: The Making and Unmaking of the Third World* (Princeton, NJ, Princeton University Press).
Fanon, F (1990) *The Wretched of the Earth* (Harmondsworth, Penguin).
Galeano, G (1997) *Open Veins of Latin America: Five Centuries of the Pillage of a Continent* (New York, Monthly Review Press).
Gilroy, P (2011) 'Shameful History: The Social Life of Races and the Postcolonial Archive' 11(2) *Moving Worlds: A Journal of Transcultural Writings, Postcolonial Europe* 19.
Green, P and Ward, T (2004) *State Crime: Governments, Violence and Corruption* (London, Pluto).
Hage, G (2012) 'Critical Anthropological Thought and the Radical Political Imaginary Today' 32(3) *Critique of Anthropology* 285.
Landry, D and Maclean, G (eds) (1996) *The Spivak Reader: Selected Works of Gayatri Chakravorty Spivak* (London, Routledge).
Maldonado-Torres, N (2007) 'On the Coloniality of Being: Contributions to the Development of a Concept' 21(2) *Cultural Studies* 240.

Merlan, F (1998) *Caging the Rainbow: Places, Politics, and Aborigines in a North Australian Town* (Honolulu, University of Hawai'i Press).
Meyer, L and Maldonado Alvarado, B (eds) (2010) *New World of Indigenous Resistance: Noam Chomsky and Voices from North, South, and Central America* (San Francisco, CA, City Lights Books and Open Media Series).
Mignolo, W (2007) 'The Decolonial Option and the Meaning of Identity in Politics' 9/10 *Anales Nueva Epoca* 43.
—— (2011) *The Darker Side of Western Modernity: Global Futures, Decolonial Options* (Durham, NC, Duke University Press).
Moreton-Robinson, A (2003) 'I Still Call Australia Home: Indigenous Belonging and Place in a White Postcolonising Society' in S Ahmed (ed), *Uprootings/Regroundings: Questions of Home and Migration* (Oxford, Berg Publishing).
Morphy, F and Morphy, H (2013) 'Anthropological Theory and Government Policy in Australia's Northern Territory: The Hegemony of the "Mainstream"' 115(2) *American Anthropologist* 174.
Niezen, R (2003) *The Origins of Indigenism: Human Rights and the Politics of Identity* (Berkley, CA, University of California Press).
Ponzanesi, S and Blaagaard, B (eds) (2012) *Deconstructing Europe: Postcolonial Perspectives* (London and New York, Routledge).
Postero, NG (2006) *Now We are Citizens: Indigenous Politics in Postmulticultural Bolivia* (Stanford, CA, Stanford University Press).
Povinelli, E (2002) *The Cunning of Recognition: Indigenous Alterities and the Making of Australian Multiculturalism* (Durham, NC, Duke University Press).
Pratt, J and Erikson, A (2013) *Contrasts in Punishment: An Explanation of Anglophone Excess and Nordic Exceptionalism* (London, Routledge).
Quijano, A (2000) 'Coloniality of Power, Eurocentrism and Latin America' 1(3) *Nepentla: Views from the South* 533.
Roach, D (2003) *Accountability in Restorative Justice* (Oxford, Oxford University Press).
Said, E (1984) *The World, the Text, and the Critic* (Cambridge, MA, Harvard University Press).
—— (2003) *Orientalism* (London, Vintage).
Simon, J (2001) 'Entitlement to Cruelty: Neo-Liberalism and the Punitive Mentality in the United States' in K Stenson and RR Sullivan (eds), *Crime, Risk and Justice: The Politics of Crime Control in Liberal Democracies* (Cullompton, Willan).
Smith, L (1999) *Decolonizing Methodologies: Research and Indigenous Peoples* (New York and London, Zed Books).
Sousa Santos, B de (2014) *Epistemologies of the South: Justice Against Epistemicide* (Boulder, CO, Paradigm Publishers).
Sousa Santos, B de (ed) (2008) *Another Knowledge is Possible: Beyond Northern Epistemologies* (London, Verso).
Stanley, E and McCulloch, J (2013) (eds), *State Crime and Resistance* (London, Routledge).
Uprimny, R and Saffon, MP (2007) *Transitional Justice, Restorative Justice and Reconciliation: Some Insights from the Colombian Case*, Coming to Terms with Reconciliation Working Paper Library.
Walklate, S (1990) 'Researching Victims of Crime: Critical Victimology' 17(3) *Social Justice* 41.

Wallerstein, I (1995) *Historical Capitalism, with Capitalist Civilization* (New York, New York Press).
Walsh, C (2007) 'Shifting the Geopolitics of Critical Knowledge' 21(2) *Cultural Studies* 224.
—— (2010) 'Development as Buen Vivir: Institutional Arrangements and (De)Colonial Entanglements' 53(1) *Development* 15.
Weatherburn, D (2014) *Arresting Incarceration: Pathways out of Indigenous Imprisonment* (Canberra, Australian Studies Press).
Zehr, H (2005) *Changing Lenses: A New Focus for Crime and Justice*, 3rd edn (Minnesota, Herald Press).

5

Outlining a Historical and Critical Ontology of Restorative Justice

GIUSEPPE MAGLIONE*

I. INTRODUCTION

THIS CHAPTER AIMS to outline a historico-philosophical investigation into the conditions of possibility of restorative justice (RJ), from a perspective informed by Michel Foucault's historical and critical project(s). Through the foucauldian lenses, RJ appears as a cultural formation constituted by three different but interlinked dimensions: 'a game of truth, relations of power, and forms of relation to oneself and to others' (Foucault, 1984: 387). Therefore, the focus of this work will be posited on historically reconstructing and critically problematising the 'true' discourses, power relationships and ethical 'potential' of RJ (Faubion, 2013). The reasons for choosing such an approach are as much epistemological as ethico-political: this perspective serves not only the purpose of diagnosing and defamiliarising the 'present' (what we take for granted or accept uncritically) of RJ but also of imagining specific forms of resistance to it (Hoy, 2004; Voruz, 2010). In this way it is possible to develop a critical tension which might make RJ a challenge to 'conventional' criminal justice,[1] from an epistemological, ontological and ethical viewpoint.

The first (archaeological) objective is to delineate the archive of RJ, ie to reconstruct and unpack the range of authoritative discourses which have shaped the 'thinkable and practicable' (Gordon, 1991: 3) about RJ over the last 30 years. The second (genealogical) aim is to critically appraise the power/knowledge embeddedness of the authoritative discourses on RJ, conceptualising their emergence within a wider context of socio-political transformations and technologies of power. The last (ethical) goal is to reflect

* I wish to thank Kirsty Boutle for her invaluable help in writing this chapter.

[1] This is a shorthand expression which refers to the legal rationality developed in Western countries at least since the Enlightenment, implemented by public prosecution, trial process and criminal punishment justified by retributivist and/or rehabilitative philosophies.

upon the possibility of re-working RJ as a space for ethical practices as a form of critical resistance to the cooptation of RJ by subjugating forms of social control (Hoy, 2004). Along these lines it is possible to take a step toward the critical development of new opportunities in the theory and praxis of RJ, beyond the taken-for-granted *récits* on why and how RJ has emerged and works. There are two main limitations to the research. The first is of a geographical and chronological nature, insofar as a distinctive emphasis is placed upon the European (especially English) context in the last 30 years. Second, the analysis is to some extent 'biased' by my interest in RJ involving adults within criminal justice settings and applied through victim-offender mediation.

II. ARCHAEOLOGY, GENEALOGY AND ETHICS

The secondary literature mostly distinguishes three periods in Foucault's scholarship: archaeology, genealogy and ethics (Davidson, 1986; Scheurich and McKenzie, 2005), centring respectively on reconstructing the conditions of possibility for the emergence of certain knowledges (*savoir*), power relationships and subjectivities (Deleuze, 1995: 91–92). The links between these phases of inquiry are, however, a matter of contention, insofar as it is disputed whether they are theoretically and meta-theoretically interrelated or instead autonomous phases of the foucauldian research (the late Foucault himself (2000: 326) seems to endorse the first option, identifying that link in his interest in studying how 'human beings are made subjects'). In this work, archaeology, genealogy and ethics are considered as feeding into each other for epistemological and ethico-political reasons, not on the ground of any philologically 'correct' reading of the restless foucauldian journey (Valverde, 2008). Hence, the legacy of the archaeology is represented by the structural technique of focusing on both discourse and speaker as constructed objects. This being a necessary step to free ourselves from taking authoritative discourses as simply expressing the way things *are* (Dreyfus and Rabinow, 1983: xxvii).

The identification of discursive objects enables the raising of the genealogical questions: how are these discourses used? Which is their political ground? What role do they play in society? Genealogy moves from archaeology, intended as an attempt to unveil the conditions of emergence of certain discursive objects, how they have reached a status of truth, and how these truths are co-extensive of relations of power (Dean, 1994: 33). In this way it is possible to add a new level of critique to the analysis of the authoritative discourses, providing a counter-memory that helps to recreate the political conditions of their existence (Foucault, 1986: 53), opening up new possibilities of understanding and action. But the outcome of this process would not be sufficient if our goal was to identify forms of critical resistance in and through RJ to subjugating forms of justice: 'if the world could not be changed by revealing the hidden matrices of discourse and practices, perhaps it could be changed by transforming ourselves, by inventing new modes of being subjects' (Voruz, 2010: 13). This means to advance a reflection on how RJ could offer spaces for dealing with conflicts by intensifying people's moral agency. The question is then how can RJ practices enable self-forming activities which work as forms of ethico-political resistance to the present, ie to the subjugating ways of dealing with social conflicts and harms? How can we nurture the capacity of RJ to be a critical (and self-critical) challenge to 'conventional' criminal justice?

In order to operationalise this methodological perspective, I will proceed as follows. First, I will identify and unpack the structure of the authoritative discourses which compose RJ's 'hard core' (Tamboukou and Ball, 2003), identifying the socio-cultural constructs which underpin the emergence of these discourses. Secondly, I will map out the political conditions for the possibility of RJ, ie the technologies of power which have facilitated the historical emergence of the authoritative discourses of RJ. Thirdly, I will reflect upon the possibility of constructing RJ encounters as spaces of ethical practice, aiming at imagining an expanded field of possible subjectivities and conducts available to people involved in social conflicts. Lastly, I will sketch out some conclusive reflections on this analytic approach and its findings, raising new questions for RJ.

Two methodological caveats are necessary here. First, I plan to work by revising (and maybe distorting) specific foucauldian research devices in order to open up different possibilities of thinking and to generate new kinds of questions on RJ. This means simplifying or reconsidering many aspects of the foucauldian legacy, without worrying about being faithful or unfaithful to any 'textbook' version of Foucault's meta-theory. Secondly, as David Garland has argued, there are potentially serious limitations to the use of Foucault's historical method. The main problem is that the foucauldian perspective is often (and paradoxically) accepted as offering a grand theory; that is, it is often accepted 'in a manner which tends to displace other interpretive accounts, rather than supplement them or add a new dimension to their explanation' (Garland, 1990: 199). Notably, Garland acknowledges that Foucault's work was not intended by him to be read as a totalising or complete analysis of any of his chosen subjects. In the same vein, my aim is not to merely replace existing accounts of the birth, meaning and application of RJ with another, opposing a different truth-account. The goal here, is to outline and problematise the processes which underlie and feed on the authority of some discourses on RJ, the ways these are contingently produced, the political conditions of their emergence, and the opportunities to re-imagine their ethical 'potential'. Ironically, such an effort might end up being as problematic as the functionalistic versions of history it contests. This is because a foucauldian-inspired study, as any form of knowledge, normally produces power effects which the researcher might not be aware of; moreover, it is necessarily incomplete because it does not search for causes or origins, but for conditions of emergence which give rise to a myriad of more problems to be diagnosed and interpreted. Thus, the undertaking of research such as this is an inherently (and deliberately) subjective, shifting and unfinished enterprise. I believe that the reflexive awareness of these limitations can help to elide their detrimental effects on the critical aspirations of this work.

III. RECONSTRUCTING GAMES OF TRUTH

Foucauldian archaeology analyses the contingent and contextual conditions for the emergence of societal discourses, disregarding the consciousness of individual subjects as a precondition of discourse-making processes (Foucault, 1970; 1972; Howarth, 2002). From this perspective, the first step reconstructs the *archive*, ie the historical and dynamic set of discourses 'that governs the appearance of statements as unique events' (Foucault, 1972: 129), in all their interrelations and transformations (Foucault, 1991: 54). Here 'discourse' equates to 'discursive practice': cultural formations institutionally situated, historically shaped, constructed (by people, institutions, etc) and constructive of people's lived experiences, conducts, knowledges. I will be focusing on the range of discourses (within the RJ archive) which over the last 30 years have achieved an 'authoritative' status influencing, theory, policy and practice of RJ (Maglione, 2013). These authoritative discourses should not be considered as discrete and cohesive entities, with neat boundaries, but rather as analytical concepts 'that the researcher projects onto the reality in order to create a framework for the study' (Jørgensen and Phillips, 2002: 143) of neglected dimensions of the phenomena under examination. As far as the identification of these discourses is concerned, this proceeds inductively from the qualitative examination of two different but connected sets of cultural artefacts: a wide range of 'founding' texts for the RJ field and the 'textbook literature' on RJ produced between 1985 and 2015 in the English (and partially North American) context. I will select sources which have informed policy and law-making processes in the context chosen (England). I maintain that the commonly recognised (by RJ scholars and practitioners) foundational texts and the textbooks used world-wide (witnessed by the many editions) incorporated into policy/legal documents which challenge the criminal justice mainstream, define some of the main authoritative discourses of RJ. The crucial point of using an archaeological approach is to de-naturalise the somehow comforting idea of RJ encompassing very different opinions and views, arguing for the primacy of some recurrent and tacit ideas at the 'bottom' of the RJ field. Once the authoritative discourses have been outlined, it is possible to explore how they have historically emerged. Methodologically this analysis (which will be complemented by the genealogical inquiry) entails the detection of the contextual factors—that is, conditions of possibility (Foucault, 1970: 168)—which have contingently contributed to create the 'authority' of that stereotype, setting the conditions for a *legitimate* RJ (Elwick, 2012: 620).

Various attempts have been made to reduce the complexity of RJ's views and understandings, for instance, distinguishing between 'civilisation', 'communitarian' and 'moral' theses (Dignan, 2005: 95) or between 'encounter', 'reparative' and 'transformative' approaches (Johnstone and Van Ness, 2007: 1). In my view, RJ is cultural formation composed of at least three main (and empirically overlapping) discourses which constitute the core of the RJ archive: 'disenfranchising the victim', 'transforming the offender', 'decentralising conflict management'. While the first two are mainly characterised by a reformist-pragmatic approach to criminal justice, the third is more related to a radical-abolitionist view. These different discourses have reached in different times and places an authoritative status, featuring in legislative measures, applicative procedures, advocacy initiatives and training programmes, with intersections, combinations and tensions.

If we look at the English context especially, it is the first discourse which seems particularly authoritative, informing the majority of relevant policy and legal documents enacted during the last 15 years.[2] The 'disenfranchising the victim' discourse seems constituted by three pivotal ideas. The idea of 'producing safety' stresses the active participation of victims, offenders and community in order to manage the conflict that ties them together, as a condition to achieve empowerment and reconciliation. The restorative encounter is regarded as a time and space where the different issues at stake can be identified, discussed and addressed, restoring the emotional, social, symbolic and material relationships among the conflict stakeholders, with a specific emphasis on the victim's needs (Strang, 2003; Strang and Sherman, 2003; Zehr 1990). This view includes, then, the necessity of a meeting, the development of a narrative which enables the participants to express and address emotion; a moment of mutual understanding; and an agreement which seals the convergence of the interests of victim and offender by giving them the ability to guide the outcome (Van Ness and Strong, 2003: ch 4).

The 'taking care' perspective refers to a theory of reparation and prevention of crimes and their consequences, based on the idea of repairing harm with healing effects. This view discards the basic and deep-seated retributive

[2] This discourse informs the Restorative Justice action plans and Progress Reports released by the Ministry of Justice from 2012 onwards, in which they deal with RJ, the Crime and Courts Act 2013 (para 2.16), the Offender Rehabilitation Act 2014 (para 15.3.8) and the Code of Practice for Victims of Crime (October 2015) (para 34). At the European level, EU Directive 2012/29/EU (art 12) is a clear example of that discourse.

idea to address a crime by coercing the offender to endure pain quantitatively related to the gravity of the crime committed. The retributive stance has to be replaced by a restorative one, ie a concrete action toward the material and/or symbolical repair of the harm caused to the victim instead of punishment to the offender (Braithwaite, 1999; Walgrave, 2003; Wright, 1996).

The idea of 'transforming relationships' is also crucial. RJ is in fact identified as a cultural perspective which can inform concrete systems of dealing with conflictual relationships in everyday life (Sullivan and Tifft, 2001). RJ must be regarded as a way of life and a mindset which might lead us to understand ourselves and others and to behave in a 'restorative' way, ie relying on peace-building through dialogue and agreement. The premise of this view is a relational understanding of humans (Johnstone and Van Ness, 2007: 17), the 'natural' interconnectedness which can be hindered by destructive and antisocial behaviours. RJ interventions must aim, then, at restoring such interconnectedness, transforming actions which threaten or weaken interpersonal relationships.

The underpinnings of the discourse of 'disenfranchising the victim' are multiple, intersecting and different. The first ground is related to the consolidation of (general) victimology as a scientific and academic discipline combined with the emergence of crime victims' movement(s) in contemporary Western societies. The rise of 'victimhood' as an academic subject and political resource plays the role of crucial discursive pillar of RJ. The victimological 'necessity' of the involvement of crime victims in criminal proceedings and the political claim of meeting the expectations of crime victims have become key categories in the language of RJ proponents. This is not a 'natural' phenomenon, but the consequence of the consolidation of mainstream victimological research and the popularisation of victim movements' claims (Walklate, 2012: 180). A second component to be considered is the so-called 'psy-discourse' and its spread during the last two decades (Rose, 1998; Richards, 2005). This phenomenon refers to therapeutic languages which have informed a range of criminal policies emerging in recent years, particularly those designed to assist victims of crime, seemingly working as the secularised version of the action of religious groups involved in penal reform. It this way, it has now become widely accepted that crime victims must be offered opportunities to tell their stories of victimisation, express their pain, fear and/or anger about the offence, and 'be heard'. The final underpinning is the discourse of the crisis of 'conventional' criminal justice. Here the emphasis is on the endemic failing of criminal justice and the penal response in particular, which is no longer able to fulfil the public needs triggered by crime. The criminal justice rationality shows a typical dichotomising attitude (Achutti, 2011: 10–11; Christie, 1986: 95), expressed by a binary classification system 'both for evaluation of acts and for evaluation of persons' (Christie, 1986: 96). This rationality is implemented by institutions and practices which are said not to be working but at the same time cannot be completely overcome without evoking the demon of anarchy or an abolitionist utopia.

IV. MAPPING OUT RELATIONS OF POWER

Genealogy, like archeology, is a way of writing history. But if archaeology is meant to re-construct and isolate certain discourses, genealogy aims at describing the patterns between relations of power and those discursive objects, describing how they have become true or unproblematic (Bailey, 1993: 120; Saar, 2002: 231–33). What is distinctive of Foucault's genealogical work is to consider discourses interpenetrated by power, adding then a fundamental layer (the critique of power relationships) to his historical project (Foucault, 1978; 1984). Power is a productive, ubiquitous set of precarious trans-individual relations which entail the possibility of freedom and resistance; it operates in and through discourses (Gubrium and Holstein, 2000: 494), producing what is taken as knowledge or considered truth (Foucault, 1977: 27).

From a genealogical perspective, the rise and spread of the authoritative versions of RJ has been possible due to the parallel emergence of a specific set of technologies of power[3] inscribed in the framework of the advanced-liberal paradigm (Pavlich, 2005; Rose, 1996; 1999a). These technologies shift government from questions of rational administration of the population to those of individual everyday morality, from taking care of collectivity to empowering individual responsibilities of self-control, over-emphasising individual agency at the expense of structural constraints (Pathak, 2014: 1–2). These technologies of power make RJ a fully 'thinkable and practicable' object (Gordon, 1991: 3), they are the RJ's political conditions of possibility.

There are three main technologies of power which have made the emergence of RJ (specifically the discourse of 'disenfranchising the victim') possible. First, the emergence of a certain technology of security. This can be conceptualised as the qualitative transformation of the processes of social protection (safety) within those of individual defence (security), through a panoply of instruments which aim to predict and thus prevent dangerous events (Foucault, 2007: 93). It expresses the 'unrelenting de-socialisation of security and the growing securitisation of personal safety mainly conveyed through the increasing use in different *milieus* of society of a wide range of techniques designed to ensure a safe and secure future' (Schuilenburg, 2012: 75).

[3] This expression refers to 'technologies imbued with aspirations for the shaping of conduct in the hope of producing certain desired effects and averting certain undesired ones' (Rose 1999a: 52).

The security at stake is then the negative/private state of immunisation from risk and dangers, as the advanced-liberal product of the celebration of a 'gated' freedom (Bauman, 1998), closely related to the retrenchment of the welfare state. As Anthony Burke contends, we should see security as 'an interlocking system of knowledges, representations, practices, and institutional forms that imagine, direct, and act upon bodies, spaces, and flows in certain ways—to see security not as an essential value but as a political technology' (Burke, 2002: 3). These technologies set in motion a particular political dynamic, empowering specific political actors, and building up strategies and instruments for making responsible subjectivities. From this viewpoint, RJ makes sense as a de-centralised strategy of providing security relying on the stakeholders' (victims, offenders and communities) capability to take care of themselves. In fact, RJ advances the fundamental claim to invest in interventions on crimes which emphasise the direct involvement (ie responsibilisation) of stakeholders. RJ is about imagining participatory decision-making processes to deal with the causes and consequences of crimes, by empowering 'victims' and 'offenders' within and through their 'communities' to address the harm experienced. The actors of RJ are at the same time providers and recipients of security as immunisation from crime's consequences. Moreover, RJ services are community-based entities, posited between the private and the public, representing the community's effort to responsibilise itself as actor/user of security.

The second technology to be considered is what we might call 're-feudalisation' of governance. This expression refers to a political technology which works toward the hybridisation of public and private governance in advanced-liberal regimes, engendering a specific 'third way' of exercising authority and control over a wide range of social issues, first of all crime and deviance. Particularly, the appeal to 'community' as a site of governmental authority in both Europe (a typical case was the 'third way' politics during Blair's mandate in England) and North America, seems to be a crucial expression of this political technology. The re-feudalisation of governance, with its reference to family and community as crucial spaces of government, as well as politico-moral ideals (Rose 1999b: 487) resonates with the emphasis in RJ on empowerment by participatory decision-making and on the role of a consensual community to manage moral order.

The last technology is the process of psy-individualisation, which involves 'a plethora of indirect mechanisms that can translate the goals of political, social, and economic authorities into the choices and commitments of individuals' (Rose, 1998: 165), contributing to governing 'at a distance', via the re-definition of individuals' subjectivity. It works by installing, through the diffusion of psy-techniques, a concept of the human subject as an 'autonomous, individualised, self-directing, decision-making agent at the heart of policymaking' (Rose, 1999b: 499). This technology offers individuals, groups and communities new opportunities to actively participate in various arenas of action 'to resolve the kind of issues hitherto held to be the responsibility of authorized governmental agencies' (Burchell, 1996: 29). Here, individuals, groups and communities are 'encouraged freely and rationally, to conduct themselves' (Burchell, 1996: 29), and to become '"experts of themselves", to adopt an education and knowledgeable relation of self-care in respect of their bodies, their minds, their forms of conduct and that of the members of their families' (Rose, 1996: 59). Individualisation through psy-discipline integrates the de-socialisation of security and the emergence of hybrid arenas (and actors) of governance. The success of RJ is therefore linked to the simultaneous emphasis on a communal network which surrounds and supports the 'victim' and 'offender' in dealing with the crime and individualisation of responsibility for individual actions. 'Victim' and 'offender' are in fact deemed to have the necessary psychological, moral, symbolic and practical skills to engage in the restoration of the relationship harmed by the crime, which is the outcome of their deliberate decisions. They are the only ones who can repair, compensate or apologise for what happened.

There is a further dimension of the technologies of power, which needs finally and briefly to be pointed out. Insofar as these technologies are the political conditions of possibility for the emergence of RJ, they also impact on the actual functioning or restorative processes by conveying a certain idea of subject to be projected on the actual users. They potentially contribute to make RJ (as expressed by the authoritative discourses) a system for shaping self-surveillant and emotional subjects, obliged to be free. Self-surveillance implies the stipulation that individuals might be dangerous to themselves, due to being emotionally 'driven'. At the same time they are portrayed as free and responsible individuals, able to make choices. They need then to constantly survey themselves, only in this way can they enjoy a wide range of possibilities in dealing with conflicts, insofar as their emotions are liberated but harnessed, enfranchised but controlled.

V. ENVISIONING FORMS OF CRITICAL RESISTANCE

Archaeology and genealogy bring to the fore and historicise the authoritative discourses on RJ, showing their political embeddedness. RJ appears, now, as a complex field where only certain discourses play the role of main reference point for policy, legislation and practitioners. These authoritative discourses are rooted in a specific political context, the advanced-liberal regime. RJ is neither a open conglomeration of views and positions nor a politically neutral entity, as often appears in the accounts of RJ movement scholars and practitioners. However, defamiliarising the present without imagining possibilities to critically resist it, would mean to reduce the ethico-political capacity of this overall project to a 'mere' epistemological enterprise. Does the presence of authoritative stances in RJ doom us to passively comply with them? Does the advanced-liberal 'nature' of mainstream RJ compel us to re-enact that governmentality? Is there any alternative to the idea of subject embodied by the authoritative discourses? As already stated, one of the main features of the genealogical analysis is that power and resistance are thought as co-extensive (Foucault, 1978: 95). From this perspective, within the authoritative discourses as well as within the advanced-liberal regime, lie the very conditions for destabilisation or even subversion. What I am interested in here is not the general plan of this form of resistance, but the critical resistance which lies in an ethical realm and aims at problematising societal discourses with subjugating effects (ie 'conventional' criminal justice but also the same authoritative discourses of RJ). If this historical ontology aims at nourishing a critical (and even self-critical) tension in RJ, we need to envision RJ processes as an opportunity for re-creating ethical selves as an alternative to the lack of genuine moral communication between parties and normalisation of identities within 'conventional' criminal justice, as well as to the unproblematic assumptions of the same authoritative discourses of RJ. The goal of this reflection is not to dictate a new account of what one ought to do, but to imagine alternatives to certain forms of subjugation[4] by reflecting upon the conditions to dissolve normalised identities, thus, opening up spaces for reinventing social relationships (Hoy, 2004: 89–90).

Foucault defines ethics as the 'reflexive practice of freedom' (1997: 281), ie the intentional self-forming activities (the 'care of the self') of an individual in order to 'subjectivise' itself, becoming in this way a moral subject (Foucault, 1986). The word 'subject' in Foucault's work entails two different meanings, with critical implications for his ethical theory: 'subject to someone else by control and dependence; and tied to his own identity by a conscience or self-knowledge. Both meanings suggest a form of power which subjugates and makes subject to (Foucault, 2000: 331). The first connotation refers to being subjected to someone else but also to intentional and not subjective discourses; the second meaning refers to the activity of subjectivation, ie the active self-fashioning ethical work. Subjectivation aims at creating productive freedom, by choosing to shape new truths about oneself, detaching oneself from the normalised identities imposed by others, generating new possibilities of being and becoming. Foucault's ethics then, does not establish a 'fixed' human nature or a 'true' self to be enshrined in moral codes (which would end up promoting another form of domination). The self is instead a ceaseless process of becoming within a cultural and social context, rather than a passive being. Accordingly, ethics is conceptualised as

[4] The domination carried out by 'conventional' criminal justice (and paradoxically endorsed by certain RJ discourses) consists in subjugating individuals to binary classifications of right and wrong and victim and offender; imposing and enforcing normalised identities linked to those labels; using pain delivery as a normal vehicle to re-establish an assumed social order; denying genuine moral communication with individuals and between them.

a transformative and relational practice of subjectivation (ie ethical fashioning of oneself) whose condition and outcome is freedom. In Foucault's view, these ethical relations which can actively contribute to shape our selves are constituted by four formal elements, whose contents are subject to historical variation: the ontological element or 'ethical substance'; the deontological element or 'mode of subjection'; the ascetic element or 'ethical work'; and the teleological element or 'telos' (Foucault, 1984: 353–55). I propose to use this framework as a blueprint for envisioning the ethical 'potential' of RJ, ie the possibility for RJ to be a space of subjectivation and not of subjugation. The ethical substance is the material or aspect of self that is morally problematic, taken as the object of one's ethical reflection, and transformed in one's ethical work. In the case of RJ encounters, the ethical substance consists of the 'problematic situations' (Hulsman, 1986: 73), ie the conflict and harm which represent the object of the ethical reflection and transformation. The mode of subjection is the way in which the individual establishes its relation to the moral code, recognises itself as bound to act according to it, and is entitled to view its acts as worthy of moral valorisation. The mode of subjection is, as Foucault refers to it, the 'deontological' or normative component of ethics. In RJ, this component consists of the outcome of the encounter, the decision to converge toward a common understanding of what happened and why, as well as to agree to a collaboratively created action plan. In order to get to this point it is necessary to carry out what Foucault calls the 'ethical work', ie the self-forming activities meant to ensure one's own subjection to a moral authority and transformation of oneself into an autonomous, ethical agent. The goal of this overall process is its 'telos', ie the ideal mode or state of being toward which one strives or aspires in one's ethical work, which in RJ could be, *inter alia*, repairing the harm of being 'subjected' to societal forces that seek to define subjectivity for individuals.

Of these four components, the 'ethical work' probably needs further elaboration and clarification due to its critical role. The 'ethical work' or 'care of the self' is a dynamic and continuing activity rather than an adherence to a pre-established system of moral codes. This activity brings the ethical self into being and can be practised only when there is sufficient freedom which, conversely, is the result of engaging in the practices of 'care of the self'. Freedom is not some end state achieved by eluding all manner of restriction; rather, to be free is to be involved in producing change in the world, and to be an ethical being is to be an actor (Infinito, 2003: 157). RJ's spaces should then, as far as possible, be free spaces, ie alien to external coercion (*ergo* the impossibility of any restorative punishment), but also free in the sense of rejecting the normalising labels offered by 'conventional' criminal justice (eg 'victim' and 'offender') as well as of critically re-thinking the labels offered by authoritative discourses of RJ ('healing', 'empowerment/disempowerment', 'reconciliation', etc). Therefore, the issue at stake is to reflect on how to shape RJ encounters as free, pluralistic and creative environments where participants' ethical work can take place, addressing proper responses to 'the other' (Infinito, 2003: 155). The 'care of the self' would be practised as resistance to that which threatens to control one's identity, considering conversely freedom as the formation of the self (Infinito, 2003: 158). As David Hoy argues, this strategy of *désassujettissement* ('desubjugation') consists not in our finding our true subjectivity behind ideological masks, but in de-subjectifying ourselves, of purging the selves produced by the forces of conformism, in order to become different from the way we normally are (Hoy, 2004: 103). This is not only desubjectification of individual identities, but of collective, communal or social identities, avoiding entrapment by externally imposed and limiting subjectivities, activating human capacities for self-creation (Infinito, 2003: 159).

From this perspective the goal of a restorative encounter would primarily be to offer a chance for engaging in an activity of 'questioning and adjusting of thought and action in relation to notions of human good and harm. It entails work on the self and consideration of how to be and act in relation to others' (Christie, 2005: 40). This is possible if restorative encounters take place within a space which is safe and experimental, where individuals can participate in the ongoing production of themselves with and in front of others, and where they can be both witness to and resource for the experiments of other selves. This space would allow for critical activities and reflections which aim at intensifying our relation with ourselves and also with others. The 'working out' of our ethical self is 'not an exercise in solitude, but a true social practice. The care of the self—or the attention one devotes to the care that others should take of themselves—appears then as an intensification of social relations' (Foucault, 1986: 53). To stipulate a list of exhaustive technologies of the self to be embodied within RJ processes in order to allow the 'ethical work' within, would be against the very basic idea of a non-subjugating ethics and would commit the very harm to individuals it seeks to overturn. At stake here is not the creation of a new moral code but of the conditions for critically resisting the limited range of possibilities available to those involved in social conflicts and harms, offered by 'conventional' criminal justice but also, foreseeably, by the 'mainstream' RJ.

VI. NOT TO CONCLUDE: THINKING RESTORATIVE JUSTICE OTHERWISE

The historical and critical ontology I have proposed consists in using Foucault (more than offering a 'correct' interpretation of his work) in order to reconstruct the truths (archaeology) and the political embeddedness of RJ (genealogy). Furthermore, this project is complemented by the normative envisioning of RJ as an ethical space alternative to 'conventional' criminal justice, and critical of the same authoritative discourses which reify that unique way of thinking and dealing with social conflicts and harms. Framed in this way, RJ finds its conditions of possibility in certain socio-cultural constructs and technologies of power. Being scaffolded by authoritative discourses does not entail necessary subjugation to them. Being thinkable in an advanced-liberal regime does not necessarily imply that RJ is doomed to re-enact that governmentality. Re-working RJ as an ethical space means to structure it as a free and safe space for detaching individuals from the normalised identities of 'conventional' criminal justice, as well as of the RJ authoritative discourses (both informed by advanced-liberal imperatives). The provisory outcome of this inquiry, in fact, is the appreciation that RJ should be different not only from 'conventional' criminal justice but also from itself, ie from its authoritative discourses which threaten its ethical 'potential' as a space for resisting predetermined ranges of possibilities of being and becoming. Turning RJ not only against the mainstream way of dealing with social conflicts and harms, but also against its own taken-for-granted forms, will likely nourish a self-critical attitude which might make RJ 'un lieu de réflexion incessante, de recherche et d'expérience, de transformation' (Foucault, 1981).

REFERENCES

Achutti, D (2011) 'The Strangers in Criminal Procedure: Restorative Justice as a Possibility to Overcome the Simplicity of the Modern Paradigm of Criminal Justice' 1(2) *Oñati Socio-Legal Series* 1.

Bailey, M (1993) 'Foucauldian Feminism: Contesting Bodies, Sexuality and Identity' in C Ramazanoglu (ed), *Up Against Foucault: Explorations of Some Tensions Between Foucault and Feminism* (London, Routledge) 99–122.

Bauman, Z (1998) *Globalization: The Human Consequences* (New York, Columbia University Press).

Braithwaite, J (1999) 'Restorative Justice: Assessing Optimistic and Pessimistic Accounts' 25 *Crime and Justice: A Review of Research* 1.

Burchell, G (1996) 'Liberal Government and Techniques of the Self' in A Barry, T Osborne and N Rose (eds), *Foucault and Political Reason* (London, UCL Press) 19–36.

Burke, A (2002) 'Aporias of Security' 27(1) *Alternatives: Global, Local, Political* 1.

Christie, N (1986) 'Images of Man in Modern Penal Law' 10 *Contemporary Crises* 95.

Christie, P (2005) 'Education for an Ethical Imagination' 24(4) *Social Alternatives* 39.

Davidson, AI (1986) 'Archaeology, Genealogy, Ethics' in DC Hoy (ed), *Foucault: A Critical Reader* (Oxford, Blackwell) 221–33.

Dean, M (1994) *Critical and Effective Histories: Foucault's Methods and Historical Sociology* (London, Routledge).

Deleuze, G (1995) *Negotiations, 1972–1990* (New York, Columbia University Press).

Dignan, J (2005) *Understanding Victims and Restorative Justice* (Berkshire, Open University Press).

Dreyfus, HL and Rabinow, P (1983) *Michel Foucault: Beyond Structuralism and Hermeneutics*, 2nd edn (Chicago, IL, University of Chicago Press).

Elwick, J (2012) 'Layered History: Styles of Reasoning as Stratified Conditions of Possibility' 43 *Studies in History and Philosophy of Science* 619.

Faubion, J (2013) 'Foucault's Ontology and Epistemology of Ethics' in C Falzon, T O'Leary and J Sawicki (eds), *A Companion to Foucault* (Oxford, Blackwell) 493–509.

Foucault, M. (1970) *The Order of Things: An Archaeology of the Human Sciences* (New York, Pantheon).

—— (1972) *The Archaeology of Knowledge* (New York, Pantheon).

—— (1977) *Discipline and Punish: The Birth of the Prison* (London, Allen Lane).

—— (1978) *The History of Sexuality*, vol 1, *An Introduction* (New York, Pantheon).

—— (1981) 'Contre les peines de substitution', *Libération*, 18 September.

—— (1984) *The Foucault Reader* (P Rabinow (ed), London, Penguin Books).

—— (1986) *The History of Sexuality*, vol III, *The Care of the Self* (New York, Pantheon).

—— (1991) 'Politics and the Study of Discourse' in G Burchell, C Gordon and P Miller (eds), *The Foucault Effect: Studies in Governmentality* (Chicago, IL, University of Chicago Press) 53–72.

—— (1997) *Essential Works of Michel Foucault: Ethics* (P Rabinow (ed), New York, New Press).

—— (2000) *Essential Works of Michel Foucault: Power* (J Faubion (ed), New York, New Press).

—— (2007) *Security, Territory, Population: Lectures at the Collège de France, 1977–78* (M Senellart (ed), London, Palgrave Macmillan).

Garland, D (1990) *Punishment and Modern Society: A Study in Social Theory* (Oxford, Clarendon Press).

Gordon, C (1991) 'Governmental Rationality: An Introduction, Discourse' in G Burchell, C Gordon and P Miller (eds), *The Foucault Effect: Studies in Governmentality* (Chicago, IL, University of Chicago Press) 1–52.

Gubrium, J and Holstein, J (2000) 'Analyzing Interpretive Practice' in N Denzin and Y Lincoln (eds), *Handbook of Qualitative Research*, 2nd edn (Thousand Oaks, CA, Sage Publications) 487–508.

Howarth, D (2002) 'An Archaeology of Political Discourse? Evaluating Michel Foucault's Explanation and Critique of Ideology' 50 *Political Studies* 117.

Hoy, DC (2004) *Critical Resistance: From Poststructuralism to Post-Critique* (Cambridge, MA and London, MIT Press).

Hulsman, L (1986) 'Critical Criminology and the Concept of Crime' 10(3/4) *Contemporary Crises* 63.

Infinito, J (2003) 'Ethical Self-Formation: A Look at the Later Foucault' 53(2) *Educational Theory* 155.

Johnstone, G and Van Ness, DW (eds) (2007) *Handbook of Restorative Justice* (London, Willan).

Jørgensen, M and Phillips, L (2002) *Discourse Analysis as Theory and Method* (London, Sage).
Maglione, G (2013) 'Problematizing Restorative Justice: A Foucauldian Perspective' in T Gavrielides and V Artinopoulou (eds), *Reconstructing Restorative Justice: Philosophy, Values, Norms and Methods Reconsidered* (Farnham, Ashgate) 67–90.
Pathak, P (2014) 'Ethopolitics and the Financial Citizen' 62 *Sociological Review* 90.
Pavlich, G (2005) *Paradoxes of Restorative Justice* (London, Glass House Press).
Richards, K (2005) 'Unlikely Friends? Oprah Winfrey and Restorative Justice' 38(3) *Australian and New Zealand Journal of Criminology* 381.
Rose, N (1996) 'Governing "Advanced" Liberal Democracies' in A Barry, T Osborne and N Rose (eds), *Foucault and Political Reason* (London, UCL Press) 37–64.
—— (1998) *Inventing Our Selves: Psychology, Power, and Personhood* (Cambridge, Cambridge University Press).
—— (1999a) *Powers of Freedom: Reframing Political Thought* (Cambridge, Cambridge University Press).
—— (1999b) 'Inventiveness in Politics: Review of Anthony Giddens, The Third Way' 28(3) *Economy and Society* 467.
Saar, M (2002) 'Genealogy and Subjectivity' 10(2) *European Journal of Philosophy* 231.
Scheurich, JJ and McKenzie, KB (2005) 'Foucault's Methodologies: Archaeology and Genealogy' in NK Denzin and Y Lincoln (eds), *The Sage Handbook of Qualitative Research*, 3rd edn (Thousand Oaks, CA, Sage) 841–68.
Schuilenburg, M (2012) 'The Securitisation of Society: On the Rise of Quasi-Criminal Law and Selective Exclusion' 38(1/2) *Social Justice* 73.
Strang, H (2003) 'Justice for Victims of Young Offenders: The Centrality of Emotional Harm and Restoration' in G Johnstone (ed), *A Restorative Justice Reader: Texts, Sources, Context* (Cullompton, Willan Publishing) 286–93.
Strang, H and Sherman, LW (2003) 'Repairing the Harm: Victims and Restorative Justice' 1 *Utah Law Review* 15.
Sullivan, D and Tifft, L (2001) *Restorative Justice: Healing the Foundations of Our Everyday Lives* (Monsey, NY, Willow Tree Press).
Tamboukou, M and Ball, SJ (eds) (2003) *Dangerous Encounters: Genealogy and Ethnography* (New York, Peter Lang).
Valverde, M (2008) 'Beyond Discipline and Punish: Foucault's Challenge to Criminology' 4 *Carceral Notebooks* 201.
Van Ness, DW and Strong, K (2003) *Restoring Justice: An Introduction to Restorative Justice* (Cincinnati, OH, Anderson Publishing).
Voruz, V (2010) 'Politics in Foucault's Later Work: A Philosophy of Truth; or Reformism in Question' 15(1) *Theoretical Criminology* 1.
Walgrave, L (2003) 'Imposing Restoration Instead of Inflicting Pain' in A von Hirsch, J Roberts, A Bottoms, K Roach and M Schiff (eds), *Restorative Justice and Criminal Justice: Competing or Reconcilable Paradigms?* (Oxford, Hart) 61–68.
Walklate, S (2012) 'Who is the Victim of Crime? Paying Homage to the Work of Richard Quinney' 8(2) *Crime Media Culture* 173.
Wright, M (1996) *Justice for Victims and Offenders* (Winchester, Waterside Press).
Zehr, H (1990) *Changing Lenses: A New Focus for Crime and Justice* (Scottsdale, AZ, Herald Press).

6

Restorative Justice is Not a Panacea Against All Social Evils

LODE WALGRAVE

I. INTRODUCTION

THE CRIME PROBLEM in all its dimensions is deeply rooted in structural dysfunctions and injustices in society. The definitions of crime, the social positions and prospects of those considered as risk groups, the selective way police and criminal justice function, all indicate that social power relations in society penetrate the way crime is dominantly seen and dealt with.

For the majority of criminologists all attempts to deal with the crime problem must rest upon more social justice. Along this line, one of the main criticisms against restorative justice is that it fails to include a strategy for correcting deprivation, inequality and discrimination (Shank and Takagi, 2004; Cheliotis, 2011). At its best, restorative justice would reiterate the unjust power relations in society. In the worst case, restorative justice would worsen injustice by extending the net of social control, inducing a discriminating bifurcation in the criminal justice responses, and favouring neo-liberal individualisation of responsibilities. Cunneen summarises the concern (2010: 156):

> There are many reasons to think that a restorative justice response will be less able to address structural inequalities because of less public accountability, fewer resources, less access to co-ordinated services and the potential perpetuation of power imbalances.

Restorative justice advocates believe the opposite. They argue that restorative justice has great potential to correct the consequences of social inequalities (Braithwaite, 2002; Hoyle, 2010). On the individual level, the restorative deliberation can include the offender's social position and perspectives in estimating his/her responsibility. His/her participation in a restorative process and the acceptance of making reparative gestures may help to stop the downward spiral more than being placed in a facility, for example. On the collective level, the respectful deliberation including the local community is supposed to be a leg up towards tackling local systematic issues, which are often the consequences of social deprivation (Pranis, 2001; Froestad and Shearing, 2013).

There is not much empirical data to illustrate one or both positions. The debate is mainly one of fears, concerns, hopes and beliefs. In this chapter, I propose a realistic view, positioning restorative justice as just one among the many social institutions for governing social life. Consequently, one must dim the expectations that restorative justice would be a vehicle par excellence for correcting social inequalities.

II. CONCERNS ABOUT THE SOCIAL IMPACT OF RESTORATIVE JUSTICE

For some, restorative justice repeats all flaws of the traditional criminal justice system, while others fear that the particularities of restorative justice would worsen the social outcome.

A. Restorative Justice is Like Criminal Justice

While its grounding philosophy may promise a fundamentally different approach, restorative justice went off the rails when it came to practice and its institutionalisation, some say. In their view, restorative justice advocates anticipating possible cooptation and resistance by the judicial and political authorities, to 'try to enhance the attractiveness of RJ for policy-makers in the criminal justice system' (Aertsen *et al*, 2006: 288). They accept, for example, the traditional deontological principles as the frame for including restorative processes in the criminal justice system, or they try to demonstrate the utility of restorative justice practices in the ongoing security rhetoric. Restorative justice is then an easy prey to becoming an instrument in the hands of the state. The perversion of the restorative justice philosophy then occurs, losing all of its originally attractive seeds for a fundamental reorientation of the way in which we respond to conflict and injustice.

(i) Built on the Same Concepts

Nils Christie criticises restorative justice for using the same words, and thus the same basic concepts, as traditional criminal justice does. In his eyes, 'justice' is an authoritative and fake concept, the notion of 'crime' deviates the approach from its original conflict among citizens, terms such as 'victim' and 'offender' block the possibilities for open dialogue (Christie, 2013). In doing so, restorative justice is offering old wine in new skins, repeating all the fundamental dysfunctions, flaws and hypocrisies that have made criminal justice the catastrophic system it actually is for social relations.

(ii) A Functionalist Approach

In a functionalist view, crime is seen as a kind of social pathology that has disrupted peace in the community. Restorative justice is then supposed to pursue correction or neutralisation of the pathology and to bring the community back to its 'normal' state of harmony and peace (Koen, 2007; Delgado, 2000). However, seeing harmony and peace as 'normal' states in society and communities denies the class differences in power and interests, which are, according to some, endemic to capitalist societies. Restorative justice then appears to pursue the conservation of existing class inequalities and to be an instrument for disciplining those who are opposed to it.

(iii) Individualising Responsibility

A particularity of the functionalist approach is that restorative justice continues to focus on the individual crime problem.[1] By addressing concrete crime events, individual criminals and specific victims, restorative justice continues to fail 'to address the socio-economic roots of crime' (Lofton, 2004). On the contrary, those who are considered responsible for the offence are confronted with their individual 'shortcomings' and wrongs. Restorative justice pressurises them to take up their active responsibility, thus to accept their guilt and to behave accordingly. As Maruna writes: 'We expect an enormous amount of the individuals we sometimes call "offenders" in restorative justice, although we are fully aware of all the social, economic and structural disadvantages they face' (Maruna, 2014: 17).

B. Restorative Justice is Different, But Not Better

Other criticisms recognise that restorative justice actually is different from traditional criminal justice, but assert that its social impact would be even worse than criminal justice.

(i) Double Track

The emergence of restorative justice within the criminal justice system has caused the existence of a double track: the traditional criminal procedure, and a diversionary path towards a restorative handling of crime. Police officers,

[1] Surprisingly, this trend seems to be in line with a famous quotation by Nils Christie that the conflict should be given back to its owners (Christie, 1977). The idea that the state has nothing to do in the solution of the aftermath of a crime (a 'conflict', Christie would insist to say) suggests that the public dimension is not really important and that only the 'owners of the conflict' (the citizens) must have a say.

public prosecutors and judges are the gatekeepers to select cases as being 'appropriate' for a restorative process and those which are not. Moreover, holding a restorative dialogue depends on the willingness of the stakeholders to participate in a restorative process. The risk is imminent that secondary class characteristics play a role in both selection mechanisms. For example, research suggests that juveniles with a 'better' profile in terms of family status and/or school career are more often offered the possibility of mediation or restorative conferencing, while juveniles with a less positive situation are more often sent directly to the traditional procedures (Franssen *et al*, 2010; Vanfraechem, 2007). Consequently, the double track has a high risk of additional discrimination.

(ii) Communication Skills

While traditional criminal justice procedures leave the direct communication to the lawyers, restorative processes involve the stakeholders personally and directly in the communication. Restorative encounters are intensive emotional events, exchanges of deep and genuine feelings, rejecting the act but respectful and supportive to the person (Harris *et al*, 2004). One of the main tools in such encounters is oral communication and body language. Cultural studies show that juveniles and other people living in a lower class situation generally have different communicative skills (Pauwels *et al*, 2011). Deprived juveniles or adult offenders may have more difficulties to explain with nuance why and how they committed the offence. Their expression of empathy, shame, remorse and other moral emotions might be less well understood. They risk feeling more defenceless in an emotional exchange than middle class people. This disadvantage adds to their general societal vulnerability when they are confronted with social institutions (Vyverman and Vettenburg, 2009).

(iii) Vulnerable to Inclusion in Safety Rhetoric

The thoughtless enthusiasm of policy-makers, police, judges and social workers for integrating a few 'restorative' techniques in traditional criminal justice systems may be one of the greatest threats to restorative justice. These techniques are stripped of their restorative justice philosophy, serving as ornaments of a system that essentially remains unchanged. Respect for the victim is promoted to underline the guilt and the punishability of the offender; restorative practices are used to deal with benign cases so that the 'hard core' justice business is unburdened. These 'restorative' practices, then, are instruments for net-widening the control under a punitive mandate, and included as part of the punitive rhetoric. Restorative practices are at risk of being dragged into the waters of safety obsession and penal populism (Pratt, 2006; O'Malley, 2006).

(iv) Flexibility and Confidentiality Threaten Legal Rights

Where and when possible, restorative justice advocates try to minimise state intervention and to consider crime through the eyes of the main stakeholders (Sullivan and Tifft, 2006). The expected advantage is that the flexible process will be more embedded in real life and that the stakeholders will be more committed to agreements in which they have had their say. But flexibility also holds risks (von Hirsch, 1998; Feld, 1999).

Some formality is needed for the checks and balances demanded by the principles of constitutional democracies. Less procedural rules may leave more space for exerting pressure on one party to accept less favourable outcomes. More flexibility means also more opportunities to influence the process. Some offenders, for example, are lucky to have a 'sympathetic' victim willing to participate in a mediation or conferencing, while others are unfortunate to be confronted with a tough victim demanding the full punitive procedure. And even within the process, the encountering parties may have unequal power and capacities to mould the intervention according to their preferences and interests. The more assertive and boastful car owner may have more impact on the deliberation process than the impressed juvenile who broke into the car. In a conference after domestic violence, the husband may intimidate his victim wife again.

The same concerns apply with regard to confidentiality. Again, confidentiality may help to avoid negative side-effects of a judicial intervention, such as stigmatisation. But it hides the procedure and the process from public and judicial control, which are generally considered as crucial safeguards against judicial misuses and mistakes.

The possible advantages linked to the flexibility and confidentiality of restorative justice processes thus risk deteriorating into being another power play outside the judicial system, and thus loosening its safeguards (Braithwaite, 2002; Koen, 2007).

III. LIMITING THE SCOPE OF RESTORATIVE JUSTICE

The reply to these critics depends on the vision of restorative justice. A number of scholars have a broad conception of restorative justice. Some even extend it to being a vehicle for transforming social life as a whole (Sullivan and Tifft, 2006). In my view, however, too wide a notion leads to confusion, an over-estimation of the restorative justice potential, and a loss of credibility. Hence, the argument for a restricted vision of restorative justice, focused on dealing with matters that qualify for a criminal justice intervention (Walgrave, 2008; 2012). While it is part of a broader social movement, it does not encompass it entirely. There are several reasons for this restriction. The main reason is, however, that dealing with criminalisable matters works in a different social context and pursues different objectives than dealing with issues of school discipline, for example.

A. Responding to Crime is a Particular Matter

In the terms of Braithwaite and Pettit (1990), dominion is the set of assured rights and freedoms granted to all citizens.[2] A good society seeks to extend dominion for its citizens. It does so through socio-economic and cultural policies, integration policies, education and welfare. All societal institutions do not do the same. There is a division of tasks, according to which appropriate power and equipment is given to each institution. Criminal justice is a very specific societal institution.

Political communities have preserved the notion of 'crime' or 'offence' for a category of conducts, which are considered as threats to the quality of social life and against which coercive responses may be used. Private violence, for example, or taking away another's possessions, do not only affect relations between two citizens, but are also of interest for the entire community and/or the state. If they were not formally prohibited, living together would be dominated by mutual threat and fear. As we are not living in a natural park populated by gentle and good willing people only, not all transgressions can be dealt with through inclusive deliberation. The eventuality of coercion cannot be erased.[3]

Coercion must be kept under strict control. Coercion and repression are at odds with the liberties granted in a democratic constitutional state, and with the aim of promoting dominion. Good democracies should permit the reduction of freedom through coercion only in exceptional situations of emergency, when social interests are considered to be threatened to the extent that they must be defended, including by the use of coercion if necessary. Criminal justice thus only intervenes as a last resort, when all other possibilities to nurture law-abidance among citizens have proven unsuccessful.

To avoid criminal justice and its coercive power overflowing its banks, it is crucial to be very clear about the strictly defensive role of the system

[2] In later publications, Braithwaite and Pettit use the term 'freedom as non-domination'. I prefer, however, the original 'dominion'. 'Freedom as non-domination' focuses on the negative, the absence of domination. In my view, it is not affirmative enough on the positive side of the concept.

[3] This position is shared by probably the majority of restorative justice advocates. See, eg most responses to Christie's 'Words on Words' (2013), and especially those by John Braithwaite, Kathleen Daly, Lode Walgrave and Martin Wright.

and about its limits. The possible use of coercion must be encapsulated in a particular institution.

B. Need for Institutionalisation

To respond to the behaviour called 'crime' and deal with the delicate balance between safeguarding civic liberties and possibly intervening coercively, a specialised institution is needed. Braithwaite and Pettit distinguish between coercive and socialising institutions (1990: 80–85). The French philosopher Louis Althusser points to the difference between '*les institutions idéologiques de l'état*' (in plural form) and '*l'institution répressif de l'état*' (in singular form) (1980). According to Althusser, the state uses most of its institutions to 'seduce', 'convince' or 'motivate' its citizens to accept the dominant norms and values and to behave accordingly. Only when these institutions fail, for one reason or another, does the state openly rely on its coercive power through its repressive institution, the criminal justice system. It then forces the citizens into conformity, or excludes them (temporarily) from the community.[4]

Whereas restorative justice itself tries to avoid coercion maximally, it operates in a field where the eventuality of coercion is at hand. Therefore, blurring the limits of restorative justice is not desirable. Restorative justice must be kept clearly distinguished from other deliberative processes after injustices or conflicts that are not categorised as 'offences' (Walgrave, 2008).

The priority for restorative responses to an offence needs to be framed into a criminal justice system, which should be reoriented towards being a restorative criminal justice system. A restorative criminal justice system shares a number of characteristics of traditional criminal justice, such as clear limits to social tolerance, the responsibility of the one who transgressed the rule, the controlled use of coercion if needed. However, the institution also has fundamental differences. Instead of the punitive premise, it is oriented to a restorative premise, and thus leaves ample space for deliberation among the stakeholders and seeks to promote it; there are strong reservations against the actual use of coercion, and if any is used, judicial coercion is placed as much as possible at the service of possible reparation.

How this would work in practice has been represented in the form of a pyramid (Braithwaite, 2000; Dignan, 2002; Walgrave, 2008), with at the broad bottom ample space for free deliberation on resolving conflicts and tensions in the community, and at the narrow top a very reduced possibility for incapacitation if all other possibilities to cope with serious threats

[4] Althusser was a Marxist. He would not agree that the state promotes dominion, but it would only function to preserve the existing hegemony.

to public life are exhausted. The pyramid provides for the possibility to increase pressure and coercion gradually. But even at the bottom level, the possibility of coercion is already implicitly present. The knowledge that the community of care, the local and wider community, and finally the criminal justice system may expect, demand, and if necessary enforce a gesture of reparation has an influence on even the most freely accepted deliberative level.[5] For the victim, it is reassuring that victimisation is not tolerated and must be repaired. For the offender, it makes clear that he/she will in any case not escape taking responsibility. For both, it is reassuring and moderating to know that the legal frame keeps the action within limits. For the community at large, it is a confirmation that the authorities take dominion seriously. After all, it would be unworldly to expect that such deliberation can ever be completely free of pressure.

But if deliberation between the main stakeholders is not possible, or considered unsatisfactory, judicial intervention can be considered, which, however, must also serve by priority the reparative objective. Wherever and whenever favourable for restoration and possible in terms of public security, the cases should be left with, or given back to, the less coercive levels. This presupposes a moderated and reserved attitude in the more coercive agencies, and especially in the justice system. The criminal justice system must transform its punitive premises and procedures focused on proportionate punishments into a coherent priority for restoration in processing and in sanctioning.

The restriction of restorative justice to dealing with the aftermath of crime and the option to define it through the restorative or reparative outcome pursued, and not by its process, is the core of the maximalist view of restorative justice (Walgrave, 2008). It is maximalist because its ambition is to penetrate the criminal justice system maximally, not because it extends to other domains of social life than criminal justice matters.

C. Imitator Paradox?

As in the current criminal justice system, also maximalist restorative justice, as I see it, focuses on the individual criminal event and individual responsibilities and keeps the possibility of using coercion. In Pavlich's terms, I may have walked into the trap of the 'imitator paradox', whereby 'restorative justice defines its governmentalities in opposition to basic concepts within the criminal justice system, but it does so by founding itself on many

[5] In a not (yet) published text on regulating (the threat of) violence in international politics and resistance movements, John Braithwaite writes: 'the display of a capability to escalate up a regulatory pyramid drives more of the regulatory action down to the less coercive base of the pyramid' (2014: 10).

of those self-same concepts (e.g. crime, victim, offender and community)' (Pavlich, 2005: 14).

However, crucial differences exist. (1) Re-establishing the harm to fellow citizens and to social life as the reason for criminalising behaviour may lead to other conduct being subjected to a restorative criminal justice system than is currently the case in the punitive criminal justice system. (2) The objectives of the enforcement focus on repairing the harm, and restoring the victim and the quality of social life, rather than on inflicting a proportionate pain on the offender. (3) The procedures in a restorative criminal justice system give priority where possible and allow ample space for inclusive deliberative solution-finding at the grass-roots. (4) The traditional principles of legal safeguards, such as equality, right of a defence, public control or proportionality, are to be reconsidered so as to be more adapted to the new paradigmatic approach of restorative justice (Walgrave, 2013).

Restorative justice in a maximalist perspective adopts a number of concepts that are also crucial in the traditional criminal justice system. Not all of that system is bad. I am glad that it is prohibited to kill me and that the authorities may use coercion to enforce that rule. One cannot resolve all problems, conflicts and injustices through inclusive deliberation. Some mechanisms in the existing criminal justice system may be inspirational in discovering how to combine giving full priority to inclusionary deliberation, with a restricted possibility of using coercion. Using partly the same building blocks does not necessarily mean the same building. With bricks and cement, churches, mosques or synagogues are built, but also nightclubs or prisons.

IV. BEING REALISTIC ABOUT EXPECTATIONS

This maximalist view of restorative justice is a ground for responding to the specific concerns about the impact of restorative justice on social inequalities.

A. Being Steadfast to the Social-Ethical Fundamentals

Restorative justice's starting point is the occurrence of an offence, as it is defined by the authorities. That may be an indication of a functionalist approach, pursuing a status quo in current social relations. In the diversionary view of restorative justice, the risk of functionalism is imminent. Characterising restorative justice through the deliberative process only leaves the hard core of dealing with crime to the traditional criminal justice system. Such a view of restorative justice indeed remains complementary to the existing system and submits to its functionalist role.

But that is not necessarily so in the maximalist approach. As maximalist restorative justice seeks to penetrate criminal justice itself, also the definition of offending is to be submitted to a restorative check. The focus on repairing the harm caused, and not on punishing a norm transgression, may provoke a shift in the selection of conducts subjected to criminal justice. Some behaviour which appear less harmful (such as the use of illegal drugs, for example) could be decriminalised, others which are very harmful to social relations might be criminalised. Current penal law is too one-sidedly oriented towards safeguarding physical integrity and individual property, and neglects crucial social goods such as respect, and social and economic equity. That may be corrected in a coherent maximalist restorative justice approach to criminalisation.

However, most essential for keeping restorative justice safe from being coopted into a functionalist mainstream is to safeguard its roots in the wider socio-ethical ground-stream. The emphasis on informal inclusive deliberation and the search for outcomes that minimise harm and strengthen relationships is grounded in a conception of social life and democracy which is also the *basso continuo* for many other theories, movements and practices. In the field of criminology, for example, the Good Lives Model in rehabilitation focuses on 'building offenders' capacity to live personally meaningful and fulfilling lives' rather than seeing the (potential) offender through the risks he/she represents (Ward, Fox and Garber, 2014: 28). Criminologists complain that criminology has fallen 'under the spell of thinking negatively about safety and security' (Schuilenburg, van Steden and Oude Breuil, 2014: 10) and explore more positive views that build on inclusion, trust and wellbeing.

These and other constructive approaches in and outside of criminology are grounded in a common awareness that the quality of social life depends on how we relate to each other. The other is not considered initially as a threat, but as a companion in the search for a better, more liveable world. That is reflected in the concept of 'dominion' advanced by Braithwaite and Pettit (1990) as a social conception of freedom, based on the mutual assurance that fellow citizens and the state will respect individual rights and freedoms. Putnam (2000) considers trust as the necessary 'lubrication' of social life, to make democracy work smoothly. Even the neuro-scientist Cacioppo (Cacioppo and Patrick, 2009) or the primatologue De Waal (2009) conclude that the ability to cooperate is far more crucial in the advancement of social life than the drive for self-interest. The quality of our lives is dependent on the extent to which we succeed in integrating the pursuit of our self-interest into a project of common interest (Walgrave, 2008). This insight is increasingly common in (social) sciences.

Restorative justice advocates must keep strong links with this wider and deeper social-ethical undercurrent. That is the most essential condition for being able to escape the risk of being coopted into a conservative functionalist tendency, and to contribute to a more socially just society, a more participative democracy, a more sustainable social life.

B. Individual Responsibility in Constructive Responses

Many offenders have in their life course suffered systematic social injustices and discriminations. This is why some scholars consider it unjust to demand from them reparative gestures when they are in fact victims themselves.

This reasoning recalls the old concept launched by Sykes and Matza (1957), 'neutralisation techniques': the moral wrongfulness of an act is neutralized through kinds of crooked reasoning in order to justify the actual commission of the act. 'Yes, I should not do it, but I was victimized first.' Injustice is not undone by more injustice. Being socially excluded does not deliver a 'wildcard' to assault, steal or use private violence. Being frustrated on the job is no excuse for the battering husband. Individual offending behaviour remains a problem for social life, regardless of the identity and the social conditions of the perpetrator.

But there is a problem indeed with the current punitive premise in criminal justice. Criminal punishments push individual offenders still deeper down in the mire through stigmatisation, worsening their social prospects and reducing still more the possibilities for social (re)integration. And it does not help the victim. In that regard, a restorative response offers more constructive opportunities. The invitation, the social pressure or even the obligation to make gestures of reparation is an opportunity for the offender to show the capacity (and willingness) for positive actions and relations, and to avoid stigmatisation. It may open the pathway towards more social acceptance, less exclusion, more motivation and more socially constructive relations.

Of course, that does not remedy structural systematic social injustice which is a major problem in our societies. But remedying structural social injustice is not the main mission of criminal justice, even if it is reoriented as a restorative criminal justice system. That is a mission for wider social policies and many other social institutions and agencies. Criminal justice as the coercive institution has to remain encapsulated, focusing on individual problems and situations. The reduced but realistic ambition is that it does not worsen social injustice and discrimination, and that it contributes to improving the prospects of individuals. A restorative criminal justice system offers better opportunities.

C. Flexibility May be Better than Rigidity

Whenever possible, restorative justice leaves the pathway of predictable, established procedures and opts for flexibility, adapted to the needs of the stakeholders. The dependence on voluntary decisions by stakeholders and the confidential flexibility of the processes reduce the possibilities for external control by checks and balances. It may reiterate the unequal power balances existing already outside the restorative process.

Two observations are to be made.

First, the pretended equality of all citizens in current judicial procedures is far from being evident. Huge sentence differences exist for the same offences. It helps to have the smartest (often the most expensive) lawyer. Wealth, status and power even influence the legislative process of whether or not to criminalise certain behaviour. Some people are better able than others to get state power on their side, including the power of the criminal justice machine.

Equality is often misunderstood in legal doctrine. If an illiterate person is subject to the same complicated judicial rules as a defendant with a diploma in law, if the rich pay exactly the same fine as the poor, this kind of equality is 'a travesty of equal justice' (Braithwaite 2002: 160). The rigidity of the traditional judicial procedures imposes a unique procedure on a very heterogeneous public, adding serious inequalities to the inequalities that already existed before.

Legal doctrine mostly understands equal as identical, whereas it should be understood as equivalent, being of equal value (Claes, 2004). People should have equal access, equal rights, be guaranteed equal possibilities before the judiciary, which means that their differences should be taken into account in assuring these equalities. The rules of the current justice system do not guarantee this equivalence better than the informal restorative justice processes.

Secondly, the flexibility of the restorative processes is also an opportunity for diluting existing unbalances in power. Equivalence of citizens may be better achieved when the protagonists are stripped of their power and status, and meet each other in a personal face-to-face dialogue, as proposed in a restorative encounter. The flexibility of the process and the respectful dialogue offer more opportunities to include an authentic reflection on the social and other dynamics that ended in the offence, and in finding the most constructive way of responding to it. The personal involvement of the stakeholders allows for more openness for particular ethnic or social characteristics in communication patterns. Compared to traditional procedures, there is more chance that the socially weak will understand better what the dialogue is about and that they will have more impact on the outcome.

Nevertheless, one cannot deny that flexibility also holds some risks for unbalanced processes. The risk can be reduced by training the facilitators in sensitivity to the more subtle expressions of unbalanced power relations and in neutralising them. Moreover, the judicial context also offers some safeguards. But still, flexibility can be misused. All in all, the opportunities and risks of flexible processes have to be balanced. Based on available experiences and research so far, flexibility appears to offer more opportunities than risks in dealing with the social dimensions in individual problem behaviour.

V. CONCLUSION

Many of the criticisms addressed to restorative justice as it currently functions keep the restorative justice advocates, researchers and practitioners awake at night. Among others, the sceptical observations make clear that restorative justice is not the panacea to resolve all social problems. But that must not keep us from continuously striving.

At its best, the dream of a fully deliberative, inclusionary way of responding to conflicts and injustices is an image of an ideal of justice in an ideal society. But in the meantime, we must get our hands dirty and think of how a less ideal version of restorative justice can function in our less ideal society. Compromises with reality are needed. Social injustice exists and it penetrates all social relations, all practices, all differences in access, in capacities. But social injustice cannot be compensated by tolerating other injustices through crime, for example. The possibility of coercion must be accepted, while trying continuously to marginalise its use and to maximise the space for free and respectful dialogue.

Combatting social injustice is a mission for all social institutions, as also is trying to maximise the space for respectful, inclusionary dialogue among all citizens on issues that matter for them. Restorative justice as a system is but one of these institutions, specialised in responding to behaviours qualified as offences.

Believing that restorative justice could address all social conflicts and injustices is unworldly. It makes restorative justice vulnerable to being caricatured as 'evangelism' or 'doing good', and loss of credibility. That is why I insist on making clear that restorative justice is not an institution meant to remedy social injustice. It is meant to respond constructively to concrete offending with concrete victims and offenders:

> The social and institutional practices that support gendered and racial violence are not going to disappear because of the relocation of a process from the court to a more informal setting. The struggle to ensure safety, to provide reassurance, to rehabilitate an individual perpetrator all involve commitment, time and resources from a range of individual actors. (Cunneen, 2010: 156)

I could not agree more.[6] Hans Boutellier compared the complex of social institutions to a soccer team (2006). Safety policy was considered the

[6] But I do not agree with the conclusions Cunneen draws from this statement.

defence, and the judicial response to offending was the goalkeeper. In that metaphorical language, complaining that criminal justice, and also restorative criminal justice, does not help to remedy social inequality and deprivation is like complaining that the goalkeeper does not score enough goals.

That does not mean that restorative justice remains blind to the structural social problems. As discussed above, the social ethics underlying restorative justice are shared with the wider social movement for a more participatory and more just society. On such a view, the bottom line is that restorative justice interventions should not worsen social injustice and that it should set the conditions to begin the gradual attainment of full participation of all stakeholders in social life. It has the potential to do so, to avoid further social degradation and to start the social uplift. Many other social institutions and agencies must take on and complete this objective, on the individual and collective level. In a good soccer team, good defenders deliver the accurate passes to launch the forward players so that they can score.

REFERENCES

Aertsen, I, Daems, T and Robert, L (eds) (2006) *Institutionalizing Restorative Justice* (Cullompton, Willan Publishing).

Althusser, L (1980) *Positions* (Paris, Hachette).

Boutellier, H (2006) 'The Vital Context of Restorative Justice' in I Aertsen, T Daems and L Robert (eds), *Institutionalizing Restorative Justice* (Cullompton, Willan Publishing).

Braithwaite, J (2000) 'Decomposing a Holistic Vision of Restorative Justice' 3 *Contemporary Justice Review* 433.

—— (2002) *Restorative Justice and Responsive Regulation* (Oxford, Oxford University Press).

—— (2014) *Limits on Violence: Limits on Responsive Regulation Theory* (Unpublished).

Braithwaite, J and Pettit, Ph (1990) *Not Just Desert: A Republican Theory of Criminal Justice* (Oxford, Oxford University Press).

Cacioppo, J and Patrick, W (2009) *Loneliness: Human Nature and the Need for Social Connection* (New York, Norton & Co).

Cheliotis, LK (2011) 'The Perils of Non-Adversarialism: Commentary on Freiberg' 8 *European Journal of Criminology* 108.

Christie, N (1977) 'Conflicts as Property' 17 *British Journal of Criminology* 1.

—— (2013) 'Words on Words' 1 *Restorative Justice, An International Journal* 15.

Claes, E (2004) 'Punitieve rechtshandhaving, herstelrecht en menselijke gelijkwaardigheid' in B Van Stokkom (ed), *Straf en Herstel. Ethische Reflecties over Strafdoeleinden* (The Hague, Boom).

Cunneen, C (2010) 'The Limitations of Restorative Justice' in C Cunneen and C Hoyle, *Debating Restorative Justice* (Oxford, Hart).

De Waal, F (2009) *The Age of Empathy: Nature's Lessons for a Kinder Society* (New York, Harmony Books).

Delgado, R (2000), 'Goodbye to Hammurabi: Analysing the Atavistic Appeal of Restorative Justice' 52 *Stanford Law Review* 770.
Dignan, J (2002) 'Restorative Justice and the Law: The Case for an Integrated, Systemic Approach' in L Walgrave (ed), *Restorative Justice and the Law* (Cullompton, Willan Publishing).
Feld, B (1999) 'Rehabilitation, Retribution and Restorative Justice' in G Bazemore and L Walgrave (eds), *Restorative Justice for Juveniles: Repairing the Harm by Youth Crime* (Monsey, NY, Criminal Justice Press).
Franssen, M, Put, J and Deklerck, J (2010) *Het beleid van de jeugdmagistraat* (Leuven, Universitaire Pers).
Froestad, J and Shearing, C (2013) 'Meditative Reflections on Nils Christie's "Words on Words", Through an African Lens' 1 *Restorative Justice. An International Journal* 31.
Harris, N, Walgrave, L and Braithwaite, J (2004) 'Emotional Dynamics in Restorative Conferences' 8 *Theoretical Criminology* 191.
Hoyle, C (2010) 'The Case for Restorative Justice' in C Cunneen and C Hoyle, *Debating Restorative Justice* (Oxford, Hart).
Koen, R (2007) 'The Antinomies of Restorative Justice' in E Van der Spuy, S Parmentier and A Dissel (eds), *Restorative Justice: Politics, Policies and Prospects* (Cape Town, Juta).
Lofton, BP (2004) 'Does Restorative Justice Challenge Systemic Injustices?' in H Zehr and B Toews (eds), *Critical Issues in Restorative Justice* (Monsey, NY and Cullompton, Criminal Justice Press/Willan Publishing).
Maruna, S (2014) 'The Role of Wounded Healing in Restorative Justice: An Appreciation of Albert Eglash' 2 *Restorative Justice, An International Journal* 9.
O'Malley, P (2006) 'Risk and Restorative Justice: Governing Through the Minimization of Harms' in I Aertsen, T Daems and L Robert (eds), *Institutionalizing Restorative Justice* (Cullompton, Willan Publishing).
Pauwels, L, Vettenburg, N, Gavray, C and Brondeel, R (2011) 'Societal Vulnerability and Troublesome Youth Group Involvement: The Mediating Role of Violent Values and Low Self-Control' 21 *Journal of International Criminal Justice* 283.
Pavlich, G (2005) *Governing Paradoxes of Restorative Justice* (London and Portland, OR, Glasshouse Press).
Pranis, K (2001) 'Restorative Justice, Social Justice, and the Empowerment of Marginalized Populations' in G Bazemore and M Schiff (eds), *Restorative Community Justice: Repairing Harm and Transforming Communities* (Cincinnati, OH, Anderson).
Pratt, J (2006) 'Beyond Evangelical Criminology: Meaning and Significance of Restorative Justice' in I Aertsen, T Daems and Robert, L (eds), *Institutionalizing Restorative Justice* (Cullompton, Willan Publishing).
Putnam, R (2000) *Bowling Alone* (New York, Simon and Schuster).
Schuilenburg, M, van Steden, R and Oude Breuil, B (eds) (2014) *Positive Criminology: Reflections on Care, Belonging and Security* (The Hague, Eleven International Publishing).
Shank, G and Takagi, P (2004) 'Critique of Restorative Justice' 31 *Social Justice* 147.

Sullivan, D and Tifft, L (2006) 'Introduction, the Healing Dimension of Restorative Justice: A One-World Body' in D Sullivan and L Tifft (eds), *Handbook of Restorative Justice* (Oxford, Routledge).
Sykes, G and Matza, D (1957) 'Techniques of Neutralization: A Theory of Delinquency' 22 *American Sociological Review* 664.
Vanfraechem, I (2007) *Herstelgericht groepsoverleg* (Bruges, Die Keure).
von Hirsch, A (1998) 'Penal Theories' in M Tonry (ed), *The Handbook of Crime and Punishment* (New York and Oxford, Oxford University Press).
Vyverman, V and Vettenburg, N (2009) 'School Well-being Among Young People: Is It Influenced by the Parents Socioeconomic Background?' 35 *Educational Studies* 191.
Walgrave, L (2008) *Restorative Justice, Self-interest and Responsible Citizenship* (Cullompton, Willan Publishing).
—— (2012) 'The Need for Clarity about Restorative Justice Conferences' in E Zinsstag and I Vanfraechem (eds), *Conferencing and Restorative Justice: International Practices and Perspectives* (Oxford, Oxford University Press).
—— (2013) 'From Civilising Punishment to Civilising Criminal Justice: From Punishment to Restoration' in D Cornwell, J Blad and M Wright (eds), *Civilising Criminal Justice: An International Restorative Agenda for Penal Reform* (Hook, Waterside Press).
Ward, T, Fox, K and Garber, M (2014) 'Restorative Justice, Offender Rehabilitation and Desistance' 2 *Restorative Justice, An International Journal* 24.

7

Restorative Justice, Procedural Justice and Care

JOSEP TAMARIT SUMALLA

I. RESTORATIVE JUSTICE AND CRITICAL THEORY

SOME OF THE criticisms levelled against restorative justice (RJ) are useful to trigger a better theorisation of this paradigm and to improve restorative practices. However, contradictions are frequent among those criticisms inspired by critical social theory. Moreover, it is sometimes unclear whether these criticisms are based on what RJ actually is or whether they are inspired by assumptions as to what RJ should be, thus entailing the risk of producing a blocking effect on the theorisation of RJ. I will focus on a simple example. The assumption that mediators should receive systemic training so they are not blind to issues of power and privilege and in order to prevent them from focusing on technicalities and short-sighted solutions is far from the reality that restorative programmes have to deal with. In fact, the problem lies in a basic failure of most critical doctrines, as far as they fail to capture the plural and diverse phenomenology of crime. Obviously, RJ does not offer a strategy to eliminate the alleged great and deep social causes of crime, such as deprivation and inequality. This is not the goal of current restorative practices, nor should it be. Most crimes, eligible or not for restorative processes, are not properly conflicts and, to the extent that they may be defined as such, they are, above all, micro human conflicts. Consequently, they should not be seen as purely symptoms of social macro conflicts, such as those related to economic, racial or gender inequalities, which are assumed, according to the 'critical' criminological doctrines, to be the actual and deep roots of crime.

I do not reject the many contributions by social theory to the analysis of crime and to the critique of how the criminal justice system operates, but critical approaches fail to explain, for example, why criminality decreased in Spain in the period 2007–2012, while unemployment increased from 8.5 per cent to 27.2 per cent, people suffering from risk of social exclusion (Eurostat) from 23 per cent to 28 per cent, and economic inequality (in terms of rent, GINI) from 31.9 per cent to 35 per cent. Similarly, those doctrines are more ideologically than empirically grounded when interpreting family violence grossly as a result of gender inequality in society, thus ignoring most forms of victimisation in domestic contexts, including bidirectional intimate partner violence, and underestimating the deep, complex and diverse roots of violence in human behaviour and the diverse, complex and subtle forms of conflict and abuse of power in close human relationships. Training facilitators and other practitioners in reductionist approaches to the causes of crime is not a good way to guarantee that restorative practices and other responses to it are able to serve the interests of the victims, repair harm, reintegrate the offender and prevent further crimes.

RJ is not the solution to violence and to other forms of criminality, but it is more concerned with victims' needs than critical criminology has ever been. I agree with those who argue that we should not burden RJ with the broad task of making a better world, although RJ, by improving the way we respond to crime, helps society to make a step forward on the right track. Promoting active responsibility is not merely attributable to neo-liberalistic tendencies. Those practices considered as mostly restorative, such as conferencing, are revealed as ambitious projects aiming to involve other actors from the community in transformative dynamics that can be initiated in the aftermath of crime.

Restorative processes are expected to reinforce the victim's position, thus empowering him or her, naming and blaming the injustice suffered by the crime. Likewise, restorative interventions encourage perpetrators to accept responsibility for his or her censurable behaviour and for its effects on other human beings and on society. Thus, by reinforcing the positions of victim and offender, RJ is exposed to be judged as a new form of essentialist discourse. Nonetheless, RJ may also be a real remedy against essentialism, as far as it helps us to capture the ambivalences and complexities that sometimes imbue the positions of victim and offender and to deal with conflicts that cannot be effectively managed by legal preconceptions.

II. TO RESTORE: THE FACE OF A NEW CONCEPT OF JUSTICE

Beyond criticisms, a consistent body of research confirms that restorative justice is able to satisfy participants and communities, and particularly victims' needs, by means of improving their wellbeing and reducing the emotional distress produced by crime. I agree with the position that conceives of RJ as a new paradigm of justice that operates in the interface between ethics of care and ethics of justice. According to this approach my research team has conducted some studies. The theoretical basis of such studies lies in the belief that providing justice for victims constitutes a basic aim of penal mediation and that resolving conflict is a secondary objective. What society needs to manage in cases which are legally described as criminal is not only, or always, conflict, but rather a demand for justice, grounded in the human needs of those who have been directly or indirectly victimised and have experienced a social event as 'injustice'. The desire for justice is one of the basic needs of those suffering from the effects of a criminal offence.

Research helps us understand what lies behind this need, which specific expectations are involved and to what extent society and institutions can meet these expectations. The notion that the criminal justice system is an expression of the punitive power of the state and that it only serves aims associated with an abstract idea of justice or the social goal of preventing future offences is now becoming outdated, or at least qualified, with acceptance of the fact that it can also have the purpose of satisfying the need for justice on the part of the victims of crime. Directive 2012/29/EU of the European Parliament and of the Council of 25 October 2012 establishing minimum standards on the rights, support and protection of victims of crime, links 'doing justice' with victims' rights and their respectful treatment (paragraph 34 of the Preamble).

Published studies do not provide a clear view of the basis of the need for justice, as far as we can conceive it as a basic human need that lies behind the recognition of a victim's right to justice. It is not expressly included in Maslow's (1943) hierarchy of basic human needs, although some authors have more recently cautioned that Maslow's famed classification is not exhaustive, and that the obtaining of justice can be regarded as a basic need. For some, it would be linked to the need for safety. In this regard, Taylor (2009) has noted that the experience of victimisation would have the effect of denying a basic need leading to a desire in victims to re-establish the status quo. Furthermore, in a systematic review of 33 empirical studies on the needs of victims of crime, Ten Boom and Kuijpers (2012) concluded that the victims of violent and serious crimes (including sexual and domestic ones) express needs associated with safety, which appear linked with justice and, specifically, with a judicial decision. This kind of expectation normally includes the need for punishment, for perception of the community's condemnation of the offence, and for the obtaining of material or immaterial redress.

Basis for the need for justice can also be found in Lerner's (1980) theory and his affirmation that, above and beyond individual differences, belief in justice is something natural and inevitable in human beings, which goes beyond the mere need for control and predictability. Thus, in the face of an offence viewed as a threat to this minimum necessary confidence in the justice of the world, there is a need for a social response that is given value as a means of re-establishing trust. The progress of civilisation entails leaving behind vindictive responses and refining punitive reactions and even an effort to avoid punitive aspects. Nevertheless, faced with deeds capable of destabilising the fundamental bases of trust and that are viewed as unjust, there is an expectation on the part of victims and society as a whole of compensatory or restorative action (Tamarit, 2013). The different expected responses to injustice have in common the search for restoration of the moral balance upset by the crime, that the offender suffer in proportion to the harm caused and that the victims may receive redress (Gromet *et al*, 2012).

These needs for justice have found their most conventional voice in retributive and preventive justice, but have also been channelled towards more innovative theoretical formulations or more refined mechanisms, as suggested by the ideas of restorative, therapeutic or procedural justice. The retributive concept of the punishment assumes that it is able to correct the imbalance caused between perpetrator and victim, which is behind the desire for vengeance. However, the way in which the compensatory mechanism of retributive justice actually works is far from being empirically proven, in contrast to the case of the expectation that the punishment act as a deterrent against future crimes, which is supported by studies showing that the punishment reduces the fear of future victimisation, particularly in cases of ongoing violence, like domestic violence. Vengeance is classed amongst the negative social reactions to victimisation, associated with rage, fear and depression and the symptoms of post-traumatic stress disorder. The reasons for revenge are associated with the wish for protection against a threat, recovery of self-esteem and the reestablishment of the balance of profit and loss of power.

According to a number of studies, the desire for vengeance and the feeling of injustice appear to be positively associated with the symptoms of post-traumatic stress disorder (Sonis *et al*, 2009). This is in line with the idea that reducing the symptoms as well as psychological adjustment by the victims can also moderate the desire for vengeance and promote forgiveness (Eaton and Struthers, 2006). Some studies have contributed information on how the need for justice can be met through victims' perception of procedural justice. They have therefore sought to test, with regard to the victims of the crime, the thesis of this form of justice, according to which the fact of being treated properly and with respect for procedural guarantees has a positive impact upon confidence and the sense of justice, irrespective of whether the outcome is favourable, defined as any benefit obtained by the individual as a consequence of the final decision on the case (Tyler, 2001; 2006). Having a voice and being treated with respect are key to bolstering victims' perception of justice, contributing to reducing secondary victimisation in the process (Laxminarayan, 2002; Van Camp and Wemmers, 2013). Research on procedural justice leads to put the focus on the 'encounter model'. From this approach, the capacity of a restorative practice to provide justice derives from it giving the different parts the opportunity to maintain a direct dialogue and to participate in the process of reconciliation; in this way it provides a sense of fairness that links RJ with procedural justice (Van Camp and Wemmers, 2013). On the other hand, the 'outcome model' highlights reparation as the key contribution that a restorative process can provide to both the victim and the community (Johnstone and Van Ness, 2007).

Examining RJ from the victims' perspective, several researchers have stressed that we need to make a greater effort to assess the extent to which RJ is currently able to satisfy the needs of the victims of crime for empowerment, psychological rebalancing, recovery of control, removal of blame, reparation, healing and a sense of justice and closure. There is empirical evidence that victims value their ability to participate in RJ practices because this provides them with information, gives them the opportunity to be heard, and allows them to experience a feeling of fairness and control (Umbreit, Coates and Vos, 2004; Sherman and Strang, 2007). Making an in-depth psychological evaluation of the evolution of the wellbeing and mental health of victims was not the main aim of most of the studies carried out. By way of an exception, Angel (2005) evaluated post-traumatic stress disorder. She observed that fewer symptoms of post-traumatic stress were found in those who took part in restorative processes, compared with a control group of victims whose cases were dealt with by conventional criminal justice.

Different studies have used a more feasible way to evaluate how the emotional states of victims evolved over time, comparing them before and after the RJ process. This is relevant because victimisation has important associated costs. Other authors have already identified a number of these costs, including fear, pain, emotional anguish and a considerable negative impact on a victim's quality of life (Mayhew, 2003; Field, Zander and Hall, 2013). Advocates of RJ assume that participation in a restorative process can have a healing or therapeutic effect on victims. These effects have been shown and/or referred to in various different studies. Several researchers have shown that the participation of victims in RJ practices reduced anxiety and fear and produced a recovery of self-esteem (Umbreit, Coats and Vos, 2004). Strang *et al.* (2006) reported reduced levels of fear and anger in victims after their participation in restorative processes compared with other more conventional types of contact with the criminal justice system. The positive contributions of RJ processes have also been reported regardless of the typology or seriousness of the crime in question. Shapland concluded that conferencing was considered significantly more useful by victims of more serious offences. Studies which compared the opinions of victims who participated in direct mediation with those of others whose cases were only indirectly mediated reported higher satisfaction rates in those involving direct mediation. In line with previous studies, and following both a qualitative and quantitative analysis of a sample of Spanish and Belgian victims who participated in mediation processes, Bolívar (2013) observed that victims of direct mediation scored highest on the majority of the scales employed, having a better perception of the social support received and a more positive opinion of the offenders. This study also found that victims of unknown offenders presented lower perceptions of damage and a better perception of the offenders themselves. They also showed a greater tendency to attend direct mediation sessions than the victims of known offenders.

III. EVALUATING A VICTIM-OFFENDER MEDIATION PROGRAMME

In order to explore the potential of restorative practices to satisfy victims' needs we evaluated the Catalan victim–offender mediation (VOM) Programme (Tamarit and Luque, 2016). We conducted a quantitative study with a larger sample of 121 people, comprising all the victims who participated in a VOM between 1 September 2011 and 31 December 2012 and who had given consent for their data to be transferred to the research team. Then we worked with a smaller sample of 90 people, comprising those victims who agreed to be interviewed by telephone. The aims of our study were: (a) to verify the hypothesis that penal mediation can satisfy victims' needs and contribute to the emotional recovery of the victim; (b) to assess the extent to which penal mediation can serve the objective of providing victims with a sense of justice, resolving the conflict, or both; and (c) to assess whether the restorative effect of penal mediation was related to the perception that the process was fair or if it was an effect of the outcome achieved.

The results of the smaller sample (n:90) revealed that the victims interviewed were generally satisfied with the mediation process. In a scale from 1 to 5, the programme was given an average score of 4.5 and the facilitator scored 4.7. The victims also expressed their general satisfaction with the police (4.2). What they valued most was having been heard, participating in a procedure in which they had been directly involved and having the opportunity to explain their feelings about the act to the offender. Obtaining an apology from the offender and having solved the conflict were not considered relevant. However, the victims' opinions of the offenders' behaviour were less positive. Only 25.7 per cent declared that they were satisfied with their attitude and 31 per cent felt partially satisfied, while 43 per cent said that they were not satisfied. Satisfaction with offenders was greatest when the offender was unknown to the victim (60 v 20 per cent in the case of relatives or known people). The offender acknowledged the offence in 60 per cent of the cases, provided information in 52 per cent and apologised in 49 per cent, but only 8 per cent of their victims felt that they assumed their responsibility. Most of the victims believed that the crime involved was serious (42 per cent) or very serious (41 per cent), with only 16 per cent qualifying it as not serious or less serious. Two out of three victims (66.7 per cent) affirmed that the offence had produced psychological harm. Physical damage was reported in 24 per cent of cases, material damage or loss in 30 per cent and indirect disadvantages, such as job loss, in 24 per cent. Psychological harm was more frequent when victim and offender had a close relationship: 82 per cent in cases in which a relative or partner was involved, but only 33 per cent when the offender was not known to the victim (p = 0.002). In contrast, job loss was more prevalent when the victim and offender did not know each other (53 per cent) than in conflicts involving relatives (17 per cent) (p = 0.017).

One of the key findings of the research was the positive emotional impact of penal mediation on the victims. They were asked to evaluate how they felt after the crime and after the mediation process with reference to six different emotional states (rage, anxiety, fear, sadness, impotence and loss of control) on a scale from 1 to 5. The main emotional effects of crime were feelings of impotence (3.85), rage (3.65) and sadness (3.14). The impact of crime, and particularly feelings of anxiety and fear, was greater in women than in men. We found a reduction in emotional distress in relation to each of the six items following mediation. In all cases, the differences between the declared values before and after the mediation process were statistically significant. This reduction was observed for both men and women, and for Spanish and foreign subjects, in all age groups and for all types of offence, and irrespective of the relationship between the victim and offender. It is worth mentioning that emotional distress decreased significantly after the mediation process in the case of offences involving family relationships for all the emotions assessed, even when the victims had declared themselves less satisfied with the mediation process. Feelings of rage and impotence particularly decreased in relation to these offences, revealing the capacity of mediation to provide empowerment to the victims of these crimes.

The results of this study gave us an optimistic view of penal mediation. The findings were in line with those reported in other studies carried out in other countries, highlighting that victims are generally satisfied with restorative practices. The evaluation revealed that high victim satisfaction was not incompatible with poor outcomes with regard to the reparation of harm or obtaining an apology from the offender. This has been interpreted as complying with the procedural justice model in which contributions such as trust, respect, participation and/or voice have all been highlighted (Tyler, 2001; Van Camp and Wemmers, 2013). However, this does not allow us to set aside some of the other benefits of the mediation process. Its restorative potential also arises from its contribution to the emotional recovery of the victims and its ability to provide empowerment. Whatever the case, the positive contributions of penal mediation are not related to the offender's attitude or to its capacity to resolve conflict. Victims may feel satisfied even though the conflict remains unsolved. This finding can be interpreted as a validation of penal mediation as a restorative practice which is able to achieve the goals of RJ. However, the capacity of penal mediation to resolve conflict must be questioned or, at the very least, its objectives need to be redefined. It could be argued that mediation allows the different parts to deal with conflict but that it is not realistic to expect it to be able to resolve this conflict. In a general evaluation of the results presented here, the benefits of penal mediation obtained by the victims are twofold: the satisfaction of participating in the process and emotional recovery. This would point to RJ being linked to both the procedural and therapeutic dimensions of justice.

This study focused on two different kinds of cases dealt with by the mediation programme: conflicts involving family and partner relationships and offences committed outside such close relationships, in which the perpetrator is a person who could be either known or unknown to the victim. The results of mediation were generally positive in both types of case, but there were relevant differences. In conflicts involving family members and partners, despite the initial disposition of victims to take part in the process, it was more difficult for the programme to achieve its objectives. In these cases, the psychological harm suffered by the victim tended to be deeper and therefore the offence committed presented the symptoms of a more serious conflict. This could also explain why, in these cases, the offender tended to be less willing to assume their responsibility and/or to apologise. Consequently, mediation tended to be less successful in cases of cross reporting in which the positions of the victim and offender were more subtly defined. Notwithstanding this, it is encouraging to see that most of the victims experienced a significant reduction in the emotional distress that they suffered and stated that they felt satisfied with the process.

We should not expect penal mediation to be able to deal effectively with the roots of deep and long-lasting problems in close relationships. Our findings confirmed that mediation is a restorative practice. However, some of the deficits observed could be interpreted as intrinsic limitations of this practice. It could reasonably be expected that more complex restorative interventions, such as those based on the conferencing model, would prove better able to achieve objectives in the case of more complex conflicts. Penal mediation should be seen as a first step in developing more complex restorative practices. Specific measures should be taken to prevent secondary victimisation, to guarantee free choice and, in particular, to provide attention to vulnerable victims. This is particularly required in cases in which there is strong psychological dependence or a perceived threat from the offender. These measures may consist of giving information and psychological assistance to the victims judged to be most at risk. Above all, we believe in implementing programmes that include practices based on the conferencing model, which permit greater dialogue.

These findings confirmed the potential of penal mediation. The emotional improvement of victims is something that had not been so clearly outlined in the research previously carried out in other countries. Penal mediation can achieve the objectives of RJ in that it can meet victims' needs by improving their wellbeing and reducing the emotional distress caused by crime. It is best able to achieve its objectives when the offence committed is not directly related to conflict. In these cases justice can particularly be valued from the procedural perspective, in that victims can feel that they have been listened to and treated fairly, with any reparation received (outcome) constituting a secondary contribution. However, RJ does not only reveal itself as having much in common with procedural justice but it also seems to be closely connected to therapeutic justice, because restorative practices are able to provide victims with emotional recovery.

IV. NEED FOR JUSTICE IN CHILD VICTIMS

Subsequently, a qualitative study was conducted to gain an understanding of the expectations and needs of the victims of child sexual abuse from the criminal justice system (CJS). The study was carried out in Barcelona in 2015. 23 victims of child sexual abuse were interviewed in depth (20 women and three men), aged between 17 and 50 ($M = 32.26$ and $TD = 10.47$), who were contacted via a victim support centre. Of them, 19 were receiving psychological treatment and four had been discharged. The study revealed that expectations of the justice system were centred particularly on the outcome of the process, something that is in line with studies that have established that the perception of the fair or unfair nature of the verdict is a key factor in the victim's experience (Regehr *et al*, 2008). Aspects associated with the justice of the procedure were of secondary importance, helping to increase or moderate the secondary victimisation this type of victim experiences when coming into contact with the CJS.

According to our study, victims' expectations of the CJS's involvement was highly focused on the verdict imposing a prison sentence. Their discourse revealed a demand for justice, which was regarded as insufficient whatever the requested sentence, largely associated with punishment of the offender and retribution for the harm suffered, in line with the results of other studies (Felson and Pare, 2008; Boateng and Lee, 2014). Also arising frequently were thoughts of the compensatory suffering that the offender should experience as rationalisation for a feeling of restorative vengeance. However, at the same time, they also expressed other needs, associated with the hope that a guilty verdict may bring them emotional relief, with the idea of justice linked with expectations of recognition, validation or closure appearing. These needs appeared to be more positively valued than the mere punishment of the abuser, or both aspects became almost inextricably intertwined.

Moreover, special attention should be paid to the need for recognition and validation. In many cases, interviewees suffered from the disbelief of their surrounding environment, including parents and others very close to them, and so they expected the CJS to validate their truth before these people and even before themselves. An official declaration of the truth would mean that their suffering had been recognised and a guilty verdict for the abuser had the effect of absolving them of guilt, a key need, especially for those victims who have blamed themselves or been blamed by their surrounding environment. On this point, the results are in line with the findings of other countries (Jülich, 2006; Koss and Achilles, 2008; McGlynn, Westmarland and Godden, 2012). The victims' demand for punishment can thus be viewed as a symbolic subrogation of a desire for justice largely associated with the need for recognition and validation. So, the demand for justice stems not only from the basic need for safety, but also from that for esteem, in the double sense of self-esteem and recognition from the surrounding environment.

The study revealed that assumption of responsibility for events by the abuser and being made aware of the damage inflicted is another need of victims, which is linked to the need for absolution from blame and the fact that, in most cases, they experienced abuse at the hands of a family member. In any case, generally speaking, victims did not regard this as something that can be provided by the conventional justice system. This is why those who state that, for their recovery process, they need this assumption of responsibility by the abuser and do not wish him to be imprisoned do not resort to the CJS, but instead believe that it is a process that they should carry out for themselves. These conclusions might lead one to consider the potential of restorative processes, especially if they take account of practices that seek the involvement of family members in the restorative dialogue and incorporate the community element, such as those based on the conferencing or family group conferencing model. Such practices can facilitate processes of recognition, assumption of responsibility and involvement of the victims' surrounding environment and act to complement the CJS or as an alternative to it in cases in which the victim decides not to make a formal complaint or in which the criminal system cannot become involved, as the offence has exceeded the statute of limitations (as is frequently the case with this type of offence, whose disclosure often comes very late). The law should also permit the CJS sufficient flexibility to facilitate restorative processes when continuing with criminal proceedings would be inefficient and detrimental to the victim. It is also worth mentioning that in any case, given the results of our study, victims' needs for restitution are generally unrelated to demands of a monetary nature and focus on the need for moral or psychological redress: so, in this type of offences, restorative justice is more closely associated with ideas of therapeutic and procedural justice rather than with outcomes associated with pure retribution.

V. NEW DEVELOPMENTS: TRANSITIONAL JUSTICE AND HATE CRIMES

RJ experiences new developments that will require further theorisation and will be a challenge for critical reviews and for empirical work.

An increased number of publications reflect the emergence of transitional justice as a new field where alternative practices of justice have been developed. A new culture of transitional justice stands to provide a theoretical background to mechanisms that are conceived as an alternative to criminal justice and also as a way to overcome the culture of impunity and the invisibility of victims in transitional contexts. Research is needed to test to what extent the principles and expectations of RJ are met by the actual operation of these mechanisms. By way of example, in Colombia the Justice and Peace Special Court created in 2005 to deal with crimes committed by paramilitary forces has issued more than 30 judgments, through which 'alternative penalties' and reparations have been imposed in cases of gross violations of human rights, most of them atrocity crimes. However, only empirical analyses can make clear how these measures fit with the ideals and expectations of RJ regarding the participation of the community, the reintegration of victims and offenders, the restoration of social bonds, and the generation of transformative inputs in the community.

A second arena where new challenges arise is the social response to hate crimes. Restorative practices provide those in the increasingly multicultural European societies good opportunities to deal with the aftermath of intercultural conflicts in cases of hate crimes. In those cases RJ may help the offender to appreciate the full impact of their actions. Furthermore, the victims can receive support through which they will better be able to overcome the additional impact of those crimes (Iganski and Lagou, 2014). Conferences can involve the community in a transformative intervention towards values of mutual understanding and integration of minorities. Therefore, it would be a useful recommendation that practitioners in restorative processes should be trained in intercultural skills.

REFERENCES

Angel, C (2005) *Crime Victims Meet Their Offenders: Testing the Impact of Restorative Justice Conferences on Victims' Post-Traumatic Stress Symptoms* (Philadelphia, PA University of Pennsylvania).

Boateng, FD and Lee, HD (2014) 'Willingness to Report Sexual Offenses to the Police in Ghana' 9 *Victims and Offenders* 436.

Bolívar, D (2013) 'For Whom is Restorative Justice? A Mixed-Method Study on Victims and (Non) Participation' 1(2) *Restorative Justice, An International Journal* 190.

Eaton, J and Struthers, CW (2006) 'The Reduction of Psychological Aggression Across Varied Interpersonal Contexts Through Repentance and Forgiveness' 32 *Aggressive Behavior* 195.

Felson, RB and Pare, PP (2008) 'Gender and the Victim's Experience with the Criminal Justice System' 37 *Social Science Research* 202.

Field, C, Zander, J and Hall, G (2013) 'Forgiveness is a Present to Yourself as Well: An Intrapersonal Model of Forgiveness in Victims of Violent Crime' 19(3) *International Review of Victimology* 235.

Gromet, DM, Okimoto, TG, Wenzel, M and Darley, JM (2012) 'Victim-Centered Approach to Justice? Victim Satisfaction Effects on Third-Party Punishments' 36(5) *Law and Human Behavior* 375.

Iganski, P and Lagou, S (2014) 'Hate Crimes Hurt Some More Than Others: Implications for the Just Sentencing of Offenders' *Journal of Interpersonal Violence* 1.

Jacobsson, M, Wahlin, L and Andersson, T (2012), 'Victim Offender Mediation in Sweden: Is the Victim Better Off?' 18(3) *International Review of Victimology* 229.

Johnstone, G and Van Ness, DW (2007) *Handbook of Restorative Justice* (Cullompton, Willan).

Jülich, S (2006) 'Views of Justice Among Survivors of Historical Child Sexual Abuse: Implications for Restorative Justice in New Zealand' 10 *Theoretical Criminology* 125.

Koss, M and Achilles, M (2008) *Restorative Justice Responses to Sexual Assault*, Applied Research Forum, Harrisburg, PA (National Online Resource Center on Violence Against Women).

Laxminarayan, M (2002) 'Procedural Justice and Psychological Effects of Criminal Proceedings: The Moderating Effect of Offense Type' 25(4) *Social Justice Research* 390.

Lerner, M (1980) *The Belief in a Just World: A Fundamental Delusion* (New York, Plenum Press).

Maslow, AH (1943) 'A Theory of Human Motivation' 50 *Psychological Review* 370.

Mayhew, P (2003) *Counting the Costs of Crime in Australia, Technical Report* (Canberra, Australian Institute of Criminology).

McCold, P and Watchell, T (2003) 'A Theory of Restorative Justice' in G Johnstone and DW Van Ness, *Handbook of Restorative Justice* (Cullompton, Willan).

McGlynn, C, Westmarland, N and Godden, N (2012) 'I Just Wanted Him to Hear Me': Sexual Violence and the Possibilities of Restorative Justice' 39(2) *Journal of Law and Society* 213.

Regehr, C, Alaggia, R, Lambert, L and Saini, M (2008) 'Victims of Sexual Violence in the Canadian Criminal Courts' 3 *Victims and Offenders* 99.

Shapland, J *et al* (2007) *Restorative Justice: The Views of Victims and Offenders, The Third Report from the Evaluation of Three Schemes*, Ministry of Justice Research 3/07.

Sherman, L and Strang, H (2007) *Restorative Justice: The Evidence* (Smith Institute).

Sonis, J, Gibson, JL, de Jong, JT, Field, NP, Hean, S and Komproe, I (2009) 'Probable Post Traumatic Stress Disorder and Disability in Cambodia: Associations with Perceived Justice, Desire for Revenge and Attitudes Toward the Khmer Rouge Trials' 302(5) *Journal of the American Medical Association* 527.

Strang, H, Sherman, L, Angel, CM, Woods, DJ, Bennet, S, Newbury-Birch, D and Inkpen, N (2006) 'Victim Evaluations of Face-to-Face Restorative Justice Conferences: A Quasi-Experimental Analysis' 62 *Journal of Social Issues* 281.

Tamarit Sumalla, JM (2013) 'Restorative Justice: A New View' 1(1) *Restorative Justice, An International Journal* 70.

Tamarit Sumalla, JM and Luque Reina, E (2016) 'Can Restorative Justice Satisfy Victims' Needs: Evaluation of the Catalan Victim-Offender Mediation Programme' 4(1) *Restorative Justice, An International Journal* 68.

Taylor, AJW (2009) 'Justice as a Basic Human Need' 38(2) *New Zealand Journal of Psychology* 5.

Ten Boom, A and Kuijpers, KF (2012) 'Victim's Needs as Basic Humans Needs' 18(2) *International Review of Victimology* 155.

Tyler, TR (2001) 'Public Trust and Confidence in Legal Authorities' 19 *Behavioral Sciences and the Law* 215.

—— (2006) 'Restorative Justice and Procedural Justice: Dealing with Rule Breaking' 62 *Journal of Social Issues* 307.

Umbreit, M, Coates, R and Vos, B (2004), 'Victim-Offender Mediation: Three Decades of Practice and Research' 22 *Conflict Resolution Quarterly* 279.

Van Camp, T and Wemmers, JA (2013) 'Victim Satisfaction with Restorative Justice: More than Simply Procedural Justice' 19(2) *International Review of Victimology* 117.

Wemmers, J and Van Camp, T (2005) 'Can Mediation be Therapeutic for Crime Victims? An Evaluation of Victims' Experiences in Mediation with Young Offenders' 47(3) *Canadian Journal of Criminology and Criminal Justice* 527.

Part II

Applying Analytical Tools and Frameworks to Research and Practice

8

Restorative Justice and Democratic Citizenship: A New Social Pedagogy or Back to 'Social Defence'?

LEO VAN GARSSE

I. INTRODUCTION

AS A SOCIAL pedagogue and a former practitioner in mediation, I very much embraced the idea of restorative justice (RJ), not so much as a friendly way to solve conflicts, but as an approach to challenge the parties involved, the public in general as well as the judiciary to 'demonstrate democracy'. The notion of democracy here does not refer to a form of state organisation, but rather to a quality of social interactions to be stimulated at all levels of society. It is about a culture of readiness to constantly learn from the otherness of the other person(s) we encounter (Biesta, 2006; 2011).

Compared to most other countries, Belgium appears to have been quite successful in implementing restorative justice. But still, Belgian mediation practice also demonstrates the slippery character of the path between success and just adoption. The more mediators tend to specialise and to diversify their methods (mediation in cases of sexual violence, family violence, neighbourhood conflicts, schools, etc), the more impressive the proportion of cases concluded 'successfully' with an agreement, the more articles on 'better' techniques of mediation or conferencing appear ... the more reason there might be to worry. No doubt, mediation implies a social-pedagogical learning process for all involved, including the mediators as a new professional group. But what kind of citizenship does it really promote, and what kind of 'democracy' does it imply?

The usual plea is for restorative justice as a 'paradigm shift' in doing justice from cold technical formalism to a warm and communicated experience. This shift is promoted to be fully elaborated and exploited to radically transform, or even abolish, criminal justice as such. Post-modern philosophers like Lyotard (1979) suggest that what we used to see as the opposite of something, should probably rather be seen as somehow a part of it, be it in the sphere of its '*différend*'. In that sense restorative justice shouldn't be put at the other side of formal criminal justice, but in the sphere of what criminal justice, seen from a certain (political) angle, *could look like*. This cautious, tentative approach might open an escape route from the claustrophobic pressure to do 'otherwise' or 'better', a pressure too familiar and too modern to be still credible. As far as Belgian experience in mediation is concerned, the complicated nature of the relationship between the formal and the informal, the private and the public way of 'doing justice', clearly reflects an (interesting type of) ambivalence people invited to participate in mediation tend to struggle with (Van Garsse, 2004; 2012).

These thoughts make a critical reflection on the current state of the art of restorative justice far from useless. But my suggestion would be to do this in a somewhat foucauldian, genealogical way, taking not the problem, but our way of defining it, as a starting point. It is facing the paradox of looking backwards to enable looking forward (Biesta, 2006).

In this chapter, I will try to explore some of the perspectives of such an approach. Hopefully, I will not be blamed for using the Belgian situation as my 'case'. In fact, about a century ago, Adolphe Prins, a Belgian legal scholar, managed to inspire amongst his national and international colleagues a great and long-lasting debate about the elaboration of a specific criminal policy, widely known as 'Social Defence' (Prins, 1910). The 1910 publication of his work *La défence sociale et les transformations du droit pénal* might be a nice point of reference for a reflection upon restorative justice today, one century and two world wars later.

The next section of this chapter briefly goes into the nature of Social Defence and tries to contextualise its appearance. Looking backwards from today, we're looking for similarities and differences. A third section is intended to trigger and to some extent complicate three familiar aspects of restorative justice, mostly taken for granted. Finally, I try to draw some preliminary conclusions in line with the attempt to further sharpen instead of answering questions on a 'critical restorative justice'.

II. ANCIENT REFLECTIONS ON A CURRENT PROBLEM

A. Young Nation-State in Turbulent Times

The young Belgian state, founded only in 1830, was a remarkable mix of liberal and catholic interests finding one another in a common goal: emancipating civil society in an era of upcoming capitalism. Massive industrialisation confronted the government with 'proletarisation', cutting off huge parts of the population from their traditional communities and their agricultural roots. Moreover, the prominence of the capitalist economy provoked migration through 'waves' which were far from politically controlled, but dependent upon the unpredictable evolution of 'the market'. The proclaimed principle of equality of citizens was brutally trivialised by social reality. Prins (1910) spends pages on describing the enormous problems of poverty, alcoholism, child abuse and prostitution amongst large groups of the Belgian population, characterised by a massive disconnection from moral values and from any feeling of national coherence. In those circumstances, the formal national system of justice appeared to be completely incapable of maintaining security and order. Prisons were condemned as being ineffective and far too expensive. Traditional penitentiaries were dramatically overcrowded and blamed for promoting instead of preventing deviance. The judiciary was criticised for being lazy, slow and blinded by a rigid procedural formality. The systematic non-execution of minor sentences tended to create, amongst large parts of the Belgian population, an atmosphere of impunity (see also Christiaensen, 2004).

For the first time in history, economic forces began to organise themselves in a universal rational way, largely independent from any national politics and local culture. Bismarkian Germany represented a seductive example of translating economic principles into social and political practices of *governance*, challenging at the same time the principle of political sovereignty. There was a growing plea to convert the state into a 'society', government into management, and 'justice' into a fluid 'criminal policy', to be constantly adapted to the ever-changing social circumstances. Being considered a valid indicator of what 'rational' governance in given circumstances would stand for, scientific knowledge could be the constitutive cornerstone of a science-based 'neutral' policy hard to question or to criticise (Sachβe, 2003; Gutwirth, 1993). The 'positivist revolt' of modern sciences criticised traditional politics based on transcendental essentialist presumptions and on values such as freedom, honour, responsibility, national unity, personal guilt and citizenship (Ancel, 1965).

B. A Call for Pragmatism Beyond Punishment

Prins' work fascinates by its attempt to compromise fire and water, social determinism and dignity and freedom, as constitutive features of democratic citizenship (Fijnaut, 1986; 2014).

On the one hand, Prins (1910) fulminates against a criminal justice system hiding itself behind all sorts of procedural formalities instead of having an open eye for social reality. He accuses the justice system of victimising the whole population in the name of just such an abstract 'idea' of justice. He insists on the mission of the state to protect its population from being victimised. This must be done by focusing not just on the criminal event as a moral evil, but on the person of the offender and on his social context:

> Pour choisir les mesures à prendre, c'est l'état permanent de l'individu qu'il faut considérer, pas son acte passager. Et il s'agit de réagir contre la routine des tribunaux qui, ayant à juger tel individu pour tel délit se bornent à appliquer la formule juridique fournie par le texte du code, sans se préoccuper du mode d'existence, du milieu, des instincts, des prédispositions de la nature psychique de l'accusé. (Prins, 1910: 75)

The poor people, the mentally retarded as well as the children, are seen as the (virtual) victims by excellence, not only of criminal events, but also of contamination by the disease of delinquency.

Therefore, Prins sees a clear link between (criminal) justice and social support as a public matter of crime-prevention:

> L'état ne peut donc passer indifférent à côté d'eux [the poor and the vulnerable] et laisser agir l'initiative privée. Même ici, il est tenu à garantir l'ordre social. Seulement, la défense sociale se manifeste alors sous sa forme la plus haute et la plus féconde. Elle n'est plus de la répression, elle est de la protection et de l'assistance. (Prins, 1910: 69)

However, Prins is not prepared to abolish the concepts of personal responsibility and punishment. But, in his view, those important notions should be preserved to be applied to real 'citizens': people with a sufficient degree of social stability and personal morality, by whom one can expect the punishment to be understood and accepted as a rational/ reasonable/ logical answer to the transgression of the social rule.

Wanting to bridge freedom and determinism, Prins strongly advocates for education as a matter of eminent public and political interest. Referring to the famous French author Victor Hugo: 'Peuplez les écoles et vous viderez les prisons!' (Prins, 1910:160).

In this approach, education should not be a matter of learning this or that, but rather ought to focus upon *'émancipation'*, a notion defined by Prins as the capacity to creatively cope with the circumstances and conditions one finds oneself in. In the perspective of this emancipation, democratic citizenship has to be 'postponed' as a perspective to strive for. It should be seen as a result of a social pedagogical project eventually directed to every member of the population, and at the same time everybody's responsibility.

For those who appear not to be affected through either punishment or education, the only solution is the one of neutralisation through isolation. And this should not be done 'post factum' but preventively, despite the breach of legal safeguards. A responsible state could not afford the obvious risk of endangering its population through being affected by crime. As such, the indirect function of pedagogy was the making of a justifiable (ie science-based) distinction between: (a) groups of citizens deserving justice; (b) groups of not-yet-citizens to be protected by social and pedagogical measures; (c) groups of non-citizens to be isolated from the population in order to avoid contamination.

C. Long Ago or Up-to-Date?

The current socio-political circumstances are easily comparable to the ones described. Political sovereignty is in danger of being over-ruled by socio-economic requirements, leaving the state with the a-political functions of maintenance, protection and facilitation (Mouffe, 2005). As in Prins' time, it is common-sense to consider the national criminal justice system ineffective, expensive, outdated, if not counterproductive. Social assistance and 'alternative measures' are appreciated above all as investments in the fight against public insecurity, far less expensive than imprisonment. As in Prins' times, the (virtual) victim is prominently present in every debate on criminal policy. Government is held accountable for public safety. In this context, the voices in favour of victims' rights tend to sound in harmony with the chorus of those criticising national policy for its laxity. The discourse of respecting the victim easily combines with a plea for more efficient punishment.

Of course, stating that nothing has really happened since Prins, would be nothing but another populist slogan. But quite rightly, the question might arise where we have got to since then, and how we did so. Looking backwards from where we are now, we might ask ourselves whether we would currently find amongst 'offenders', as well as amongst the (virtual) 'victims', distinctions between groups of 'citizens', 'non-citizens' and 'not-yet-citizens'. One could question the role of an offering like mediation as an unspoken contribution to this societal stratification (Eliaerts and Bitoune, 2001; Gutwirth and De Hert, 2011). What about the mechanisms in selecting cases 'suitable' for mediation? What about the current popularity of specific offerings of mediation to vulnerable groups, such as children or long-term inmates, mentally disturbed offenders, all obviously not in the best position to take up in a credible way any tangible responsibility (Van Garsse, 2015)? What about the implicit and often unspoken effects of a refusal to accept a mediation offer?

Further on, we might indeed presume in any restorative offering an aspect of pedagogy attempting to bridge freedom and determinism, or doing justice, on the one hand, and offering protection, on the other. Despite all claims of neutrality, it would be hard to deny that restorative justice in any event shows a normative mission (Duff, 2001). At least partly, mediation is pedagogy, as much as Prins' 'social assistance' was. An offering of mediation in the aftermath of a crime is different from just the provision of a free public service. It is a representation of an ethical challenge, the more difficult, the more honourable.

Social Defence saw social order as an absolute precondition for human freedom and development. As such, it may sound outdated and disciplining, incompatible with current views on democracy. Restorative justice is seen as holding a learning opportunity for participating in 'doing justice' and therefore to be a matter of democratic citizenship. In fact, this might be one of the reasons for its current political popularity. Far less clear is the nature of the idea of 'democracy' and 'justice' hidden behind this common enthusiasm for participation. Mouffe (2005) and Žižek (1998) strongly problematise the current normative pressure upon consensuality in dealing with contradictory interests and opinions. Rosanvallon (2011) and Mouffe (1989; 2005) point to the fluid nature of the concept of democracy, likely to be understood as the approach fitting best with historical (and economic) circumstances. Biesta (2006; 2011) sharply questions the idea of democratic citizenship being a status to obtain through learning. He criticises it as a de-politisising neo-liberal manoeuvre (compare Mouffe, 2005). For him, democracy should be seen as a continuous confrontation with the unexpected other, a 'happening' in 'real time', a quality of intersubjective dialogue.

III. RESTORATIVE EVIDENCES REFLECTED IN HISTORICAL DYNAMICS: A BRIEF EXPLORATION

A. Restorative Justice and/as Criminological Paradigm

Restorative justice finds itself in a delicate balance between being an emerging penal practice, a grass-roots 'movement' and a promising new criminological 'branch'. From experience we know that this multi-dimensional feature of restorative justice can be of considerable strategic benefit, above all in the stage of implementation (Van Garsse, 2008). Depending on the public he has to convince, a promotor of restorative justice can emphasise one or other dimension as a way to empower the restorative message. One cannot blame anybody for using all he/she has available to fully *represent* the values he/she is standing for in order to *affect* others. Still, an ethical limit is to be respected. This limit forms a constitutive element in the positioning of the educator, the criterion of success not being found in the transfer of the message, but in the regular and eventual experience to be properly conveyed (Biesta, 2006). Absolute transparency, even if not possible at every stage of the debate, should therefore be a permanent goal. A theory may sound like poetry, but, ethicallyspeaking, it might be better not put into effect (Verhoeven, 1988). And this also goes for testimony, as honest as it might be, in relation to the notion of 'truth' (Lyotard, 1979).

In the post-war welfare state, the balances in the power triangle of (legal) practice, (scientific) knowledge, (cultural) values had to change drastically. The promotion of individual legal safeguards and positive rights moved to the centre of policy attention, knowledge was promoted as a precondition to freedom, but also suspected as a source of power (Gutwirth, 1993). Confrontation with totalitarianism virulently questioned the modernist identifying the 'rational' with the 'logical', and the 'logical' with the 'good'.

In this context, the 'Popper-Kuhn debate' has to be situated, focusing on the status of the scientific search for truth. In this debate Kuhn launched the notion of 'paradigm' in an attempt to breach the common idea of linear scientific progress through a gradual discovery of 'truth' (Kuhn, 1976). The introduction of the concept of paradigm situates the value of a (scientific) insight in a cultural and provisional perspective, rather than considering it 'truth'. In this respect, a paradigm is nothing to be proud of, or to strive for. So, stating that restorative justice is just (another) paradigm, is a way to emphasise the relative, contextual nature of it.

If this were really the common understanding, the focus should be not so much on further *proving* or 'exploiting' this paradigm's potential, but rather on the question: what happened to us and to our societies that this paradigm shift has taken place and that we are even likely to 'promote' it?

Not by coincidence, the struggle for recognition of restorative justice as a new paradigm refers to the register of science. In promoting restorative justice, academic support obviously is of utmost importance, partly because it provides the fragile pilot projects on mediation and restoration with a certain authority. The other way round, it is fair to say that the stories of concrete experience gave quite a boost to the credibility of the exotic theories on talks between victims and offenders as a way to deal with issues of crime, justice and security. This mechanism of mutually legitimising theory and practice, described in unfriendly terms by some as a 'parasitical symbiosis' (Depaepe, 2005: 441), dates back to the origins of modern human sciences. It brings us back to the era of the German '*Kathedersocialismus*', the coming modernity and the common appeal therein to science as a strong source of authority of progressive social/criminal policy (Sachβe, 2003). This reasoning also was the motor of the conception of criminology, an applied science *par excellence*, in service of (and paid for by) governments (Walgrave, 2009). German scholars were very explicit indeed in their confidence in scientific knowledge as a cornerstone of the '*Bildung*' of a whole society and of every citizen's personality (Natorp, 1964; Nohl, 1965). And so, until decades after Prins, were some prominent promoters of the original Social Defence doctrine (Gramatica, 1964). As demonstrated during the Interbellum, from a democratic viewpoint this positioning of science is not without danger (Arendt, 2005; Gutwirth, 1993; Fijnaut, 2014).

The dramatic loss of political innocence was reflected in post-war developments of human sciences. Pedagogy, psychology as well as criminology were all compromised by authoritarian ideology. And this also went for the whole idea of Social Defence as a science-driven state doctrine focused upon steering and protecting the collective (Ancel, 1965). Prins' dilemma of integrating individual rights and public interests was back on stage. In his notorious plea for a 'New Social Defence', Ancel (1965) explicitly blamed criminologists, as well as legal policy-makers and practitioners, for having selfishly withdrawn from the challenge of collaboration, each of them trying to monopolise the field of criminal policy. In the concept of criminal policy he had in mind, he therefore foresaw not two, but three constitutive elements:

(1) criminology as building knowledge on the phenomenon of crime and its causes;
(2) law as the constant elaboration and adaptation of a proper legal framework as a tangible and justifiable answer by society to the event of crime;
(3) criminal policy, a science and an *art* alike, with as a double goal:
    (a) first, to enable and improve clarification and re-formulating of the rule;
    (b) secondly, to guide lawyers and all kinds of legal practitioners.

Ancel (1965) saw criminal policy as an area of negotiation between knowledge and law, between the principle of equality and the respect for the particularity of each situation. He described it as an area of responsibility of everyone involved, including the offender and society as a whole, their involvement being alike a goal and a precondition.

The whole idea of restorative justice, seen as a way of making the search for justice a common mission for all involved, corresponds with it. But, what is the logic of restorative justice being mainly a *criminological* matter? Where does knowledge end to give space to art? And where then is the reflection on the 'art' as such?

In the 1970s, the young Belgian association for criminology had dreams of a fluid scientific enterprise with the ambition of becoming a critical social movement, strongly refusing to build another fortress of expertise. The aim, at the same time as the prominent political mission, was to promote emancipation from an oppressive notion of criminal justice (Houchon, 1990). This idea has faded since then, even if some still call for a criminology not afraid of engaging in a utopian mission (Walgrave, 2008: 2014). Currently, criminology indisputably carries fully-fledged scientific ambitions and a corresponding social status. Mixing 'registers' of power, like the one of knowledge with the one of ethics, might be too close to manipulation to be something that the credibility of restorative justice or criminology can afford (Eliaerts and Bitoune, 2001; Gutwirth and De Hert, 2011).

B. Democratic Citizenship and the Right to Feel/Be Satisfied

Current restorative justice is linked to a focus on responding to needs. This 'needs-approach' is a feature of criminal policy and of public policy in general.

The official system is criticised as not being responsive to the citizens' needs and therefore is lacking credibility.

In the context of the establishment of the United Nations and the Universal Declaration of Human Rights, the needs approach was put forward as a matter of *rights*. The figure of the state itself was in significant measure deprived of its *raison d'être*, unless in the figure of a mediating provider of equal access by its citizens to efficient public services (Dean, 2004). The reasoning behind this was that international conflicts often resulted from long-term failure to satisfy needs combined with persistent inequalities in the capacities to meet them (Donzelot, 1994; Rosanvallon, 2011). The borders between the political and the social fields faded. Something known as 'political economy' was born. The public authority shifted from execution of sovereignty to management of interests (Donzelot, 2008; Huyse, 2014). The notion of human rights as *universal* rights opened a perspective on the overall evaporation of national sovereignty as a remainder from the past. Criminal justice, considered as a field by excellence ruled by the sovereign state, has found itself under pressure to show it is of use. The credibility of state punishment is measured by evaluating its effect on the offender's conduct, on the satisfaction of the victim and on the reassurance of the public. This approach holds a risk of slipping away into a totalitarian rationality (Foqué and 't Hart, 1990). Gutwirth and De Hert (2002; 2011) state that satisfaction of needs, however defendable it might be to strive for it, is just the wrong category from which to approach criminal justice. The current plea for victims' 'right to be restored', often heard in restorative justice circles, appears hard to combine with principles of legality and equality, and even more with the unpredictable nature of what the notion of 'restoration' in any particular case appears to consist of (Van Garsse, 2004).

This brings us back in the midst of the tensions between political principles and pragmatic effects that Social Defence was struggling with 100 years ago. The main focus was on defending and protecting the victim and all those at risk by offering assistance. In this context, a right to public assistance, '*un droit à l'assistance social*', was mentioned and a duty of the state to guarantee it for all in the danger-zone of being victimised. The emphasis was rather on prevention then on cure. The victim in focus was the dangerous victim, likely to radically call into question the credibility of the social order. The provision of 'assistance' was at the same time a matter of state security. The goal of it was peace and 'satisfaction', rather than justice. Principles of justice were indeed somehow suspended as ineffective instruments to master the threat of social disintegration and political instability. The example *par excellence* for a new approach of national policy-making was the German model of the '*Fürsorgestaat*' originating in the Bismarkian success in linking national identity and citizenship to performance in the international economic dynamics (Sachβe, 2003). This model inspired the post-war United Nations and the nation-states worldwide in their promotion of social security as the key instrument of the '*état de providence*'/ '*verzorgingsstaat*'. 'Capacity to consume' was the new feature of citizenship and the notion of 'need' the motor of any policy (Rosanvallon, 1995; 2011; Donzelot, 1994; 2008).

But how do those needs-based policies, hard to contradict, relate to politics? Some scholars question whether in the country of need and necessity, there's any place left for freedom or politics (Mouffe, 2005; Dean, 2004; Valverde, 1999). And, as far as doing justice is a matter of politics and of democratic sovereignty, a radical needs approach leaves little space for justice, seen as a result of a contradictory debate. Democracy and satisfaction have a most complicated and somehow even contradictory relationship (Arendt 2007; Mouffe, 2005; Foqué and 't Hart, 1990). In this way of reasoning, some scholars continue to warn of the bottomless, pretty normative and even authoritarian aspect in a plea for a victims' needs oriented criminal justice system (van Dijk, 2008; Gutwirth and De Hert, 2011; Fijnaut, 1983; Fattah, 1981).

C. Criminal Justice as a Matter of 'Agreement'

Restorative justice promoters criticise punishment and retribution for using violence to obtain justice. Instead, in the name of humanity and democracy, they plead for a consensual approach, with parties involved in crime coming to agreement upon the terms and conditions to put an end to any further conflict or claim (Zehr, 1990). The implicit pedagogy is towards democratic citizenship, understood as a personal capacity and preparedness to estimate a conflict as a problem to be solved, in mutual interest. Seen from this angle, restorative justice responds not so much to morality or altruism, as to a certain pragmatic self-interest, talking up responsibility being a common good, in the interest of all (Walgrave, 2008).

This whole idea very much echoes the spirit of probation, the way it was launched in the United States at the end of the nineteenth century. The concept consisted in making use of the capacities within the concrete community to conceive the social reaction to a crime in a way that would be rehabilitative, educative and restorative at the same time. It was built upon the very Anglo-Saxon presumption of common interest of all citizens as partners of a community, based upon common-sense. In this vision, needs and responsibilities eventually (sort of) merge under the umbrella of a commonly understood mutual self-interest. The appeal to the offenders' (and the community's) free collaboration is essential (Cornil, 1937; Verheyden, 1975). Conceiving justice as a dynamic communicative enterprise, eventually leading to pragmatic solutions, was seen to be a motor for 'another', more civilised justice.

The introduction of probation, however many years discussed and prepared, appeared to be a development away from justice and politics and towards prevention, security and cure, reflecting the turn at the beginning of the twentieth century (Winkel, 1980; 1981; Fijnaut, 1983; Peters, 1993). In fact, probation never escaped being identified as a public service focused upon orienting the potential offender towards social adaption, a last chance to get away from punishment (Van Garsse, 2016).

An inspired minority (many of them Dutch) warned of the eventual political consequences of a bottomless empowerment of the state-bureaucracies reducing the citizen to either a (potential) offender to be educated, or a (potential) victim to be protected. Their plea was one for de-criminalisation through active involvement of the citizen in the juridical decisions concerning him/her. Under the provocative notion of 'abolitionism' the old principle of subsidiarity was revisited and radicalised (Hulsman, 1972; 1975; Christie, 1977; Blad, 1996). The old concept of the modern preventative '*Fürsorgestaat/état de providence*', fuelled by the rediscovery of the vulnerable (virtual) victim, found itself confronted with a revival of an even older concept of a dynamic deliberative democracy, with origins dating back to the French Revolution and even further.

In this complicated context, the reception of the Anglo-Saxon notion of restorative justice, including dialogue and an 'agreement' as a new type of criminal justice outcome, could not be but layered. It simultaneously allowed tapping into a neo-liberal pragmatism and into an upcoming democratic radicalism.

The Belgian RJ development has been fascinating, in both its speed and its ideological ambiguity. Pragmatism and radicalism, educational opportunities as well as political perspectives, they were all ingredients of the complex motivation behind the sudden popularity of mediation in circles of RJ promoters and policy-makers. Depending on the programme, one out of two kinds of citizenship was in focus, as well as two corresponding definitions of 'humanisation'. The first drew upon the modern societal relevance of education (Dewey, 2009), as a tool to teach people to adapt, to think and act like a 'mature' person should, ready to respond constructively to societal requirements. The underlying humanising call to people in conflict was: 'Let's (learn to) agree, so life can continue as usual! Let's avoid public intervention by doing this privately'. The client who is not ready to come to terms, or the offender (materially) not capable of doing so, represents a problem. The other vision connected the notion of democracy as well as that of education to plurality, to conflicts of opinions and interests, and to continuous debate (Arendt, 2007; Mouffe, 1989; 2005). The underlying humanising message to people in conflict then is rather: 'Let's (learn to) disagree! Let our precious conflicts not be stolen from us! Let's explore to what extend they appear to be an opportunity for change and growth! Let's critically question the social rule! Let's provoke a deepening of public attention on this!' (Christie, 1977; Foqué and 't Hart, 1990; Van Garsse, 2008; 2012; 2016; compare Biesta, 2006; 2011).

The remarkable speed and the far-going extent to which the Belgian legislator embraced a notion such as 'restoration' as a central perspective of any juridical intervention didn't leave much space for a fundamental ideological debate. It enabled the development of several practices, but at the same time it delivered restorative justice to a multitude of 'domain-specific applications', professionally referred to through a proper selection of suitable cases, but leaving the more complicated files aside, unless post-trial. Adolphe Prins (1910) could almost not have been any closer.

IV. SOME CONCLUDING REMARKS

In the context of this chapter, the focus is on estimating the nature and the weight of the recent rise of restorative justice in the dynamics of the quest for a democratically defendable and sustainable criminal policy. Paradoxically, however, questioning the questions, it is hard to deny critical theory itself, as well as the rise of restorative justice, which was an almost predictable part of the dynamics within which criminal policy found itself. Our exploration brought us in the midst of the rise of modernist thought, with a multitude of social sciences in service of a pragmatic search for promoting progress by the use of 'better', more effective methods. The common goal of 'improvement' in some way connected the economic, the scientific and the ethical rational. This powerful pact between the three discourses tended to marginalise the ancient ontological connection between the nation-state and sovereignty, and thereby the essentialist concept of 'justice'. Justice tended to be considered as a 'function' in society, not as a matter of identity and sovereignty, but as an aspect of social management focused on social order and stability. The brand new science of criminology situated itself at the frontline of this approach. In this context, the challenge of post-war 'Social Defence' was not so much in the promotion of a determinist view of human behaviour, but more than ever in the attempt to combine a respect for socio-genetic determinants with a call for citizenship as a matter of personal responsibility (Ancel, 1965). Behind this challenge was a (too?) implicit idea of intersubjective dialogue as the foundation of a democratic criminal policy and as the proper space of 'doing justice' as such (Foqué and 't Hart, 1990; Biesta, 2009). However, even a superficial comparison of Prins' thoughts and remedies with the current focus on issues of security, crime prevention and efficiency is sobering.

We recalled the delicate post-war quest of criminology trying to position itself in the midst of the triangle between the domains of science, ideology and executive policy. In this respect, in line with the Belgian development of Social Defence, restorative justice risks producing an image of a promising academic doctrine, founding a bunch of ambivalent practices based upon a mix of findings, convictions and values. Indeed, restorative justice seems to shift between claiming the status of a science, a social movement and a cluster of practices. What exactly is there of restorative justice to evaluate, and who is in a position to do so? The current popularity of restorative justice seems to profit from, and the attempts to promote 'best practices' seem to fit very well with, the overall neo-liberal de-politisation which authors like Mouffe (2005), Donzelot (1994; 2008) and Biesta (2006; 2011) are pointing to.

This brings this chapter to a final thought. Having witnessed extensively the enormous potential of an open communication of parties involved in crime, one cannot but advocate what generally goes under the umbrella of 'restorative justice'. But a look at the historical and contextual positioning of restorative justice urges us to combine any critical analysis of restorative justice with questioning the ideology behind any use of the notion and its methods. Our plea is to radically reconsider the social positioning of restorative justice, rather than the effects of its methods. A good starting point might lie in a reflection on the notion of democratic citizenship situated in the political sphere as opposed to the social (Foqué and 't Hart, 1990; Fitzpatrick and Joyce, 2007; Valverde, 1999; Derrida, 2003). In those terms, restorative justice should be seen as expressing a political commitment, rather than as a science-based new type of feasible response to crime.

REFERENCES

Ancel, M (1965) *Social Defence: A Modern Approach to Criminal Problems* (London, Routledge & Kegan Paul).

Arendt, H (2005) *Totalitarisme* (Amsterdam, Boom, orig pub 1951).

—— (2007) 'Filosofie en politiek' in H Arendt, *Politiek in donkere tijden, Essays over vrijheid en vriendschap* (Amsterdam, Boom) 117–51.

Biesta, G (2006) *Beyond Learning: Democratic Education for a Human Future* (London, Paradigm Publishers).

—— (2009) 'Deconstruction, Justice and the Vocation of Education' in M Peters and G Biesta (eds), Derrida, Deconstruction and the Politics of Pedagogy (New York, Peter Lang Publishing) 15–38.

—— (2011) *Learning Democracy in School and Society: Education, Lifelong Learning, and the Politics of Citizenship* (Rotterdam, Boston, NJ, Taipe, Sense Publishers).

Blad, JR (1996) *Abolitionisme als strafrechtstheorie* (Arnhem, Gouda Quint).

Christiaensen, S (2004) *Tussen klassieke en moderne criminele politiek, Leven en beleid van Jules Lejeune* (Leuven, Universitaire Pers Leuven).

Christie, N (1977) 'Conflicts as Property' 1 *British Journal of Criminology* 1.

Cornil, P (1937) 'L'organisation de la rééducation morale et de la réadaptation sociale des délinquants' *Revue du Droit Pénal* 381.

Dean, H (2004) 'Human Rights and Welfare Rights: Contextualising Dependency and Responsibility' in H Dean (ed), *The Ethics of Welfare* (Bristol, Policy Press) 7–27.

Depaepe, M (2005) 'Praktijkgerichte theorie versus theoriegerichte praktijk: een "historische" paradox in de pedagogiek' in M Depaepe, F Simon and A Van Gorp (eds), *Paradoxen van de pedagogisering* (Leuven, Acco) 440–66.

Derrida, J (2003) *Voyous* (Paris, Éditions Galilée).

Dewey, J (2009) *Democracy and Education: An Introduction to the Philosophy of Education* (Milwaukee, WI, WLC Books, orig pub 1916).

Donzelot, J (1994) *L'invention du social, Essai sur le déclin des passions politiques* (Paris, Editions du Seuil).

—— (2008) 'Michel Foucault and Liberal Intelligence' 37 *Economy and Society* 115.

Duff, RA (2001) *Punishment, Communication and Community* (Oxford, Oxford University Press).

Eliaerts, C and Bitoune, R (2001) 'Herstelrecht voor minderjarigen, Theorie en praktijk' in L Dupont and F Hutsebaut, (eds), *Herstelrecht tussen toekomst en verleden* (Leuven, Universitaire Pers Leuven) 225–45.

Fattah, A (1981) 'La victimologie: entre les critiques epistémologiques et les attaques idéologiques' 5 *Déviance et Société* 72.

Fijnaut, C (1983) 'Averechtse mobilisatie van slachtoffers' 13 Delikt en delinkwent 193.

—— (1986) *Verleden, heden en toekomst van de geïntegreerde strafrechtswetenschap* (Antwerpen, Kluwer).

—— (2014) *Criminologie en strafrechtsbedeling* (Antwerp and Cambridge, Intersentia).

Fitzpatrick, P and Joyce, R (2007) 'The Normality and the Exception in Democracy's Empire' 34 *Journal of Law and Society* 65–76.

Foqué, R and ' t Hart, AC (1990) *Instrumentaliteit en rechtsbescherming* (Antwerp and Arnhem, Kluwer and Gouda Quint).

Gramatica, P (1964) *Principes de défense social* (Paris, Éditions Cujas).

Gutwirth, S (1993) *Waarheidsaanspraken in recht en wetenschap* (Brussels, VUB-press and Maklu).

Gutwirth, S and De Hert, P (2002) 'Grondslagentheoretische variaties op de grens tussen het strafrecht en het burgerlijk recht. Perspectieven op schuld- risico- en strafrechtelijke aansprakelijkheid, slachtofferclaims,buitengerechtelijke afdoening en *restorative justice*' in K Boonen, CPM Cleiren, R Foqué and Th de Roos (eds), *De Weging van' t Hart. Idealen, waarden en taken van het strafrecht* (Deventer, Kluwer) 121–70.

—— (2011) 'Punir ou réparer? Une fausse alternative' in F Tulkens, C Guillain and Y Cartuyvels (eds), *La peine dans tous ces états* (Brussels, Larcier) 67–88.

Houchon, G (1990) 'Pratiques et réseau: éloge de l'ambiguïté' 14 *Déviance et société* 213.

Hulsman, L (1972) 'Kriteria voor strafbaarstelling' in E de la Porte, C de Boer, H de Doelder, W van Gelder, M Mulder, F Orie, H de Ruijter, L Smoor-van Son and P Veling (eds), *Strafrecht te-recht? Over dekriminalisering en depenalisering* (Baarn, In den Toren) 80–92.

—— (1975) 'Justitie en welzijn' 5 *Delikt en delinkwent* 599.

Huyse, L (2014) *De democratie voorbij* (Leuven, Van Halewyck).

Kuhn, TS (1976) *De structuur van wetenschappelijke revolutie* (Amsterdam, Boom and Meppel, orig pub 1962).

Lyotard, J-F (1979) *La condition postmoderne* (Paris, Les éditions de minuit).

Mouffe, C (1989) 'Radical Democracy: Modern or Postmodern?' in C Mouffe, *Universal Abandon? The Politics of Postmodernism* (Durham, NC, Duke University Press) 31–45.

—— (2005) *Over het politieke* (Kampen, Klement and Pelckmans).

Natorp, P (1964) *Pädagogik und Philosophie* (Paderborn, Schöningh, orig pub 1905).

Nohl, H (1965) 'Die Sozialpädagogik in der Wohlfahrtsplege' in *Aufgaben und Wege der Sozialpädagogik, Vorträge und Aufsätze vor Herman Nohl* (Weinheim, Verlag Julius Betz, orig pub 1926) 17–19.

Peters, T (1993) 'Slachtofferschap: probleemanalyse, sociale en penale reacties' in T Peters and J Goethals (eds), *De achterkant van de criminaliteit* (Deurne, Kluwer Rechtswetenschappen) 5–90.

Prins, A (1910) *La défence sociale et les transformations du droit pénal* (Brussels and Paris, Misch et Thron).

Rosanvallon, P (1995) *La nouvelle question sociale, Repenser l'état-providence* (Paris, Éditions du Seuil).

—— (2011) *La société des égaux* (Paris, Seuil).

Sachβe, C (2003) *Mütterlichkeit als beruf. Sozialsarbeit, Sozialsreform und Frauenbewegung 1871–1929* (Weinheim, Basel and Berlin, Verlagsgruppe Beltz).

Valverde, M (1999) 'Derrida's Justice and Foucault's Freedom: Ethics, History, and Social Movements' *Law and Social Inquiry* 655.

Van Dijk, JJM (2008) *Slachtoffers als zondebokken* (Antwerp and Apeldoorn, Maklu).

Van Garsse, L (2004) 'Bemiddeling in de strafrechtelijke context: suggesties voor regelgeving op basis van jaren bemiddelingspraktijk' 25 *Panopticon* 47.

—— (2008) 'De implementatie van de herstelbemiddeling: veranderingsmanagement in samenspraak' 29 *Panopticon* 14.

—— (2012) 'Daders en herstel: tussen plicht, behoefte en capaciteit' in I Weijers (ed), *Slachtoffer-dadergesprekken in de schaduw van het strafproces* (Den Haag, Boom and Lemma) 59–72.

—— (2015) 'Restorative Justice in Prisons; "Do Not Enter Without Precautions"' 22 *Ljetopis socijalnog rada* 15.

—— (2016) 'Has Probation Any Impact on Reparation to Victims and Communities? Complicating a Simple Question' in F McNeill, I Durnescu and R Butter (eds), *Probation: 12 Essential Questions* (London, McMillan Pubishers) 85–106.

Verheyden, R (1975) 'De probatie tussen toekomst en verleden' *Rechtskundig weekblad* 51.

Verhoeven, C (1988) *Het medium van de waarheid. Beschouwingen over Plato's houding tegenover de poëzie* (Baarn, Ambo).

Walgrave, L (2008) *Restorative Justice, Self-interest and Responsible Citizenship* (Cullompton, Willan Publishing).

—— (2009) 'Criminologie en strafrechtelijk beleid' in W Bruggeman, E De Wree, J Goethals, P Ponsaers, P Van Calster, T Vander Beken and G Vermeulen (eds), *Van Pionier baar onmisbaar, Over 30 jaar Panopticon* (Antwerp and Apeldoorn, Maklu) 524–54.

—— (2014) 'Reflecties over de maatschappelijke verantwoordelijkheid van de criminologische wetenschap(per) (en andere maatschappijwetenschappen)' 35 *Panopticon* 288.

Winkel, FW (1980) 'Generale preventie: het gelijk van voor- en tegenstanders' 22 *Tijdschrift voor Criminologie* 113.
—— (1981) 'Sociopreventie- de rol van de samenleving in het tot stand komen van een delict' 23 Tijdschrift voor Criminologie 53.
Zehr, H (1990) *Changing Lenses: A New Focus for Crime and Justice* (Scottdale, NY, Herald Press).
Žižek, S (1998) *Pleidooi voor intolerantie* (Amsterdam, Boom).

9

*Old Goffman as a New Research Strategy in Restorative Justice**

IDA HELENE ASMUSSEN

I. DOUBLE CHALLENGE

RESEARCH WITHIN CLASSIC qualitative approaches such as phenomenology and hermeneutics seeks to immerse itself in a subject and thereby be able to uncover some kind of truth in its regard. There is thus a form of authentic core, which, though varying over time, exists prior to and independent of the researcher. Roughly put, however, no such stable kernel is found within ontological constructivism.[1] According to a constructivist approach, reality is contingent and ambiguous: it is constructed first and foremost in the meeting with the researcher (Järvinen and Mik-Meyer, 2005). Participants' needs and feelings therefore cannot be considered as expressions of stable, inherent truths, nor mediation as a process of discovery or disclosure.[2] Seen in this light, research in the area of mediation and restorative justice (hereafter RJ) presents a 'double challenge'. The assumption of truth as a social construction conflicts with the basic, classical logic inherent in both the object of the research (mediation meeting) and the research process.

* This chapter is based on a PhD thesis published as a book in Danish (Asmussen, 2014). The overall result from the PhD study is published in English (Asmussen, 2015). The case examples and quotations used in the chapter derive from the empirical part of the thesis. The data consist of observations of victim-offender mediations in Denmark in 2010, observations of RJ conferences in Norway in 2011, and interviews with the participants in both settings.

[1] This fundamental notion of truth is found among symbolic interactionists, eg, Mead, Blumer and Goffman; poststructuralist-inspired researchers, eg, Latour and Fairclough; structuralist constructivists, eg, Bourdieu; and classic American constructivists, eg, Berger and Luckmann (Järvinen and Mik-Meyer, 2005).

[2] Given their dominance, I refer to the interest-based and problem-solving mediation models (Wall and Dunne, 2012). However, other mediation models based on constructivist social theory have been developed and practised, most consistently in narrative mediation (Winslade and Monk, 2008; Winslade, 2006).

What follows is a suggestion for how this 'double challenge' can be dealt with. As later elaborated upon, I consider Erving Goffman's role theory and his theory of interaction order as particularly relevant, though I will also draw upon additional theories that explore linguistic interaction as the purest expression of social constructivism (ie, ethnomethodology; conversation analysis (CA); positioning theory; discourse psychology).

II. AN INTERACTIONIST VIEW AT THE RJ MEETING

Becker's book, *Outsiders* (1966), which is a classic in interactionism,[3] redirects our attention from the individual deviant's background and personality, to the interactions and control processes that contribute to the creation of deviance. Becker shows that deviance is a relative phenomenon that is created and modified primarily via processes of social definition (Järvinen and Mik-Meyer, 2005). Deviants are created through a process of definition: 'The world is continually remade as it is expected to be' (Potter, 2012: 66). The processes of definition are thus more worthy of study than the deviants themselves. Becker therefore believes that a scientist with an unresolved analytical perspective risks subconsciously adopting official or other established positions on social deviance and thereby reproducing existing knowledge (Järvinen and Mik-Meyer, 2005). This critique is used as a more general objection to phenomenological research, which, without formulating a theoretically-grounded analytical framework, conducts empirical research with an underlying ideal of atheoretical, value-neutral, inductive positions and thereby risks re-confirming the researcher's own presuppositions (Bourdieu, 1993). The researcher herself is therefore by no means immune to these definitional processes and is herself a product of social definition. Scientists run the same risks when exploring the concept of mediation theory in mediation sessions: 'Description becomes inscription' (Denzin, 1999: 312–13). This could also be described by Potter's words that one never 'just' describes something objectively 'as it is', but always 'does' something by the way of describing (Potter, 2012: 47).

Let me provide an example. The following passage is drawn from an exchange between an offender and a series of victims whose houses he has broken into. The exchange is taken from the end of a victim-offender mediation session (hereafter 'VOM session'):

(Case 1)

Heather (victim): It is very commendable of Ray to participate in this.

[3] Other classics include Mead (1934); Blumer (1969); Goffman (eg, 1968); Holstein and Miller (1993); Gubrium and Holstein (eg, 2004).

Stone (victim): This has been a positive experience. I hope you get your life together.

Harry (victim): I am hungry. I can't wait to get home.

Ray (offender): Thank you for letting me be who I am. I see this meeting as a sign of new times.

Joe (victim), sharply: All we need now is your apology, Ray.

Ray (offender): I'm so very sorry.

Heather (victim): I hope we haven't been too harsh on you.

Joe (victim): Let's not make things too rosy.

Scanning the dialogue for needs that victims might be expected to express at an RJ meeting, one can consider Joe's first statement as a need for an apology. But is it possible that Joe's request for an apology was provoked by the altruistic comments of the other participants? Is Joe just as likely to have asked for an apology if the others had expressed anger towards the offender?

An interactionist approach focuses on shared meaning created in the course of interaction. When the interaction is considered meaningful and truth-producing, the actions and expressions cannot be interpreted without reference to their context. While research suggests that dialogue cannot in and of itself be considered solely as positive or potentially liberating for the participants (Adelswärd, 1995; Jacobsson *et al*, 2012: 230), there is only a limited amount of qualitative, micro-sociological research in RJ processes (Vanfraechem *et al*, 2010). Researchers have therefore called for more in-depth studies of RJ process dynamics (Braithwaite, 2002; 2006; Daly, 2001; Daly and Stubbs, 2006; Harris *et al*, 2004, all as cited in Rossner, 2011: 95).

A limited number of newer, qualitative studies that borrow from Goffman are already available (eg, Asmussen 2014; 2015; Bruce, 2013; Rossner, 2011; 2013; Dignan *et al*, 2007; Shapland *et al*, 2006). Yet as I will try to show here, I see especially fruitful possibilities in combining Goffman's interactionist take on the production of the self with the Chicago School's empirical, micro-sociological approach to interactionist research. The interactionist premise on shifting the focus from individual motivation and intentionality to social interaction leads to Goffman's explorations of the ways in which interaction is used to maintain and create specific impressions of one-self and others.

The applied notion of context concurs directly with the CA term *doing-being* in the construction of identity (Sacks, 1984). The point is that we can only observe what individuals do, not what they 'are', for example, doing-tired by yawning or doing-happy by smiling. Identity is thus rather what we project in the presence of others than an expression of who we 'are'.

III. THE PERFORMING SELF

The background for Goffman's interest in face-to-face meetings is his thesis that the moment 'an individual enters the presence of others' (Goffman, 1959: 13) a series of projective and interactive processes are initiated that set the framework for human expression and the understanding of the self and the world around one. This implies that the way one presents oneself is always situated and relationally contingent upon how 'the other' is perceived. Goffman illustrates this by reference to Willard Wallner's study of a girls' dormitory: 'It has been reported by many observers that a girl who is called to the telephone in the dormitories will often allow herself to be called several times, in order to give all the other girls ample opportunity to hear her paged' (Goffman, 1959: 4). As I shall explain below, the idea of 'the other' is central to Goffman's idea of the self as resulting from a mutual interpretative and projective process.[4]

Goffman distinguishes between two types of face-to-face meetings: the *unfocused* and the *focused*. The unfocused meetings are the brief, casual, interpersonal communications that arise when two people find themselves in the same sphere, as when two strangers pass one another observing each other's appearance and adjusting their own demeanour in response (Goffman, 1961c: 7). A focused meeting, on the other hand, is an interaction where the parties temporarily agree to focus upon one another. There is a common focus, an agenda (at least, in a broad sense) and norms of behaviour. Norms, for example, define how a meeting should begin and end (eg, whether one gives a handshake, a hug, a nod, or simply arrives or leave). Parties to focused meetings favour one another with face-to-face attention, which optimises opportunities for perceiving the processes of definition. The mere 'setting' of an RJ meeting is, according to Goffman's thinking, likely to instil an expectation among participants that they should orient themselves toward each other. This orientation towards each other means that 'a "we rationale" is likely to emerge, that is a sense of the single thing that *we* are doing together at the time' (Goffman, 1961c: 18).

According to Goffman, we assume an interpretive stance in any social context. This stance becomes the basis for each individual to lay down a 'line—that is, a pattern of verbal and nonverbal acts by which he expresses his view of the situation and through this his evaluation of the participants, especially himself' (Goffman, 1982: 5). This line we lay down establishes a range of possibilities and limitations that to a certain extent become fixed: 'Once the person initially presents a line, he and the others tend to build

[4] The notion that human behaviour involves the calculation of how others will interpret one's behaviour, and that the positioning of the self inherently implies a positioning of others, is inspired by Mead (1934).

their later responses on it, and in a sense become stuck with it' (Goffman, 1982: 11).

Construction of the line may proceed more or less consciously, and those present will attempt to decipher what *face*, ie, positive self-image, the person is communicating and attempt to help him maintain that face. Goffman uses the concept of face as a kind of visualisation of the social self-image a person wishes to convey in a particular context. Inspiration for the face one adopts is based on rituals and codes of normative behaviour. The notion that one should help others to maintain face is itself one of these normative rules—what Goffman terms 'the traffic rules of social interaction' (Goffman, 1982: 12).

Face is seen as an emotional issue, a delicate expression of the whole person (Jacobsen and Kristiansen, 2002: 112). Face is therefore inviolable, and the interaction order, ie unspoken norms and rituals of interaction, can be seen as the membrane we all guard in order to protect our own and others' faces. This also entails temporarily accepting the lines presented by others: 'It is typically a "working" acceptance, not a "real" one, since it tends to be based not on agreement of candidly expressed heart-felt evaluations, but upon a willingness to give temporary lip service to judgments with which the participants do not really agree.' (Jacobsen and Kristiansen, 2002: 11). Facework is connected to the process of definition, and it is this dimension of the RJ session that I wish to put the focus on. The perspective is of course also relevant in mediation sessions in general, but I find it especially important with regard to RJ, because the focal point in a criminal case is less likely to be a case of two 'morally equivalent' parties.

IV. RJ STAGE

William Shakespeare may have been the first to call the world a stage, but Goffman was the first sociologist to use the *stage* and the *play* (Goffman, esp. 1959) as a metaphor for the behaviour that people exhibit when others are present. With his drama metaphor, Goffman emphasises that the person has, on the one hand, been given a role—a limited framework for action defined by the context's normative expectations, and that he is constantly forced to both play his role and act as audience to the roles of others: 'No audience, no performance' (Goffman, 1974: 125) and vice versa. The drama can therefore be regarded as the result of a mutual and continuous process of interpretation that takes place on a particular social stage, for example, at an RJ meeting. This puts the focus on the fundamental question: what is created on an RJ stage? What expectations do the participants have for themselves and each other at an RJ session? This can be clarified by analysing positioning, self-presentation and interactional strategies by means of methods like discourse analysis, positioning theory and conversation analysis (CA).

Goffman differentiates *front stage* from *back stage* behaviours, ie those one exhibits in the presence of others versus those performed in non-social settings where 'impression management' is not a concern. These concepts can be used to distinguish between interactions that take place during an RJ meeting (front stage) and those that occur before the start of the meeting, during breaks or after the meeting's conclusion (back stage). The RJ session's front stage also includes 'props' such as the coffee, tea, fruit, cake and candy that is prepared for the meeting before the actors arrive. Backstage the session's mediator has the possibility to express critiques of himself, other participants, or other aspects of the session without being considered unprofessional or unethical (Åkerstrøm, 1995). For example, I observed a mediator who having said goodbye to the session's participants, closed the door and turned to me with resignation and heaven-turned eyes (Asmussen, 2014). Similarly, there were some mediators who informed me of their preconceived notions concerning some of the participants prior to a meeting. For example, I was told that one of the parties had seemed 'heavy' on the telephone.

A backstage analysis could explore the mediators' discussions concerning the physical arrangement of the meeting locale, such as the placement of chairs and tables, who should sit where etc to shed light on the mediators' expectations and agendas.[5]

V. FRAMING

With his book, *Frame Analysis* (1974), Goffman sets focus on what the players bring to the concrete, social interaction. For this purpose he uses yet another metaphor: when we form an opinion about events and people, we *frame* what we see in a specific way. We organise what we experience based on some normative principles that suggest that one interpretation is more plausible than another. The frame is something the actors both produce and are a product of (Goffman, 1974; Branaman, 2004: ixxiv).

In 'Felicity's Condition' (1983), among other works, Goffman further elaborates on the notion of framing and describes the presuppositions or implicit background assumptions that condition a meaningful interaction. Let me provide an example. In this situation I had just observed a VOM session and immediately afterwards one of the participants and I went together while talking, because he had agreed on an interview with me. During our conversation he told me that he was 'dying for a cup of coffee', but hadn't

[5] Recent studies employing front-stage/back-stage analytics include Bruce (2013) and Portillo *et al* (2013), though the latter does so only in connection with judges in problem-solving courts.

taken a single sip at the meeting because he was 'a bundle of nerves'. When we sat down in a room with a coffee machine, I said: 'Milk or sugar?' to which he replied 'black'. On its own, this exchange of words is incomprehensible and meaningless. Nonetheless, neither he nor I had any doubt that what I meant was that I wanted to buy him a cup of coffee and needed to know whether he used anything in his coffee. Likewise, there was no doubt that his answer was that he didn't use anything in his coffee. It is therefore the underlying set of rules 'that leads us to judge an individual's verbal acts to be not a manifestation of strangeness. Behind *Felicity's Condition* is our sense of what it is to be sane' (Goffman, 1983: 27). Goffman is not simply saying that we 'fill in' the blanks when a person utters a limited number of words. He is also talking about our presumptions. For example, in the scenario just described, I presume that the interviewee has also noticed the coffee machine, that he would like a cup of coffee and that he is not 'a bundle of nerves' when talking to me. None of these assumptions are explicit in the question I asked him. Yet the fact that the question still makes sense and can be immediately answered indicates that 'we are forced beyond that which appears to be the primary surface of meaning, the utterances themselves. We must address not another's words, but their mind, their capacity to understand what is going on' (Lemert, 2004: xi).[6]

Empirical observation of presuppositions can, for example, contribute to the analysis of positions and strategies. Take a look at the following exchange recorded at a VOM session:

(Case 2)

Mediator: Why did you do it [commit crime]?

Sam (young offender): It just happened. I didn't think so much about it.

The mediator here assumes that Sam knows why he committed the crime and that he will be willing to explain his actions at the meeting. An interpretation focused solely on the topic of interaction would probably conclude that the crime was a straightforward act of impulse. With an answer related to the process of definition, Sam's reply can be interpreted as an expression of his unwillingness to let himself be positioned in roles as 'the child, who should be ashamed of himself', 'the criminal, who should explain himself', or 'the sinner, who should repent his sins'. In light of a tendency found in

[6] It was the desire to explicate such unspoken norms and expectations in specific social contexts that formed the basis for Harold Garfinkel's (1967) noted analytical method, 'Garfinkeling'. The method consists of doing something other than that which is expected in a given situation and then observing people's reactions. For example, Garfinkel asked his students to go home to their parents and behave like hotel guests. In addition to exposing various norms that are taken for granted, Garfinkel used his experiments to demonstrate that the social order is not determined from above, but that it is people who maintain and/or revise it.

the data for young men to demonstrate a recurring pattern of withdrawal and disengagement (Asmussen, 2014), Sam's answer might be seen as an expression of resignation or resistance to letting himself be controlled by the VOM session's expectations of self-reflection and emotional articulation—expectations that can be difficult to reconcile with traditional notions of masculinity as expressions of strength, authority and control (Kiesling, 2005).

Another central concept is *keying*. Keying is the framing of a situation on the basis of a similar situation. Goffman borrows this concept from Gregory Bateson (Jacobsen and Kristiansen, 2002: 148), who developed it in connection with his studies of primate behaviour. Bateson's main contention is that when apes play, they borrow meaning from a different, yet similarly-structured situation: the fight. 'In play, apes bite as if it were serious, but they don't bite hard' (Jacobsen and Kristiansen, 2002: 148). Likewise, Goffman argues that when framing a given situation, people transfer meaning from analogous known situations. For example, young offenders at an RJ conference in Norway introduced themselves in a way that seems to reflect the keying of an Alcoholics Anonymous meeting (Case 3): 'My name is Robert and I have done something stupid'. The mediators then looked at the second offender in the room, who said: 'My name is Kim and I have also done something stupid'. When the young men key the RJ session as an AA meeting, they seem to be framing it on the basis of some kind of 'confessional situation' (Asmussen, 2014; 2015).

As shown, Goffman presents two sides of the self: the self as a product of social structure, that transcends the situation and defines guidelines for and limitations on individual expression (Branaman, 2004: xlvii; Manning 2000; Mik-Meyer and Villadsen, 2013: 31), and the self as manipulatively and considerately supporting specific lines and faces. As Branaman describes it: 'The self is the mask the individual wears in social situations, but also the human being behind the mask who decides which mask to wear' (Branaman, 2004: xlviii). This dualistic approach to the self as both producing and produced by social norms[7] is analytically fruitful, since it keeps the researcher open to diverse ways of interpretation.[8]

[7] It has been pointed out that his early writing, especially *The Presentation of Self in Everyday Life* (1959), seems to stress a more autonomous individual than his later writings, where the individual seems more structurally limited. Goffman thus seems to distance himself both from reducing interaction to nothing more than the sum of two peoples' situated conduct and from seeing the actors as transparent 'agents of structure' (Giddens, 2000: 169).

[8] From my perspective, Goffman's stance is also a result of his penchant for provocation and a tendency to put his views bluntly using heuristic and metaphorical clarifications. It is thus clear that expressions such as [one's] 'face' 'is only on loan to him from society' and 'approved attributes and their relation to face make every man his own jailer' (Goffman, 1982: 10) do not leave much room for an autonomous self. Yet meanwhile, role theory focuses on how the individual actively attempts to construct a specific impression of himself (Goffman, 1959; 1961a).

An obvious objective for the qualitative analysis of RJ sessions is an examination of the participants' positions as both models for and expressions of the meeting's norms. Goffman describes this as the primary purpose of role analysis (Goffman, 1961a: 86–87).

VI. POSITIONS

Roles are assigned on the basis of a particular definition of the situation. A particular definition is 'in charge of the situation', as Goffman puts it (1961a: 133). By this, he refers to the basis for interpretation that the immediate situation gives rise to. The basis for interpretation can be examined, for example, by looking at how the definition of the situation and the relevant positions are negotiated. Goffman speaks of an interactional *modus vivendi* and uses it to clarify his thesis that all interacting attempts to contribute to a common, general definition of the situation, reflect not a real consensus, but rather a consensus on avoiding open conflict and loss of face.[9] Conversational exchanges are therefore not only expressions of a theme, but also attempts to adapt one's face to the normative expectations of the situation (Goffman, 1982).

Rom Harré's notion of positions can be useful in regard to the situation-specific and dynamic interactionist perspective where roles are continuously constructed and negotiated in social life (for example, Harré and Slocum, 2003: 104), while 'role' as used by both Goffman and traditional social psychological and sociological role theorists has a more determinant and stable character.

Harré and Moghaddam (2003: 5) define a position as 'a loose set of rights and duties that limit the possibilities of action'. The notion of position is related to positioning.[10] Inspired by Goffman, positioning is what one does when one puts oneself or others in specific positions (Bronwyn and Harré, 1990). For example, I observed a mediator initiate an RJ session by stating: 'I am neutral and I'm not on anyone's side'. With this, he presupposes that the parties are in conflict (that there is a need for a 'neutral' person) and positions himself as one capable of maintaining a neutral stance. At the same time, he positions the parties as 'biased'. The mediator here draws on the narrative that 'warring parties need a neutral third party'.

[9] Goffman elaborates on the concept of losing face as being in *wrong face*, *out of face* or *shamefaced*.

[10] The notion of 'positioning' was first used by Wendy Hollway in her 1984 analysis of gender and subjectivity (Harré and Langenhove, 1991: 395). Since then, the concept has been refined, especially within positioning theory, as formulated in particular by Rom Harré, Bronwyn Davies, Luk Van Langenhove and Fathali Moghaddam.

VII. FACE TESTING

Goffman has exhaustively described the positioning of others in socially and culturally *discredited roles*. In his books *Asylums* (1961b) and *Stigma* (1968) he explores the ways in which *discrediting* and *stigmatising* characteristics are managed within the interaction order.

That the concept of stigmatisation is particularly relevant to the RJ context stems from the fact that VOM sessions are conducted *precisely because* one person has committed a crime against another. It therefore lies in the meeting's 'nature' that the offender per se bears a stigma. Stigma is defined as a deeply discrediting characteristic that leads to stereotype labelling (Goffman, 1968: 13). Moreover, given that the meeting focuses on a criminal event, the alleged offender cannot just pass it off. *Passing* is Goffman's expression for when a potentially discredited actor attempts to conceal stigmatising information about him or herself. Likewise, the victim can hardly avoid (simply by virtue of his or her presence in the room) to be witness to a face-threatening situation and thereby embarrassed. And it is precisely these situations that Goffman says we try to avoid because of identification with others and a tacit social understanding that we as civilised people protect each other's faces. If exposed, the stigma becomes, as Goffman would say, *obtrusive* in the situation (Goffman, 1968: 66).

Goffman defines stigma as the discrepancy between a person's *apparent* (as in observable) and *actual* identity (Jacobsen and Kristiansen, 2010: 20). Those who violate the law constitute a textbook example of a group which, due to labelling and definitional processes discussed earlier, is transformed from having committed a criminal act to belonging to a marginalised, stereotyped category: *the criminal*: 'A stigma, then, is really a special kind of relationship between attribute and stereotype' (Goffman, 1968: 14). In the Case 1 example provided above (where multiple victims approach the alleged offender, Ray, with an altruistic discourse), the victim Heather says: 'It is very commendable of Ray to participate in this'. It is the unspoken 'criminal' stigma that makes this statement meaningful. This makes it all the more impressive that Ray lets himself be confronted even though it reveals his stigma.

Stigma is both a deprivation of positive personal characteristics (*role dispossession*, Goffman, 1961b) and an attribution of various negative characteristics ('role ascription', Asmussen, 2014). This implies a number of obviously adverse consequences, but what is most relevant in the current context is the import it has for the interaction between the parties. Goffman argues that the ambivalence that is embedded in an individual's relation to the stigmatised category (for example, the criminal) can encourage *information control* by discredited actors. In other words, the discredited actor may monitor and control what he says about himself because of its explosive implications for the interaction's process of definition. The offender at an RJ session will normally have acknowledged having committed the criminal offence and will typically be reluctant to allow 'more of the same crap' to come out. This applies especially to circumstances which, when viewed in light of conventional standards, might suggest *other* characteristics associated with criminality such as unemployment, lack of education, alcohol or drug abuse, or a deviant or non-existent social network: 'It is a fact that persons who are ready to admit possession of a stigma (in many cases because it is known about or immediately apparent) may nonetheless make a great effort to keep the stigma from looming large' (Goffman, 1968: 125).

The interaction may become especially tense in the built-in asymmetry between 'normal' and 'stigmatised' individuals (Goffman, 1968). After all, it is hard to imagine a situation in which an offender's face is more vulnerable than when he is placed together with the victim he has violated. To some extent this also applies to the victim, for as Goffman points out, no one enjoys being present when a face is threatened (Goffman, 1982). From Goffman's perspective, RJ sessions may therefore be seen as a comprehensive form of 'face-testing' (Asmussen, 2014; 2015). Goffman describes that confusion and uncertainty arises in both parties when someone's face is threatened. Should the victim, for example, 'avoid noticing' more stigmatising information about the offender?

VIII. CONCLUSION AND PERSPECTIVES

As shown, Goffman is not including notions of the personal psyche or intentions of the participants, but focuses on expressions and representations of feelings in interactions and their impact on relational dynamics. These expressions of feelings are interpreted as responses to the specific context and not as stable expressions of a permanent state of mind. From an interactionist perspective, the human frame of reference is conditional and ever-changing. It is therefore more expedient to explore which frames of reference appear in which contexts and how they interact than to examine the 'private' experience of the individual (Järvinen and Mik-Meyer, 2005). This focus is one of the limitations of the sociological enterprise (inspired by Waksler, 1989): we only have an indirect, filtered understanding of the human psyche, since our knowledge rests on assumptions made on the basis of behaviour (Goffman, 1959).

The purpose of a conversation may be the exchange of views, problem solving, task resolution, or in the case of RJ mediation sessions, the deliberation of a certain episode, but for the interaction to 'run smoothly', that is without anyone losing face, both parties concurrently carry out the so-called face-work. According to Goffman, this practice of a system of mutual understanding is enacted due to the inherent expectation in any human encounter that we, through spontaneous identification, will strive to assist the other person in maintaining face.

If the process of definition, including face-work, is not included in research into RJ sessions, their statements and actions will be interpreted as a direct expression of how they feel. For example, if a participant apologises, I will have to assume that this indicates that the person feels guilty—not just at some point during the meeting, but on the whole. However, doing so would cause us to overlook that which Goffman in 1964 called 'the neglected situation', ie what the participants do to protect themselves, the others and the situation. If words and actions are considered expressions of context as opposed to manifestations of stable and inherent personal authenticity, the research will say more about the context and less about persons as private or psychological selves. Attention to the interaction's process of definition not only opens up a more reliable analysis, but also for contributions to understanding the complex, micro-sociological processes that can deepen and clarify the norms and patterns that characterise RJ meetings.[11]

CASES QUOTED

Case 1: Break-in at summerhouses, one offender (Ray) with supporter, 11 victims (among these, Joe), Denmark.

Case 2: Repeated thefts, two offenders with one and two supporters, respectively, one victim with one supporter, Denmark.

Case 3: Vandalism on private property, conference, three offenders, one with supporter, one with a government representative and two victims with one supporter, Norway.

REFERENCES

Adelswärd, V (1995) 'Institutionella Samtal—struktur, moral och rationalitet' ['Institutional Conversation: Structure, Ethics and Rationality'] 36 *Folkmålsstudier* 109.

Åkerstrøm, M (1995) 'Sociologisms and Sarcasm in Swedish Shelters' 28(2) *Sociological Focus* 147–159.

Asmussen, IH (2014) *Fra Retsstat til Omsorgsstat—om syndsforladelse i konfliktråd* [*From State of Law to State of Caring: On Absolution in a Conflict Mediation Setting*] (DJØF).

—— (2015) 'Performing Absolution Narratives in Restorative Justice' 3(1) *Restorative Justice, An international Journal* 28.

[11] The normative pattern, which appeared by exploring constructions of selves in a study of VOM sessions in Denmark, was drawn from the Christian absolution, see Asmussen, 2015.

Becker, W (1966) *Outsiders* (New York, Free Press).
Blumer, H (1969) *Symbolic Interactionism* (Berkeley, CA/Los Angeles, CA/London, University of California Press).
Bourdieu, P (1993) *Sociology in Question* (London, SAGE Publications).
Branaman, A (2004) 'Goffman's Social Theory' in C Lemert and A Branaman (eds), *The Goffman Reader* (Oxford, Blackwell Publishing).
Bronwyn, D and Harré, R (1990): 'Positioning: The Discursive Production of Selves' 20(1) *Journal for the Theory of Social Behaviour* 43, available at www.massey.ac.nz/~alock/position/position.htm.
Bruce, J (2013) 'Understanding "Backstage" and "Front Stage" in Restorative Justice Conferences: The Benefits of Using Ethnographic Techniques' 25(1) *Current Issues in Criminal Justice* 517.
Davies, B and Harré, R (1990) 'Positioning: The Discursive Production of Selves' 20(1) *Journal for the Theory of Social Behaviour* 43.
Denzin, NK (1999) 'Evaluating Qualitative Research in the Poststructural Moment' in A Bryman and RG Burgess (eds), *Qualitative Research* (London, SAGE Publications).
Dignan, J, Atkinson, A, Atkinson H, Hoes, M, Robinson, G, Shapland, J and Sorsby, A (2007) 'Staging Restorative Justice Encounters against a Criminal Justice Backdrop: A Dramaturgical Analysis' 7(1) *Criminology and Criminal Justice* 5.
Dingwall, R (1997) 'Accounts, Interviews and Observations' in R Dingwall and D Miller (eds), *Context and Method in Qualitative Research* (London, SAGE Publications).
Garfinkel, H (1967) *Studies in Ethnomethodology* (Cambridge, Polity Press).
Giddens, A (2000) 'Goffman as a Systematic Social Theorist' in GA Fine and GWH Smith (eds), *Erving Goffman*, vol 4, Sage Masters of Modern Thought (Thousand Oaks, CA, SAGE Publications) 151–75.
Goffman, E (1959) *The Presentation of Self in Everyday Life* (New York, Anchor Books).
—— (1961a) 'Role Distance' in E Goffman, *Encounters* (New York, Cornell University Press).
—— (1961b) *Asylums: Essays on the Social Situation of Mental Patients and Other Inmates* (Chicago, IL, Aldine Publishing Co).
—— (1961c) *Encounters* (New York, Cornell University Press).
—— (1964) 'The Neglected Situation' in 66(2) *American Anthropologist.*
—— (1968) *Stigma: Notes on the Management of Spoiled Identity* (London, Penguin Books).
—— (1974) *Frame Analysis* (New York, Harper & Row).
—— (1982) *Interaction Ritual: Essays on Face-to-Face Behaviour* (New York, Pantheon Books).
—— (1983) 'Felicity's Condition' 89 *American Journal of Sociology* 1.
Gubrium, JF and Holstein, JA (2004) *The Active Interview* (Thousand Oaks, CA, SAGE Publications).
Harré, R and Langenhove, L (1991) 'Varieties of Positioning' 21(4) *Journal of the Theory of Social Behaviour* 393.
Harré, R and Moghaddam, F (2003) 'Introduction: The Self and Others in Traditional Psychology and in Positioning Theory' in R Harré and F Moghadam, *The*

Self and Others: Positioning Individuals and Groups in Personal, Political, and Cultural Contexts (London, Praeger).

Harré, R and Slocum, N (2003) *Disputes as Complex Social Events* (Durham, NC, Duke University Press).

Hasund, IK and Hydle, H (2007) *Ansikt til ansikt—konfliktrådsmegling mellom gjerningsperson og offer i voldssaker* [*Face to Face: Conflict Mediation Between Perpetrator and Victim in Cases of Violence*] (Oslo, Cappelen Akademisk Forlag AS).

Holstein, JA and Miller, G (eds) (1993) *Reconsidering Social Constructionism: Debates in Social Problems Theory* (New Brunswick and Piscataway, NJ, Transaction Publishers).

Jacobsen, M and Kristiansen, S (2002) *Erving Goffman—Sociologien om det elementære livs sociale former* [*Erving Goffman: Sociology of the Social Forms of Elementary Life*] (Copenhagen, Hans Reitzels Forlag).

—— (2010) 'De ødelagte identiteters sociologi' ['The Sociology of Destroyed Identity'], Foreword to Danish translation of E Goffman, *Stigma* (Frederiksberg, Samfundslitteratur).

Jacobsson, M, Wahlin, L and Andersson, T (2012) 'Victim-Offender Mediation in Sweden: Is the Victim Better Off?' 18 *International Review of Victimology* 229.

Järvinen, M and Mik-Meyer, N (2005) 'Indledning' ('Preface') to *Kvalitative metoder i et interaktionistisk perspektiv* [*Qualitative Methods in an Interactionist Perspective*] (Copenhagen, Hans Reitzels Forlag).

Kiesling, S. F. (2005) 'Homosocial Desire in Men´s Talk: Balancing and Re-creating Cultural Discourses of Masculinity', *Language in Society*, vol 34, p. 695–726.

Lemert, E (2004) 'Goffman' in C Lemert and A Branaman (eds), *The Goffman Reader* (Oxford, Blackwell Publishing).

Manning, P (2000) 'Credibility, Agency, and the Interaction Order' 23(3) *Symbolic Interaction* 283.

Mead, GH (1934) *Mind, Self and Society: From the Standpoint of a Social Behaviorist* (Chicago, IL, University of Chicago Press) 178.

Mik-Meyer, N and Villadsen, K (2013) Power and Welfare: Understanding *Citizens' Encounters with State Welfare*, Routledge Advances in Health and Social Policy (New York, Routledge).

Portillo, S, Rudes, D, Viglione, J and Taxman, F (2013) 'Front-stage Stars and Backstage Producers: The Role of Judges in Problem-Solving Courts' 8(1) *Victims and Offenders Journal* 1.

Potter, J (2012) *Representing Reality: Discourse, Rhetoric and Social Construction* (London, SAGE Publications).

Rossner, M (2011) 'Emotions and Interaction Ritual: A Micro Analysis of Restorative Justice' *British Journal of Criminology* 95.

—— (2013) *Just Emotions: Rituals of Restorative Justice* (Oxford, Oxford University Press).

Ryding, A (2005) *Välviljans variationer—moraliske gränsdragningar inom brottsofferjourer* [*Variations in Benevolence: Moral Boundaries in Victim Support*] (Dissertation in Sociology, Lund University).

Sacks, H (1984) 'Notes on Methodology' in JM Atkinson and JC Heritage (eds), *Structures of Social Interaction: Studies in Conversation Analysis* (Cambridge, University of Cambridge) 21–27.

Shapland J, Atkinson, A, Atkinson, H, Colledge, E, Dignan, J, Howes, M, Johnstone, J, Robinson, G and Sorsby, A (2006) 'Situating Restorative Justice within Criminal Justice' 10(4) *Theoretical Criminology* 505.

Stax, T (2005) *Duetter fra anden sal—et interaktionelt perspektiv på samtaler mellem hjemløse og socialarbejdere* [*Duets from Another Room: An Interactional Perspective on Conversations Between Homeless People and Social Workers*] (PhD Dissertation, Institute of Sociology, University of Copenhagen).

Vanfraechem, I, Aertsen, I and Willemsens, J (2010) *Restorative Justice Realities: Empirical Research in a European Context* (The Hague, Eleven International Publishing).

Waksler, CF (1989) 'Erving Goffman's Sociology: An Introductory Essay' 12 *Human Studies* 1.

Wall, J and Dunne, T (2012) 'State of the Art, Mediation Research: A Current Review' *Negotiation Journal*.

Winslade, J (2006) 'Mediation with a Focus on Discursive Positioning' 23(4) *Conflict Resolution Quarterly* 501.

Winslade, J and Monk, G (2008) *Practising Narrative Mediation* (New York, Jossey-Bass).

10

Lifeworld, Law and Justice

KATRIN KREMMEL AND CHRISTA PELIKAN

I. INTRODUCTION: RESTORATIVE JUSTICE AND THE IMPORTANCE OF THE LIFEWORLD

WE HAVE TAKEN recourse to the concept of the lifeworld quite early in our attempts at delineating core elements of restorative justice. We have used it deliberately in an effort to transcend the common prevalent use of concepts like 'harm' and 'need'. It was an effort to denominate those essential features that make for the difference between restorative justice and the criminal justice system (CJS), in other words: to catch those differences that make a difference! (Bateson, 2000: 453).

We have arrived at distinguishing three core elements of restorative justice, caught as differences. They are: lifeworld versus system-oriented; participation versus delegation; and reparation versus retribution/punishment. We will further explain these core elements.

(a) *The 'lifeworld' element.* In restorative justice discourse, crime is considered disruption or disturbance of human relations, and therefore a response to crime means starting from and attending to the immediate experience of the persons involved, the experience of doing, of hurting or harming somebody and the experience of suffering from somebody else's doing, of being done-to (Benjamin, 2004). The emphasis is on the interaction, ie what happened in-between these persons or groups of persons.
(b) *The participatory element.* This implies the active participation of those concerned and affected by the conflict to become part of the effort to achieve reparation and reconciliation, and promotes 'taking responsibility', especially on the part of the offender.
(c) *The reparative element.* Concentrating on the conflict, understood as a disruption of social relations, will lead the search for ways of making good, for reparation and for transformation. The active involvement of victim and offender in this process makes it possible to meet the 'real' needs of both of them.

The three elements are inextricably linked, more precisely, they are interdependent. It affords the perception of an act of wrongdoing as an interaction of doer and done-to to provide the ground for the active involvement of those concerned and/or affected. Since it is about their relationship and the disturbance, or the break of trust (Ragazzi, 2015) that has occurred, they are called to enter a dialogue. And it follows from this concern about their concrete experiences that this exchange evolves about reparation, around setting right the wrong that has occurred and the reparation of its consequences in a very concrete way (Pali and Pelikan, 2010; 2014).

While the participatory and the reparative element of restorative justice are well established and generally accepted by researchers and practitioners, we have sensed some apprehensions and also confusion concerning the concept of the lifeworld.

We will therefore raise the following questions: What is the 'lifeworld'? What does the Habermasian concept of the lifeworld entail? What is its place within Habermas' theoretical edifice? And why do we use it as a core element of restorative justice? How is justice achieved via attending to the lifeworld of those involved in an act of wrongdoing—both as victim and offender?

II. ATTENDING TO THE LIFEWORLD IN RESTORATIVE JUSTICE PROCEDURES: EMPIRICAL EVIDENCE

We will, in order to answer these questions, draw from empirical evidence produced in the course of two research projects targeted at one of the most controversial topics in restorative justice practices, the topic of domestic violence. Austria was one of the first countries to apply victim-offender mediation (VOM) rather widely in those cases, and has very early met with the critique of the protagonists of the women's movement. The research projects, commissioned by the Austrian Ministry of Justice, the first one jointly with the Ministry of Family Affairs and the Ministry of the Interior, the second one by Neustart, the organisation responsible for carrying out VOM, were designed to supply the policy-makers of the Ministry and the practitioners of the VOM services with solid evidence as to the effects of this practice on the victims and the offenders in cases of domestic violence.

The first research effort, executed in the years 1998–2000, was based on the observation of VOM procedures, on the one hand, and of criminal procedures, on the other hand, as well as on interviews with victims and offenders that were repeated after a time interval of six to 12 months. The result of this first study had evoked the author's provocative summarising statement that 'Men don't get better, but women get stronger' (Pelikan, 2010; 2012). In other words: it was the women whose claim to a partnership free of violence had been confirmed and reinforced by the VOM intervention, while a deep-reaching inner change of the men had occurred only very rarely.

This kind of result deviated from a preconceived notion of individual prevention as the most important effect of any intervention within criminal law. We had to face up to the inconvenient fact that the expected and desired effect of 'making the offender a better human being' did not come true—at least not to the extent protagonists of restorative justice might have hoped for.

But, listening very closely to the women and the men in the VOM process and in the interviews, the authors of the study had arrived at a typology of the restorative process (Pelikan and Hönisch, 1999; Pelikan, 2002). Summarising, Christa Pelikan contended:

> VOM with its potential for empowerment can play an important role within an on-going process that can be characterized as a 'spiral of empowerment'; this spiral empowerment corresponds and counteracts the (well-known) spiral of violence that often affects the lives of women. Only very rarely does a 'conversion', or a reformation of the alleged perpetrator take place. In that case, the short term intervention that is VOM by definition, produces an effect in the way of an incentive, or a take-off event that starts more long-ranging and deep-reaching effects or even better: processes of change. (Pelikan, 2002)

In the light of these results, the picture that emerged from the second study was even more remarkable. Ten years later the quantitative part of the new study, ie the results from the questionnaire sent out to women victims of partnership violence, provides empirical evidence that it has been possible to contribute to the prevention of violence both by way of an empowerment of women, but also by an effect towards a change of attitude of perpetrators (Pelikan, 2010; 2012).

Eighty-three per cent of all responding women experienced no further violence. Of those, 80 per cent contended that VOM had contributed to this effect, in 40 per cent of those cases even to a substantial degree. This contribution was brought about by way of direct or indirect empowerment: direct empowerment implying the increased capacity to state one's demands and claims for a life without violence, or the increased capacity to handle conflicts through communication, ie by talking and deliberating and by an enhanced capacity to insist on one's demands and one's claim to live free of violence. Indirect empowerment is pointing to VOM as an impetus to seek further support and help.

In addition, 40 per cent of those women whose partnership continued or who still had contact with an ex-partner and who had experienced no further violence stated that their partner had changed as a result of going through VOM.

How and why did this happen? The qualitative part of this research was to shed light on this question. We were able to trace the processes that led up to such an inner change, as observed in the course of the VOM procedure and as related by the women.

The most impressive effect occurred when and where in the course of the procedure, men were brought to confront themselves with what they had done to their woman partner.[1] The researcher could observe this happen during the VOM procedures and she was told in more detail about this effect in the course of the interviews with women.

The process of arriving at an in-sight of something that has been set out as wrongdoing by the law, of recognising the 'you ought not' (*das Sollen*) has been very beautifully described by Frau Wellner:

> Listening to his story ... I learned and realised things I had not known ... I had the feeling that my husband only then ... had realised that he cannot contend any longer that what had happened in reality was not as stated in the files and that it was not he himself and only he himself responsible—that's what I heard. I am sure that this was a topic in this talk, because afterwards and later at home as well, the whole story as told from his side had become different. I guess that had happened in the individual talks. Of course, I was not present, but I know my husband pretty well—his tendency not to use the 'I'-form but talking about 'one' that does things or perceives them as such. I guess that the social worker he was with had told him: 'no: it is not "one" it is "you"'—something like that.

To give a bit of the background of this case: Frau Wellner went to the police after the hospital she visited had already informed the police about the injuries her husband had caused. This was the first experience of this kind for her, it was dramatic and it had traumatising consequences for her. She had attended a trauma therapy in the aftermath and she said that she did not want to talk about the incident in more detail at the '*Tatausgleich*'. In addition to going to the police, she had used the emergency hotline for women and there she had received valuable support. She had realised that her husband had tried to belittle the event, and to suppress all memory of it.

Pelikan's observation and the transcript of the interview contribute in a complementary manner to convey the story of a man going from 'one must not' to 'I have done this'. On the basis of this knowledge he arrives at the feeling of remorse and the readiness to compensate for the harm by doing something good and beneficial to his wife—as an act of restorative justice, one could say.

We will come back to the larger societal changes that provide the background for these changes that have occurred between 1999/2000 and 2009/2010.

Within both studies the qualitative data analysis has focused on the dynamics of the relationship between victim and offender. It is about the concrete experiences of the victim and the offender—the doer and the done-to!

[1] As has already been shown in the reformation case from the first study.

This is about understanding power relationships, not as preconceived perceptions of a fixed and inescapable demonstration of male dominance, but as a complex pattern of inter-acting, of searching for survival, for self-preservation, for conciliation and a bit of peace. We clearly have traced processes of empowerment, concretely and not as a mere slogan.[2] We contend that this is the lifeworld perspective.

How to assess theoretically the role and importance of the lifeworld approach marking the restorative justice procedure? What is the 'added value', or the necessity of resorting to the lifeworld experience of both victim and offender? Let us first look at the way Habermas has conceptualised 'lifeworld'.

III. HABERMAS' CONCEPT OF THE LIFEWORLD

As an integral part of Habermas' theory of 'communicative action' we find the notion of the lifeworld.[3] Communicative action, bound to the lifeworld, is 'oriented toward mutual recognition' ('*verständigungsorientiert*', sometimes termed consensus-oriented, which we regard as a problematic translation). The sphere of the lifeworld is 'the intuitively present, in the sense of familiar and transparent, and at the same time vast and incalculable web of presuppositions' (Habermas, 1987: 131). Put in more simple words: the lifeworld is the background consensus of our everyday lives, the vast stock of taken-for-granted definitions and understandings of the world that give coherence and direction to our lives (Habermas, 1987: 133). And further broken down: it is about the immediate closer and wider surrounding people move, the family, neighbourhood, networks of friends and mates, about a world that subjects may experience together.

Turning to the notion of system, we have attempted to explicate what 'system' for Habermas implies by focusing on the 'colonisation of the lifeworld', addressing the relationship between system and lifeworld. The understanding of this relation has undergone transformations in the course of Habermas' writings.

Moreover, we have to admit that in the realm of law, and more specifically in criminal law, Habermas' concepts, including the colonisation of the lifeworld theory, are not adequate theoretical tools to catch the contradictions and the shortcomings of modern criminal law. Or rather, such usage

[2] On the importance of careful empirical research and the necessity to 'learn' from it, cf the article of Ellen Pence referred to in Pelikan, 2012.

[3] He is not the one who has invented the term; it surfaced within the phenomenological theory of Edmund Husserl (1936) and of Alfred Schütz (Schütz and Luckmann, 1973) and was further elaborated by various authors.

does not do justice to Habermas's highly complex and changeful theorising about law.[4]

The colonisation thesis pertains, first and foremost, to money and power, the sphere of politics and economics. The term 'juridification', as kin to 'colonisation', is used by Habermas mainly to denounce a development 'when law comes to invade more and more areas of social life, turning citizens into clients of bureaucracies with what Foucault might call "normalizing" effects' (Bohman and Rehg, 2014: 10).

Here again, Habermas discerns different waves of juridification. The first wave is taking place during the formation of the absolutist bourgeois state in Europe; it regulated the sovereign's monopoly over force and the contractual rights and obligation of private persons, resulting in the legitimisation of the co-existence of a strong monarchical state and a 'free' market. The following waves, according to Habermas, indicate how lifeworld demands attempt to resist the autonomous workings of state and economy. This is achieved first by claiming individual rights against the sovereign, then by democratising the political order, and finally by guaranteeing freedoms and rights against the economic system.

Overall, Habermas attributes to law an important mediating function between lifeworld and system by negotiating between the demands of everyday communicative actions, on the one hand, and the functional needs of the economic and administrative/political systems, on the other, says Mathieu Deflem (Deflem, 2013: 7).

It is also important to see that Habermas is mainly concerned with the law in general, with welfare laws, with constitutional law, and with legislation, almost never with criminal law. Insofar as theories of justice figure in his thinking and writing, eg in his discussion of Rawls (McCarthy, 1994), his theorising pertains to social justice or distributive justice (cf Finlayson and Freyenhagen, 2011).

We have put forward the difference of lifeworld and system, applying it to characterise the perceptions, the different lens of restorative justice, on the one hand, and the CJS, on the other hand. Lifeworld orientation appears as the opposite of system orientation. Concluding, we think that the lifeworld concept adequately catches this core element of a change of lenses that goes with a movement towards restorative justice. On the other hand, the constitutive difference of lifeworld vs system cannot be grounded in Habermas' thinking about the law. It is too differentiated, it is too complex and it has undergone vast changes that make it difficult to reduce Habermas' conceptualisation of law to a system approach opposed to a lifeworld orientation.

[4] We would also like to mention the critique put forward by Nancy Fraser (1985) who has attacked the distinction as covertly ideological, concealing forms of patriarchal and economic domination.

We are therefore still confronted with the task of theoretically adequately catching the essence of the lifeworld—system difference. In other words: what is the relationship between the CJS and restorative justice at the level of the perception of wrongdoing? And in what way does this lifeworld approach contribute to conveying justice for victims and offenders?

IV. ON THE FUNCTIONS OF LAW

At this point, we will turn to the thinking and the work of the late German sociologist of law, Detlev Frehsee. He starts from the notion that law's potential as a regulatory instrument has to be generally judged as very modest only; at the same time, the mechanisms of regulation are quite subtle, not working directly as cause and effect, but as a catalyser of change inside the system. Frehsee has discerned three different levels (or categories), where law becomes effective and relevant: the level of law-making (setting the norm); the level of the procedure (the implementation or evocation of the norm); and the level of enforcement, ie the sanction that is the outcome of the procedure (Frehsee and Bussmann, 1994).

The legal norm is the most important element of the system of law. The legal norm 'the law' serves and becomes effective as a 'medium of communication'. Frehsee traces this concept back to Luhmann, but also to Habermas. These are the main steps of argumentation: in complex, highly differentiated and pluralistic societies, the system of law becomes separate from the lifeworld. It creates and develops its own reality. It symbolises 'the ought' (*das Sollen*) in society and in social reality. Law becomes a medium of communication about everyday social acting. It provides the space for interpretations and constructions of reality through its code that serves as a semantic instrument for these constructions. Frehsee states that in this communication the rationality of the law (carrying also moral implications) with its claims to universality comes to bear upon society and its subsystems. This way the law exerts its influence and becomes effective. By mobilising the norm, ie by turning to the institutions of the law, conflicts become externalised and relevant beyond the internal private sphere. The law works as an external structure of reference. Especially with an individual in a situation where she is subjugated to the domination of another individual or group, this resource of law as a medium is of great importance, since other resources, such as money or power, are lacking.

The level of the procedure is essential insofar as it puts procedures at the disposal of those mobilising the law. According to Frehsee, these procedures ought to be flexible, they should allow for 'inner learning' and for a joint effort at working towards solutions. In this respect, the criminal procedure strictly adhering to the principle of legality (as is the case in the German criminal law tradition) can prove dysfunctional: coercion prevents reference to the other (*Fremdreferenz*), ie a confrontation with the perspectives of the others, says Frehsee. 'Once you experience coercion, you will not develop different orientations by yourself, out of your inner drive' (translation, Christa Pelikan) (Frehsee and Bussmann, 1994: 164). This is a core sentence of restorative justice; in other words, the very fact of coercion prevents individuals from developing new orientations—it suffocates the inner drive! More immediate problems stem from the level of the procedure being bound to the level of execution, ie the level of the sanction. Whereas law enforcement is indeed an indispensable constitutive feature, the effectiveness of law is in the last instance dependent on its being mobilised, and not on its being executed! And mobilisation increases where and when alternative procedures are at the disposal of the parties, not least potential victims.

Let us repeat the main tenets of this chain of argument: the power of the law lies with the legal norm being used as a mean of communication. It is backing up the claims of individuals and groups of individuals, especially of weaker parties; they can refer to the norm as an orientation, as an 'ought' agreed by society in democratic processes of norm-setting, ie of law-making. This effect is not dependent on a court procedure taking place, in fact this is rather the exception. Its potential accessibility is essential, though. But at this level as well, it needs procedures that allow the norm to enfold a potential of inner re-orientation, one could say for learning. And in the last instance, ie the level of execution, the sanction has to be there in order to become evoked, whenever the communication and the learning processes fail. We have thus a vast field of influence or efficacy of the law that lies before the procedure taking place and, given the availability of alternative procedures open for communication, an equally vast field of law becoming effective before any sanction is imposed.

This whole chain of arguments can therefore be understood as strongly supporting restorative justice, not only in the field of criminal law but also in other fields where legal regulation is deemed important.

Frehsee (1996) was able to underpin the contention that the prime function of law becomes manifest as the norm providing the potential claimant/aggrieved party with a means or a medium of communication by empirical research. This research dealt with the introduction of new laws ruling the use of violence against children by their parents 'illegal'. Children and child protectors could then refer to this interdiction of violence, using it as a 'medium of communication'. This proves an important resource for curbing the actual use of violence, more important than 'going to the courts'. The pivotal function of legislation, ie of law-making, becomes evident. At the same time, by introducing the concept of law as a medium of communication, Frehsee connects the 'functioning' of law and of law-making with the level of the beneficiaries, their actions and considerations.

This is indeed the realm of the lifeworld. We could now state that the alternative procedures where learning can take place, because they are devoid of coercion, are circulating around the lifeworld. Reference to the lifeworld is opening a space for learning.

V. HABERMAS AND THE DISCOURSE FREE FROM DOMINATION

The level of the norm and norm setting is also of paramount importance within Habermas' 'discourse ethics' and the concept of a discourse free from domination (*herrschaftsfreier Diskurs*).[5]

Within discourse ethics, justice is achieved whenever the requirements of a discourse free from domination are met and provide the grounds for the decisions society rests upon, first of all decisions regarding the constitution, but also regarding all kinds of political decisions that become manifest as law-making in various fields of society.

The core sentence referring to the discourse free of domination is: 'Only those norms can claim validity that could meet with the acceptance of all concerned in practical discourse' (Habermas, 1990: 66).

Being idealistic and detached from any political reality is one of the most frequently heard critiques of these constructions (cf Benhabib, 1985; Heller, 1985; Rorty, 1994). Becoming more specific, several authors have accused Habermas of losing sight of and/or avoiding the issue of power. In addition, by stating the requirement of inclusion and participation, the power processes that result in the exclusion of marginalised groups are implicitly treated as non-existent. In contrasting Habermas and Foucault, Bent Flyfbjerg (1998) emphasises another shortcoming or object of critique expressed by Foucault: Habermas' holding on to the juridico-discursive model of society and of societal change. This implies that for Habermas the authority of law remains untouched.

We will here point to the later work of Habermas, the essay 'The Struggle for Recognition in the Constitutional State' contained in the book *The Inclusion of the Other* (1998). We think that there he has adopted some of Foucault's ideas and he has also reacted to the critique of neglecting the importance of the 'new movements'. He pays special attention to the women's movement, using it as an example of the necessity to solve the tension between the protection of individual rights and the requirement to attend to specific life contexts, ie to compensate for structural inequalities and for crass power imbalances. Habermas contends that a correctly understood theory of rights requires a politics of recognition that protects the integrity

[5] We have to admit that the connection we establish here with Habermas' discourse ethics rests on an eclectic, highly condensed reading in this vast field. We focus on the discourse theory of law and politics and the role discourse ethics play within Habermas' deliberative democratic model.

of the individual in the life contexts in which her identity is formed. Referring to Nancy Fraser (1989) he states that the exercise of individual liberties must be clarified in the political public sphere, specifically in public debates about the appropriate interpretation of needs (Habermas, 1998: 210).

So, there Habermas returns to the core requirement of a discourse free from domination, namely the participation of those concerned and affected by a specific piece of legislation. But he arrives also at an understanding of the discourse free from domination that is far from 'idealistic'. It is located in the political arena and it is about power and power struggles. We would even contend that it approaches Foucault's 'grand goal', namely 'not to try to dissolve relations of power in the utopia of a perfectly transparent communication, but to give the rules of law ... but also the ethics ... which would allow these games of power to be played with a minimum of domination' (Foucault, 1988: 18).

It so happens that in the field of domestic violence, an important piece of law-making has happened in the 1990s in Austria that can serve to illustrate the political struggles that closely resemble this kind of a discourse free from domination.

VI. ALMOST A DISCOURSE FREE FROM DOMINATION: THE GENESIS OF THE AUSTRIAN ACT OF PROTECTION AGAINST DOMESTIC VIOLENCE

Understanding this piece of law-making[6] and its effects is important for understanding the empirical results presented above, especially the differences that we could observe between 1999/2000 and 2009/2010.

In October 1993, a joint conference of the Austrian Minister of Women's Affairs and the Minister of Justice took place on the theme of 'Women and the Law' that resulted in a first proposal drawn up by the Minister of Justice stating his intention 'to provide help to the victim in a prompt and effective way and to offer the perpetrator—dependent on certain conditions—the possibility for therapy'.[7] And he expressed his conviction that the implementation of this proposal would promote cooperation between various institutions and groups concerned. For this purpose, a working group was to be constituted in order to further discuss how to proceed with efforts to achieve these goals. In the months to follow, an effort of truly innovative law-making started and held the centre-stage of legal policy for three years. This innovative way of working toward a new piece of legislation consisted, first of all, in setting up a steering group that later distributed

[6] In this chapter we draw on Haller, Pelikan and Smutny, 2004.

[7] Letter of invitation from the Minister of Justice, 4.214/26-I 1/1993, 2 November 1993.

responsibility for different parts of the legislative package among different working groups: police law, civil (execution) law, criminal law, and one dedicated to the design and establishment of the new 'Interventionsstellen', the intervention-centres. These working groups consisted of civil servants of the relevant departments of the Ministries of Justice, of the Interior and of Family Affairs, of representatives of the police force, of judges and state prosecutors, of attorneys, and of 'the women' as representatives of the shelters and other institutions working in the field of domestic violence. Thus, the working groups were not restricted to professional law-makers, nor even to 'jurists'. That meant that, at a very early stage, the law-makers were forced into (or had the benefit of) confrontation—if not with the beneficiaries of law and especially the victims themselves, but at least with those who are immediately concerned with their plight. The participation (and a very active participation it was indeed!) of the representatives of the women's movement proved that civil society has found a place within the democratic institutions of the wider society and its law-making processes.

During the three years to follow, and in the course of quite a number of group and plenary sessions, the new legislation, as well as the first new intervention-centres designed to coordinate the efforts for the protection and support of women, took shape. It was the result of a remarkable cooperation. It was also the result of a struggle that very often was hard, even embittered, a struggle over demands and requests, over needs and over interests, over rights to fight for and over rights to protect.

A main point of controversy was the role of victim-offender mediation, more precisely, its application to cases of domestic violence. From its very beginning when this practice was introduced in Austria in 1992 it had met with the opposition of the women's movement, who raised quite powerful arguments: the potential lack of sufficient norm confirmation; the potential neglect of power imbalances, inextricably present where violence has occurred; and the short-term character of the VOM intervention, which neglected control and after-care. The controversy found its solution by concentrating on alternative, innovative strategies that proved more do-able and more effective. Summarising this remarkable process of law-making, Pelikan ventured the contention that, on the one hand, the demands of the women's movement on the criminal justice system forced the law-makers to scrutinise the array of traditional legal instruments and to invent new answers to this challenge. On the other hand, the apprehensions of the conventional law-makers motivated those who had challenged 'the law', to go beyond mere requests for a tighter grip of penal law. The prime goal of immediate effective protection, as well as of effective support, came more clearly into view. From the background of a struggle that had touched upon far-reaching questions of the function and the potential of (criminal) law interventions, a very pragmatic solution had emerged.

This was power play and quite openly so. Was it free from domination? Looking at its results, we can answer in the positive. Was it the force of the stronger argument, meaning the more rational argument, that prevailed? We regard as most important the need to become outspoken and clear about the aims of the effort, namely to develop an instrument that would effectively protect women from violence inside their homes. This aim could be and had to be shared by the experts of criminal procedural law. Clarifying and openly explaining goals and intentions is one of the requirements of the discourse free of violence.

But most importantly, the genesis of the Act can be ascribed to the requirement of 'the law becoming subject to the deliberation of citizens, who thus author the laws to which they are subject' (Bohman and Rehg, 2014: 10).

In the following years, the participation of different stakeholders, most importantly representatives of civil society (in this case the women's movement) in the process of law-making were shaping the 'mentalities' and the awareness of a wider public. This was then to become the background and the reference point of the deliberations going on within the restorative justice procedure.

VII. CONCLUSION

In the material from the two empirical studies, we have seen that the specific framing of the event, taking recourse to the lifeworld of the participants that occurs in the restorative justice procedure, paves the way for transformation. It is a transformation of the general awareness and knowledge of the rightful claim to live free of violence into the individual experience as victim and as an offender. Societal awareness of the rightful claim has been enhanced by specific legislation, the Austrian Act on Protection Against Domestic Violence. We have interpreted it as an example of law-making that approximates the requirements of a discourse free from domination: as a piece of legislation it serves as a means of communication, which is to be regarded as the most important function of law. This way, 'justice' is effectuated for the beneficiaries, most importantly for victims in disadvantaged positions.

In the restorative justice procedure, reference to the concrete lifeworld experiences of the other becomes the lever for a transformation of the norms set out in legislation to the individual level. This dialogical restorative justice process opens the path to an actively acquired understanding of rights and rightful claims on the part of the women, and of insight into one's individual responsibility for having infringed on the right of this concrete person, one's partner, on the part of the male perpetrators. Resorting to the lifeworldly experience of the parties involved and affected serves to bring home the message of 'this ought not to have happened'. It means translating a generally accepted norm, a societal understanding of a '*Sollen*': you ought to refrain from violating your partner, into the experience of 'this is what I have done and what has affected my wife in this way!'.

Reference to the *Sollen* as enshrined in legislation is one part of this process; reference to 'the Other' is the other side. This is different from being told through the verdict that you have acted against the law; it is, at its very best, a deep-reaching process grounded in cognition and recognition of having done something wrong and hurtful to one's partner.

As regards the women, they gain the confirmation of 'their' right as the individual experience of a validation of their rightful place in the world and within their relationship. It is acquired through dialogue as a kind of inter-action, through '*Auseinandersetzung*'. Jointly tackling and disputing the issue at stake proves more persuasive than a mere verbal assertion that you have this right. The restorative justice process has the capacity to deeply convince women of their rights. Whereas the personal has become political as a consequence of the women's struggle, this process now brings the political back 'home' to become a personal experience.

REFERENCES

Bateson, G (2000) *Steps to an Ecology of Mind, Form, Substance and Difference, Collected Essays in Anthropology, Psychiatry, Evolution and Epistemology* (Chicago, IL, University of Chicago Press, orig pub 1972).

Benhabib, S (1985) 'The Utopian Dimension in Communicative Ethics' 35 *New German Critique* 83.

Benjamin, J (2004) 'Beyond Doer and Done-to: An Intersubjective View of Thirdness' 73 *Psychoanalytical Quarterly* 5.

Bohman, J and Rehg, W (2014) 'Jürgen Habermas' in EN Zalta (ed), *The Stanford Encyclopedia of Philosophy* (Fall 2014 edn), available at http://plat.stanford.edu/entries/habermas.

Coleman, J (1971) *Resources for Social Change* (Hoboken, NJ, Wiley & Sons).

Dalton, S (2008) 'Beyond Intellectual Blackmail: Foucault and Habermas on Reason, Truth, and Enlightenment', *Electronic Journal for Philosophy*, E–Logos, ISSN 1211-0442.

Deflem, M (2013) 'The Legal Theory of Jürgen Habermas' in R Banakar and M Travers (eds), *Law and Social Theory* (Oxford, Hart Publishing)70–95.

Finlayson, JG and Freyenhagen, F (eds) (2011) *Habermas and Rawls: Disputing the Political* (New York, Routledge).

Flyfbjerg, B (1998) 'Habermas and Foucault: Thinkers for Civil Society?' 49 *British Journal of Sociology* 210.

Foucault, M (1988) 'The Ethic of Care for the Self as a Practice of Freedom' in J Bernauer and D Rasmussen (eds), *The Final Foucault* (Cambridge, MA, MIT Press).

Fraser, N (1985) 'What's Critical about Critical Theory?' 35 *New German Critique* 97.

—— (1989) 'Struggle over Needs' in N Fraser, *Unruly Practices* (Oxford, Oxford University Press) 144–60.

Frehsee, D (1996) 'Introduction' in D Frehsee, W Horn and KD Bussmann (eds), *Family Violence Against Children* (Berlin, De Gruyter) 3–19.
Frehsee, D and Bussmann, KD (1994) 'Zur Bedeutung des Rechts in Familien. Der Rechtsstatus von Kindern und Gewalt gegen Kinder' 15 *Zeitschrift für Rechtssoziologie* 153.
Habermas, J (1981) *Theorie des kommunikativen Handelns*, vol 1, *Handlungsrealität und gesellschaftliche Rationalisierung* (Frankfurt am Main, Suhrkamp).
—— (1987) *The Theory of Communicative Action*, vol II, *Lifeworld and System* (Boston, NJ, Beacon).
—— (1990) *Moral Consciousness and Communicative Action* (Cambridge, MA, MIT Press).
—— (1998) *The Inclusion of the Other: Studies in Political Theory* (Cambridge, MA, MIT Press).
Haller, B, Pelikan, C, and Smutny, P (2004) 'The Austrian Protection Against Domestic Violence Act 1996' in F Dünkel and H von Hofer (eds), *Crime Policy in Europe: Good Practices and Promising Examples* (Strasbourg, Council of Europe) 37–49.
Heller, A (1985) 'The Discourse Ethics of Habermas: Critique and Appraisal' 10(1) *Thesis Eleven* 5, available at http://caae.phil.cmu.edu/Cacalaier/Forum/meta/background/hab_rawl(html.
Husserl, E (1936) *The Crisis of European Sciences and Transcendental Phenomenology* (Evanston, IL, Northwestern University Press).
Luhmann, N (1993) *Das Recht der Gesellschaft* (Frankfurt am Main, Suhrkamp).
McCarthy, T (1994) 'Notes on the Contrast between Habermas and Rawls' 19(5) *Ethics* 44.
Pali, B and Pelikan, C (2010) *Building Social Support for Restorative Justice: Media, Civil Society, and Citizens* (Leuven, European Forum for Restorative Justice).
—— (2014) 'Contexting Restorative Justice and Abolitionism: Exploring the Potential and Limits of Restorative Justice as an Alternative Discourse to Criminal Justice' 2 *Restorative Justice, An International Journal* 142.
Pelikan, C (2002) 'Victim–Offender Mediation in Domestic Violence Cases: A Comparison of the Effects of Criminal Law Intervention, the Penal Process and Mediation: Doing Qualitative Research' 3(1) *Forum Qualitative Sozialforschung / Forum: Qualitative Social Research*.
—— (2010) 'On the Efficacy of Victim–Offender Mediation in Cases of Partnership Violence; Or, Men Don't Get Better, But Women Get Stronger: Is It Still True? Outcomes of an Empirical Study' 16 *European Journal on Crime Policy and Research* 49.
—— (2012) 'Partnership Violence and the Role of Restorative Justice: An Austrian Case Study' in T Gavrielides (ed), *Rights and Restoration Within Youth Justice* (Whitby, De Sitter) 149–77.
Pelikan, C and Hönisch, B (1999) *Die Wirkungsweisen strafrechtlicher Maßnahmen bei Gewaltstraftaten in Paarbeziehungen. Das Strafverfahren und der Außergerichtliche Tatausgleich* (Vienna, Forschungsbericht des Instituts für Rechts- und Kriminalsoziologie).
Ragazzi, M (2015) *Report on the Comparative Analysis in the Action Research Sites*, ALTERNATIVE Project, http://alternativeproject.eu.

Rorty, R (1994) 'Habermas and Lyotard on Post-Modernity' 13 *Praxis International, A Philosophical Journal* 32.

Schütz, A and Luckmann, T (1973) *Structures of the Lifeworld*, Studies in Phenomenology and Existential Philosophy, vol 1 (Evanston, IL, Northwestern University Press), available at www.qualitative-research.net/fqs-texte/a2324/1-02pelikan-e.htm.

11

'Cultural' Problematisations in the Restorative Justice Discourse

BRUNILDA PALI

I. INTRODUCTION

THERE ARE MANY forces that push a field or a discourse in a certain direction, like political debates, policy reforms and requirements, socio-economic conditions, concrete cases and events, and sometimes global or supranational forces. Depending on these forces, and the ways the discourse bends to or resists them, matters start to be problematised in certain manners, and not in others. The focus of this chapter is to examine discursively the way 'culture' is thematised and problematised in restorative justice, both by a critical literature review and through analysing empirical data. In other words, it asks questions such as: how and why does 'culture' become a problem in restorative justice; what solutions do these forms of problematisations lead to; and how can we think of other forms of 'cultural' problematisations in the restorative justice discourse?

Compared to endless volumes written on other topics, the literature on restorative justice and its applications in intercultural cases is extremely limited and can be said to be in its infancy. The chapter has two main objectives. The first objective is to trace in the restorative justice literature the 'cultural' problematisations. I will discuss this literature under two headings: first application of RJ to 'hate crime and interracial violence', and secondly, application of RJ to cases involving 'immigrants and refugees'. The second objective is to argue for prioritising certain forms of problematisations rather than others by presenting some findings from my empirical data gathered through interviews conducted within mediation programmes in Europe.

II. TRACING 'CULTURAL PROBLEMATISATIONS' IN THE RESTORATIVE JUSTICE DISCOURSE

A. Application of Restorative Justice in Cases of 'Hate Crime', Interracial Violence and Conflicts

The topic of hate crime in relation to restorative justice starts to be explicitly addressed around the beginning of the twenty-first century. What characterises the first writings is the critique of the criminal justice system (CJS) and the retributive measures it amplifies, like penalty enhancements, especially in the call to combat hate crime (Whitlock, 2001; Tubman-Carbone, 2007), and the failure of this system to keep the needs of the victim in focus (Shenk, 2001; Tubman-Carbone, 2007). The authors mainly argue that hate violence has deeper roots, and that imprisonment and retribution can be meaningless interventions, unless the community is involved and the 'perpetrator' is also healed together with the 'victim'. Nevertheless, the authors propose restorative justice as a supplement (instead of a replacement) to the current criminal justice system, especially given the seriousness of hate crimes. The methods proposed are use of victim-offender mediation (VOM) (Shenk, 2001), and Circle Sentencing (Sapir, 2007).

The best case known in literature on the relation of restorative justice and hate crime is the Hate Crimes Project (HCP) at Southwark Mediation, South London, a project set up over 10 years ago to deal with conflict in local communities where an incident of hate or prejudice has been reported (Gavrielides, 2007; 2011; 2012; Walters and Hoyle, 2010, 2012; Walters, 2011). The cases showed that hate conflicts make up just one dimension of a complex social relationship between the parties that is exacerbated by socio-economic conditions. The authors argue that an adversarial court system would not be able to understand and root out the many intersecting prejudices or to do justice to the varied socio-economic factors that provided the crucial context for the conflict. At the same time, the authors argue that structured dialogue that involves all parties to a dispute, that reveals myriad harms and exposes prejudice for community condemnation, is more likely to reduce the likelihood of repeat victimisation than a purely punitive anti-social behaviour order, or punishment imposed by a court, and removed from the concerned community. Further, based on their observations, the authors argued that the mediation process clearly promoted emotional benefits for the majority of victims. Nevertheless, they argued that it would be naive to think this was enough. In fact, in several cases the involvement of local organisations, including housing associations and social services, became central to resolving the conflict, allowing participants to move on with their lives peacefully. Unlike some other restorative processes, the HCP often engaged in multi-agency partnerships. This allowed the mediation process to capitalise on both a dialogic process between the parties, who frequently found resolution between themselves, but also inclusive communication between the parties and other relevant organisations. Although they are confident that mediation meetings do help to break down cultural and identity differences between the parties, they argue that such a process is unlikely to undo years of learnt prejudice, change any of the socio-economic, socio-structural and other cultural factors which give rise to individuals' prejudiced behaviours, or prevent the influences of the media, contemporary politics and broader ideologies (Walters, 2011; Kelly, 2002).

Not under the explicit construction of 'hate crime', but under the concept of 'interracial violence and conflict', Mikhail Lyubansky and Dominic Barter (2011; 2013) have written on the potential of 'restorative circles' (RC), which originally developed in urban Brazil in the mid-1990s with favela residents, to these types of cases. The authors argue that such cases have three characteristics: (a) the use of a specific incident to explore underlying issues; (b) the explicit involvement of 'community' members; and (c) the fostering of power-sharing. The authors argue that in addressing deeply rooted structural violence, such as that characterised by racism, the ability to maintain a balance between the specificity of an act and the immensity of the context in which it occurred (rather than focusing only on either the act or the societal context), is a key feature of RC.

There have been many advocacy calls in the United States to foster restorative justice as a response to terrorism and post-terrorism impacts. The National Association for Community Mediators (NACM) and other organisations advocated a restorative justice response to such incidents. Additionally, the US Department of Justice Community Relations Service offered mediators free of charge to community officials concerned about hate crimes. Mapping efforts of these initiatives have explored the extent to which RJ was utilised in response to hate related crimes, or anti-Arab and anti-Muslim harassment and after September 11-related hate crimes (Umbreit *et al*, 2003b; Volpe and Strobl, 2005). The situations identified included a cross burning at a residence; interracial conflicts in a school; post 9–11 threats against a mosque and its leaders; the murder of a transgendered youth; promoting understanding between Somalis and non-Somalis in an urban setting in the United States; racism across reservation boundaries; and building relationships between Arabs and Jews in an urban area addressing, among other issues, the conflicts in Israel and the occupied territories. The forms of the 'community' gatherings ranged from intimate victim-offender meetings in small groups to very large 'community' gatherings. The restorative processes included facilitated dialogue, circles, and open forums. In a practical guideline, *Multicultural Implications of Restorative Justice: Potential Pitfalls and Dangers*, Umbreit and Coates (2000) argue that the key to adaptation of restorative justice frameworks is increased sensitivity to cross-cultural issues and dynamics that affect restorative justice programmes and the administration of justice.

B. Application of RJ to Cases Involving Immigrants and Refugees

In the limited literature from continental Europe, the main matter of concern is the application of RJ in cases when immigrants (or immigrant background clients) and refugees are involved (Albrecht, 2008; 2010; Del Campo *et al*, 2011). Based on the concern of over-representation of both adult and adolescent minority groups in serious criminal cases in Norway and Finland, Albrecht (2008; 2010) argues, on the one hand, for the advantages of restorative justice for refugees and immigrants compared to the criminal justice system, and on the other hand, on the importance of establishing restorative justice practices that take the needs of these minority groups into consideration. She has pointed out several obstacles during mediation with these groups, among which are language; communication style; denial of guilt on the part of offenders; 'loss of face or honour' due to conflict; punitive attitudes of some of the victims; cultural stereotypes by mediators; and lack of cultural knowledge on the part of mediators. One of the central issues that came up in this research was the dilemma on the part of mediators between openly addressing cultural issues in mediation (the cultural specificity argument) versus mediating each of the cases in an equal way regardless of culture (the generalist argument).

The research conducted by Del Campo *et al* (2011) on mediation among young immigrants in the juvenile penal justice system in Spain highlighted the difficulties of young immigrants in attaining access to alternatives such as mediation. Both ignorance of the judicial system, and a lack of stability and bonding which allows for the fulfilment of the penalty, represent serious obstacles and this orients the judge instead towards measures of physical control. Additionally, many of the young immigrants involved in the mediation process have only a very basic and rudimentary knowledge of the languages currently in use, and this poor quality of communication makes it harder to achieve the level of abstraction and reflection required in mediation, thus producing an excess of ambiguity. Additionally, the mediator may be unfamiliar with the cultural and social context from which the young person comes, and as a result the relational asymmetry which exists often passes unnoticed, with the mediator simply being left with a frustrating feeling of being unable to establish a relationship based on trust. The families of the young people often seem to experience their encounter with the judicial system with a feeling of panic, and as a consequence, the family cannot offer the young people involved the emotional and material aid they really need. The mediator is seen as a legitimate agent of the judicial system itself, and their function is conceptualised as one of repression and control. The result is a tendency to adopt a defensive attitude, and often to create obstacles in an attempt to avoid the entry of the child into the mediation process. Another aspect which favours the asymmetry in power relations in the context of mediation is the cultural difference that exists between the two parties, and at the same time also between the young offender and the mediator. Normally, the mediator belongs to the same culture as the other party in the mediation, which adds to the perception and feeling of lack of confidence towards the institutional structure.

Furthermore, in relation to the precariousness of immigrants, Albrecht (2008; 2010) has mentioned cases when immigrants and refugees may be willing to accept, first, participation in mediation, and secondly, unfavourable and disproportionate deals in mediation in order to avoid formal legal action, given that these proceedings can have a negative impact on their right of residence, a vulnerability that might be abused by the other conflict party. This type of cases clearly illustrate the need for procedural safeguards for immigrants and refugees regarding proportionality of restitution and (in)voluntary participation. These principles are not only relevant for the 'culturally different', but for all people who are in a state of vulnerability, who can be young, old, traumatised, mentally ill, violated, etc. The challenges that stem from heightened precariousness and vulnerability are not particular to mediation, but can be reasons for under-representativeness of such people in mediation and other alternative measures. For example, young immigrants have greater difficulty in attaining access to such alternatives. One of the basic principles of access to mediation is the capacity for the compromise that the young aggressor should accept in making retribution for the harm caused to the victim. Both ignorance of the judicial system, and a lack of stability and bonding which allows for the fulfilment of the penalty, represent serious obstacles and this orients the judge instead towards measures of physical confinement.

In relation to precariousness and restorative justice, the opposite has also been argued. For example, Albrecht (2008; 2010) has argued that despite their vulnerability, or precisely because of that, immigrants and refugees can profit from restorative justice interventions for two main reasons: (a) procedures are easier to understand and to relate to compared to the regular formal justice systems; and (b) they are more accessible since they are free of charges. Refugees and immigrants are groups that are assumed to have more problems in relating to legal systems. The legal terminology of experts can alienate and exclude them from the justice processes, while restorative justice is a less complex system, more flexible, and more responsive towards the needs of the participants. At the same time, refugees and many immigrants usually have scarce financial means, thus are more suitable for restorative justice which is offered free of costs. During the interviews, especially in systems where restorative justice works as a diversionary method or where it clearly intersects with other probation-related measures, the advantage of this system becomes unquestionable from the simple fact that entry into it means avoidance of imprisonment. During these kind of efforts and initiatives, which attempt to be a clear alternative to punishment for young people, it becomes of paramount importance for the mediation services to learn to work with such cases despite the challenges (language, cultural difference, lack of bonds and circle of support for the offender, etc) and not to use these challenges as justification for dropping the case, especially when 'dropping' the case for the young offender clearly means a return to or entry into prison.

III. WHAT ARE THE 'INTERCULTURAL CHALLENGES' FOR RESTORATIVE JUSTICE?

Based on my own data, I argue that the 'intercultural' engagement of restorative justice has been so far with regard to the question of 'cultural competence'. In my interviews with mediators, leaders and advisors in four mediation services (Austria, Belgium, Norway and Hungary), I found that 'cultural difference' proves to be a strong filtering mechanism in participating in mediation. The most important factor seems to be the language. Often young immigrants involved in the mediation process have only a very basic knowledge of the national language, and the poor quality of communication makes it harder to achieve the level of abstraction and reflection required in mediation, producing thus an excess of ambiguity, which makes mediators uncomfortable. Most of the time translation is needed and this seems to create several problems. One can be the financial aspects. Translation is an expensive option that the organisation is not always able to take. Often, to counteract the financial costs, family members may be asked to translate. In these cases, the lack of 'neutrality' is mentioned as a problem. Mediators seem also to have issues of lack of trust when this option is used and do not like to 'lose control'. In both cases (professional translator and family member) however, mediators say clearly that it is very difficult for them to conduct mediation under translation as this makes the process extremely slow and difficult to follow. One case partly illustrates the lack of trust and suspicion of mediators when another language is involved, and also how this in their view jeopardises the principles of mediation:

> Mediator: I had a case when the son had to translate all the time to the mother. I tried to talk to her in Norwegian, but he said 'no, she doesn't understand Norwegian'. I was not sure, as I thought he was lying to me about that. And I was not prepared to have one of the parties talking to a support member in another language which neither I nor the other party understood. In the end there was the agreement, and when I asked him to translate it to her, he told me 'there is no need, she understands very well Norwegian, so she will read it herself.

Another issue with translation seems to be that often, given the small scale of some of the communities, even requesting an official translator from the same community can cause 'loss of face'.

Sometimes, besides the language, extreme 'cultural specificity' was mentioned as a reason to drop the case. The mediator's unfamiliarity with the cultural and social context from which the people come can leave the mediator with a frustrating feeling of being unable to establish a relationship based on trust. Mediators often referred to specific problems with participants from other cultures, which some identify as obstacles to mediation, others identify as different elements they have slowly learned to handle. Examples were given regarding offenders from some cultures who were said to be extremely reluctant to admit to their guilt; offenders who feel ashamed both about having created a conflict and about having to talk to strangers about it; participants who do not accept and easily appreciate the fact that the mediators have to be neutral; participants for whom the very concept of mediation is difficult to understand because they instead expect the mediator to make authoritarian decisions; participants who do not respect the strict scheduling by the mediation services; participants who do not respect the legitimacy of the mediators; mediators' own cultural stereotypes and implicit biases; and the cultural background of mediators.

As Ida Hydle (2006) has argued, with the rise of 'intercultural' cases, communication becomes extremely complex in restorative justice practices, mainly because of language and communication styles, but also because of socio-historically embedded knowledge and meaning making. The mediator's unfamiliarity with the cultural and social context of the parties can leave the mediator feeling unable to handle the situation. In the words of a mediator tackling a conflict between two Palestinians:

> Mediator: I was mediating between two people from Palestine. One of them was sincerely responding to mediation, while the other was non-responsive, so it was very frustrating, until at some point I realised because of something he said that he could not change his point of view. He had a political position that he could never bargain. And mediation is bargaining. But in this case it was more important for him to keep his established position rather than solve this concrete conflict. So I had to accept, and they did too, that we had to conclude because it was not going anywhere. I felt so impotent, and subject to not-knowing, very important and necessary knowledge about the situation, so that I could have handled it another way

Particularly telling in this case is the description of the parties, one 'sincerely responding' to mediation, and the other 'non-responsive'. Research done on mediation with Aboriginals shows how White-Settler mediators interpret the constantly shifting positions of the Aboriginals as inconsistency. Furthermore, Aboriginal peoples' disputing behaviour challenges Western mediators, mediation processes and accompanying political ontology by clashing with the expectations that selves should be peaceful rather than combative, rational rather than emotional, self- rather than otherwise-oriented, and focused on the task at hand rather than on wider issues (Brigg, 2007). In the case above, it becomes clear that the mediator is trying by all means possible to decouple the macro-context from the individual context of the concrete conflict in order to reach an agreement, which ignores the fact that this might often be impossible.

Mediators often referred to specific problems with participants from other cultures. For example, offenders from mainly Middle East and Arab countries were said by mediators rarely to openly admit their 'guilt'. Some mediators hold that acceptance of 'guilt' on the part of the offender is a precondition for the victim to participate in mediation, and therefore they will not take up the case if this condition is not fulfilled. Other mediators seem to have their own strategies for handling this problem, which may be by debriefing the victim, and focusing on the willingness of the offender to repair the damage rather than focusing on the explicit acceptance of 'guilt':

> Mediator: I had a case between a young Norwegian girl, who had a Pakistani boyfriend, who had had a quarrel. In one event, she had remained alone with the father of the boyfriend, who out of anger had tried to strangle or suffocate her. In mediation were present the mother of the girl and the father of the boy. He continued denying he had done anything, and the mother kept showing the marks on her daughter's neck. He kept saying 'How can I ever do that, that's not right'. We had to come to a conclusion and his denial was certainly not helping. This went on for some time. And then I asked him, I think for the eighth time, 'But so and so happened?', and he did not reply, he did not protest. That was his way of admitting what had happened. We were able to reach an agreement after that.

Such cases serve to contrast the perception of restorative justice as a universal approach and to demonstrate that guilt, shame, justice, reconciliation are social constructs with diverse meanings and significances assigned to them. Albrecht (2010) has argued that the conceptual approach to restorative justice in the Nordic countries, often considering mediation a rational and linear decision-making process, is not necessarily shared by all ethnic migrant minorities. Furthermore, in the above quotation, what is striking is the persistent technique used for 'moving on' with the case towards an agreement. The mediator uses the word 'denial' and repeats her version of the story eight times before she is convinced that there is no more resistance.

Many mediators also mentioned that some participants from other cultures do not accept and appreciate the fact that the mediators have to be neutral or impartial. Within a Western context, the mediator is usually expected to be impartial, with no relationship to any disputant. But a Western cultural concept of mediation requiring neutrality is not necessarily the norm across cultures. Among other cultural contexts, there is less of a concern about professional credentials and impartiality, but more of a concern that the mediator be an insider, someone who knows the parties or at least the context of their dispute (Augsburger, 1992; Lederach, 1986; Avruch, 2002). In one of the interviews with a 'victim of forced marriage' from Iraq, it became clear that she would have preferred the mediators to advise her more, and to be more proactive in proposing solutions to her problems, while the pure listening and impartial attitude was considered helpful but also frustrating. A mediator articulated this dilemma as follows:

> Mediator: Sometimes, it happens that during the preparatory meetings they [what he calls: 'the new country men'] will think I am on their side. Then we go into the big meeting, and they see I am on everybody's side, I am a friend to everybody. Then they get frustrated and angry and disappointed. But they have to understand that this is my job, to be impartial and kind to everybody.

The mediator here constructs himself as a friend of everybody, kind, and impartial. As Christa Pelikan (1992; 2007) has explained, mediators have to attend to the requirement and high demanding task of making oneself redundant by remaining in the background and standing 'between' offender and victim. They act as instigators or catalysts that enable the parties to take care of the conflict and the matters arising from wrongdoing by bringing forth their capacities to find a solution themselves. Many mediators argued that the neutrality of the mediation service has to be protected at all costs, as its loss could jeopardise the legitimate position gained within the criminal justice system and therefore put funding at risk. Others believe that neutrality has been misused and abused to the detriment of accepting the status quo. According to these (minority) voices, the sheer fact that mediation services accept mainly minor cases of urban disturbances and property protection without questioning them makes them the accomplice of a security oriented capitalist system.

Most mediators do not report differences between non-intercultural and intercultural cases. They use a generic approach, in combination with a cultural sensitivity or cultural 'knowhow', which is looked at on an individual basis. On the one hand, a few mediators suggest that it would be beneficial to have 'specialists' for cultural mediations, just as there are specialists for domestic violence, and that cultural conflicts must be well understood, unearthed and openly targeted (the cultural specificity argument). On the other hand, most of the mediators argued that every mediator should be able to mediate every case and every case is equal (the generalist argument). Mediators do not actively address cultural diversity as an issue, and according to them it is up to the conflicting parties if stereotypes and prejudices appear during mediation. The 'genericity' of the mediation seem to rely on a universal idea of human nature and human conflict. For example, one mediator said:

> Mediator: The starting point is a human level. We are all human beings. On that ground it is possible to recognise what is happening in mediation. We have all been in situations of conflict. We can all relate to how guilt, impotence, and fear feel like. We know how it is to feel small, to doubt our capacities. Once I recognise these difficulties my task is to show respect, to accompany people through that hardship, at least for a little while. It is about attitudes, you can train about attitudes, although you cannot know every human culture. It is about an attitude

of equality. Culture comes in only when these human feelings and difficulties have to be expressed.

The idea that we are all the same also reflects a fear of stereotyping or being prejudiced on the grounds of racism, or in particular, given the mediators' official role, institutional racism. It is part of an official role, according to which they have to make sure they do not stigmatise anyone based on their culture.

When asked whether 'culture', 'racism' or other similar topics should become a topic for discussion within the mediation room, the mediators take a step back and say it is not for them to decide, depending on what the parties 'bring to the table'. Taking a clear distance from the role of a prosecutor or a judge, mediators say:

> Mediator: We received a case from the police. Between an Ethnic Norwegian and a Pakistani. The Pakistani has been stalked and violated. It is not written in the documents from the police that the background is racism. This is what we take as the starting point of what happened. If racism as a topic comes up in mediation, it will certainly be dealt with, but the mediator will not take the initiative to say openly 'this is racism'. It is not the role of the mediator to investigate the case or to interpret it.

> Mediator: The focus should be on the situation, not on the people. Before going into a mediation it is not up to a mediator to think 'I am a feminist, and this is really a bad man'. A mediator has to be free of his or her own positive and negative knowledge about somebody. We are not here to judge.

Nevertheless, in one of the previous quotations, we have seen how the mediator did 'push' towards the investigating role, as she asked the offender eight times in order to mould his answer into what was necessary to move on with the mediation. Mediators do seem to have many judging capacities when they express their opinions about the parties, so both the non-judging and non-investigating attitudes are unattainable. Most of the mediators seem focused on and eager to conduct mediation 'from the heart rather than from the mind', which implies a focus on human feelings as compared to ideological or systemic themes (like racism or feminism). Likewise, the most difficult reported cases for a mediator are cases when they 'cannot reach the person' emotionally.

The issue of legitimacy is an interesting one to consider. Some mediators mention the fact that some participants question the authority of young women mediators. Despite this, they also say that their position as criminal justice professionals and their standing as representatives of the majority in the (host) society, counterbalance the 'lack of respect' and illegitimacy that both gender and age could cause for them when dealing with offenders and victims form more 'patriarchal' cultures. But institutional and 'cultural' legitimacy can be a knife with double edges. The fact that the mediator is seen as a legitimate agent of the judicial system itself, and their function is conceptualised as one of repression and control, can result in a tendency to adopt a defensive attitude, and often to create obstacles for one's own child, or spouse, or other relative to enter into the mediation process. At the same time, the fact that the mediator belongs most of the time to the same culture as the other party in the mediation, can add to the perception and feeling of lack of confidence towards the institutional structure. Richard Delgado (2000) has been very critical of the fact that in many cases the mediators share the same background and have more in common with the middle-class victim than with the lower-class offender. Young offenders, both in mediation practices and in detention centres, report the presence of 'barriers' which have their origin in the stereotypes and prejudices, including even explicit cases of discrimination, that these young people have perceived in their relations with the institutional context of juvenile justice (Del Campo *et al*, 2011).

Most mediators are anxious to claim that for them, any case is like another, and that 'they don't have any problem' with other cultures, that they respect everybody and have no stereotypes. To question 'innocent' claims like this, it suffices to take a look at psychological research on stereotypes, prejudice and implicit bias. Pettigrew (1998) describes the modern form of prejudice in Western Europe as 'subtle prejudice', which means being cool, distant and indirect. Although subtle prejudices are often not verbalised, they have the capacity to influence mediation. Besides research on prejudice, there is by now a large amount of research on implicit social cognition, or implicit bias, which refers to the attitudes or stereotypes that affect our understanding, actions and decisions in an unconscious manner. These biases, which can encompass both favourable and unfavourable assessments about others, are activated involuntarily and without an individual's awareness or intentional control. Everyone possesses implicit biases, even people with avowed commitments to impartiality such as mediators, and other social workers (Banaji and Greenwald, 2013; Rudman, 2004; Richeson and Nussbaum, 2004).

Often co-mediation is used as a balancing model intended to counteract misunderstandings and biases when different cultures are involved. A Norwegian mediator reflected on the usefulness of having had in one case a co-mediator from Iran:

> Mediator: We had a case of a son-in-law who had hit the mother-in-law during a family gathering from the Middle East. There were a lot of supporters in the room from both sides. We were trying to recollect what happened, but the son-in-law would not enter at all into discussions on what he had done and what had happened. At some point, my co-mediator proposed to take a break, when he proposed to take the son-in-law and the mother-in-law separately in mediation for a while. That was a fantastic move. They could speak openly to each other, and afterwards tell the most important points and decisions back to the supporters.

Employing mediators of 'different' background is not the policy of the organisations in any of the four countries where I conducted my interviews. The question whether they think a Roma mediator could be employed to deal with the Roma-related conflicts, for example, shocked the respondents in Hungary. The job of a mediator is an important one, and opening the field of probation and mediation to 'others' was even interpreted by some as a de-legitimising factor for the authority of the organisation with respects to their 'clients'. A few mediators nevertheless seemed unhappy with the lack of colleagues from other origins, and wished for this kind of 'diversity' to become part of the policy of the organisation. The only exception on this issue was Norway. Given the fact that Norway has a volunteer-based mediation system, explicit efforts were made in the recruitment of the volunteers to include mediators with different background, and these efforts were quite successful. Clearly, there is no difference in the Norwegian system from the other countries when it came to the official positions where we find only white and middle-class Norwegians.

IV. CONCLUSION

As mentioned in the introduction, the forces that push a field in a certain direction can be political discourses, policy reforms and requirements, socio-economic situation, historical and societal differences, concrete cases and events that become salient, and sometimes global or supranational forces.

There has been for a decade now a rising interest in restorative justice in reacting to 'hate crime' (Whitlock, 2001; Shenk, 2001; Umbreit *et al*, 2003a; 2003b; Vos *et al*, 2002; Coates *et al*, 2006; Umbreit and Ritter, 2006; Volpe and Strobl, 2005; Sapir, 2007; Tubman-Carbone, 2007; Gavrielides, 2012; Walters and Hoyle, 2010; 2012; Lyubansky and Barter, 2011; Lyubansky, 2013). This is due to a multitude of factors, such as the creation of a discourse on 'hate crime', criminalisation of acts that are defined as 'hate crime', and penalty enhancement on the part of the criminal justice system. Once the justice system starts reacting to these cases, on the one hand, its inability to deal with their complexity, and on the other hand, the lack of a victim's perspective, have been the main reasons for addressing hate crime by restorative justice. Other reasons for addressing racial violence, mainly in the United States, have been the repercussions created by the discourse of the 'war on terror', where we see the government financing and promoting restorative approaches to deal with violent acts against Muslims, Blacks, and their communities. These developments clearly make a distinction between hard measures that are taken when dealing with 'terrorists' themselves as part of the security discourse, and soft approaches that deal with the repercussions that such discourses have on the suspect population.

In Europe, on the other hand, a similar trend has been noticed with regard to domestic violence cases, and more recently with family violence, forced marriages, 'honour'-based killings, and female genital mutilation cases. Several mediation services have started dealing explicitly with these matters because of national- or international-based policies and requirements. Similarly, there has also been a movement in several mediation systems to address punishment of minors, where this is blended with and dependent on various ideologies and influences. One reason was to offer alternative measures for what were framed as 'high-risk' youth; another reason was to appease public opinion with regard to the death and sexual abuse of such children in remand prisons; and another was certainly the influence of European Union policies and regulations.

Another reason for the rising interest (mainly of a few researchers) in exploring the implications of restorative justice in cases involving immigrants and refugees in continental Europe and other minorities in Australia, Canada and United States is, on the one hand, the over-representation of these groups in the criminal justice system and, on the other hand, the under-representation in the alternative and diversionary measures (Albrecht, 2008; 2010; Del Campo *et al,* 2011; Waites *et al*, 2004; Bargen, 1995; Blagg, 1998; Brigg, 2007). Research in Spain (Del Campo *et al,* 2011) has shown that young immigrants have greater difficulty in attaining access to such alternatives.

The other major difference between the US and the continental European restorative justice field was the engagement of the English-speaking colleagues in what can be perceived as 'proper' 'intercultural' conflicts. In my own research in the mediation services, nothing in Europe indicated the engagement of the restorative justice field with this category, nor even the intention or the ability to do so. This difference, I believe, has two main causes. One is that continental Europe, because of its history, has a certain difficulty in speaking openly and loudly about race and racism, and even about the seemingly softer concept of 'cultural difference'. There are strong anti-discriminatory discourses in Europe, and often this shows even in the lack of statistics on immigrant background citizens, who are simply considered citizens by the formal system, to the advantage of promoting a certain sense of belongingness, and to the disadvantage of not being able to map properly racism and discriminatory practices. At the same time, when cultural diversity is referred to in Europe, it may relate to a 'totally' different culture, so totally different that it has to be protected, for example, cultural and linguistic minorities. The rest of diversity requires a certain 'blindness', requires to be downplayed and not emphasised.

The other reason, I think, is the way restorative justice is structured in the different continents: in Europe, it is mainly a state-bound and diversionary system, while in the United States it is more flexible, not diversionary, and 'community' based, which makes it easier to experiment with larger conflicts and cases, and also to be more flexible regarding the use of different methods and practices. Serious cases need a restorative intervention that is more of a supplement rather than a total replacement of the criminal justice system.

The 'cultural competence' claims are the less politically oriented claims regarding the topic of 'interculturality', in the sense that they often sound like anthropological social-psychology, or even common-sense insights. The concept has had a better reception in rather more private-oriented fields such as business, counselling and therapy, and also mediation as applied to civil and family matters. With regard to the fact that 'cultural competence' has developed in other fields, including mediation in civil and family matters, this is an indication that the restorative justice field in Europe is bound to the state and criminal justice approach, and therefore less flexible and less in need of improvements on that side. While 'culture' has been 'borne in mind' in other fields in order to increase the quality of negotiations, agreements and interventions, the fund-raising techniques, the legitimacy of the practices, etc, in restorative justice cases are referred to by the criminal justice agencies and funding is provided by the Ministry of Justice, so unless the referrals from the criminal justice system will be drastically reduced or the funding cut, the field will not have the same need to increase its 'cultural competence' to the same degree as other fields have or have had. Nevertheless, I predict the increasing use of this concept in continental Europe, given, on the one hand, the over-representation of foreigners in the prison system, and, on the other hand, the increasing use of the language of clientele, and assume that it will begin to resemble the other continents and other fields which have used the concept to acquire legitimacy.

What is certainly relevant and common to all the continents is the over-representation of minorities, foreigners, immigrants, and people with an immigration background in criminal justice institutions, and even though less represented in diversionary measures compared to the majority population, still in high and increasing numbers also in probation services and restorative justice practices. Discriminatory and filtering mechanisms especially influence foreigners, who are often not considered sufficiently suitable for alternative measures, mainly because of a lack of residence permit, lack of job, lack of community ties, and language difficulties, and who instead are over-represented in remand or pre-trial detention and once there, consequently more likely to go to prison. The reaction towards a 'culturally-appropriate' restorative justice is certainly not a politically motivated one; with few exceptions, there is little indication in the field of restorative justice that the over-criminalisation and over-punishment of these groups is of any concern. Rather,what is of concern for the field is the fact that they increasingly 'have' to deal with participants who are of a mixed background, and this creates challenges which have to be tackled, and which the field might not be prepared for. This clearly illustrates how and why a problem becomes problematised and framed, and urges us to think in an alternative way about these problematisations.

To conclude, I argue that while the concern of mediators in relation to inter-culturality seem mainly to be in relation to matters of 'cultural competence', my own concern is that this emerging problematisation will only be pursued in order to legitimate mediation and enable mediators to deal with the difficulties they will encounter. I have argued that other issues have to be problematised instead, such as over-representation of minorities and foreigners in penal institutions and their low representation in probation and restorative encounters; the use of cultural specificity and language as a filtering mechanism; the lack of representation of different groups from the profession of mediation; the refusal and inability of mediators to engage with more systemic issues and their focus on minor urban disturbances and property cases; the centrality of the concept of neutrality in mediation practices; and the separation of mediation 'from the heart' with mediation 'from the mind'. While I predict that a sector of 'cultural competence' will arise both in Europe and among mediators in the criminal justice system, I argue that the main problem is not lack of 'cultural competence', but more complex types of problematisations.

REFERENCES

Albrecht, B (2008) *The Cultural Dimension of Restorative Justice: The Case of Immigrants and Refugees in Norway and Finland*, Centre for Peace Studies Working Papers No 11 (University of Tromsø).

—— (2010) 'Multicultural Challenges for Restorative Justice: Mediators' Experiences from Norway and Finland' 11(1) *Journal of Scandinavian Studies in Criminology and Crime Prevention* 3.

Augsburger, D (1992) *Conflict Mediation Across Cultures: Pathways and Patterns* (Louisville,KY, John Knox Press).

Avruch, K (2002) 'What I Need to Know About Culture? A Researcher Says …' in J.P Lederach and JM Jenner (eds), *A Handbook of International Peacebuilding: Into the Eye of the Storm* (San Francisco, CA, Jossey-Bass) 75–78.

Banaji, M and Greenwald, A (2013) *Blindspot: Hidden Biases of Good People* (New York, Delacorte Press).

Bargen, J (1995) 'Critical View of Conferencing: Australia and New Zealand' *Journal of Criminology, Special Issue* 100.

Blagg, H (1998) 'Restorative Visions and Restorative Justice Practices: Conferencing, Ceremony and Reconciliation in Australia' 10(1) *Current Issues in Criminal Justice* 5.

Brigg, M (2007) 'Governance and Susceptibility in Conflict Resolution: Possibilities Beyond Control' 16(1) *Social and Legal Studies* 27.

Coates, R, Umbreit, M and Vos, B (2006) 'Responding to Hate Crimes Through Restorative Justice Dialogue 9(1) *Contemporary Justice Review, Issues in Criminal, Social, and Restorative Justice* 7.

Del Campo, J, Vila, R, Marti, J and Vinuesa, MR (2011) 'Mediation among Young Immigrants in the Juvenile Penal Justice System' *Journal of Social Work* 1.

Delgado, R (2000) 'Prosecuting Violence: A Colloquy on Race, Community and Justice; Goodbye to Hammurabi: Analysing the Atavistic Appeal of Restorative Justice' 52(4) *Stanford Law Review* 751.

Gavrielides, T (2007) *Restoring Relationships: Addressing Hate Crime Through Restorative Justice* (London, Race on the Agenda).

—— (2011) 'Restorative Practices and Hate Crime: Opening Up the Debate' *TEMIDA* (December) 7–19.

—— (2012) 'Contextualizing Restorative Justice for Hate Crime' 27(18) *Journal of Interpersonal Violence* 3624.

Hydle, I (2006) 'Ungdom, film og kommunikasjon–et dialogisk persepsjons-perspektiv' ['Youth, Film and Communication: A Dialogical Perception Perspective'], paper presented at the Annual Conference of the Norwegian Anthropologic Association, Trondheim, Norway, 19–21 May.

Kelly, T (2002) 'Is Restorative Justice Appropriate in Cases of Hate Crime' in *Western Pacific Association of Criminal Justice Educators Conference Papers* (Lake Tahoe, NV).

Lederach, JP (1986) 'The Mediator's Cultural Assumptions' 5(1) *Conciliation Quarterly* 2.

Lyubansky, M (2013) 'Restorative Justice for Trayvon Martin Special Issue on Violence Against Individuals and Communities: Reflecting on the Trayvon Martin Case' 5(1) *Journal for Social Action in Counseling and Psychology* 59.

Lyubansky, M and Barter, D (2011) 'A Restorative Approach to Interpersonal Racial Conflict' 23(1) *Peace Review, A Journal of Social Justice* 37.

Pelikan, C (1992) 'The Austrian Juvenile Act 1988: A New Practice and New Problems' in M Heinz and O Hans-Uwe (eds), *Restorative Justice on Trial: Pitfalls and Potentials of Victim Offender Mediation: International Research Perspectives* (Dordrecht, Kluwer Academic Publishers) 163–78.

—— (2007) 'The Place of Restorative Justice in Time and Space' in R Mackay *et al* (eds), *Images of Restorative Justice Theory* (Frankfurt am Main, Verlag für Polizeiwissenschaft) 35–56.

Pettigrew, T (1998) 'Reactions Toward the New Minorities of Western Europe' 24 *Annual Review of Sociology* 77.

Richeson, J and Nussbaum, R (2004) 'The Impact of Multiculturalism Versus Color-Blindness on Racial Bias' 40 *Journal of Experimental Social Psychology* 417.

Rudman, L (2004) 'Social Justice in Our Minds, Homes, and Society: The Nature, Causes, and Consequences of Implicit Bias' 17(2) *Social Justice Research* 129.

Sapir, B (2007) 'Healing a Fractured Community: The Use of Community Sentencing Circles in Response to Hate Crimes' 9(1) *Cardozo Journal of Conflict Resolution* 207.

Shenk, A (2001) 'Victim-Offender Mediation: The Road to Repairing Hate Crime Injustice' 17 *Ohio State Journal on Dispute Resolution* 185.

Tubman-Carbone, H (2007) 'The Use of Restorative Justice to Inform Penalty Enhancements for Hate Crimes', paper presented at the annual meeting of the American Society of Criminology, Atlanta, GA.

Umbreit, M and Coates, R (2000) *Multicultural Implications of Restorative Justice: Potential Pitfalls and Dangers* (St Paul, MN, Center for Restorative Justice and Peacemaking).

Umbreit, M, Coates, R and Vos, B (2003a) *Final Report: Community Peacemaking Project: Responding to Hate Crimes, Hate Incidents, Intolerance and Violence Through Restorative Justice Dialogue* (St Paul, MN, Center for Restorative Justice and Peacemaking).

Umbreit, M, Lewis, T and Burns, H (2003b) 'A Community Response to a 9/11 Hate Crime: Restorative Justice Through Dialogue' 6(4) *Contemporary Justice Review, Issues in Criminal, Social, and Restorative Justice* 383.

Umbreit, M and Ritter, R (2006) 'Arab Offenders Meet Jewish Victim: Restorative Family Dialogue in Israel' 24(1) *Conflict Resolution Quarterly* 99.

Volpe, M and Strobl, S (2005) 'Restorative Justice Responses to Post-September 11 Hate Crimes: Potential and Challenges' 22(4) *Conflict Resolution Quarterly* 527.

Vos, B, Coates, R and Umbreit, M (2002) *Community Peacemaking Project Roundtable Report* (St Paul, MN, Center for Restorative Justice and Peacemaking).

Waites, C, Macgowan, MJ, Pennell, J, Carlton-LaNey, I and Weil, M (2004) 'Increasing the Cultural Responsiveness of Family Group Conferencing' 49(2) *Social Work* 291.

Walters, MA (2011) 'A General Theory of Hate Crime? Strain, Doing Difference and Self-control' 19(4) *Critical Criminology* 313.

Walters, MA and Hoyle, C (2010) 'Healing Harms and Engendering Tolerance: The Promise of Restorative Justice for Hate Crime' in N Chakraborti (ed), *Hate Crime: Concepts, Policy, Future Directions* (Cullompton, Willan Publishing) 228–49.

—— (2012) 'Exploring the Everyday World of Hate Victimization Through Community Mediation' 18(1) *International Review of Victimology* 7–24.

Whitlock, K (2001) *In a Time of Broken Bones: A Call to Dialogue on Hate Violence and the Limitations of Hate Crimes Legislation*, A Justice Visions Working Paper (American Friends Service Committee).

12

To Talk or Not to Talk?

The Limits and Potential of Restorative Justice in Addressing Social Inequalities

BORBÁLA FELLEGI, GÁBOR HÉRA AND GABRIELLA BENEDEK

I. INTRODUCTION

THE INITIAL QUESTION of this chapter was whether restorative justice (RJ) can—in any way—influence the very social processes that produce inequalities and that can be regarded as the main determinant cause of the criminal activity itself. Since this question is highly relevant in the current Hungarian context, we first analyse the main historical and sociological processes that led to the current state of social inequalities in our society, with special emphasis on the situation of the Roma population.

Our analysis also discusses the emerging discourses that link poverty, ethnicity and criminality. As a next step, we move on the 'micro level' to give a deeper insight into the situation of one particular village, including one of its (still ongoing) conflict cases. Following this, we take our 'researcher lenses' off and put on our 'restorative justice practitioner lenses'. Through this particular case we raise some of the potentials and limitations/obstacles that we can face while experimenting with the restorative justice approach. The case study leads us to discuss some more general findings concerning the applicability of the restorative justice approach.

To conclude, on the one hand, we do not think that restorative justice can visibly change the very social structure that reproduces crime. On the other hand, we still think that there are a number of reasons why restorative principles should be taken into consideration while working towards reducing social inequalities.

II. THE 'MACRO LEVEL': ROMA IN HUNGARY

This chapter gives a brief description about the historical and social background of the Roma people in Hungary. Taking the findings of research programmes into consideration we follow how the social circumstances of the Roma have changed in the last few decades. In addition, we introduce the general attitudes of the majority of the society towards the Roma. Finally, we focus on the possible link between the minority and crime and reveal our own approach regarding this issue.

A. Historical Perspectives

The economic situation in Hungary became worse after the fall of the communist regime in 1989, and the situation of the Roma has also worsened dramatically. The employment rate of the general population became considerably higher in comparison with the Roma population (Kertesi, 2005: 194). As the FRA Roma pilot survey confirmed, the rate of paid employment of the Roma aged 20 to 64 was significantly lower (around 35 per cent) in 2012 compared to the non-Roma (nearly 50 per cent) (European Union Agency for Fundamental Rights, 2012: 16–17). There are several reasons behind the high unemployment rate but discrimination is surely one of them. As the ENAR Shadow Report underlines:

> 42 % of the Hungarian Roma respondents aged 16 and above looking for work in the past 5 years said that they experienced discrimination because of their Roma background. (Bodrogi and Kádár, 2014: 12)

Those people, who are trapped in the low-paid segments of the labour market or excluded from it, suffer from the risk of becoming excluded from society (Council of Europe, 2001). Social survey data has confirmed this trend in the case of the Roma in the fields of education (Kemény *et al*, 2004; Molnár and Dupcsik, 2008); housing (Marketing Centrum, 2010; Letenyei and Varga, 2011; Babusik 2004); and health (Országos Egészségfejlesztési Intézet, 2001; Babusik, 2004; European Commission, 2014).

A significant part of the Roma minority (around 8 per cent of Hungarian citizens, about 800,000 people, Marketing Centrum, 2010: 31) suffers also from prejudice. According to a survey conducted in 2011, two-thirds of Hungarians would not let their children play with Roma children (NOL, 2011). In 2009, the percentage of non-Roma agreeing with the statement 'there are respectable Roma, but the majority of them are not respectable' was 80 per cent. Negative attitudes are mirrored by the media representation of the Roma (Bernáth and Messing, 2011; Monori and Kozma, 2010) as well. The lack of tolerance was highlighted not only by research findings but also by the existence of hate speech and hate crime incidents. In 2008 and 2009, a series of murders resulted in the death of six Roma people and several injuries.

B. Roma Crime?

While we are describing the situation of the Roma, the possible link between the minority and crime should also be introduced. This is a 'patchy area' since due to the over-representation of Roma people within the criminal justice system, many people simplistically link criminality to Roma origin. We agree with Kerezsi (2011) who pointed out that in Eastern Europe 'members of the ethnic minorities are commonly considered as "criminal", "thief" which opinion suggests that they are associated with the traditional, typically not serious, so-called "livelihood crime"'.[1] As several research programmes have underlined (Jogifórum, 2008; Gimes *et al*, 2009; Publicus Research, 2009) Hungary is not an exception; many citizens of the country share similar ideas about the Roma.

Scholars and researchers face difficulties in Hungary when they try to confirm or deny these ideas as ethnic origin is considered as sensitive information. Accordingly, a signed consent form would be required for anyone to collect, record, organise or store data concerning people with Roma origin. This has resulted in a lack of crime statistics with special regard to the Roma. In the last 30 years, only three research programmes have analysed this issue. At the end of the 1980s, Tauber and Balogh elaborated the statistics of the police and the prosecution concerning Roma. They declared that the rate of criminal activities of the Gypsies was higher than that of the majority of society, at least in the case of specific types of crimes (such as crimes against property) and within specific groups (such as juvenile offenders) (Tauber and Balogh, 1988). About 10 years later, Huszár pointed out that 'Roma people ... are unprecedentedly overrepresented among the population who are in prison' (Huszár, 1999: 131). In 2000, Póczik conducted a survey in the prison at Vác where a high number of the population (41.5 per cent) belonged to the Roma minority (Póczik, 2000).

Taking these descriptive statistics into consideration, we may conclude that the Roma are significantly over-represented in prisons and have more conflicts with the police. However, we would like to refer to scholars who emphasise that crime is a social problem, closely related to other social conditions, for which not only one individual but the whole of society is responsible. Researchers (Hough and Sato, 2011; Kerezsi, 2011; Mohácsi, 1987) have shown that being influenced by social deprivation and discrimination can lead to criminal offences. As research programmes have already revealed, negative attitudes towards the Roma have been expressed by the police (Bólyai, 1997; Csepeli *et al*, 1997; Fleck *et al*, 2012; Fridrik, 2007; Geskó,

[1] 'Livelihood crime' is a frequent term which is used not only by (extreme) right-wing politicians but by ordinary people as well. It describes petty thieving as a profession and presupposes that the Roma do not have a job as they would not like to work.

2000; Hera, 2015; Kádár *et al*, 2008; Krémer and Valcsicsák, 2001; 2005a; 2005b; Tarján, 1999). Probably, this attitude also contributes to discriminatory behaviour by police officers (Roma Sajtóközpont, 2014; Kőszeg and Králik, 2008; Pap and Simonovits, 2006; Tóth and Kádár, 2011), which practices also increase the number of Roma imprisoned.

III. THE 'MICRO LEVEL': LIFE OF A VILLAGE

In the following, we introduce a village where researchers of the Foresee Research Group were working within the framework of the European ALTERNATIVE project between January 2013 and December 2015.[2] The method of the investigation was action research.

Kulacs is an average village. It is almost in the middle of the country. It has its own soccer field, kindergarten, primary school, small library and church, while a family doctor is available. Local grass-roots organisations (Home Guard, a club for retired residents, a choir, etc) are active. The number of the local inhabitants is around 2,800 so the settlement is average. Roma residents also live in the village but their number is not significant; in 2001, about 4 per cent of the people considered themselves Roma (Központi Statisztikai Hivatal, 2012) but in the opinion of the leader of the Roma Minority Government, this percentage is 8 per cent today, again consistent with the national average. During socialism, 50 per cent of the local residents worked in the industry and many people worked in the capital. This was the period when even the local Roma had jobs and did not have to worry about income and living standards. However, after 1989, industrial workers faced unemployment. Nowadays even the non-Roma villagers have limited opportunities; they can only work mainly at institutes of the local government or travel to Budapest to work and have a job in the surrounding villages or at the few local companies. And Roma residents are either unemployed or, with a few exceptions, work exclusively within the public work system.

Our fieldwork started in January 2013. We prepared interviews with local residents. All kinds of information about Kulacs was collected from libraries, Internet, local residents, local newspapers and local government. Moreover, we personally took part in events, such as the ball of the Catholic Church, soccer games, Roma Day, graduation, consecration of a local monument, etc. As our research already in the first few months revealed, most of

[2] Action research conducted within the ALTERNATIVE project ('Developing alternative understandings of security and justice through restorative justice approaches in intercultural settings within democratic societies'), funded by the European Commission's Seventh Framework Programme (FP7), SEC-2011.6.5 (www.alternativeproject.eu).

the local villagers considered the settlement peaceful where the (subjective) perception of security was positive. However, at the end of the year, at least according to some of the villagers, the number of burglaries had increased in the village. As a reaction, one of the local leaders decided to establish a new 'Civil Guard' in order to 'make the sense of security of the local residents in Kulacs stronger'.

A. Antecedents of the Current 'Civil Guard'

Tibor, the leader of the Roma Self Government and also a member of the local government, revealed the antecedents of the story. He shared with us that members of the Young Residents of the Village Association initiated the establishment of a civil guard a few years ago. They organised a workshop in Kulacs and invited civil guards from the neighbouring villages where they discussed the topic of local security. At that time, several local residents joined the initiative who, as Tibor put it, 'took part in the work but only for several months. After that the enthusiasm decreased'.

As Tibor shared with us, a dissent emerged at that time as members of the current Civil Guard were clearly against involving Roma residents in the work of the only grass-roots organisation which dealt with local security. However, some members of that organisation invited Tibor to join the civil guard but:

> no other Roma from the village were welcome. I resented that, as for the local Roma local security was as important as for the non-Roma. It would have been great if the village had believed that the local Roma had been also for the local security, tranquillity and peace.

Finally, the conflict and harms which arose due to the Roma's exclusion from the Civil Guard were not discussed. Tibor (and other local Roma people) did not join the initiative.

B. Attempt to Establish a New 'Civil Guard' Organisation

Tibor was motivated to do something about the local security after the number of burglaries increased in Kulacs at the end of 2013. He initiated the establishment of a new Civil Guard. He was not alone in this attempt, because Henrik also supported the initiative. The two villagers informed the members of their informal network about their intention, and they advertised the plan on Facebook and in one of the local newspapers. They planned to recruit altogether around 30 to 60 participants.

The originators invited those who were prepared to take part in the work of the new Civil Guard not for a salary but as volunteers. In addition, they wanted to involve villagers who would have been able to support the work by covering the costs of the petrol. According to Tibor, lack of a criminal record had also been a criterion. Henrik emphasised that they had mainly been interested in those applicants who had a driving licence and/or a car. Tibor tried to mobilise and involve even Roma residents in the work of the new organisation.

As Tibor and Henrik emphasised, they had several problems with the current Civil Guard because the number of burglaries increased in 2013. As only two civil guards were on the street at nights, and as their technical equipment was poor, they were not able to catch criminals. According to Henrik, members of the Civil Guard were not dedicated to their work. Despite the discontents, Tibor and Henrik wanted to avoid conflicts with the current Civil Guard. As Tibor underlined: 'I would like to work not against but for them'. He got in contact with the mediators[3] of the Foresee Research Group, as he was afraid of the emergence of a new dissent. As Tibor thought, members of the current Civil Guard which worked in the village would probably have resented the new initiative.

C. How Could RJ Help in this Case?

By now, based on the research interviews, we had been able to gain a rough picture of the themes and tensions concerning the Civil Guard organisation. Since Tibor, as the main stakeholder in this issue, was open and willing to use the help of mediators, we could consider this stage as a 'referral' by him to a RJ procedure. Hence, the next step was that we started the preparation of the case as mediators. To quickly jump to the end, the mediation finally did not take place; the case was closed during the preparatory stage upon the request of Tibor due to the lack of activity of the people he was supposed to represent.

However, the preparatory discussions with the affected parties shed light on several underlying causes and dilemmas. In the following, we will discuss a few of them through 'RJ practitioner lenses'. The next section is more a list of our questions, rather than clear answers to them. Nevertheless, we think that these questions well represent the limitations and obstacles of the RJ approach, specifically in this case as well as in general.

[3] In this chapter we use the term 'mediator' interchangebly with 'RJ practitioner' to make the text easier to understand (although in a methodology-focused chapter we obviously should differentiate between the two terms).

D. Past versus Future

Originally, as RJ practitioners, our primary question was: knowing that there had been past incidents that had caused harm to our 'referral' agent, Tibor, and some others around him, did they actually wish to discuss what had happened in the past and how it had affected them? After several conversations with Tibor, we could conclude that he did *not* prefer the idea of talking about the past. Instead, he constantly highlighted the importance of talking only about the *future*, namely, how to create a better functioning Civil Guard system and who can do what to make it happen.[4]

The preference and choice of Tibor unquestionably had priority in identifying the core topic of a possible dialogue, and as intervening mediators we needed to accept that. Certainly, we could propose different alternatives and argue for their (risks and) advantages, but the final decision was made by Tibor. Still, it raised the question for us: has RJ any added value (compared eg to a 'community planning' activity) if affected people are not interested and motivated to talk about their past harms? Or, in this case are they merely *afraid of* turning back to past atrocities? Or do they not have the *trust* that anyone would listen to them with respect and empathy? At this point, further questions remained for ourselves: can we focus on future solutions and possible ways of cooperation without actually going through what had happened in the past and considering those effects that inevitably influence our present attitudes?

In this case, we accepted the request of Tibor to focus only on the future and leave the past un-discussed. However, we think that this showed one of the important obstacles to applying RJ practices. Namely, we have to discover whether people are ready and trusting enough to face the people who harmed them, before they turning to how to build the future together. Or, from another angle, we have to ask whether we as practitioners are able to build the necessary trust and empowerment to reduce the fear in people and make them able to talk about their pains to each other? And if so, in what ways can we help with this? And can we do this work in cases in which parties differ so much regarding their social and economical statuses within a community? Furthermore, can RJ practices, which aim at *repairing the harm and restoring relations*, be successful at all, if parties do not discuss what they had felt as unjust and painful. And lastly, even if parties come to an agreement about the future needs and offers, will that be sustainable and doable if their mutual understanding of the other side's 'victimisation'

[4] We can also say that there was more openness towards the 'proactive' (future planning) than the 'reactive' (past restoring) restorative interventions.

is lacking. Certainly, we had doubts about where the process could go, but we accepted the preference for future-orientation.

E. Representation

Who owns the conflict in this case? Our 'referral agent' was Tibor, but he represented several others: people who previously wanted to join the Civil Guard? Or those who are interested in it now? Or those suffering from local crime and willing to contribute to this discussion? On the other hand, Tibor constantly communicated that *he* needed to see who were the people supporting this idea, and how many of them would come forward. While this need was absolutely understandable, in practice it resulted in travelling down a dead end street. He was not able to efficiently motivate 'his people' to join this initiative, the interest stayed very low. But meanwhile, he refused the help of mediators in this motivational/empowerment phase, saying that if there were not enough people, this initiative was unnecessary and he did not want to embark on a failed action due to the lack of interest from others. Although we offered our help in mapping and supporting the potentially interested people, Tibor wanted to do it alone, which was understandable again. However, at the end of the day, the result was that due to Tibor's conclusion—'I have realised that there is hardly anyone who is now willing to actively join this initiative'—none of the members of the Roma community could gain more information about our offer of a dialogue process. Hence, we did not have information about *their* needs: would they have wished to talk about their past experiences and were they ready to talk about future solutions? All we know is that they did not show interest to the invitation of Tibor. It is certainly more than acceptable that if the local community leader is not able to effectively motivate the people who he/she represents, an outsider mediator has to accept this situation. However, this still raised the question for us: if the leader stops the dialogue process, does it mean the opportunity for dialogue has to be stopped for all the others concerned in this issue?

F. Voluntariness, Neutrality and the Level of Intervention

The case of the Civil Guard raised further questions concerning the level of intervention and the neutrality of the mediator. These are not only additional questions, but also consequences of the previously discussed dilemmas. This case can be considered as an entirely voluntary, bottom-up approach (unlike RJ, eg penal cases) in which citizens articulate a certain problem and wish to find solutions to that based on their own resources and participation. However, when we get beyond the individual 'venting' level, people would ideally take steps: they might collect allies (by discovering who are committed and interested in further discussing this issue), and initiate personal meetings to share their needs and decide about next steps. While we do not think that it was a surprising and unique experience in this case, we can conclude that active participation and commitment was absolutely lacking even though the issue indeed concerned the entire community. At this point, the question becomes: to what extent can and should the mediator, as an external eye, further 'push' this civil initiative? Initially, we had thought to stay neutral in this regard and instead of *proactively* offering services we rather planned merely to *respond* to requests being made to us. However, in this case we evidently faced the limitations of such a 'reactive' approach. Hence, we can say, we stepped beyond our borders by occasionally suggesting certain actions as next steps and offering help (eg using the mediators' help in recruiting potentially interested people). Also, on several occasions we were the ones initiating discussions even when we had not received calls from people. So in other words, we can say, in Christie's words (Christie, 1977), that we were in danger of taking away the conflict from the people who owned the conflict, because we so much wanted to help and resolve their conflict. Certainly, it did not work. But it raised the question: when a truly bottom-up initiative is started in a context in which civil participation hardly exists, to what extent can and should a dialogue-facilitator stay neutral in not proposing further steps? In other words, what are the effective ways of empowering the parties without actually taking the process out of their hands?

Without answering all these open questions, we found it useful to list some upcoming dilemmas, since they well illustrate the possible obstacles to restorative justice in this context. In the next section, we would like to refer to the title of the chapter and highlight one of the primary challenges that we have faced in this work, namely, people's unwillingness to talk openly, or in short: silence.

G. Silence

The question of silence has already been in focus in previous studies exploring conflict in Kulacs. These reports (Hera *et al*, 2015; Hera, 2016) revealed that the cultural view of conflicts in Kulacs is based on avoidance: villagers avoid open discussion about their problems and 'prefer silence'. Residents consider a 'debate' not as an opportunity for change but as a risk. This is despite the fact that within the community there are several disagreements or even harms that have not been discussed or resolved and are still remembered.

Several conversations confirmed this observation. According to a non-Roma resident, the Roma have a 'different culture and we have to accept it. We shouldn't argue with them and in that event they will not hurt Hungarians either'. Somebody else declared while she was talking about a particular rivalry: 'I forgive but I will never forget it'. Another interviewee maintained that 'I do not think you should deal with this conflict. If we focus on it, it will be worse'. Another person was talking about the clashes among native villagers. In his opinion 'all the time, native villagers were also talking about these oppositions. However, they were not loud as they were sisters-in-law, sons-in-law … They knew it but they did not talk about it'. We met the headmaster of the school who disclosed that about conflicts 'officially there is no communication. They are drowning. There is a drowning and everybody feels their own truth. However, it never comes up to the surface'. A Roma resident shared with us information about a violent conflict. Although someone was hurt seriously, that rivalry has never been resolved, since 'if we do not offend each other, we do not tell it into the face of them, it is not such a big deal'. All in all, participants thought that it was better not to talk about conflicts, not to break with accepted practices that were based on avoiding.

We framed this set of attitudes as a 'culture of silence'. This is what we identified in the case of the Civic Guard as well. The so-called 'pro-Roma' villagers, those who supported the local Roma community, avoided talking about burglaries which might have been committed by the local Roma. On the other hand, Gyuri the leader of FFLE, also made it clear that 'I will tell you nothing about the Roma issue'. His opinion would have been important for us not only because FFLE initiated the establishment of the first Civil Guard in the village, but also due to the supposed anti-Roma characteristic of the organisation. Unfortunately, Gyuri expressly forbade the members of the association to talk openly about problems with the local Roma.

H. Reasons for Silence

There are probabe, reasons why both the 'pro-Roma' and 'anti-Roma' groups avoid open communication about the possible links between crime in the village and the local Roma. On the one hand, the former group would not have liked to strengthen the negative attitudes and accusations of 'Gypsy crime'. According to their interpretation, the Roma do not take part in burglaries at all, especially not in their own village. On the other hand, non-Roma people would like to avoid being stigmatised as 'racist', despite the fact that some of the residents warned that the thefts in their opinion were committed by the Roma:

> There is a lot of conflict about firewood. While white people buy the wood Roma people steal the forest. I know somebody … they went to measure the forest …

> they realised that the trees could be cut so they hired people to work there. One month later ... they arrived at the forest but it was not there. The gypsies stole it.

Another interviewee emphasised that local Roma are seen as contributors to several burglaries. As he put it:

> I consider 100% sure that Roma from Kulacs are involved. Here is my neighbour who let some of the local Roma take away the metal from his garden. They looked around and observed everything ... two weeks later they robbed him.

According to an interviewee, the Roma commit crime because they need money, they are lazy and just live on social benefits. Moreover, committing crime 'somehow it is a kind of code ... it is in their blood'. This is the reason why '90% of the Roma are in prisons'. In short, in both groups avoiding being labelled seemed to be common factor leading to silence.

I. Consequences

Through attempts to avoid conflict and because of the 'culture of silence', there is no public and open discussion about the conflict itself. Reasons, responsibilities and motivators behind crime cannot be identified. Local residents do not discuss questions such as 'Why does somebody commit a crime?' 'What is the reason for burglaries?' 'Is only the perpetrator, the individual responsible for crime?' 'What should the local community do for human or existential security?' Accordinly, there is only symptomatic treatment and the problem of crime cannot be solved either by the Civil Guard or the police.

In addition, lack of open discussion results in a lack of information, which only strengthens the stereotypes, assumptions and suspicions about the Roma, who, at least according to some of the villagers, are involved in burglaries. All in all, lack of information and open communication makes the villagers more prone to create stereotypes about the 'others'. This is how the local 'Roma', the 'FFLE', the current or the new 'Civil Guard', etc become homogeneous groups which consist only of the same kind of people without any exceptions. If the 'other group' is considered to be 'hostile', 'unfriendly', an 'enemy', etc, its initiatives or ideas will not be accepted by 'our group'.

IV. THINKING RJ FURTHER

'Yes, we are mediators. No, we are not into politics.' This could be the starting point of our next section. But we need to move close to the borders of several fields, including politics, if we wish to analyse the possible impact of RJ on changing existing social structures. The current political tendencies in

Hungary[5] are resulting in significant changes in the ways in which communities with disadvantaged and minority background are treated, both within the social welfare and the criminal justice system. It has evident impact on the question whether RJ has any potential to be applied at all, and if so, whether it can reduce social inequalities in such a social climate. However, as we are wearing our RJ lensess and the focus of this chapter is different, we would like to avoid providing any political analysis. Rather, we would like to think aloud about the ways in which RJ can contribute to a stronger sense of social justice within this context.

Returning to our initial question, we asked whether RJ can, in any way, influence the very social processes that produce inequalities and that can be regarded as the main determinant cause of the criminal activity itself. In this regard, our short answer would be: no, we do not think that applying the restorative approach between individuals or even communities has the potential to effectively influence or change the dominant social structures resulting in criminal activities, at least not in the Hungarian context. Based on the previous arguments, we could conclude that several of the necessary conditions for an RJ intervention (eg readiness to talk face to face), are lacking.

Based on the presented case, we could also say that the conflict around the Civil Guard organisation can be perceived as just the tip of the iceberg: it illustrates the difficulties of discussing the causes and solutions to crime on the local level, as well as of bringing people to the same table in order to share their different views and find their own solutions in cooperation with the others. Nevertheless, the question remains whether the RJ approach is able to result in reducing social inequalities and give a greater chance for disadvantaged people to avoid the criminal path.

In short, we would state that if we are searching for ways to find 'respectful' and 'effective' answers to respond to a symptom (crime), even with the RJ approach, but do not address the very phenomena that generates the symptom, the impact of our answer will be very limited. Nevertheless, we still believe in some potentials of RJ. At this point, we return to the 'macro' level, since, if it happens at all, these potentials will probably not be perceived 'here and now', but more in the long term and in broader societal processes. In the next section, we describe four main potentials of the RJ approach that we define as: (1) its community-building function; (2) its delabelling and thematising function; (3) its applicability in advocacy work; and (4) the messages it delivers to us about the notion of responsibility-taking and recognition of the 'other'.

[5] This can be simplistically summarised as a shift from a supportive, equal opportunities-oriented approach towards punishment and strong centralisation concerning the treatment of poor or 'deviantly' labelled social groups.

(1) First, we raise the question whether RJ can be applied without a sense of community with the 'other' side. In our research, we could see that many of the people who are interconnected by a conflict do not feel as if they are interconnected with the others. Hence, any response that promotes mutual respect and dialogue is questionable due to the lack of care about the other. However, the existence of community ties can be considered not only as a precondition (*input*) of RJ. We can look at it also as a possible *output* of RJ: if we somehow manage to bring people together and allow them to share stories and work on solutions together in a respectful and personalised manner, that might result in a sense of community between the involved people. And it gives some hope, especially when the extent of social inequalities are increasing and it is becoming more and more difficult for anyone to 'shield' him/herself from the 'disadvantaged other'.
(2) Secondly, as discussed previously, prejudices and negative labels are both causes and consequences of growing social tensions. What we have seen from our practice is that RJ dialogues can provide safe environments for people in conflicts in order to share their personal stories, pains and strengths with an equal chance for every participant to talk and to listen. Such dialogues allow the participants to focus on a theme (eg crime) and step away from their initial positions (eg I am the victim/the blamed person/the neighbour who understands and feels solidarity with people in need/the respected law-abiding neighbour who 'just' expects others to 'behave normally', etc). If the outcome of an RJ practice is that participants (even if only slightly) move from their initial positions and better understand the underlying causes of the other side's decisions, dilemmas and perspectives, then the result is a more accepting and less labelling community.
(3) Thirdly, before moving to the potentials of RJ in advocacy, we would like to highlight what we mean by applying RJ in advocacy. Basically, it refers to any social dialogue processes (with citizens and relevant stakeholders) which, amongst many others, primarily aims at:

— finding *common points* (identifying links) and not just listing the differences (highlighting what separates us);
— providing a neutral dialogue-*facilitator* who makes sure each perspective is balanced and has an equal opportunity to talk and listen;
— acknowledging that every participant might have their own *pains*, *traumas*, unmet *needs* and *fears* that the dialogue has to address at certain points, therefore the discussion is not about finding compromises between different positions, but about understanding the needs of each participant;
— looking at each participant as a unique *human being* and by this avoiding the use of any labels, such as 'racist', 'gypsy', 'liberal', 'conservative', etc.

In reading this list, one can ask regarding advocacy work: Can we follow these principles as a guiding approach while doing policy work? Can we carry out our discussions in this way while talking to citizens, policy-makers, local mayors, police, judges, prosecutors about how to work together against growing social inequalities and crime?

We think we can. But further questions arise: is it realistic, and even more, is it ethical to put on a 'neutral' hat and approach different stakeholders in such a non-labelling, non-judgemental, understanding, supportive and acknowledging way, regardless of their position in a certain debate? Don't we even further strengthen the dominating position of the ruling classes and weaken the position of the suppressed classes?

We don't yet know the answers to these questions. However, what we have seen while working with criminal justice, social justice and school practitioners is that there are many colleagues who also suffer from being labelled (eg as racists), and have many fears regarding such categorisation and feelings of failure in providing effective help for their clients. And when legal right advocates face clients with the unacceptability of their behaviour and attitudes, they show the same resistance, neutralisation, denials and aggression as offenders do when they are harshly blamed for their acts and no one is listening to their stories before condemning their acts and identity.

To avoid any misunderstanding, we do not think that legal advocacy is not an essential activity. In many of the cases these organisations provide a gap-filling and highly empowering help for certain groups (Roma, children, women, etc) in fighting for their rights and in helping their own awareness about their rights in a democratic society. However, we think that besides such 'battles', we have to map the possibilities for applying less adversarial and more cooperation-focused approaches based on RJ principles. This is the path through which people might become open to planning together in partnerships towards reducing social inequalities. But in order to reach it, each stakeholder needs to have the opportunity to honestly share their individual (and not political!) past harms, present fears and future needs.

(4) Finally, concerning all these issues, the main potential of the restorative justice approach is the way it teaches us about 'responsibility-taking' and its acceptance by those receiving it. In several of our fieldworks we have become aware how stakeholders (representing any and all sides) are afraid of (resistant to) taking responsibility and showing regret for acts that resulted in enlarging and not reducing the social gaps between conflicting groups. It is not because of their individual 'weakness'. In our opinion, it is mostly because we as a community can easily perceive some responsibility-taking by someone belonging to 'our group' as a 'betrayal' against our group. Gaps can only be bridged if we become supportive towards those who are brave enough to take responsibility and ready to take some steps towards the 'other group'. But in many cases, such people receive

condemnation from their community allies, saying that they were not tough enough, they have betrayed their group and made compromises for their own individual interest.

Also, in many cases we might feel that taking responsibility is weakening ourselves. On the contrary, we should learn that it is one of the most difficult things to do and it shows our strength. To put it in the daily context, for example, without taboos, we should be able to admit that there are indeed schools that have segregatory and discriminatory practices. And, on the other hand, we have to face that there are people with Roma origin who are indeed involved in rule-breaking and crimes. But this does not equate to saying that 'white' Hungarian teachers are racist and Roma people are criminals. It merely frees us from taboos and being afraid of not being politically correct all the time. And it is essential, since the lack of dialogues and this kind of fear and taboos are among the main reasons behind average citizens openly adopting discriminatory attitudes and behaviours.

Furthermore, the equivalent task is the recognition (and acceptance) of the other side's responsibility-taking towards us without re-strengthening our stereotypes. Yes, it means that from our strong and sustained 'complainant' position (which can be highly 'beneficial' in the political arena), we should recognise small gestures from the other side and acknowledge those steps. This is again difficult. But it would show our strength and not our weakness and could further generate dialogue and empathy.

In short, the most significant potential of restorative justice in social justice issues is that it shows a model, a principle, which, whatever our role is in a situation, allows us to have different assumptions, make mistakes, recognise the harmful consequences of our acts on others, and have another chance to make something good together with the other side. Admittedly, these are very limited potentials alongside several limitations, but if we are able to move down this path while working with different stakeholders who have the willingness and knowledge to reduce the feeling of injustice within the society, we might have added something to help people in disadvantaged positions.

REFERENCES

Babusik, F (2004) 'Hozzáférési különbségek az egészségügyi alapellátásban' 54 *Esély* 82, available at www.esely.org/kiadvanyok/2004_5/babusik.pdf.

Bernáth, G and Messing, V (2013) *Pushed to the Edge, Research Report on the Representation of Roma Communities in the Hungarian Mainstream Media, 2011* (Budapest, Centre for Policy Studies), available at http://cps.ceu.hu/sites/default/files/publications/cps-working-paper-pushed-to-the-edge-2013_0.pdf.

Bodrogi, B and Kádár, A (2014) *ENAR Shadow Report, Racism and Related Discriminatory Practices in Employment in Hungary* (European Network Against

Racism, ENAR), available at http://cms.horus.be/files/99935/MediaArchive/publications/shadow%20report%202012-13/Hungary.pdf.

Bólyai, J (1997) 'A rendőrség és a cigányság viszonya Magyarországon' 12 *Belülgyi Szemle* 35.

Christie, N (1977) 'Conflict as Property' 1 *British Journal of Criminology* 15.

Council of Europe (2001) *Trends in Social Cohesion, No 1, Promoting the Policy Debate on Social Exclusion from a Comparative Perspective* (Germany, Council of Europe Publishing), available at www.coe.int/t/dg3/socialpolicies/socialcohesiondev/source/Trends/Trends-01_en.pdf.

Csepeli, Gy, Örkény, A and Székely, M (1997) 'Szertelen módszerek. A megkülönböztetésmentes viselkedés lehetőségei és akadályai' in K Csányi (ed), *Szöveggyűjtemény a kisebbségi ügyek rendőrségi kezelésének tanulmányozásához* (Budapest, Alkotmány- és Jogpolitikai Intézet a Nyílt Társadalom Intézet Társintézete).

European Commission (2014) *Roma Health Report, Health Status of the Roma Population: Data Collection in the Member States of the European Union*, available at http://ec.europa.eu/health/social_determinants/docs/2014_roma_health_report_en.pdf.

European Union Agency for Fundamental Rights (2012) *The Situation of Roma in 11 EU Member States: Survey Results at a Glance* (Luxembourg, Publications Office of the European Union), available at http://fra.europa.eu/sites/default/files/fra_uploads/2099-FRA-2012-Roma-at-a-glance_EN.pdf.

Fleck, Z, Krémer, F, Uszkiewicz, E and Navratil, Sz (2012) *Technika vagy érték a jogállam?* (Budapest, L'Harmattan).

Fridrik, J (2007) *Sociological Questions of the Management of Ethnic Minority Conflicts in and in the Area of Gyöngyös* (Thesis, Zrinyi Miklós Nemzetvédelmi Egyetem), available at http://portal.zmne.hu/download/konyvtar/digitgy/phd/2008/fridrik_jozsef.pdf.

Geskó, S (2000) *Rendőrök és romák: konfliktusok vagy párbeszéd?* (Mediátor Tanácsadó Iroda), available at www.konszenzus.org/tanulmanyok/zarotanulmany.pdf.

Gimes G *et al* (2009) *Látlelet 2009. Kutatási összefoglaló a magyar szélsőjobboldal megerősödésének okairól* (Budapest, Political Capital), available at www.politicalcapital.hu/wp-content/uploads/latlelet_2009.pdf.

Hera, G (2015) 'The Relationship Between the Roma and the Police: A Roma Perspective' 1 *Policing and Society* 15.

—— (2016) *Counteracting Social Exclusion Through Restorative Approaches* (Unpublished manuscript).

Hera, G, Benedek, G, Szegő, D and Balla, L (2015) *Deliverable 5.5: Comprehensive Final Report on RJ in Intercultural Communities* (Budapest, Foresee Research Group).

Hough, M and Sato, M (2011) *Trust in Justice: Why It is Important for Criminal Policy, and How It Can be Measured, Final Report of the Euro-Justis Project* (Helsinki, European Institute for Crime Prevention and Control), available at www.icpr.org.uk/media/31613/Final%20Euro-Justis%20report.pdf.

Huszár, L (1999) 'Roma fogvatartottak a büntetés-végrehajtásban' 124 *Belügyi Szemle* 133.

Jogifórum (2008) '*Cigánybűnözés' mint közvélemény-kutatási kérdés?*, available at www.jogiforum.hu/hirek/18478.

Kádár, AK *et al* (2008) 'Justified ID Checks' 106 *Belügyi Szemle* 132.
Kemény, I, Janky, B and Lengyel, G (2004) *Roma of Hungary 1971–2003* (Budapest, Gondolat Kiadó), available at www.mtaki.hu/A-magyarorszagi-ciganysag-1971-2003/4/121/2.
Kerezsi, K (2011) *Konfrontáció és kiegyezés a helyreállító igazságszolgáltatás szerepe a közpolitikában. Akadémiai Doktori Értekezés*, available at http://real-d.mtak.hu/492/4/dc_231_11_doktori_mu.pdf.
Kertesi, G (2005) 'The Roma' in J Köllő (ed), *Monitoring of the Hungarian Employment Politics in the Context of European Employment Strategy Based on Experiences in the Last Five Years* (Budapest, Magyar Tudományos Akadémia Közgazdaságtudományi Intézet), available at www.mtakti.hu/doc/felhiv/zarotanulmany_teljes_mtafmm.pdf.
Kőszeg, F and Králik, L (eds) (2008) *Final Report on the Strategies for Effective Police Stop and Search (STEPSS) Project* (Budapest, Hungarian Helsinki Committee), available at helsinki.hu/wp-content/uploads/books/en/Controlled-group.pdf.
Központi Statisztikai Hivatal (2012) *Magyarország Helységnévtára*, available at www.ksh.hu/apps/!cp.hnt2.telep?nn=32230.
Krémer, F and Valcsicsák, I (2001) 'Előítéletesség a főiskolai hallgatók körében. Vélemények, meggyőződések a cigányságról' 91 *Társadalom és Gazdaság Közép- és Kelet-Európában* 126.
—— (2005a) 'Cigánysággal kapcsolatos attitűdök' 3 *Magyar Rendészet* 27.
—— (2005b) 'Cigánysággal kapcsolatos attitűdök' 39 *Magyar Rendészet* 58.
Letenyei, L and Varga, A (2011) '*Roma Társadalom' TÁMOP— 5.4.1-8/1 'B' komponens* (Unpublished manuscript).
Marketing Centrum (2010) *Roma Society 2010*, available at uccuprojekt.files.wordpress.com/2010/04/romak-marketing-centrum.pdf.
Mohácsi, K (1987) 'Magyar Hírlap interjú Dr. Tauber Istvánnal. A Cigányság bűnözéséről—reálisan' *Magyar Hírlap* 92.
Molnár, E and Dupcsik, Cs (2008) *Country Report on Education: Hungary*, Edumigrom Background Papers, available at www.romaeducationfund.hu/sites/default/files/documents/edumigrom_background_paper_hungary_educ.pdf.
Monori, Á and Kozma, K (2010) *Ezek az emberek nem tudják elfogadni a szabályokat, nem képesek a beilleszkedésre*, available at www.mediakutato.hu/cikk/2010_02_nyar/02_monika_joshi_bharat_roma.
Népszabadság Online (NOL) (2011) *Még az LMP-szimpatizánsok fele is előítéletes nol.hu/belfold/20111205-a_rejtett_ketharmad.*
Országos Egészségfejlesztési Intézet (2001) *Roma felnőtt népesség egészségállapota, egészség magatartása és a romák valamint az egészségügyi szolgálatok közötti kapcsolat vizsgálata* (Unpublished manuscript).
Pap, LA and Simonovits, B (2006) 'Ahogy a lakosság és ahogy a rendőr látja: az igazoltatási gyakorlat tapasztalatai' 125 *Fundamentum* 139.
Póczik, Sz (2000) 'Magyar és cigány bűnelkövetők a börtönben', *Magyar Tudomány*, available at http://epa.oszk.hu/00700/00775/00017/426-435.html.
Publicus Research (2009) *Cigányellenesség a norma*, available at www.publicus.hu/blog/ciganyellenesseg_norma/.
Roma Sajtóközpont (2014) *Nincs rajtuk kalap!*, available at http://romasajtokozpont.hu/nincs-rajtuk-kalap/.

Tarján, G (1999) 'Milyenek is azok a cigányok ...?' in K Csányi (ed), *Szöveggyűjtemény a kisebbségi ügyek rendőrségi kezelésének tanulmányozásához* (Budapest, Alkotmány- és Jogpolitikai Intézet a Nyílt Társadalom Intézet Társintézete).
Tauber, I and Balogh, S (1988) 'A cigányság bűnözése továbbra is aktuális társadalmi probléma' 13 *Belügyi Szemle* 23.
Tóth, MB and Kádár, A (2011) 'Ethnic Profiling in ID Checks by the Hungarian Police' 383 *Policing and Society* 394.

13

Digital Stories and Restorative Justice in Brussels

ERIK CLAES, IMAN LECHKAR, MINNE HUYSMANS AND NELE GULINCK

I. INTRODUCTION

This chapter aims to explore the potentials of digital storytelling for restorative theory and practice in urban areas.

Digital stories are short, participative, produced videos that combine voices, photos, images from magazines and paintings. Digital storytelling is embedded in a tradition of oral history, in which people tell their own stories, of their past, future, their hopes and aspirations. Digital storytelling is therefore designed as a strongly biographical process, in which people can express themselves, unfold their stories, create their scenario, choose, and assemble their images, sketch their drawings, use their voices to convey their message, and even, in the final stage, edit the short films themselves. Modern multi-media techniques, accessible software, allow people to become the movie-makers of their own life stories. The methodology of digital storytelling is highly structured, and staged, and is strongly intertwined with a collective, participative process in which people support each other in the individual process of digital storytelling. Digital storytelling as a space of self-expression also becomes a space of exchange and dialogue.

Restorative justice (RJ) refers to a complex web of practices, aiming at responding constructively to conflicts, or to criminal wrongdoing, by means of mediation practices, family group conferences, peace-making circles. These practices and programmes, with clear, indigenous roots, have been redesigned, refined and monitored, through the last decades. They have been developed in parallel with, in the margin, or, even, in the very centre of the criminal justice system.

The background ideas underpinning these developments refer to strong criticism with regard to the existing concepts, procedures and institutions of the criminal justice system. The current legal environment still has a strongly punitive dimension, is offender-focused, rule-based, institutionally complex. It organises and regulates vertical communication between state officials and the conflicting parties. Restorative justice offers an alternative, more participative view. It proposes an alternative lens to crime, and to responding to crime, by focusing on restoring the harm, and on restoring broken trust between victims, offenders, communities. Storytelling, communication and participation of the conflicting parties in an informal and neutral setting are seen as core features of the process of restoring harm and trust. Proponents of restorative justice perceive and construe their project as an alternative, or as complementary to the criminal justice system, with victim-offender mediation, family group conferences, peace-making circles, as their most powerful instruments of social change.

At first sight, both digital storytelling and restorative justice present interesting similarities. They are both rooted in an empowerment philosophy. Their programmes are structured, staged, and they are often highly monitored by qualitative research. Empirical evidence has strengthened the credibility and legitimacy of both fields of practice. Both fields derive their intuitive force from the power of storytelling that has the potential to move, bond and bridge. And, finally, digital storytelling and restorative justice are strongly embedded in a grass-roots tradition with a strong focus on rediscovering and reinventing indigenous wisdom, in order to respond to the challenges of our times.

So, a multitude of reasons can be offered to organise knowledge-exchange between scholars and practitioners of digital storytelling, on the one hand, and expertise in restorative justice, on the other hand. But as far as we know, neither literature nor innovative practices have taken steps to bring these fields of experience together.

In this chapter, we will fill this gap. While it definitely deserves our full attention to examine the potentials of restorative justice techniques for the process of digital storytelling, we will restrict our analysis to tease out the potentials of digital storytelling for restorative justice theory and practice. The reason for this choice stems from the nature and purpose of the actual research project in which the potentials of digital storytelling emerged.

Since 1 November 2013, the School of Social Work of Odisee (Brussels) launched a practice-oriented project on restorative justice in intercultural settings (until November 2015). The purpose of the project was threefold. We, first, aimed at rethinking the conceptual framework of restorative justice in order to make RJ theory responsive to urban challenges. The second purpose was to develop innovative practices to test restorative justice concepts, intuitions, and techniques in complex, urban settings, full of multilayered, intercultural conflicts. The third aim was to connect the expertise of community work with mediation techniques.

It was the power of an encounter (and not active, systematic research) that brought digital storytelling into the research project. By experimenting with this method, and by combining it with other interventions, the relevance (as well as the limitations) of digital storytelling for restorative justice became gradually visible.

This chapter reconstructs the trajectory of 10 months' research from an internal point of view. In 'thick' descriptions and from a 'we'-perspective the researchers narrate some crucial, transformative scenes of research in which important milestones have been set. These scenes reveal a storyboard of research leaps that have been made with regard to connecting digital storytelling with restorative justice.

The central hypothesis of the chapter comes down to the idea that digital storytelling has ground-breaking potential for restorative justice theory, practice, but also for restorative justice research.

But let us begin with sketching a first, transformative scene. It is in fact our last one and it represents our most recent experience in the field that urged us to rethink the place and role of digital storytelling in our overall research scheme on restorative justice in Brussels.

II. *MOKAFÉ* AND URBAN CRACKS IN ANNEESSENS

It is one of the last days of August 2014. We were sitting in a cosy cafe '*Mokafé*' in *les Galleries Saint Hubert* at hardly 200 metres from our research office. The café is located in the centre of Brussels, in a beautiful nineteenth-century gallery, near by *La Grande Place*, highly frequented by tourists and inhabitants. It is about 9 am in the morning, there is still a quietness hanging over the gallery, which brings its charm to its full expression. We were on our way to a meeting with Virginie, a social mediator at BRAVVO (a social mediation service organised by the City of Brussels focused on prevention and community work). Virginie's office is in the very heart of the Anneessens quarter, our research site, our focus for our project on Restorative Justice in Brussels. One of the offices of BRAVVO is located in the *Rue Vautour*, on the ground floor of a social housing complex.

But, there was still time for a coffee in *Mokafé*. Time to chat, to fill our minds with fresh ideas, and to prepare the meeting in a public space, at the terrace outside the café. We talked about urban cracks, lost spaces in the city, abandoned or waiting for a destination. Brussels is a city full of these depressing spaces, but at the same time, they attract curiosity and creativity. Their emptiness, ugliness trigger people's imagination. In these cracks unexpected possibilities open up, ideas and projects grow. One of us conveyed his enthusiasm about *Alleedukaai*, a city project grown out of an abandoned shack. 'This is what we have to do in Anneessens', he said. 'And I discovered an urban crack, I'll show you'.

Anneessens is the site of our research on restorative justice. We explore the field, in order to spot conflict-zones. The recently discovered crack is such a zone, it is a filthy corner, bordering one of the social housing complexes, behind the football square. It's a space with no real use, except for smoking pot and dumping garbage. It is full of weed and puddles, and a lamppost lying on the ground. Here and there, you can see signs of arson.

So we went there, after having paid for our coffees. We discovered the spot during a house visit to Catherine, a 70-year-old lady living on the seventh floor of the social housing building, with a beautiful view of the skyline of Brussels, but also with an ugly view of the dumping zone. This corner is a source of frustrations, it is filthy, it attracts illegal activities at night, groups of youngsters are hanging out there, a smell of urine spoils your morning feeling. And it feels unsafe.

Catherine's precarious living conditions in Anneessens are not exceptional. Her restless search for a calm and quiet space, her frustrations about an accumulation of incidents with youngsters, the bad housing facilities, all these personal needs reflect broader and deeper urban challenges. Brussels is a metropolitan city, marked by extreme socio-economic and cultural diversity of groups and individuals. There is a strong duality between the rich and the poor, and this is reflected in the urban geography of the city. While the east side of the capital is inhabited by wealthy habitants, the western part of the city is marked by impoverished, dense areas where unemployment is very high.

The Anneessens quarter, although located in the city centre of Brussels and with its strategic location between Central station and Midi station, is one of these impoverished areas. The area is characterised by high population density (24,948.16 per square kilometre); a young population (average age 26.35 per cent of the Anneessens population is younger than 18 years old, compared to 6.31 per cent of the population who are 65+); a high unemployment rate (36.4 per cent and among youngsters, over 40 per cent); a low property ownership rate (20 per cent live in property that is rented and not owned; the quarter is dominated by tenants; 8 per cent of accommodation is social housing); limited living space (52 per cent live in housing smaller than 55 m^2, while households are numerous); super-cultural diversity (39.8 per cent of the population is foreign, of which 12.84 per cent have roots in North Africa and 6.33 per cent in Sub-Saharan Africa).

And here we were standing, in the midst of this 'shit hole', 20 metres below the window of Catherine, and 15 minutes before our meeting with Virginie. Here we were, reflecting how in this ugly place, so many urban transitions come together:

(1) poverty, unemployment, leading to all kinds of illegal economy, breeding in dark and invisible spots;
(2) high density of the population, living in small apartments, permanently confronted with each other's own presence, seeking for spaces of leisure, spaces of self-expression, and for Catherine a space of tranquillity;
(3) blocked channels of communication between different generations.

We looked at each other, and nodded. Yes, this is it. This is the place to plant our chalet. This will become the centre of our action research. Here, we will continue our walking and weaving. Here we will experiment with digital storytelling. Here we will test, and rebuild the grounding concepts of restorative justice. And in a few minutes time we felt our research project shifting, a new direction was set. The spot opened new connections on restorative justice and urban challenges. But why build a chalet in an urban crack? From where came the idea of organising and collecting digital stories on this spot?

III. RESTORATIVE JUSTICE, GROWFUNDING AND URBAN CITIZENSHIP

We started our research project on restorative justice in Brussels, in the beginning of November 2013. The first work package of our research project consisted of developing a theoretical framework that connects the grounding concepts of restorative justice with the complex urban setting of Brussels. We planned two and a half months to draft a concept book that could serve as a guide map for our interventions. Our initial idea was to (a) define key concepts around restorative justice; (b) define key concepts with regard to the urban context of Brussels; (c) integrate both concepts into a coherent whole; (d) clarify the role of arts based methods; (e) formulate principles for innovative, urban restorative practices.

A. Restorative Justice

Pinpointing restorative justice to its essential concepts is not a sinecure. Many restorative justice theories and models exist, and sometimes they compete in their claims and ambitions. But there are at least three elements that recur in each restorative justice story. Pali and Pelikan (2010) distinguish a lifeworld element, a participative element, and a restorative element.

Restorative justice stresses the *lifeworld* element because it sees crime and conflict not only as unlawful behaviour, but also as a disturbance of human interactions, as a web of frictions and frustrations, that beg to be told and heard by the stake-holding parties. A respectful restorative response aims at constructing a safe space in which these personal stories can be told, and respectfully listened to. The underlying restorative intuition comes down to the idea that exchange of stories through a dialogical setting generates a context in which conflicting parties can be moved by each other's story. Finding an appropriate practice that embodies this life element is one of the key steps to conflict-transformation.

RJ stresses the participative element, for the simple reason that restorative justice is shaped by democratic ideals of ownership, participation and deliberation. It strongly believes that conflicting parties are affirmed, and even grow in their dignity, self-respect and autonomy, if they are given a stake in responding to crime or conflict. Participation in finding solutions for conflicts, or in negotiating conflicting interests, are seen as expressive of shared ownership. Conflicting parties are becoming the owners of their conflicts, and thereby gain again some control over their lives.

And, finally, RJ stresses the restorative element. It conceives its practices with the aim of restoring 'something'. What this restorative element precisely contains is not always clear. But the common idea is that the response to crime is something constructive, something that gives victims, offenders, the conflicting parties a chance to open new perspectives for the future. By doing so, restorative justice focuses on mobilising moral emotions such as empathy, repentance, forgiveness, hope. These emotions risk being obscured in a punitive climate that is dominated by fears, resentment and retribution. In rediscovering these restorative emotions, proponents of restorative justice hope to transform conflicts into new chances for human interactions in the future. Exchange of personal narratives (the lifeworld element), actively participating in finding a response to conflicts are seen as important vehicles in releasing and channelling these restorative emotions.

One of the main challenges of our research project on restorative justice in Brussels was to rethink these three key elements, to free them from the narrow framework of crime and criminal justice, and to make these RJ elements fully responsive to the urban setting of Brussels, and its challenges.

B. Growfunding and Urban Citizenship

In January 2015, during our thinking process, we were asked to write and present a paper that critically reflects on another research project, named 'Growfunding'.[1] The project was launched by colleagues from our social work research group at Odisee. Our colleagues developed a digital platform (a website) to help people, collectives, associations in crowd-financing their projects. They coached 10 creative, small-scaled city projects that popped up from the belly of Brussels. Each project presented a promotion film on the website, posted its desired amount of money, but also its counter-engagements corresponding to a certain amount of donation.

The researchers also gave advice as to how to stimulate the donations through activating the social networks of the project-holders, online, as well as offline. By doing so they transformed crowd-funding from a financial instrument into an empowering, participative instrument. The try-out of Growfunding was quite successful. Through the website, the media buzz,

[1] See www.growfunding.be/bxl/streetexpo.

the response of organisations in Brussels, but also in other cities, it became visible that Growfunding responded to real social needs. It included a a need for alternative financing, but also for making hope and aspirations visible around pressing social issues, such as lack of green urban space, healthy food for deprived children, but also around mobility and traffic safety. Growfunding shows to project-holders, their networks, but also to public officials that urban ideas and urban innovation are possible in small, concrete projects: producing sheep cheese in the city, building mobile kitchens to cook with children on the market, building a pop-up park in an abandoned space at *Porte de Ninove*.

And so our fellow-researchers asked us to reflect on their Growfunding project from the perspective of urban citizenship. Their request came in the middle of our conceptual exercise on restorative justice in Brussels, and we were hesitant to accept. Precious research time risked being used for other purposes than our own project. In order to manage time and energy efficiently, we decided to integrate reflection on Growfunding and urban citizenship into the building of our conceptual framework on restorative justice. As a consequence, teasing out ideas on urban citizenship from Growfunding (a project, with a completely different dynamics and purpose) became an important starting point for building our own ideas on RJ in Brussels. We were learning from an existing experiment to help ideas grow for another experiment.

Three dimensions of urban citizenship emerged from analysing Growfunding, its underlying ideas, platform, its coaching strategies, and networking environment, and not least from analysing the creative city projects that were posted on the Growfunding website.

Consider the following city project. In mid-January 2014 a socio-cultural organisation Cultureghem launched the idea of KOOKMET on the Growfunding platform. The project holders hoped to collect 10,000 Euros for building mobile kitchens. Their idea was to invite children and youngsters in Brussels to learn to buy healthy food cheaply, and to cook themselves a tasty and healthy meal. By making the kitchen mobile, project-holders hope to lower the threshold for children and youngsters to take part in their activities. The kitchens could be placed in the market of the Abattoir, amidst fresh cooking ingredients, and amidst the lifeworld of deprived children.

What Does This Project Teach Us about Urban Citizenship?

(i) The marketplace in which the mobile kitchens will be placed reminds us first that *urban citizenship aligns with urban interventions* in which social networks cross, meet, and often hurt. In these spaces, urban innovations, such as KOOKMET, emerge. In these hectic zones the diversity of cultures, and lifestyles, inspire people, citizens and associations to find creative solutions for pressing social needs. Growfunding with its digital platform amplifies this creative potential in public space, by helping to make inspiring city projects visible.

(ii) The idea of cheap and healthy cooking reminds us of the fact that this city project aims to connect people around pressing social problems and needs: child poverty and the precarious access of children to cheap and healthy food, and to the knowledge of how to prepare such food. Urban citizenship refers then to a web of practices in which people *support each other in giving access to their human needs, rights, and capabilities*. Not responsibilities but *helping people grow in their human capabilities* is the key expression of urban citizenship.[2] Growfunding broadens and deepens this social support, by helping to mobilise social networks in making city projects happen.

(iii) The idea of organising workshops with children in the market around a mobile kitchen makes us aware that hope for a better future is not a vague and fluffy aspiration, but a concrete project, with concrete actions, build around a concrete technology (mobile kitchen). Urban citizenship refers to the *capacity to aspire*, the capacity to navigate in the future by turning desires and needs into concrete operational projects.[3] Growfunding nurtures aspirational citizenship. Its underlying coaching support enables the project-holders to acquire concrete strategies of communication, to build social networks, thereby increasing their chances to connect the crowd with their project (and collect the money).

(iv) And, finally, KOOKMET invented a practice that unfolds in public space. It gives children tools, knowledge and a framework (through workshops) to move into public space, and to make in a dignified way their basic needs and rights visible. Urban citizenship refers then to the right of the city to a set of practices that allow people to claim a spot in the urban scene, and to express one's right to have rights.[4] Growfunding strengthens *this right to the city*, because it furnishes a digital version of the urban scene that can be shared and viewed through social media.[5]

From this reflection, three dimensions of urban citizenship emerged: urban citizenship as a participative practice that stimulates development of human capabilities (first dimension); as an aspirational practice in which citizens learn to make their hopes and aspirations concrete (second dimension); as a capacity to makes one's needs and rights visible in public spaces (third

[2] We were also inspired by M Nussbaum, *Creating Capabilities* (2011). We fully embrace the link between urban citizenship and Nussbaum's list of 10 capabilities.

[3] For the importance of stimulating the capacity to aspire, see A Appadurai, *The Future as Cultural Fact* (2013).

[4] Compare H Arendt's notion of citizenship as a right to have rights in her book on *Totalitarianism* (1958).

[5] For this version of H Lefèbvre's right to the city, see Plyushteva (2009).

dimension). Through our reflection on the Growfunding project, it became clear to us that our action research on restorative justice in Brussels should use this three-layered notion of urban citizenship as its guiding concept. The conceptual challenge was now to revisit the lifeworld element, the participative element, and the restorative element, and take urban citizenship as its centre of gravitation.

On 14 February 2015, the research team of Growfunding organised a concluding workshop, named 'Growfunding Bazar'. The concept of Growfunding, and its results were presented to an audience of about 100 people. We presented our paper on 'Growfunding and Urban Citizenship', as a prelude to a panel debate. The feedback was positive, and we decided to stick to our idea of citizenship, and introduce it as the central aim of our restorative justice story. This decision led to the following scheme of ideas.

C. Urban Citizenship and Restorative Justice

We first revisited the *lifeworld* element. In line with proponents of restorative justice (RJ), exchange of stories, and lived experiences of stakeholders in conflicting relations are an important element of our conceptual framework. These stories reveal different perspectives of how conflicts are lived, defined and contextualised from the first person perspective of the narrator. In line with restorative justice theory, we believe that exchange of these stories has the power to generate mutual respect and understanding. But our perspective of urban citizenship invites us to make this storytelling expressive of urban citizenship. We're looking for a narrative environment in which the stories of conflicting parties make needs and rights visible, and in which seeds of hope are sowed. And this narrative environment should not only be a private, confidential one, it should also have a public counterpart.

Secondly, we discussed the *participatory* element. Again, we reaffirmed the idea of ownership of the conflict. But we discovered that the participatory element should be expanded and deepened. If our aim for this project is to help people to collect their skills and imagination in order to get access to their needs, rights, we have no other choice than to expand the participatory element, beyond talking, negotiating and deliberating. The participatory element should also include a process of co-learning, and co-building, as in the city projects of Growfunding.

As to the third, the *restorative* element, we fully embraced the idea of mobilising restorative emotions, instead of narrowly focusing on resentment and retribution. We, also, fully embraced the idea of facilitating stakeholding parties to see their conflicts, their stance through another mirror, through a different angle that makes a more constructive space of encounter possible in the future. Our central notion of urban citizenship invites us to make this power of hope more operational, more concrete, and also more visible, so that it can circulate in the city and inspire people. This, inevitably, implies that our urban restorative justice practices should be explicitly output oriented. Aspirational citizenship brings us to the idea of creating an environment in which hopeful ideas grow into operational city projects.

After this conceptual exercise, we realised that having stepped temporarily out of one's own project, and having entered into the very core of another project, was not at all a waste of time and energy. On the contrary, it accelerated the thinking process and brought RJ to the context in which it is supposed to grow: Brussels.

D. Growfunding and Principles for Innovative Restorative Justice Practices

Besides our insights on urban citizenship, the intense cooperation with the research team of Growfunding helped us to take other elements into consideration that were worthwhile to integrate in our restorative justice interventions. These elements inspired us to formulate a few principles for our restorative justice practices.

The Growfunding project showed us, first, the importance of *proximity*. The ties of solidarity prove to be more effective if the potential donors identify themselves with the city project, if there is a proximity between the supporting networks with regard to values, interests, location of the project. Bringing this principle of proximity to restorative justice in Brussels, we decided to restrain our restorative justice practices to clearly demarcated urban zones in Anneessens, and to bring our interventions as close as possible to the lifeworld of the inhabitants of and visitors to Anneessens.

Secondly, we discovered the importance of a *digital environment* as a powerful way to communicate ideas, to mobilise people and networks. We became fascinated by the little promotion films of the city projects which were posted on the website of Growfunding, and circulated on our Facebook pages. Our hunch was that restorative justice practices might discover new horizons through new digital tools and structures. Growfunding awakened a desire to provide a new digital skin for the well-established practices of mediation and family group conferences.

Thirdly, we discovered the power of *connecting networks*, groups, around a *commonly shared project*. And so we decided to design our restorative justice practices according to the principle of weaving networks and project-building. Researchers from Growfunding coined a fascinating image: acupuncture of the city, evoking the idea that Brussels is a network city, in which a multitude of networks are living next to each other. Networks are crossing each other, or rubbing against each other. In a multi-diverse city, numerous networks co-exist. Often, tensions emerge, interests clash.

'Acupuncture of the city' refers to a limited set of social work interventions in the city, in analogy with a precise prick of a needle, pinned to a spot where networks cross, meet and collide. The intervention, like acupuncture, aims at releasing participative energy through different networks, in order to revitalise the city. This metaphor was a strong narrative for us. It inspired us to rethink crime and conflict spatially, as a friction between people and networks, but also as an opportunity for the acupuncturist (the mediator) to plant his needle, to release the energy of the conflicting parties to transform their conflicts by focusing on common grounds and a common project.

Fourthly, the metaphor of acupuncture of the city invited us also to share our broad story of restorative justice in Brussels, not only as a conceptual narrative, but also as a story that can immediately be grasped by means of a metaphor, an image, not least a set of powerful public interventions in the city that can be remembered, that can be recorded, and that can circulate in the city. Growfunding taught us the importance of communicating publicly ideas and solutions through powerful images (a mobile kitchen, a pop-up park). We were eager to learn how the conceptual building stones of our research project (the exchange of stories between stake-holding parties, the process of participation, and the dynamics of restoration) might be made visible in the city through the restorative practices we were at a point to reinvent. So we decided to take the power of imagination in *public space* as a leading principle for our project. This is a real challenge since restorative practices are traditionally organised into safe, confidential spaces, far away from publicity, and from the public realm.

IV. WALKING AND WEAVING CITIZENS

A. Reconstructing a Web of Walks

In mid-December 2013, Buurtwinkel, a community centre in Anneessens (one of our research partners in the field), celebrated its 30th anniversary: 30 years of community work around poverty, housing issues, lack of public space and over-regulation. We were invited. One of our researchers went to the event, and met Jacques, a man in his 40s, actively engaged in Anneessens, who migrated to this place from East Flanders about 25 years ago. Jacques consented to guide us into his world, his neighbourhood, his network. Two walks issued from this encounter, each time with a stop into a café. Jacques was our first interviewee, our first intervention in a series of 17 walks.[6] In the following months, one of our researchers interviewed Elke, a Flemish migrant living

[6] Only those interviewees who explicitly consented to our revealing their story are mentioned with their true names. The other names are all fictitious.

in an apartment of GOMB; Vincent (Elke's neighbour), a Spanish migrant living almost his whole life in Anneessens. Our researcher took a little walk with S, *Mr Falafel*, who runs a Falafelbar in the Rue LeMonnier. He walked with Guido, also living in a GOMB building. Guido shared his fascination for urban planning, and showed the potentials of a new park from porte de Ninoven to porte d'Anderlecht. Our researcher also met Badya, Odette and Pamela, all actively engaged in Buurtwinkel. He also contacted Daryl, a photographer and artist, who lives near by the *Palais du Midi*. And finally, he encountered Catherine, Willy and Melanie, older people, with a long history in Brussels and Anneessens.

At the end of April 2014, a second researcher started her walks with park visitors of Anneessens. *Parc Fontainas* has a reputation for drug dealing, of groups of youngsters guarding their territories. But it is the only green space in the neighbourhood where mums can chat and children can play. It's the only place in Anneessens where grass, trees and space invite people to relax and enjoy the sun. In her first intervention, this researcher encountered two French students, studying the art of graphic novels at the *Académie des Beaux Arts*, about 500 metres from Anneessens. She also walked with two 14-year-old girls who lived in *les cinq blocs*, a social housing in the Dansaert quarter, a neighbourhood bordering Anneessens. In May, our researcher met three 16-year-old boys, of Moroccan origin, at the entrance of *Athenée Le Page*, not far from Anneesssens. Like the girls, they were living in *les cinq blocs*. One of the boys brought her into contact with Medi, the coordinator of a small NGO, aiming at strengthening social cohesion in the quarter, by giving linguistic tools to parents and children. He gave his view on the problems and challenges of the neighbourhood. A few hours later, our researcher met two young women, walking in the park, two students, engaged in an association that distributes food to the poor. They have the base of their association in a house just in front of the park. The last intervention in the park revolved around an encounter with Sub-Saharan young adults, who were smoking and dealing. One of them, Daniel, wanted to tell his story.

So both researchers followed their research track. The first weaved a web of walking interviewees, by asking whether one interviewee was willing to provide a contact person in his network, as a new step for another interview. His walks were prepared in advance. He fixed a date, walked for an hour, ended with a conversation in a café. He took a half open interview, with a structured list of a few open questions. He sealed the meeting with a request: whether the interviewee consented to him taking a photo. The approach of the second researcher was quite different. She sat in the Parc Fontainas, or walked around in the quarter, and asked youngsters, who happened to be there, to show their quarter, to tell their story. The interventions were less structured, and strongly depended on what unexpectedly happened at that moment. Contrary to the first researcher, there was no existing network (friends, association) from which she could build trust. Her interactions grew out of the unexpected, with the risk of being felt to be intrusive.

Both approaches, combined with analysis of the demographic data, constituted what we initially framed as our second work package: a field analysis of Anneessens. Such a field analysis would allow us to map the conflicting zones, the conflicting parties, the broader context of the conflicts, as well as the needs and interests that might furnish a common ground for discussion and dialogue. Such a field analysis would also give us an idea of the diversity of views in the quarter. How are people living in, or visiting Anneessens? What is their engagement in the neighbourhood? Against which background of meaning are they walking through the streets? And what are their reference-points in the quarter? What is their social network, their social space in Anneessens?

A lot of issues surfaced during the walks: lack of calm, green space, bad housing conditions, garbage on the streets, drug dealing, vandalism, youngsters hanging around, criminality. One of the more global topics that recurred in the interviews concerned the bad reputation of the quarter, and especially of the park. Some responded to this issue by simply avoiding Parc Fontainas. Others expressed a desire to transform this bad image.

Asking a 14-year-old schoolgirl who was born and bred in the quarter about the challenges and the possibilities of the quarter, Selma explained that she'd rather hang out in the city centre, near the bourse and the shopping street Rue Neuve instead of in Anneessens. In the distance, she pointed to the five social housing projects where she lived. When asked whether we could go closer, the girl confessed that she would rather stay at a distance:

> If I come closer and they see me, they will oblige me to enter the house while I will want to go into the city with my girl friend.

The social control was apparently very tangible in the life of the 14-year-old girl. She referred to Parc Fontainas as Philips Park because until recently the light-producing Philips factory was situated there:

> The park is just behind the corner but I never go in there because I don't want to be associated with the park. Most young girls don't go there because there are too many guys that show wrong behaviour.

There are also young guys that don't frequent the park. The 17-year-old Ahmed elucidates the bad image of the park:

> In the past mothers with their children went to the park to enjoy a lovely afternoon but nowadays, the park is dominated by guys with whom it's better not to have contact. The park is also known because of the many police actions, in which the police block all the exits and start frisking park visitors. Because of such actions the park has received a bad reputation.

Walking towards the park, Ahmed drew our attention to a patrol car. During the quarter of an hour that we spent in the park, three other patrol cars drove by. Ahmed refused to solely associate his quarter with conflict-zones and frictional networks and emphasised the reinforcing networks that also exist in the quarter:

> There is good understanding between neighbours in the social housing. We can even speak of solidarity. If someone needs help, that person will receive help. For example if I see an old man carrying something heavy, I will help him out.

Ahmed criticised the role of the media in the image formation of the Quarter:

> This area has good and bad youngsters but unfortunately not much positive is being said about exemplary youngsters. Only the bad guys appear on TV. In that sense I wouldn't mind the Flemish or francophone TV channel to visit so we can tell our story.

Instead of tackling the source of the problem, media focuses on the visible actions that are seen out of context, Ahmed argued:

> We would like to have more green spaces and the area should become more social. A football field is really desirable because since we don't have one, we tend to play football in the parking space and might annoy other people.

B. Performative Potentials of Storytelling

Quite rapidly, we discovered that our interviews largely surpassed the borders of a field analysis. Initially designed as a research method, our walks and interventions acquired another meaning, which non-intentionally came to us through the encounters with our interviewees. Our reflection on the role of the field analysis in the global strategy of our restorative justice research brought us to radically redefine the status of these walks. One of the interviewees inspired us to conceptualise this mind shift. It was Daryl, the photographer. When walking through Anneesens he told how he was struck by the living room feeling of some spots in the quarter. People, because of the tiny living spaces, occupy public space as if it were their living room. They 'perform' these spaces as living rooms. Daryl made us understand that urban space shifts in meaning according to the manner in which people use this space, and represent themselves in this space. In other words: their talks, actions, bodily gestures perform public space. They make the meaning of public space true. Consequently, public space is something dynamic, something that needs to be performed, and in which people need to perform themselves, in order to bring to life a public space. The notion of performance (coming from linguistic theory and having entered art theory) is also nicely chosen, because the act of performing is something inherently public, it is an act that is destined (or doomed) to be seen, and assessed.

The notion of performance inspired us to understand the talking and walking as a performative process. Of course, given our background of restorative justice, and our acquaintance with the stages of mediation, we were sensitive to the importance of the lifeworld, and life stories of the interviewees, but what we didn't expect was that the combination of storytelling, meeting, walking, listening, communicating released such a strong self-expressive energy from the side of the interviewees. Inhabitants as well as visitors performed their engagement with regard to Anneesens, they consciously, or unconsciously, revealed themselves, or tried to better understand themselves through the talks and walks.

In some cases, the unfolding narrative became expressive of power relations. The smoking and dealing young adults affirmed their power with regard to their territory, and only allowed access under conditions. Interviewer and interviewee came to a point of negotiating these power relations. In what follows we will illustrate all these different performative potentials of storytelling.

C. Storytelling and Self-expression

All walks revealed a certain connectedness with the Anneessens quarter. Some of the walkers were really actively engaged in their neighbourhood: they volunteered, or thought they should engage more intensively. Others passed through the quarter to observe, to visit, to meet, or just have to lunch with friends. Their relation was more episodic. Still others felt stuck in the quarter. For them, staying in Anneessens, meant waiting, waiting to move, to escape, or even to die. Some of them were on the run; they avoided being associated with the park, or with their living place. Others stayed in the park, to deal, smoke and survive. Anneessens was the symbol of homelessness. Still others responded ambiguously: with an alternation of love and frustration.

It was remarkable to see how the walking and talking through the streets and places became an occasion for a few walkers to reflect upon their connectedness with the quarter. Vincent's interview exemplifies beautifully how his walking dialogue allowed him to reflexively redefine his stance towards his living environment. During the walk, he articulated his view on Anneessens as a quarter with a lot of potentials, that has changed positively through shops, bars and terraces, but, unfortunately, with a bad reputation. Vincent used strong but powerful images, such as Annneessens covered by a black veil, that only needed to be lifted up. The walk seemed to trigger also a stronger awareness that actions and interventions are needed to restore the image of Anneessens. Through his storytelling, we saw Vincent reflecting on his position regarding the neighbourhood, but we also encountered him as an awakening active citizen, ready to give something back to his daily life environment.

This reflexiveness surfaced even in the narratives of the 14-year-old girls. The brief intervention of our second researcher revealed how the girls are constantly repositioning themselves in urban spaces: Parc Fontainas is a 'no go'zone; *cinq blocs* are spaces of parental control; Saint Goriks hall is a lunch space; Rue Neuve and Boulevard Anspach are places of meeting and consuming. Through their narratives, the girls gave sense to their actions and to the directions of their actions. Their short replies and brief assessments betrayed their aspirations, but also the expectations of their parents. It is as if their dynamic position in urban space somehow revealed a deeper personal stance in our contemporary world.

The idea that storytelling, while moving through public spaces, invites people to express and perform their identities is a classic one, strongly elaborated in the writings of Hannah Arendt (1958). But, at least some of our interviews make this idea very concrete. Take, for example, Jacques, our first interviewee. When revisiting our research notes, we discovered how Jacques' walking and storytelling were in line with his deep Christian beliefs, of modestly, silently helping people, as a devoted *ambassadeur de la paix*. It is not surprising, then, that one of his talks took place in a Franciscan monastery. When Jacques traced his trajectory through his quarter, he also performed an inner trajectory through the inner spaces of his own strongest beliefs, convictions and aspirations. Jacques' narrative unfolded a strong civic engagement, but at the same it was a strongly personalised engagement. It was an act of self-expression, an act of expressive citizenship.

D. Shifting Roles

In their storytelling, our walking interviewees reflected on their relatedness with Anneessens, but responsive to their guiding tour, they also dynamically performed their stance to their environment, to its issues, challenges and hopes. In and through the storytelling, the interviewees not only conveyed interesting information about our research field, they revealed themselves and how they give meaning to their actions and reactions as actors in the public realm. But their walking storytelling was also strongly interactive, in the sense that it altered the relation between interviewee and interviewer. In the case of the first researcher, the process of storytelling often transformed the interviewee into a guide, a walking and narrating citizen, having the opportunity to raise his voice, to appropriate his environment, to think and judge. The dynamic process of storytelling redefined also the researcher's position: his role as a researcher shifted into the role of a companion, a listening ear in a joined journey of an hour (or two).

In the case of the second researcher, the process of storytelling, and the shifting roles, were more complex. In her encounter with Sub-Saharan youngsters, her role as a researcher was initially perceived as an intrusion. The narrative was hostile, sometimes provocative. The youngsters conditioned the encounter, clearly defined the power relations in their territory.

They negotiated a deal (we talk, if you buy us alcohol). However, one young men, Daniel, was willing to tell his story, he saw the interest of trusting his story to the researcher. Through his storytelling Daniel revealed himself as a needy welfare client, and placed the researcher in the role of a social worker. Here, the performative power of storytelling, in a dynamic urban setting, challenges the borders of restorative research. Are we, as researchers, observing, or also taking responsibility? And how far does this responsibility reach?

E. Walking and Weaving: An Innovative Restorative Justice Practice?

But there is more. The walking interventions, and the discovery of the narrative power of these interviews, invited us to discuss and reflect upon the impact of the walks on the totality of the project. As already mentioned, we were sure about the fact that these walks exceeded their status of a preparatory field analysis. But we were already fully embarked on the action stage of our research. However, we were unsure about the status of these actions. And so we asked ourselves three questions:

(1) To what extent can these walking interventions be introduced as an element of our new urban restorative justice interventions?
(2) To what extent can we embody our conceptual framework around restorative justice (RJ) and urban citizenship, but also our set of principles, into these walking interventions?
(3) Do these walks, and their strongly performative narratives, add new insights with regard to the key concepts of our broad restorative justice story?

These are serious questions. And we confess, we're still digesting these issues. In what follows we will only give a few hints that need to be fleshed out in another publication. These hints point to the potentials of the walking and weaving strategy, but also to its vulnerabilities.

(i) As to the promise of an innovative restorative justice practice, the walking strategy shows similarities with preparative conversations between conflicting parties, and conflicting views in a mediation process, with a strong focus on storytelling. One could even say that the walking talks are even doing justice more explicitly to the idea of bringing the conflicts back to informal settings. Our walking citizens are tracing their trajectories through the public realm, letting their life stories emerge from the city. Another advantage is that the walking interviewees point out themselves their zones of conflict. There is no referring instance that defines and delineates the conflict (or criminal behaviour), or the conflicting parties. This is of course also a disadvantage because the walks do not necessarily map conflicting views around which a process of conflict resolution could be started. Another disadvantage is that in the walking strategy, only the walker and his companion dialogue, but there is not yet any dialogue, any group process between the walkers themselves. So, if this walking intervention is to transform itself into a fully-fledged restorative practice, then this communicative connection should be made.

(ii) As to the image generating capacity of the walking strategy, it invites us to rethink restorative justice practices, not only based on the image of a circle, but also of an itinerary, a *parcours*, in which people respond dynamically to their environment.

(iii) As to the idea of making these narratives of inhabitants and visitors visible in public space, we have already argued how walking through public spaces activates the performative potentials of storytelling, which becomes more responsive and expressive in a city environment. But, and here comes the weak side, the narrative leaves no visible trace in the quarter. The recordings stay safely in the offices of the researcher, and with reason, of course, from the perspective of privacy and confidentiality. So we need a supplementary practice in which the stories of citizens can be given back to the public space, without compromising privacy issues. And here digital storytelling comes in.

V. RAVAGE, DIGITAL STORYTELLING AND THE DREAM OF A FOUR-LAYERED METHODOLOGY

A. Ravage

After the Easter holidays, we met each other in Leuven, a famous University town, 25 km from Brussels. In a dynamic local Museum *(Museum M)* we discovered the outcome of a recent digital story process. An annex to the central exhibition, Ravage (on art in times of war and destruction), *Museum M* also organised an exposition showing digital stories of victims and offenders. One of our researchers animated the group sessions and contributed to the final editing of the digital stories. The stories were powerful, and triggered positive reactions from the audience, not least from the victim groups who reframed their position towards offenders after having seen their digital stories.

'Yes, this is it', we said. This turns digital storytelling into a concrete project, tightly knit to restorative justice. This is innovative because it embeds restorative justice in a digital environment. On the spot, we reaffirmed the conviction that bringing digital stories to the field of mediation and restorative justice offers new and promising horizons. And that our research project on restorative justice in Brussels serves here as an important entrance gate.

From that day we became convinced about digital stories as a successive stage in the methodology of RJ in urban settings. We planned four sessions in May and June, aiming at an output of six digital stories that we could present to the two-year conference of the European Forum of Restorative Justice in Belfast. The target was ambitious, but the visit to the exposition in Leuven shortly after Easter convinced us again of the importance of realising these ambitions. From the end of February to the end of March, we regularly met and discussed the potentials of digital storytelling for the project. During these sessions we projected a whole web of virtues (and expectations) on digital storytelling.

B. Promises of Digital Storytelling

(i) *Educational and empowering potentials.* We were invited to believe in the educational and empowering potentials of digital storytelling: people grow in their self-esteem; people acquire digital competences; people become the film-maker of their own stories; and even more, people are discussing, communicating, supporting, encouraging each other, and they learn to bring their skills together. Moreover, these educational benefits have been shown to have a scientific basis. Many researches have emphasised the educational benefits of using digital storytelling. Digital storytelling is viewed as a deep learning tool that improves literary and writing skills (Robin, 2006; Sylvester and Greenidge, 2009). It also enhances academic achievement, critical thinking and learning motivation (Yang and Wu, 2012) and proved to be able to bridge the digital divide in a rural community school (Gyabak and Godina, 2011).

(ii) *Instrument of participation and co-creation.* Digital storytelling has the capacity to bond and bridge, as a strong instrument of participation, co-creation and cooperative learning. This is in alignment with literature that points out how digital storytelling contributes to strengthen democracy (Hull and Katz, 2006; Couldry, 2008). Through mediatisation and mediation, digital stories evoke dialogical processes that lead to change (Couldry, 2008). Also Lambert (2013) illustrates the societal impact of digital storytelling. By giving voice to people that normally don't have access to media channels, 'we are all somebodies'. Digital storytelling goes hand in hand with authorship and since authorship is intertwined with agency, new doors to civic participation are opened. Digital storytelling captures lives and when relationships are strengthened through deep stories, the sense of belonging and connectivity is enhanced and the creation, building and consolidation of community is fostered. In this regard, digital storytelling promises to create a strong digital environment for restorative justice.

(iii) *Narrative instrument of self-expression.* Digital storytelling is a powerful narrative instrument of self-expression, and therefore completes the storytelling process of the walks. It brings the process of engaged positioning in Anneessens to its essence, and makes the ephemeral narrative walking process more palpable and sustainable. In this respect, digital storytelling is truly innovative for restorative justice because it brings the lifeworld element of restorative justice to the surface, in a manner that totally respects the ownership of the stake-holding individual. Inhabitants, passing visitors, they all remain master over their storytelling process.

(iv) *Instrument for embracing plurality in public space.* Digital storytelling creates a digital environment through which a plurality of views can be made visible in public space. The stories can be projected on walls and can serve as an inspiring context in which restorative group discussions in public spaces could be organised. Digital storytelling is innovative for restorative justice practices, because it has the potential to bring a plurality of short self-expressive narratives to the public space, and this in a short sequence of strong images. It promises to offer narratives in which citizens can make their rights and needs visible. Or, in other words, similar to the Growfunding environment, digital stories have the potential to weave a digital environment into public spaces (digital storytelling can be projected on walls, and can be spread and shared on the Web), thereby giving citizens a public platform to express their rights and needs. Again, digital storytelling is expected to embody the idea of urban citizenship, seen as the right to the city.

(v) *Instrument for balancing privacy and public issues.* Bringing the digital stories into public space promises to give a public dimension to the lifeworld element of restorative justice practices, without sacrificing privacy interests. Participation in digital storytelling is voluntary, explicit consent for rendering digital storytelling public is requested, and the methodology of digital storytelling anonymises the narrator. Moreover, it is the narrator themselves who is the author of their own appearance.

(vi) *Potential for conflict transformation.* And, finally, the digital storytelling process promises to be conflict transforming itself. If you could organise a digital story-process around a conflict-zone and with conflicting parties, then the process of digital storytelling could bring people with diverging views and interests together, around a common goal: making each narrative powerful, supporting each other in this creative process, and thereby creating a space for being moved by each other.

C. The Four-Stage Methodology

With these promises and high expectations, we set out a four-stage methodological framework, in which digital storytelling is embedded. Still very enthusiastic about Growfunding, we decided to attach this participative instrument to our methodology, in order to create a strategy of gathering citizens around a common city project. Connecting digital storytelling with Growfunding would allow us to construct a tool that could tie networks and activate solidarity.

(i) *Walking and weaving.* In a first stage, we discover conflict-zones and conflicting networks, and mobilise engagement through the process of walking and through the performative power of narratives. We aim to have diversity and variety of views in our web of walking citizens.
(ii) *Digital storytelling.* From our web of walking citizens we select, in a second stage, one, or more groups of six participants. Participation is, of course, completely voluntary. These groups are supporting each other to go through the process of digital storytelling.
(iii) *Widening the circle.* In a third stage, a public event will be organised focusing on bringing the digital stories to the public. The digital stories will be discussed and the participants are asked to brainstorm on city projects.
(iv) *From city-project to Growfunding.* In a last stage, city ideas will incubate into the Growfunding trajectory, coached by the Growfunding research team and supported by the crowd.

D. Challenges of Integrating the Stages into Each Other

The four-stage methodology sounded great, at least on paper. But quickly, all kinds of hesitations popped up. How to lead the walking citizens to the digital story-sessions? How to ensure diversity in the sessions? Are we going to attract youngsters into digital stories? How to hear the voice of those that are often perceived as trouble-makers? Is it deontologically correct to bring conflicting views together, without these people being fully informed about the potentials of tensions? And how to go from a confidential setting of digital storytelling to an open, public space of an encounter? And how to open a creative space for developing city projects that respond to people's needs?

After the walking and talking, we asked our respondents to participate in the digital storytelling trajectory, consisting of four sessions from 7 to 10 pm (and one Saturday morning session). Out of 16 respondents, four people (Elke, Badya, Vincent, Medi) participated. Since we aimed at a group of six, Jonas, an intern of the Buurtwinkel, was allowed to participate. Also Ainara, the secretary of Medi, director of the educational organisation ASE Anneessens, accompanied him to the sessions and took part. Two of the researchers also joined in the process of making their own digital stories. During the first session the group consisted of eight people. Ainara and Medi left after the second session. All the sessions took place in Buurtwinkel Anneessens.

VI. *MR FALAFEL* AND THE DIGITAL STORY-SESSION

A. Waiting for Daniel

Each Wednesday, we sat together one hour before the digital session took place. *Mr Falafel* was our dinner and meeting place. It was a lapse of time, allowing us to rehearse the structure, to manage the stress, and to check whether all the participants were coming. One Wednesday, one of our researchers told us that she met Daniel, a Sub-Saharan African, in his late 20s, temporarily living in *L'Armée du Salut*, unemployed, released on parole for drug dealing. Daniel had a prison past related to theft with violence. He was willing to come to our session, that evening. We were excited, but also nervous and hesitating. Our feelings and reactions were contradictory.

On the one hand, his surprise visit might disturb the group dynamics and the learning process. There was also a risk that problems of power balance might arise between Daniel and the others, an 'us versus them' logic, which would make the vulnerable social position of Daniel even more fragile.

On the other hand, we were more than welcoming of his voice, the voice of youngsters and young adults who are pointed out as problematic, damaging the reputation of the park and quarter. During the first digital story-session, it became clear that youth and social deviance were one of the key topics. The participants had sharp, diverging views on the subject. Tensions and frustrations emerged. At a certain moment the discussion took on vehement proportions (and because of our digital story focus, unfortunately, our mediation skills remained in the background of our minds). We were surprised, unprepared and paralysed.

Badya ascribed the youth problems to a lack of parental responsibility. She argued that parents, and particularly fathers, have abandoned their responsibility of raising their children because they are too little acquainted with the urban realities. Youngsters are left to construct their own reference framework on the streets and end up taking, stealing, dealing and seeing unemployment as normal and normative modalities. Medi strongly disagreed. As the director of an educational organisation, ASE Anneessens, he focused on improving the linguistic tools of the residents of Anneessens. Medi viewed family cohesion as quintessential for social cohesion and argued that language forms the basis of both types of cohesion:

> We are convinced that there is no social cohesion without family cohesion. It's not that parents abandoned their children. In reality, we see that they lack the tools to communicate with them. The majority of the parents speak Berber and came to Brussels with a particular cultural luggage, while the children spend most of their time at school where they construct another linguistic and cultural frame. Since language is the basis of culture, we created children who speak and think different than their parents. This causes fractures in certain families and often also leads to societal breaches.

Giving Daniel the opportunity to raise his voice, to tell his story, but above all, to take part in the process as an equal partner, would undoubtedly bring us closer to a restorative setting in which a dynamics of talking *about* could shift into an authentic talking *with*, and *from within*.

B. Two Challenges

But Daniel didn't show up, and the digital story-session didn't transform into a classic restorative justice setting. For all of us a relief maybe, but definitely also a missed opportunity to learn. One thing became clear, though: our digital stories experiment faces two methodological challenges.

(i) Starting from our methodology of voluntary walking trajectories, it seems quite difficult to orchestrate digital storytelling in which conflicting parties embark on a process of digital storytelling. The access to digital storytelling is free and voluntary. And too much orchestration truncates the authenticity of the participatory process. So our promise that digital storytelling would offer us a digital skin for conflict mediation, and for a reiteration of a classic mediation or conference scheme, seems quite difficult to realise and to reproduce, given the voluntary and often unexpected participation of inhabitants. For some of us, these methodological difficulties were a reason to drop this ambition and frustration. But then, of course, you could ask what makes the digital story process restorative, if it does not start from conflicting interests between people. How then are we going to integrate digital storytelling in practice, which focuses on conflict-zones, reproduces a lifeworld, participative and restorative element? This is a crucial challenge that we distilled from our first digital story experiment.

(ii) Daniel's absence from the session symbolised another difficulty: the threshold for participation in digital storytelling seems to be too high for the vulnerable groups of youngsters that we want to include in the process. How to make digital storytelling more attractive? How to attune it to the needs and interests of these groups? What are the barriers, and how to remove them?

C. Groundbreaking Potentials

Apart from these challenges, our first digital stories experiment was successful, because it fulfilled many expectations. One of the advantages of having a limited number of participants in our sessions was that we, as researchers, could position ourselves differently in the digital storytelling process, by assigning ourselves different roles. One of us took the role of facilitator.

Another researcher observed the process trying to get a grip on the similarities and differences between mediation and digital storytelling. Two other researchers left their research role, and became fully-fledged participants. This insider's perspective gave us a deep understanding of how the process feels from the inside, starting from this first experiment. We see three ground-breaking axes, from which digital storytelling could be further developed, as part of a broader urban restorative justice practice.

D. Digital Storytelling Meets Methodological Expectations (First Axis)

Digital storytelling promised to be a powerful instrument of narrative self-expression. This promise came true. One of the ingredients of this success was undoubtedly linked to the fact that the methodology focuses more systematically on what Pali and Pelikan (2010) called the lifeworld element. As already mentioned, digital storytelling is a staged and structured process that teaches the participants gradually to shift from talking *about* something to talking *from within*. The group exercises that stimulate our capacity to associate inner thoughts with images, lead the participants from a judgemental stance to an self-expressive stance. Moreover, the group dynamic allow people to learn from each other. So it is not the mediator himself who has to invite each of the parties to tell their stories: it is the structure of the digital processes itself, and its collective dimension, that brings about this speech-shift. Another important point of difference is that the process of digital storytelling, in contrast with mediation, is circular and not linear. The narrative shift from speaking *about* to speaking *from within* oneself recurs, again and again, in different stages of the process (in the explorative stage, in the writing stage, but also in storyboard stages when the participants choose and create their images). This strong focus on narrative self-expression can be illustrated by two examples. In the early stage of the sessions the facilitator asked the participants to stand up and to choose three pictures, one picture that inspires you, another that represent your personality, and a third one that represents the Anneessens quarter. Through this simple exercise you see an immediate shift in the nature of speech: the timid Ainara breaks her silence. She shows a photo with sunrays, informs the group that her photo refers to her romantic nature, her optimistic and hopeful character: 'I love to give much in life', she says blushing. It was also surprising to see how Medi, who has clear views and judgements on the challenges of Anneessens, transformed his discourse from an objectifying into an expressive one. 'I am someone classy', he said, 'who is well educated, someone who thinks ahead'.

For these reasons digital storytelling is much more than a digital skin around classic restorative justice practice. It alters the very nature of the restorative justice practice, because of its systematic focus on the narrative, self-revealing part of the empowering process.

E. Digital Storytelling is Conceptually Groundbreaking (Second Axis)

There is another reason why the digital storytelling experiment in Buurtwinkel Anneessens proved to be ground-breaking. Introducing its circular structure into restorative practices breaks up the linear connections between the key-concepts of restorative justice. So, experiencing the sessions from within also triggered reflection on a more theoretical level. Here are some sketchy thoughts. In restorative justice, we are inclined to start our theory from the notion of conflict, which presupposes a demarcation of the conflict. Then people involved in the conflict are invited to narrate their experience of the conflict. And then participation and communication is supposed to issue in a solution, an agreement that makes the practice restorative, because it restores the broken trust, the harm, etc. So there is a sequential link between conflict, life-element, participation and restoration.

The logic of digital storytelling, though outcome oriented (editing a digital movie in different steps) is quite different: the conflict is not the starting point, though conflicts and tension might emerge in the conflict-zones of Anneessens. The stage of self-expression is not preparatory to the negotiation stage; narration and self-narration is considered as an end in itself, which is encouraged through participation. The restorative element (reconnecting between people) is neither a goal, nor an aim. It emerges the digital story process. So this circular movement between concepts, with self-expressive narration as its pivotal concept, is undoubtedly innovative for classic restorative justice theories. Digital storytelling invites us, friends of restorative justice, to revisit the connections between our grounding concepts, and to rethink them in a circular way.

F. Digital Storytelling is Ground-breaking for Restorative Research (Third Axis)

And, finally, digital storytelling has profoundly altered our style of restorative justice research. As we already betray in the structure of our chapter, our ideas and insights are much more intertwined with scenes and images. The narrative, subjective and intersubjective character of our research becomes more explicit. We have come to a point at which we've set ourselves the challenge to communicate our research insights not only from an outsider's perspective, but also from within. Questions like 'Why do you want to experiment with restorative justice in Brussels?' are also resonating from within.

Digital storytelling brings restorative justice research closer to personal strong evaluations, inner beliefs and convictions, on which we stand and around which we grow. We, as researchers, are still reflecting on why, and in what respect, and to what extent, such a more narrative and self-expressive research approach could be more valuable than a more objectifying approach. We have a vague intuition why this could be so, but no clear-cut arguments can be offered yet.

VII. BACK TO VIRGINIE AND THE URBAN CRACK (CONCLUSION)

So we are back where we started, revisiting our initial scene, on our way to Virginie, social mediator in BRAVVO. We took a halt at the dumping place behind the football square. Our interest was attracted by this conflict-zone, around which a variety of points of view come together. On this spot, in the immediacy of youngsters, sometimes causing nuisance, we would like to start one of our follow-up digital storytelling experiments, to explore how the experiment succeeds in reconnecting people without giving the conflict the central place, but by focusing on the process of self-narration, the process of narrating one's view on Anneessens from a personal, a lived perspective. In doing so, our aim is to lower the threshold for digital storytelling (our methodological challenge), and to refrain from too much orchestrating digital stories into a classic logic of conflict-mediation (our conceptual challenge). In our next digital stories interventions, we will restart our preparatory walks and talks. During our sessions, conflict will not be the starting point, but part and parcel of the environment.

Launching our digital stories experiment on a spot in the open air requires a shelter in to which we could organise (at least part of) our sessions. Building the shelter, with the youngsters and supporting associations, is already a public statement, expressive of urban citizenship, thereby claiming the right to the city. By building our shelter, our chalet, we are performing (and transforming) a filthy spot into a public space, where people can meet, where associations can organise, where activities can unfold, etc. Again, here, with these new ideas, which grew on the spot, we're not following a sequential, but a circular logic. Different from our initial plan to let city projects grow from the process of digital storytelling (see our four-stage methodology), we have now discovered the opportunity to transform our chalet-project already into a city project.

So we went to Virginie, that morning, to set out our new restorative justice plans in Anneessens (crossing the borders of mediation and community work). We met, talked and explored possible cooperation. Some of the explanatory remarks (not the circular thing, of course) that we pronounced in our last paragraph came up in our talk with Virginie. And she sounded curious and enthusiastic.

REFERENCES

Appadurai, A (2013) *The Future as Cultural Fact: Essays on the Global Condition* (Verso, London).

Arendt, H (1958) *The Human Condition* (Chicago, IL, Chicago University Press).

Couldry, N (2008) 'Mediatization or Mediation? Alternative Understanding of the Emergent Space of Digital Storytelling' 10(3) *New Media and Society* 373.

Dominelli, L (2014) *Citizenship and Voluntarism: A Meaningful Combination or the Basis for Exploitative Relationships?* (FOS, forthcoming).

Dworkin, R (1986) *Law's Empire* (London, Fontana Press).

—— (2000) *Sovereign Virtue: The Theory and Practice of Equality* (Cambridge, MA, Harvard University Press).

Gyabak, K and Godina, H (2011) 'Digital Storytelling in Bhutan: A Qualitative Examination of New Media Tools Used to Bridge the Digital Divide in a Rural Community School' 57 *Journal of Computers and Education* 2236.
Harvey, D (2008) 'The Right to the City' 53 *New Left Review* 23.
Honohan, I (2002) *Civic Republicanism* (London, Routledge).
Hull, GA and Katz, M-L (2006) 'Crafting an Agentive Self: Case Studies of Digital Stories 41(1) *Research in the Teaching of English* 43.
Lambert, J (2013) *Digital Storytelling: Capturing Lives, Creating Community* (New York, Routledge).
Lamote, F and Ampe, S (2013) *We are a Growfunding Platform* (Concepttekst).
Lefèbvre, H (1996) 'Writings on Cities' in E Kofman and E Lebas (eds), (Oxford, Blackwell Publishing).
Malita, L and Martin, C (2010) 'Digital Storytelling as Web Passport to Success in the 21st Century' 2 *Procedia Social and Behavioral Sciences* 3060.
Nussbaum, M (2006) *Frontiers of Justice* (Cambridge MA, Harvard University Press).
—— (2011) *Creating Capabilities: The Human Development Approach* (Cambridge, MA, Harvard University Press).
Pali, B and Pelikan, C (2010) *Building Social Support for Restorative Justice* (Leuven, European Forum for Restorative Justice).
Plyushteva, A (2009) 'The Right to the City and Struggles over Urban Citizenship: Exploring the Links' 1(3) *Amsterdam Social Science* 81.
Raco, M (2009) 'From Expectations to Aspirations: State Modernization, Urban Policy, and the Existential Politics of Welfare in the UK' 28 *Political Geography* 436.
Rawls, J (1988) *A Theory of Justice* (Oxford, Oxford University Press).
Robin, B (2006) 'The Educational Uses of Digital Storytelling' in C Crawford *et al* (eds), *Proceedings of Society for Information Technology and Teacher Education International Conference 2006* (Chesapeake, VA, AACE) 709–16.
Sylvester, R and Greenidge, W-L (2009) 'Digital Storytelling: Extending the Potential for Struggling Writers' 63(4) *The Reading Teacher* 284.
Taylor, C (1995) *Philosophical Arguments* (Cambridge, MA, Harvard University Press).
Vanderbeeken, R and De Bruyne, P (2014) 'Growfunding: een gieter vol ideologisch gemanipuleerde organismen?', available at www.dewereldmorgen.be/artikels/2014/02/21/growfunding-een-gieter-vol-ideologisch-gemanipuleerde-organismen.
Yang, Y-TC and Wu, JJ (2012) 'Digital Storytelling for Enhancing Student Academic Achievement, Critical Thinking, and Learning Motivation: A Year-Long Experimental Study' 59 *Journal of Computers and Education* 339.

Part III

Philosophical Explorations for Restorative Justice

14

Restorative Justice and the Potential of 'Exemplarity'

In Search of a 'Persuasive' Coherence Within Criminal Justice

CLAUDIA MAZZUCATO

I. INNOVATIVE TRENDS IN CRIMINAL LAW AND CRIMINAL JUSTICE SYSTEMS

SOMETHING IS CHANGING. Like a subterranean river, something is slowly, yet steadily, moving in the depths of criminal law and criminal justice, underneath massive and antique layers of punitive rocks and retributive debris.

Something is (finally) moving in new directions. Yet, it is not easy to unearth what lies beneath a system which still has at its core the deprivation of liberty as a paramount punishment, nor to weaken the strength of the millennial idea that justice deals with harming those who harmed, nor to subvert the equation that 'to make things right' the offender has to suffer a wrong. It is also difficult to move away from widespread zero-tolerance policies and from a rooted enemy criminal law.

In international and national debates, however, there are clear signs that new concepts, theories and policies are emerging. There seems to be quite a transnational desire to 'turn the page': a desire to really reform criminal law and criminal justice systems in their inner structures, in favour of up-to-date models that can succeed in being more adequate to the ideals and principles of modern democracies and to human rights, and in favour of systems that are able to more effectively incentivise and foster compliance, and therefore ensure lower crime rates and less victimisation. In other words, to 'civilise criminal justice' (Cornwell *et al*, 2013), that is, to lessen the persistently *violent* nature of criminal justice, and to strengthen ways to respond to crime based on participation (instead of segregation); consent (instead of coercion and imposition); compliance (instead of enforcement); respect for the dignity of both the victim and the offender (instead of the isolation of the former and the stigmatisation of the latter).

It is, of course, a very small portion of the current actual criminal justice world: criminal justice and criminal law *in action* are still massively driven by the dogma of security (nearly) at all costs, and are still strongly punishment centred. *De facto*, both criminal justice and criminal law rely globally, over and over again, on aggressive retributive practices.

The new trend we are referring to is that of the innovative theories and proposals that have in John Braithwaite (*et alii*) one of its most persuasive and bright supporters: that is, the 'republican' theory of justice and 'responsive regulation', and their open support for restorative justice (Braithwaite and Pettit, 1990; Ayres and Braithwaite, 1992; Braithwaite, 2002).

In the light of these theories and in the light of restorative practices, penal paradigms can no longer be divided into retributivist and instrumentalist or consequentialist conceptions, into retribution or prevention as separate fronts.

Once we have 'changed our lenses' (Zehr, 1990; 2015), classical theories of punishment (and of criminal law), which managed to survive through centuries, are forced to reveal their common nature and their inner truth: retribution and prevention (deterrence and neutralisation, including 'armed' forms of rehabilitation as a mean of incapacitation) are not so distant from each other and were not so different, as Kant and Beccaria would argue, in the past. As practically performed, both retribution and prevention share the same imprint: punishment, coercion and the use of force. In a word: violence. This is a further evidence of the 'original' connection between law and violence as underlined like no other by Walter Benjamin (1920–1921).

As widely recognised, restorative justice is not just a matter of alternative dispute resolution. It is a matter of *justice* (and of course a matter of *in*justices). In this sense restorative justice has ideas and proposals on how to respond to crime. In some ways, though, restorative justice does not deal only with *responding* to criminal offences *ex post* (ie, once they have already been committed); restorative justice has something interesting to say *ex ante*, even before the crime is committed. Restorative justice has to share ideas about (criminal) law and (criminal) justice as a whole. In our perspective, this is a key point: here lies a potential for criminal law theory and innovative crime policies, which we dare say is not yet sufficiently addressed in studies and research.

There is more to restorative justice, in fact, than victim-offender dialogue (or other programmes), more than reparation of the consequences of a criminal behaviour. The proposal to *react* to crime through a voluntary participation of victims, offenders, and (where adequate) their communities, to an encounter from which reparation and commitments for the future may voluntarily spring, brings about a whole new 'grammar of criminal law'

(I borrow this expression from Fletcher, 2007). This 'grammar' is still quite unseen and largely undeveloped among criminal law scholars.

Following restorative justice's lead, our theoretical quest will move 'upstream', leaving punishment aside for a moment. We will move from the crime committed, with its victims and perpetrators, and its harmful and disruptive results to be repaired and responded to, 'upwards' and 'counter-current', towards the legal norms, or rules, that recommend(ed) not to commit the criminal offence in the first place and that strive against re-offending thereafter.

From our 'upstream' and 'counter-current' location, we can try to take an overview of what restorative justice has to say (and, maybe, has to teach) regarding the domain of criminal law itself, even *before* a crime is perpetrated and *before* a demand for some sort of *reaction* is presented. In our view, an interesting new architecture of the concept of criminal law, not only of criminal *justice*, stems, in fact, from the theoretical proposal of restorative justice and the connected theory of responsive regulation.

Following Walgrave's suggestion, it is high time to step 'from civilisation of punishment towards civilisation of criminal justice' (where 'civilisation' stands here for 'making criminal law more civilised' and not 'making criminal law into civil law': Walgrave, 2013: 359–72).

What model, or paradigm, of criminal law (*not* just of criminal sanction/reaction/response) is hidden inside the philosophy of 'responsive-restorative' justice? What sort of relation between the citizens and the law is connected to the wisdom of 'responsive-restorative' justice? What kind of idea of criminal offence comes along with it?

For criminal law scholars, the discovery of responsive regulation models and of restorative justice is an extraordinary chance of theoretical (not only practical) evolution. At the same time, responsive regulation and restorative justice luckily confirm the fundamental principles and guarantees associated with criminal law (seen as the *Magna Charta libertatis*). The democratically 'healthier' parts of criminal law and criminal justice, those devoted to protection, not to punishment or control, receive a strong and further validation from responsive regulation and restorative justice's theory and practice. The 'dark sides' of the criminal justice system, those related to repression and punishment, are instead questioned and put under severe scrutiny: their persistent and counter-productive violent nature is revealed (and criticised) by a 'responsive-restorative' approach.

Tout se tient, maybe.

II. RULES OF CONDUCT, NOT PUNISHMENTS

Both responsive regulation and restorative justice make an interesting step forward from where abolitionism, on the one hand, and neo-retributivism (and related adaptations) on the other, had left us. In brief: abolitionism criticises punishment as pain, suffering and violence deliberately inflicted on the offender, and as a form of external control on citizens (Christie, 1981). Neo-retributivism underlines punishment as a (necessary) tool to reinforce the blameworthiness of the criminal act, and in doing so punishment is welcomed as a means to 'communicate' a strengthening of the message that criminal law addresses to citizens (Duff, 2001).

Either to disapprove of it or to praise it, yet punishment has attracted all the attention so far: it remains the 'guiding star' of criminal law and criminal justice, their unit of measurement, and their benchmark.

The new theoretical frames designed by responsive regulation and restorative justice underscore innovative elements that change all the variables on the table: compliance and consent to the rules become key concepts; the relation (a *certain* relation) between criminal law and its addressees plays a crucial role; dynamism in law and justice is introduced. Punishment is in the background. By marginalising punishment, light is shed on the 'other' pole of the criminal law 'magnet', ie, the 'rule of conduct'. The rule of conduct contains the description of the expected behaviour together with the 'invitation' to follow it and to abstain from other conducts. Furthermore, restorative justice's victim-sensitive attitude and its ability to hold offenders accountable through 'transformative' encounters, empowerment and mutual recognition with victims (Baruch Bush and Folger, 1994) disclose how the intellectual and social journey in search of justice starts and moves from injustices, which are tragically much more concrete and 'matter of fact' than the speculative, abstract and ultimately unattainable, notion of justice. Restorative justice shows how 'rights' (and rules) come from *real* 'wrongs' (Dershowitz, 2004).

Although the everyday practice of criminal justice shows unfortunately the opposite, criminal law deals (*must* deal) more with crimes than with sanctions and punishments.

This issue is immense and densely philosophical, and we can here only sketch some rough ideas. As said, we will use the term 'rule of conduct' to refer to the portion of the criminal legal provision in which, in civil law systems especially, the model fact situation is described (Ferrajoli, 2007: 217–55). This 'preceptive' dimension of the norm logically precedes the penal sanction. Despite their aggressive (and often brutal) characteristics, in fact, criminal sanctions are theoretically and logically ancillary to rules of conduct: punishments do not (*must not*) come first in the scale of priority of criminal law, if it were not for the necessity to keep their suspicious and dangerous nature under strict surveillance with adequate legal guarantees and constitutional/fundamental principles. The 'preceptive' element of the legal provision, that is, the part of the norm telling us what we should (not) do, is far more important than the punitive part of it. It is on compliant behaviour that security and low crime rates finally rest. The 'crime' is legally described in the rule of conduct, not in the punishment. If avoiding crimes (and preventing victimisation) is what really matters, then rules containing indications and directions for the behaviour of citizens are far more crucial than sanctions: sanctions per se do not tell us anything about what the correct behaviour expected from us is; sanctions are 'limited' to repression and to reaction without fostering any real 'normative competence' in us (Forti, 2013; Bagnoli, 2007; 2011).

But there is even more to it. As underlined by Jacques Derrida in *Force de loi* (1994) (along with many other studies in legal philosophy), the law does not practically prevent me from doing what I can actually do: one can still kill someone, even if criminal law asserts that I *must* not, and even if it may deter or punish me for doing so. Legal assertions are binding in a very peculiar way, since the law always expresses itself in the form of a *thou ought to* or in the form of a *thou shall not*: the way the law 'forbids' is, in the end, shaped into a (particularly impressive, socially relevant, morally demanding and appealing) *request* for a compliant behaviour addressed to citizens. The 'preceptive' rule indicates a model conduct: even in the harshest criminal law, the *ought* (or *ought not*), the *Sollen* (or *Sollen nicht*), has little to do per se with coercion, and it can never really be en*forced*, ultimately relying solely on individual will. Rather, the *ought*, the *Sollen*, is strictly dependent upon and stems from liberty, self-governance, responsibility, and accountability (Cornacchia, 2004: 76–78). Punishment can force me, incapacitate me, even kill me, but it will never be able to impose my 'normative' consent, my involvement and my commitment.

The legal 'preceptive' request is strongly associated with juridical and social expectations of compliance. In a democratic legal system, criminal law 'only' describes, through its rules, wrongful/harmful actions, and it forbids them *because* these actions are (meant to be) wrongful and/or cause harm, not because they are 'deviant', or unfaithful to authority, or solely because they are 'against the law'. By forbidding, criminal law is in fact truly just *asking* people not to commit those offences (once again, this claim is based on the reason that those behaviours *are* offensive and harmful, not on the basis that they are 'illegal' or 'transgressive', see, eg Fletcher, 2007: 37 ff, 151 ff).

The 'core business' of a democratic criminal law, we may say, is to have people comply (hopefully voluntarily), respecting each other and avoiding victimising others. The aim is not to have overcrowded prisons and intimidated societies for the sake of security. As said, in democratic human rights-oriented systems, compliance is expected because non-compliance is offensive and harmful.

For the scope and the limits of this chapter, we cannot address here the vast issue of how conducts are selected for criminalisation, what are the reasons to do so, and what risks and pitfalls for democracies may hide behind criminalisation. We have to leave in the background both the thorny issue of the balance between rights, freedoms and security and the problems arising from the 'culture of control' (Garland, 2001) in democratic societies. These questions, though relevant, draw our attention away from our primary topic. For the topical focus of this chapter, we will therefore have to assume here that criminalisation is properly decided through democratic processes and procedures, within a framework of fundamental and/or constitutional principles. It will suffice to stress that in 'civilised' (in the above-mentioned meaning of this term) democratic, non-dictatorial, societies, criminal law serves the people, not the authority: criminal law systems *must* therefore have reasons to criminalise. We will assume that these reasons are good and valid. Interestingly enough, the more restorative and responsive a system becomes or is, the less it risks over-criminalisation, prison overcrowding, illiberal forms of social control, and so forth.

At the theoretical level of our discourse, a crime is therefore not the mere transgression or violation of the law: there is more to a criminal conduct than being law non-abiding. As victims know far too well, sadly, when it comes to crime it is not (just) the breach of the law that matters: it is the breach of (better: the harm or offence to) certain relevant legally protected interests, rights or 'goods' (in the German doctrine's meaning of *Recthsgüter*: see, eg Fletcher, 2007: 40, 168). A crime is legitimately such (only) *if* the forbidden behaviour causes otherwise an offence/harm.

Put simply: in a democratic human rights-sensible criminal law system, the rule of conduct is not an 'order' to obey. The norm of conduct is more like a binding indication, or direction, not to harm/offend others (ie, to respect others). In democratic legal systems, obedience is neither a legal nor a moral virtue: respect, rather than obedience, is the virtue and the value fostered by laws in democracies. The memory of the horrors associated, even in the recent past, with the 'crimes of obedience', and the mass atrocities that these crimes provoked, is still too vivid to conceive crimes as a mere disobedience of the law. From the age of Enlightenment onwards, and mainly after Nazism and *Shoah*, the theory of crime has developed around either a harm principle or an offence principle (Feinberg 1984–1990). Either way, the theory of crime has developed in a manner that is extremely distant from the authoritarian view of crime as 'unfaithfulness' to the legal provision.

Going back to our primary topic, how does criminal law address citizens?

In the 'responsive-restorative' scenario we are supporting, criminal law systems pivot around citizens' consent and consensus to norms, and around the capacity of rules of conduct set by criminal law to respectfully 'persuade' citizens and to obtain their compliant behaviour: compliance and participation, persuasion and consent become the main assets of this crime policy (cf Braithwaite, 1985; Braithwaite and Pettit, 1990: 79 ff, 137 ff; Ayres and Braithwaite, 1992: 20 ff, 38–53, 92 ff; Sherman, 1993; Braithwaite, 2002: 33 ff, 81 ff).

To build such crime policy around consent and persuasion, rather than deterrence and incapacitation, means to 'take rights [and democracy] seriously' (Dworkin, 1977).

Impositions, orders, custody, life imprisonment, deprivation of liberty, death penalty, prison walls, prison cells, handcuffs, electronic bracelets, chemical castration, and so forth—that is, the whole punitive arsenal (still sadly actual)—are simply so dramatically distant from democratic ideals, whereas responsiveness, consent, compliance, 'voluntarity', participation, 'deliberative habits' seem so much more 'tuned' into democracy, and much more human-rights 'sounding'. Restorative justice and responsive regulation, and the theories thereafter, are no less than 'democratic' responses to the quest for justice: in the very moment in which, facing criminalisation and crime, it is so easy to 'pay back' and be violent in return; in the very moment when, facing criminalisation and crime, faithfulness to ideals, principles and democracy seems a luxury societies cannot afford, responsive and restorative regulatory systems confirm that the best 'exit strategy' from the risks, damages and harms caused by criminal offences is not on the dark violent side in which crime and justice end up being *mimetic* and symmetric, but on the bright one where rules and sanctions are 'actively' and 'dynamically' coherent with each other (Ayres and Braithwaite, 1992: 38 ff; Braithwaite, 2002: 33 ff). The challenge for criminal law and criminal justice is to dare some sort of profound coherence between norms *and* sanctions, and democratic and human rights premises: a coherence 'all the way along', from the 'birth' of the rule of conduct to the provision of the abstract sanction, down to the actual application of the punishment to the single case.

The 1995 landmark judgment of the South African Constitutional Court invalidating capital punishment (*S v Makwanyane and another*, CCT/3/94, South Africa Constitutional Court, 6 June 1995) provides an outstanding lesson in this regard, showing how coherence between principles, rules of conduct and sanctions is necessary for both the credibility of the law and its effectiveness in ensuring real protection to all:

> It is only if there is a willingness to protect the worst and the weakest amongst us, that all of us can be secure that our own rights will be protected. (para [88])

Furthermore, in Justice Langa's concurrent opinion (para [229]) we read:

> The test of our commitment to a culture of rights lies in our ability to respect the rights not only of the weakest, but also of the worst among us. A person does not become 'fair game' to be killed at the behest of the State, because he has killed.

In line with this interesting 'test' of the commitment to a culture of rights, restorative-responsive forms of justice ultimately aim to resemble what they want to *promote*, not what they want to *deter*.

To build a crime policy around consent, persuasion, responsiveness and participation is of course not an easy task: a demanding, complex, mid- or long-term strategy has to be put in place (including education, welfare, etc). Complex 'extra-legal' conditions and reasons for compliance, pertaining also to the domains of moral reasoning and emotions, must be well understood and taken into account (Forti, 2013; Bagnoli, 2007; 2011; see, eg literature on procedural justice: Tyler, 1990; 2007; 2010; Lind and Tyler, 1988; Tyler and Huo, 2002).

Such a policy is not for the 'good Samaritans', though: it aims at being (more) effective (albeit not 'tough') in reducing crime thanks to compliance, instead of deterrence and incapacitation, intimidation and punishment.

III. NEED FOR COHERENCE BETWEEN 'RULES' AND 'SANCTIONS' AND FOR A CONSTANT 'NORMATIVE DIALOGUE' BETWEEN THE CITIZENS AND THE LAW

In our perspective, a different type of criminal sanctions is demanded than the usual aggressive punishments incorporated everywhere into criminal justice systems.

A responsive-restorative model, in fact, brings about (and pushes for) a *coherent* system of sanctions in which sanctions need to speak the same language as rules of conduct do. Sanctions too, *ex post*, should be able to 'invite', 'ask', 'request' and 'incentivise' *further* compliance, and not just en*force* it (nor just deter/neutralise further criminal deviance). Sanctions too, *ex post*, should be able to 'flatter' persuasion among their addressees in order to stimulate to the extent possible their voluntary and responsive (though late) compliance, and therefore avoid or reduce re-offending.

The *ex ante* (rule of conduct) and the *ex post* (response to crime) perspectives should not be incoherently contradictory as today, and so different (like the sun and the moon) in what and how they 'communicate' to citizens (and deal with them).

The responsive-restorative paradigm stimulates criminal law and criminal justice systems to move away from 'negative' passive punishments towards 'positive' active sanctions.

The distinction between 'positive' and 'negative' sanctions is clearly depicted by Norberto Bobbio (1976: 533 ff). Negative punishments can only be 'inflicted' and passively 'suffered'. In many cases, negative punishments end up being contradictory, and counter-productive, if compared to the message outlined by the same norms of conduct these punishments were designed to support and reinforce, and the violation of which they want to stigmatise and to sanction. Paramount is the paradox and the ambiguity of the death penalty: designed to en*force* precisely the respect for life and to rein*force* the provision not to kill, it results in a sinister 'state of exception' (Agamben, 1995) in which the state decides over the life of a person, deliberatively causing their death and therefore reversing its own legal precept not to do so. Quoting the South African constitutional justices, we may ask what proof of the state's commitment to a culture of life protection does the death penalty entail.

In 'positive' responses to crime inspired by a restorative-responsive insight, offenders are held accountable, meaning that compliance from them is *still* an expectation on the part of the justice system and on the part of society as whole (victims included) even after the offence has occurred. Offenders therefore remain active and *responsible* 'interlocutors'—'fully' citizens, we may say—vis-à-vis both the rule of conduct and the response to its violation. Rules and positive sanctions await the voluntary participation of offenders, their responsible involvement and direct engagement in responding to what they have done: in other words, rules of conduct and sanctions mutually await (and promote) compliance as future behaviour and reparation for past actions.

Responsive regulation and restorative justice share a common understanding *before* and *after* the crime: they prefer to incentivise compliance, citizens' cooperation, community involvement, the least use of imposition and coercion, and a true 'parsimony' (Braithwaite and Pettit, 1990: 87 ff) in resorting to (classical) punishments. The principle of *extrema ratio*, so frequently quoted in theory, but so rarely put into practice, is taken seriously.

Responsive-restorative criminal justice systems become more flexible and better able to adapt to the responses of citizens as measured by compliance with the rule of conduct, *ex ante* or *ex post*. In these systems, it is never too late to (spontaneously, or at least voluntarily) comply (although, the later compliance takes place, the more engagement in reparation is required and the more probable an infliction of a classical punishment is). In so doing, responsive regulation and restorative justice bring a new 'compliance-centred' *dynamism* into criminal justice, as described by Ayres and Braithwaite (1992) and Braithwaite (2002) (eg, the 'responsive regulatory pyramid').

Usually, punishments stand in the foreground as they have to deter and intimidate *ex ante*, and to incapacitate *ex post*. Regardless of how much they are actually applied, punishments are logically meant to be the 'ordinary', the deserved course following offending, and only 'exceptionally', we may say, the system deflects and diverts from them in favour of some 'alternatives': the term 'diversion' overtly confesses a deviation from the ordinary way. Responsive and restorative answers to crime, on the contrary, overcome and overturn this logic in favour of a more sophisticated and articulated system, in which positive active sanctions, albeit 'mild' on offenders, entail in the first place a 'tough' stand on taking responsibility for *past* and *future* actions, but leave classical punishments in the background. This approach enriches and renovates diversion strategies.

While escalating the enforcement pyramid towards the classical punishments located at its top, responsive regulation systems are well aware of progressively losing the most noble and effective ingredients of a crime prevention strategy, ie the motivational appeal of the norm of conduct and the positive 'response' to its violation by its addressee. While escalating the pyramid, the relationship between the citizen and the law shifts from an optimal and virtuous area of ample freedom, self-regulation and self-responsibility to a less virtuous zone of compliance due to self-interest and convenience, ending in the problematic, yet last resort, areas of deterrence and of incapacitation as *ultima ratio* (Ayres and Braithwaite, 1992; Braithwaite, 2002).

In a responsive-restorative model of justice, however, criminal law engages in the first place in a *constant* dialogue with citizens, including victims and offenders, seen as active 'interlocutors', not passive recipients of orders, impositions and enforcement. This is much more than a 'stick and carrot' policy: new concepts about sanctioning emerge and new ideas and ways to respond to crimes are conceived. The crucial point is that at the core of this model lies a dialogue between the law and the citizens. The topics and arguments of this normative dialogue are rules of conduct, not reactions to offending. Sanctions 'incorporate' the rule of conduct, by expecting a compliant behaviour at least *ex post*.

This 'legal' and 'normative' dialogue around and about the rules (ie, about the expected compliant behaviour, and about the wrongful and harmful nature of the law-breaking conduct) dynamically influences the functioning of the legal and justice systems, harmonising (for once!) *favor rei* with victim support and social defence. What happens between victims and offenders inside and during restorative justice programmes to attain mutual recognition and to reach commitments towards reparation, also occurs, in a responsive model, between the law and those 'in conflict with the law'.

A continuous dialogue is carried out, *ex ante* or/and *ex post*, around and about those 'matters arising from the crime' that stand in the UN definition of restorative process (UN ECOSOC, 2002). This normative dialogue proposes a 'thinking over' of the criminal offence that has its source in freedom and its consequence in accountability (I borrow and adapt Jankélévitch's words on forgiveness, 1968: 74). This significant and *unending* 'normative dialogue' *also* with those who committed criminal offences entails the quest to restore the conditions for compliance.

IV. EXEMPLARY LAW, EXEMPLARY JUSTICE

In the responsive-restorative scenario that helps us foresee a new legal grammar and helps us design new architectures in criminal law and criminal justice, punishment is put far in the background. Importance is given, instead, to all the communicative and dialogical dimensions of the law lit up by this particular approach, before and after a crime occurs: rules of conduct with the description of the offensive/harmful behaviour are much more crucial than sanctions; and sanctions, when needed, must be capable of 'restating' (literally: 'sanctioning') the rule of conduct by being *similar to it* with their own message, therefore reaffirming (over and over again) the state's 'commitment to a culture of rights', on the one side, and, on the other, the need for voluntary and participatory compliance by citizens.

Alongside this argumentative path, we come to the crucial point of our thesis: what seems to govern the observance of criminal law and its 'republican' legitimacy has surprisingly some interesting similarities with what governs the realm of aesthetics and the forms of judgements typical to this domain. The way works of art, and especially masterpieces, attract our approval is thought-provoking.

Philosophical studies about aesthetic judgement, starting from Kant's difference between *determinant* and *reflective* judgements (especially Kant, 1790: para 6 ff) through Hannah Arendt's political developments (Arendt, 1961; 1978; 1982; 2003), provide fascinating hints also for legislators, criminal law scholars, lawyers and other legal practitioners. As stated by political philosopher Alessandro Ferrara, these studies concern more the 'judgment paradigm' itself rather than only the aesthetic judgement: these studies ultimately help us reflect on 'normative validity', 'well beyond the realm of aesthetics', providing 'a coherent and inspiring model for a large range of disciplines' (Ferrara, 2008: 17).

Reflective judgement has in fact attracted the attention of legal philosophers in the attempt to solve the eternal and very practical tension between abstract 'general' norms and 'particular' cases, and analyse legal imagination (see, eg Ost, 2014; 2016). Yet, there are other aspects too that prove extremely significant for a 'validation' of the responsive-restorative regulatory model we are proposing.

It will suffice here to briefly recall that Kant's *determinant* judgement is a speculative way of judging, in which judgement 'coercively results' from a given *a priori* principle which is rigidly applied to the particular case. *Reflective* judgement, instead, involves and activates an *insight* which enables us to discover the *universal* 'in' the *particular*: only the particular is given, but within this particular, *under certain conditions*, the universal can be 'traced', without having to 'coercively' recur to a 'determinant' *a priori*. This is how beauty shines through works of art and reveals itself to the observer.

Hannah Arendt (1982: 72) explains that:

> The validity of [reflective] judgments never has the validity of cognitive or scientific propositions … one can never compel anyone to agree with one's judgment—'This is beautiful' or 'This is wrong' …; one can only 'woo or 'court' the agreement of everyone else. And in this persuasive activity one actually appeals to the 'community sense'. In other words, when one judges, one judges as a member of a community.

The mysterious *particular*, through which the *universal* filters, is the philosophical concept of 'example'. Examples have an evocative nature, but their power to recall the universal inside the particular is so stringent that examples are capable of inspiring agreement, without ever forcing it: this is 'exemplary validity'.

The book *The Force of the Example* by Alessandro Ferrara is extremely stimulating for the development of our reasoning. According to Ferrara (2008: 23, 2–3):

> The notion of reflective judgment allows us to export this form of exemplary universalism without principles beyond the realm of aesthetic, into the realm of moral judgment, political judgment, legal judgment, and even theoretical judgment.

> Alongside the force of what is and of what ought to be, a third force gives shape to our world; the force of *what is as it should be* or the force of the *example*. For a long time unrecognized and misleadingly assigned to the reductive realm of the aesthetic, the force of the example is the force of what exerts appeal on us in all walks of life ... by virtue of the singular and exceptional congruence that what is exemplary realizes and exhibits between the order of its own reality and the order of the normativity to which it responds.

Examples are:

> atoms of reconciliation where *is* and *ought* merge, and in so doing they liberate an energy that sparks our imagination. (Ferrara, 2008: 1–2)

The ability of examples to 'reconcile' opposites is underlined also by Giorgio Agamben (1993: 9–12; 1995: 26–27)[1] who, while stressing how examples are the symmetric opposite of exceptions, points out that the example is:

> one concept that escapes the antinomy between the universal and the particular. In any context where it exerts its force, the example is characterized by the fact that it holds of all cases of the same type, and, at the same time, it is included among these. It is one singularity among others which, however, stands for each of them and serves for all.

Examples help us move *intuitively*[2] from what is particular to what is universal, thanks to the authenticity, coherence and congruence that spring from them: it is thanks to their 'inner and exceptional congruence that does not need to rely on an *a priori*' that examples persuade us (Ferrara, 2008).

The category of 'example' and 'exemplary validity' may be extremely useful in designing and understanding how legal rules in criminal law (should) address citizens, and vice versa. In brief: criminal law and criminal justice, especially in democratic and intercultural societies, should be(come) exemplary, that is, valid because of their exemplarity, not because of the force of authoritative imposition and/or the force of deterrence or incapacitation.

[1] I owe this reading suggestion to Brunilda Pali and Mario Ragazzi, whom I thank.

[2] On the importance of intuition for moral reasoning and for connections between moral reasoning and aesthetic judgement, see, eg Haidt and Joseph, 2004 and Bagnoli, 2007; 2011.

If both rules of conduct and (positive) sanctions are 'reflectively' and 'exemplarily' drafted, and therefore let justice 'shine through' them, either in the moment of criminalisation or in the moment of crime response, they can *appeal* to the consensus of citizens and can aim to persuade them, fostering their normative competence, while creating voluntary compliance without resorting to coercion and force. Compliance too, just like agreement in *reflective* judgement, can ultimately only be 'wooed' appealing to a common belonging to the community of mankind.

To do so, criminal law should pay attention, on the one hand, to the 'positive' exemplarity of what fulfils human dignity: this will be the realm of the *ought to* (the *Sollen*) or, in other words, the domain of human rights and of the legal protection of persons and their interests also (although not necessarily *only*) through criminal law (Ferrara, 2008: 121 ff). On the other hand, criminal law should be extremely sensitive to the 'negative' exemplarity of those 'particular' human experiences that recall a 'universal' lack of fulfilment of human dignity and lack of justice (Ferrara, 2008: 81 ff): this will be the realm of the *ought not to* (the *Sollen nicht*) in which criminalisation may select behaviours to be forbidden *because of* their harmful and offensive character. As pointed out by Judith Shklar (2000: 107), the sense of *in*justice is a universal distinguishing mark of our humanity, and it is the fundamental experience that entitles us to claim our dignity. A question posed by Avishai Margalit (2002: 78) is insightful, and astonishing is its reference to examples:

> So what should humanity remember? The short answer is: striking examples of radical evil and crimes against humanity.

Margalit's words echo in Tzvetan Todorov's chapter dedicated to memory and justice in *Les abus de la mémoire* (1959; 2001: 44 ff). Todorov distinguishes between *mémoire littérale* and *mémoire examplaire*. The former is 'risky' because it prevents the overcoming of past events. The latter is instead 'potentially liberating': exemplary memory is in fact capable of giving hospitality to a 'particular offence' within a 'general' category, permitting us to 'use the past in view of the future', profiting from the 'lessons' of past 'injustices' to fight today's ones (Todorov, 2001: 46). Todorov simply calls this exemplary memory: 'justice'. He defines it, strikingly, as a dynamic movement towards the 'Other'.

Yet, Hannah Arendt brings this reasoning even further forward, devoting her last studies to the thorny problem of 'the very mysterious nature of human judgment' in times of horrors that 'transcend all moral categories and … explode all standards of jurisdiction', leaving us 'without the help of categories and general rules under which to subsume our experiences'. Is judgement possible in the face of 'occurrences that spell the breakdown of all customary standards and hence are unprecedented in the sense that they are not foreseen in the general rules, not even as exceptions from such rules'

(Arendt, 2003: 23, 25–27)? Arendt shows how something close to responsiveness, in its most noble expression, emerges when facing the negative exemplarity of radical evil: it is a 'human faculty' which 'functions *spontaneously*' (emphasis added) and deals with thinking, moral reasoning, imagination, judgement, and 'personal responsibility' (Arendt, 2003: 27, 159 ff and *passim*). Interestingly for us, according to Hannah Arendt, under the said circumstances, behind this faculty there is not an 'obligation' under 'the threat of a sanction enforced', but rather a unique 'self evidence' of moral propositions (Arendt, 2003: 76–77). As Arendt explains (2003: 77–78), in Nazi Germany the very few who behaved righteously 'never doubted that crimes remained crimes even if legalized by the government'. These righteous persons:

> In other words … did not feel an obligation but acted according to something which was self-evident to them even though it was no longer self-evident to those around them. Hence their conscience, if that is what it is, had no obligatory character, it said 'This I can't do', rather than, 'This I ought not to do'.

'*I can't do it*', and not 'I ought not to do it': this is crucial.

Independent judgement, personal responsibility, normative competence in perceiving the harmful or offensive nature of an act, and spontaneous compliance with the evidence of exemplary evil and exemplary good are exactly the key elements of responsiveness which restorative justice also builds on.

But, if possible, there is even more inspiration for our thoughts.

Exemplarity and exemplary validity applied to criminal law show a double normative aspect worth mentioning, as explained by Ferrara throughout his book. First, in fact, there is a *creative* aspect of the reconciliation between *is* and *ought to be* in which light is intuitively shed on *new* profiles of the *ought to be* (the *Sollen*), until then unseen and unknown. This is part of Arendt's theoretical construction of judgement of unprecedented occurrences for which no rule, nor exception, applies. Secondly, there is a *validation* aspect of the said reconciliation in which the example confirms a *Sollen* that is already known, but which requires and claims a renovated agreement.

The picture is not yet complete, though, since sanctions too, in our perspective, must comply with the 'paradigm of exemplarity'. Put simply: sanctions should also manage to reconcile *is* with *ought to be*, by keeping away from punitive means that, on the contrary, resemble the same *ought not to be* of the crime in a sinister and mimetic way. The experience of fairness and justice should clearly—*exemplarily*–filter from sanctions, and be perceived by victims, but *especially* by offenders, with its persuasive (and preventive) 'exemplary validity'.

Responsive regulation and restorative justice (with the support of the results of procedural justice studies) seem very close to the patterns of exemplarity and exemplary validity: in fact, responsive and restorative theories appear as a sort of practicable fulfilment of the 'paradigm of exemplarity' in the field of criminal law and criminal justice.

When John Braithwaite (1989; 2002) evokes the importance of 'moral reasoning', 'intrinsic motivation', 'reintegrative shaming' in obtaining and improving compliance, rather than 'stick and carrot' strategies, he describes a sort of *reflective* judgement at the basis of the choice of a law-abiding behaviour. And so do Tom Tyler and others (Tyler, 1990; 2007, 2010; Lind and Tyler, 1988; Tyler and Huo, 2002) when they underline the impact on compliance of internal normative commitment, 'social motivation' and 'legitimacy' of norms and institutions. Also, when the risks of defiance and reaction associated wih sanctions which are perceived as unjust or illegitimate are pointed out (Sherman, 1993; Braithwaite, 2002), the mechanism of *reversing exemplarity* caused by the 'wrong' punishments is stressed.

To carry out more effectively their social goals—in other words: 'to work', or to work better—rules of conduct and positive sanctions in criminal law systems should, in our view, be 'exemplary' in the above-mentioned strict philosophical meaning, which is exactly the opposite of the common use of the term 'exemplary' in the realm of criminal justice.

Norms in criminal law should therefore tend to communicate in the same 'gentle', yet effective, way as examples do: they should involve their addressees in a normative dialogue on how to reconcile *is* and *ought to be* that does not postulate a coercive *a priori* (so dangerous in the hands of criminal law). Norms should therefore stimulate citizens' consensus and consent by means of an 'exemplary validity'; that is, a special, peculiar self-congruence of the rule with the original *Sollen* necessary to protect the legal interests from offences and/or harms. This validity rests only a little (or not at all) on authority and fully, instead, on the 'negative exemplarity' of human experiences of wrongs and injustices, and on the 'positive exemplarity' of human dignity, equality and human rights.

So far, the models and theories that have been able to come closer to the paradigm of exemplarity, and to structurally design a system in which fostering voluntary compliance, not inflicting punishment, is crucial, appear to be those of responsive regulation and of restorative justice.

It is high time that criminal law and criminal justice leave the throne where they have been sitting for too long, and move lower down to the place where injustices occur in concrete human reality: here, where the broken and harmed lives are, criminal law will need to speak a less violent, brutal (and less pompous) language. From here, the force with which the criminal law will 'affirm' and 'confirm' the expected compliant behaviour will be the 'force of the example', which is inextricably woven with citizens being a community and with citizens' agreement and participation to the incessant quest for justice from injustices, for rights from wrongs.

REFERENCES

Agamben, G (1990) *La comunità che viene* (Turin, Einaudi).
—— (1993) *The Coming Community* (M Hardt (trans), Minneapolis, MN, University of Minnesota Press).
—— (1995) *Homo sacer. Il potere sovrano e la nuda vita* (Turin, Einaudi, 2nd edn 2005).
—— (1998) *Homo Sacer: Sovereign Power and Bare Life* (D Heller-Roazen (trans), Stanford, CA, Stanford University Press).
Arendt, H (1961) *Between Past and Future* (New York, Viking Press).
—— (1978) *The Life of the Mind* (New York, Harcourt Brace Jovanovich).
—— (1982) *Lectures on Kant's Political Philosophy* (R Beiner (ed), Chicago, IL, University of Chicago Press).
—— (2003) *Responsibility and Judgment* (J Khon (ed), New York, Shocken Books).
Ayres, I and Braithwaite, J (1992) *Responsive Regulation: Transcending the Deregulation Debate* (New York, Oxford University Press).
Bagnoli, C (2007) *L'autorità della morale* (Milan, Feltrinelli).
—— (2011) 'Emotions and the Categorical Authority of Moral Reason' in C Bagnoli (ed), *Morality and the Emotions* (Oxford, Oxford University Press).
Baruch Bush, RA and Folger JP (1994) *The Promise of Mediation: Responding to Conflict through Empowerment and Recognition* (San Francisco, CA, Jossey Bass).
Benjamin, W (1920–1921) 'Critique of Violence' in *Reflections: Essays, Aphorisms, Autobiographical Writings* (E Jephcott (trans), New York, Shocken Books, 1986).
Bobbio, N (1976) 'Sanzione' in *Novissimo Digesto Italiano* (Turin, UTET).
Braithwaite, J (1985) *To Punish or to Persuade: Enforcement of Coal Mine Safety* (Albany, NY, State University of New York Press).
—— (1989) *Crime, Shame and Reintegration* (Cambridge/New York, Cambridge University Press).
—— (2002) *Restorative Justice and Responsive Regulation* (New York, Oxford University Press).
Braithwaite, J and Pettit, P (1990) *Not Just Deserts: A Republican Theory of Criminal Justice* (Oxford, Oxford University Press).
Christie, N (1981) *Limits to Pain: The Role of Punishment in Penal Society* (Eugene, OR, Wipf & Stock Publishers, 2nd edn 2007).
Cornacchia, L (2004) *Concorso di colpe e principio di responsabilità penale per fatto proprio* (Torino, Giappichelli).
Cornwell, DJ, Blad, J and Wright, M (eds) (2013) *Civilising Criminal Justice: An International Restorative Agenda for Penal Reform* (Sherfield-on-Loddon, Waterside Press).
Derrida, J (1994) *Force de loi. Le fondement mystique de l'autorité* (Paris, Galilée).
Dershowitz, A (2004) *Rights from Wrongs: A Secular Theory of the Origin of Rights* (New York, Basic Books).
Duff, RA (2001) *Punishment, Communication and Community* (New York, Oxford University Press).
Dworkin, R (1977), *Taking Rights Seriously* (London/New York, Bloomsbury, 2nd edn 2013).
Feinberg, J (1984–1990) *The Moral Limits of the Criminal Law* (New York, Oxford University Press).

Ferrajoli, L (2007) *Principia iuris. Teoria del diritto e della democrazia*, vol I (Bari, Laterza).
Ferrara, A (2008) *The Force of the Example: Explorations in the Paradigm of Judgment* (New York, Columbia University Press).
Fletcher, GP (2007) *The Grammar of Criminal Law: American, Comparative, and International*, vol I (New York, Oxford University Press).
Forti, G (2013) 'Le ragioni extrapenali dell'osservanza della legge penale: esperienze e prospettive' 3 *Rivista italiana di diritto e procedura penale* 1108.
Garland, D (2001) *The Culture of Control: Crime and Social Order in Contemporary Society*, 2nd edn (New York, Oxford University Press).
Haidt, J and Joseph, C (2004) 'Intuitive Ethics: How Innately Prepared Intuitions Generate Culturally Variable Virtues' 133 *Daedalus, Special Issue on Human Nature* 55.
Jankélévitch, J (1967) *Le pardon* (Paris, Aubier Montaigne).
—— (1968) *Il perdono* (L Aurigemma (trans), Milan, Istituto di Propaganda Libraria).
Kant, I (1790) *Critique of the Power of Judgment*, Cambridge Edition of the Works of Immanuel Kant (P Guyer (ed), P Guyer and E Matthews (trans), Cambridge, Cambridge University Press, 2000).
Lind, EA and Tyler, TR (1988) *The Social Psychology of Procedural Justice* (New York, Plenum Press).
Margalit, A (2002) *The Ethics of Memory* (Cambridge, MA/London, Harvard University Press).
Mazzucato, C (2006) *Consenso alle norme e prevenzione dei reati. Studi sul sistema sanzionatorio penale* (Rome, Aracne).
—— (2010) 'Appunti per una teoria "dignitosa" del diritto penale a partire dalla restorative justice, in *Dignità e diritto: prospettive interdisciplinari* 2 *Quaderni del Dipartimento di Scienze Giuridiche Università Cattolica Sacro Cuore* (Tricase, Libellula), available at http://dipartimenti.unicatt.it/scienzegiuridiche-tutte-le-pubblicazioni-dignita-e-diritto-prospettive-interdisciplinari.
—— (2011) 'Giustizia esemplare. Interlocuzione con il precetto penale e spunti di politica criminale' in M Bertolino, G Forti and L Eusebi (eds), *Studi in onore di Mario Romano*, vol I (Naples, Jovene).
Ost, F (2014) 'Penser par cas: la littérature comme laboratoire expérimental de la démarche juridique' 73(2) *Revue interdisciplinaire d'études juridiques* 228.
—— (2016) '"Retour aux humanités": la letteratura come laboratorio sperimentale del ragionamento giuridico' in G Forti, C Mazzucato and A Visconti (eds), *Giustizia e letteratura III* (C Mazzucato (trans), Milan, Vita e Pensiero).
Sherman, LW (1993) 'Defiance, Deterrence and Irrelevance: A Theory of the Criminal Sanction' 30 *Journal of Research in Crime and Delinquency* 445.
Shklar, J (1990) *The Faces of Injustice* (New York, Yale University).
—— (2000) *I volti dell'ingiustizia. Iniquità o cattiva sorte?* (R Rini (trans), Milan, Feltrinelli).
Todorov, T (1959) *Les abus de la mémoire* (Paris, Les Editions Arléa).
—— (2001) *Gli abusi della memoria* (A Cavicchia Scalamonti (trans), Naples, Ipermedium libri).
Tyler, TR (1990) *Why People Obey the Law* (Princeton, NJ, Princeton University Press, 2nd edn 2006).

—— (2010) *Why People Cooperate: The Role of Social Motivations* (Princeton, NJ, Princeton University Press).

Tyler, TR (ed) (2007) *Legitimacy and Criminal Justice: International Perspectives* (New York, Russell Sage Foundation).

Tyler, TR and Huo, YJ (2002) *Trust in the Law: Encouraging Public Cooperation with the Police and Courts* (New York, Russell Sage Foundation).

UN Economic and Social Council (ECOSOC) (2002) *UN Economic and Social Council Resolution 2002/12: Basic Principles on the Use of Restorative Justice Programmes in Criminal Matters*, E/RES/2002/12 (24 July).

Walgrave, L (2013) 'From Civilising Punishment to Civilising Criminal Justice: From Punishment to Restoration' in DJ Cornwell, J Blad and M Wright (eds), *Civilising Criminal Justice: An International Restorative Agenda for Penal Reform* (Sherfield-on-Loddon, Waterside Press).

Zehr, H (1990) *Changing Lenses: A New Focus for Crime and Justice* (Scottsdale, Herald Press).

—— (2015) *Changing Lenses: Restorative Justice for Our Times*, 4th edn (Harrisonburg, VA, Herald Press, 25th Anniversary Edition).

15

The Broken Tablets of Moses and the Exodus from (Post-) Modernity

On Rethinking the Role and the Rule of Law in a Dialogical Way

FEDERICO REGGIO

I. ON RETHINKING ALTERNATIVENESS: THE CONTROVERSIAL RELATIONSHIP BETWEEN RESTORATIVE JUSTICE AND CRIMINAL JUSTICE

THE QUESTION ABOUT the relationship between restorative justice (RJ) and criminal justice has been highly debated and still seems quite controversial.

Such conceptual tension is found at the origin of RJ: Howard Zehr, for instance, depicted it as an autonomous 'paradigm of justice' (Zehr, 1990), embodying an entirely different understanding of crime and of the reaction to it. The restorative approach was not, therefore, confined to a number of alternative programmes, as its promise and challenge were said to affect the way crime, punishment and criminal justice are envisioned.

Scholars would probably agree that the majority of its proponents have depicted the restorative approach as a perspective that challenges both the theory and the practice of criminal justice by suggesting different goals and focuses, as well as different ethical concerns, or even a different underlying philosophy (see, for an overview, Johnstone and Van Ness, 2007).

Questions arise regarding how these different elements relate to the traditional theories and practices of criminal justice, and thereby with criminal law itself. Restorative justice's 'alternativeness' emerges, here, as a kaleidoscopic notion, which allows, within its 'ring of vagueness' the cohabitation of different, sometimes mutually alternative conceptions (see Roche, 2001; Wright and Zernova, 2007).

Drawing from Aristotelian categories, 'alternativeness' can be viewed as an 'essentially contested concept', or as an *endoxon*, a commonplace which can be taken as a premise of an argumentative reasoning, whose vagueness of meaning does not offer sufficient guarantees about the consistency of the conclusions that can be drawn from such starting point (see respectively Gallie, 1964 and Cavalla, 2007). RJ's alternativeness emerges as a problematic issue, as a starting point, which requires further debate and further inquiry in order to clarify the conceptual borders of RJ's innovative proposal.

An interesting example of this issue can be found in a central debate that took place in the early 2000s, featuring on opposite sides Paul McCold's 'Purist' approach and Lode Walgrave's 'Maximalist' approach (see, for an overview, McCold, 2000; Walgrave, 2000).

McCold's proposal was intended to preserve RJ's purity from contaminations with substantive and procedural criminal law, and, more generally, with the categories around which such legal regulation are usually shaped.[1] This shows an underlying concern about the risk of undermining RJ's innovative proposals by formalising and structuring them within the 'gears' of legal systems.

As a critique, nevertheless, such focus on informality, voluntariness and consensus might dilute the notion of 'restoration', reducing it to the proposal of de-formalising criminal justice.[2] As Walgrave remarked, on the other hand, informal processes are justified if aimed at granting a reparatory outcome, but the latter can (and should) be pursued also by processes that may require some degree of formality and coercion and therefore some interaction with traditional tools of the criminal justice system (see Walgrave, 2007; And similarly, although external to the movement of RJ, Zanuso, 2009). There is, otherwise, the risk of confining RJ to some sort of diversionary track of the judicial system: an 'addendum' that remains outside the 'hard-core' of criminal justice systems, applicable to a minority of cases and lacking any impact in the process of rethinking the entire edifice of criminal justice (Walgrave, 1999: 12–13). According to the Belgian scholar, we should instead try to integrate RJ within the criminal justice system, or, more precisely, reform the latter in restorative terms (see Walgrave, 2007).

Drawing from George Pavlich's influential contribution on the 'paradoxes' of restorative justice, conceptualising RJ's alternativeness in opposition to criminal justice might lead to a paradoxical outcome, as it qualifies RJ as complementary, if not ancillary, to the system to which the

[1] His perspective (consistently with a process/encounter centred attitude to RJ) outlined four fundamental elements characterising a restorative approach to justice: voluntary cooperation among the parties (victim and offender); mutually agreed-upon solutions; justice mainly intended as satisfaction of individual needs as expressed by the stakeholders; the justice process designed around an informal and flexible model. Such approach is presented as opposed to the highly formalised, adversarial, adjudicative, punitive and state-centred character that traditionally informs criminal justice in the majority of Western legal systems.

[2] Such accent can be seen in various authors. To mention two who influenced the early debate in the field, see Zehr, 1990 and Cragg, 1992.

restorative paradigm promised to offer a full-fledged alternative (Pavlich, 2006: 18–20).

Moreover, one should not forget that some functions traditionally devolved to criminal justice, and usually connected to the idea of the 'rule of law', 'emerged out of centuries of struggle—with its emphasis upon due process and individual rights—by imposing effective inhibitions upon power and defending of the citizen from powerful claims' (Bošnjak, 2007: 100; see also Crawford, 2002). As Marko Bošnjak (2007: 101) points out, criminal law has offered specific and non-renounceable legal safeguards (eg access to court, right to a fair trial, presumption of innocence, privilege against self-incrimination, rights and freedoms limiting access of the state to repressive measures against the defendant). Criminal law (substantive and procedural) cannot be depicted, therefore, only in negative terms, since it is connected to fostering and protecting appreciable goals.[3]

Some safeguards and regulatory schemes provided by criminal justice, and more generally by the legal system, are not necessarily opposed to restorative justice's values and goals: they are sometimes complementary, or even functional to them.[4] It is not surprising, then, that despite the polarisation expressed in his earlier writings, Howard Zehr has suggested that RJ and traditional criminal justice can be seen within a 'continuum' (Zehr, 2002: 60).

Still, the idea of integrating RJ within the criminal justice system is highly problematic, since the changes invoked by the restorative approach involve the overall architecture of criminal justice as a system (see, on this point, Aertsen, Daems and Robert, 2006).[5]

Do we risk, then, to remain 'stuck in the desert' during the 'exodus' from the traditional approaches to crime and justice, unable to reach the promised land that many proponents of RJ are longing to finally achieve?

[3] As the author points out, nevertheless, 'an implicit consensus seems to exist among restorative justice advocates that fundamental rights ought to be respected in restorative justice processes' although 'the argument is about what the list of rights ought to consist of' (Bošnjak, 2007: 101).

[4] In his pioneering work, Nils Christie suggested that the necessary function of ascertaining the facts requires procedural instruments which are better granted in the legal trial. See Christie, 1977. Therefore, restorative practices could better take place at the moment of sentencing.

[5] Daniel Van Ness has outlined four models of conceiving the relationship between RJ and the traditional approaches to criminal justice: a 'unitary model', in which the whole system is restorative-oriented; a 'dual track model', in which RJ and conventional criminal justice operate as parallel tracks with pre-determined connections and channels between them; a 'safety net model', in which the conventional criminal justice approach operates as second or last resort, when restorative practices fail or turn out to be impossible perform; the final, 'hybrid model', links conventional criminal justice with restorative justice, mostly by distinguishing their roles: the former would mostly be appropriate in ascertaining facts, the latter in defining restoratively the reaction to crime. See Van Ness, 2002. See also, for other reconstructive proposals, Bosnjak, 2007.

The reference to words like 'exodus' and 'promised land' is not accidental. Restorative justice proponents might sometimes feel like the Hebrews when they were crossing the desert: they were willingly leaving the highly hierarchical, static, repressive, 'pyramidal' legal order of the Pharaoh and moving towards a land where they had been promised they could live in peace as free people. Yet, while they were facing the harshness of the desert, they often needed to recall what they were escaping from, and towards which promise they were directing their exodus. As the narration from the book of *Exodus* reminds us, in the emptiness and hollowness of the desert, the Hebrews needed a new law: the law of the Pharaoh was no longer applicable nor desirable, but they needed regulatory schemes that enabled them to deal with interpersonal relationships and, of course, with interpersonal conflict.

Similarly, RJ's proponents often need to remind themselves and others what they are suggesting to escape from (a punitive, repressive criminal justice system to which persons and interpersonal relationships are peripheral if not even irrelevant) and towards which promised land they are moving, and yet the journey appears to be rather long and full of obstacles.

But as much as it is useful to focus on the weak spots, failures and contradictions of the 'pyramidal legal order' that RJ wishes to replace, we often come to realise that we still need rules, legal safeguards, procedures, regulatory schemes.[6]

On the other hand, much of the critiques that the legal system receives from a restorative perspective emphasise how those legal concepts and tools, especially the way they have been conceived and practised throughout modernity until our times, might be used in a way that suffocates elements, values and goals that the restorative approach seeks to promote.[7]

Is it the regulatory potential of law that is at stake here, or rather the way such role and rule have been conceived and practised?

By claiming the central role of people and relationships, by promoting a participatory process and the reparation of harms, possibly outlined in a consensual way, RJ puts at stake the relationship between the 'technical'

[6] Such tools are needed, eg: to outline which rights and freedoms are legally protected; which type of violations cause a harm that needs to be restored (which type of violations can be defined as crimes); how responsibilities can be ascertained; how restorative processes can be regulated and how they interact, in the individual case, with other more conventional processes; which rights must be protected throughout the justice process and which legal remedies are available. See, for some wider considerations, Hartmann, 2007.

[7] Such values are, eg: attention to the victims and their needs; promotion of the offenders' active and constructive responsibility; involvement of their entourages or, more generally, of the community; the attention to conflict as an experience that concretely harms interpersonal relationships and that therefore requires a participatory approach.

element of law and the 'human dimension' which underlies it, and which is tangibly involved when conflict happens.[8]

If we agree on this, we must also notice that in this way, the restorative perspective endorses (although frequently in an implicit manner) a deep question that trespasses on the borders of the wider criminological debate and that involves, more generally, the role and the rule of law.[9]

II. RJ AND THE LAW IN THE EXODUS FROM MODERNITY

The width of the above-mentioned radical question seems to be summed up in a quotation taken from the biblical wisdom: 'The Sabbath was made for man, not man for the Sabbath' (*Mark*, 2:27). With much respect for the religious implications of this sentence (which will not be taken into account here) the question about the relationship between a rule (the Sabbath) and its receivers reaches the 'bone-marrow' of both legal theory and practice, as it questions the justifications, the limits and the goals of law.

As François Ost explains in his 'law & literature' reading, it should not be forgotten that the Sabbath as a holiday was one of the first rules introduced during the Exodus, and even before the Law stipulated between God and the Hebrews by means of the Covenant. Such rule was meant to remind the Hebrews that they were no longer slaves: once a week, on the day dedicated to God, who had liberated them, they had to rest and let everyone (servants and animals included) do so. Only slaves, in fact, are never allowed to rest.[10]

Reminding that such rule was made for man, and not the opposite, was meant to prevent formalistic and even fundamentalist applications of the rule itself. If that rule was intended as a safeguard 'for' the people, the good of the people must be the leading concept when it comes to interpreting and applying it.

[8] As Robert Mackey puts it, RJ (in common with the ADR movement) is 'promoting the value of dialogue which is in sharp contrast not to law as an entity, but to its established mechanisms and dominant practices' (Mackay, 2007: 114). See, on RJ and such 'human dimension', also Mazzucato, 2010.

[9] As Mackey observed, RJ can be seen as a 'catalyst in helping us to rethink the purpose o law' (Mackay, 2007: 121). He also previously maintained that 'the current state of theory in the restorative justice movement' does 'not provide … sufficient arguments to enable us to speak coherently of a restorative theory of justice or a restorative theory of law' (Mackay, 2007: 114). On the other hand, however, the vitality of the debate among restorative justice scholars and advocates shows that such issues are being frequently discussed, in favour of a theoretical development which benefits the whole concept of RJ. See, on this point, Walgrave, 2002b.

[10] In the various references to the Exodus and the Covenant for the purposes of this chapter I am following, in particular, the interpretation of Ost, 1999 and Ost, 2004. See also, Drai 1992 and Jacobson, 1990. My reading is, nevertheless, in debt to the studies of Wiesnet, 1980; Zehr, 1990; Marshall, 2001.

Similarly, when RJ claims to rediscover the importance of persons and interpersonal relationships, it critically points out how these elements have become peripheral to the modern and contemporary theory and practice of law, mostly in the sector of criminal law.

It is no surprise, then, that the proposal of a participatory, reparative and possibly consensual model of dealing with crime and its aftermath is indeed frequently treated with suspicion in the legal debate. These ideas challenge consolidated mental schemes and explanatory narratives which typically characterise the domain of law, especially when it is rooted in a norm-centred approach.

Despite the changes occurring in the 'post-modern' shift, it should not be forgotten that the predominant configuration of legal systems, and of a remarkably large part of legal theory as well, stems from rather old philosophical premises, rooted in the so-called 'modern' mentality.[11] This leads us to hypothesise that the above-mentioned resistances might originate from such mentality, and mostly from the significant traces of it that still characterise the 'legal world'.

The times of the Baroque and Early Enlightenment saw the development of the modern conception of the state, thereby promoting a new configuration of the role and the rule of law. It was a moment of deep transformation, characterised by a fracture with the classic and medieval times, which mirrored quite a remarkable shift in the mentality affecting all the sectors of theoretical reflection and human experience.[12]

Early Enlightenment doctrines of natural law tended to share very specific anthropological (individualistic and utilitarian) and epistemic (rationalistic) premises. Such premises led, through different argumentative paths, to the 'geometrical' demonstration of the necessary presence of the state as owner of the monopoly of the use of force, grantor (and sometimes creator) of a political order whose guarantee relied upon the capability of the state to enforce its order by means of legal tools.[13] As Christa Pelikan observes,

[11] The 'modern' approach is characterised by a highly systematic and transformative attitude to (the factual, social, political legal) reality, which stems from a highly rationalistic approach to knowledge, which tends to reduce the world to the merely phenomenal: a ground for the manipulative attitude of human beings, in the sense of the '*homo faber*' depicted by Hannah Arendt (see Arendt, 1958). My analysis is here in debt to a consolidated interpretive tradition that has been developed by the legal-philosophical school of Francesco Cavalla. See, eg Cavalla, 1990; 2011; Zanuso, 1993; Zanuso and Fuselli, 2004; Zanuso, 2013; Manzin, 2008; Moro, 2013.

[12] Without attempting any cause-effect analysis, we can underline how those times witnessed a significant convergence of anthropological and epistemic premises with political and legal theories and with the factual development of a model of state to which the modern idea of law was quite functional. See, on this point, Lenman and Parker, 1979; Berman, 1983; Cavalla, 1996; 2011; Montanari, 2005.

[13] As a result of its individualistic anthropological model, which is strictly bound to a rationalistic epistemology, the modern understanding tended to consider human beings as unable

'the state, as the new sovereign, extends its realm of power and establishes its monopoly of the use of force by promising equality of all those new subjects, now "citizens" that come under its sole rule' (Pelikan, 2007: 39).

On one hand, this idea of 'role' and 'rule of law' is placed at the origin of further developments which are probably still to be interpreted as a civilising process within Western history, including the modern constitutional states, the codification of law, and, more generally, the systems of checks and balances that were designed to prevent the arbitrary use of power also within and by the state. This helps to show how much of the contemporary political and legal architectures are still related to the modern roots also by positive outcomes.

On the other hand, nevertheless, 'different theories portraying the essence of these developments contribute' (according to Pelikan) 'to making visible the "Janus face" of criminal law in society' (Pelikan, 2007: 39). The development of modern legal and political theories not only witnesses to the affirmation of the 'rule of law' as a condition in which 'the rights and liberties of each legal subject are equally protected' (Blad, 2013: 216), but also the theoretical justification of a sort of 'law of rule', in which law is instrumentally bound to providing the state's political order with effectiveness (see, on the images of Justice, Mannozzi, 2003).

In the latter framework, criminal justice plays a central role, as effectiveness depends on the possibility of enforcing law through the threat of applying a sanction to the non-abiding (so-called 'non-homologated') citizens (see, on this point, Cavalla, 1979; 2000).

Modern theories of punishment have offered a variety of theses about the justification and the goal of the penal sanction. Despite relevant differences, theories such as retribution, deterrence and special-prevention also show some important commonalities (see Cavalla, 2000; Zanuso and Fuselli, 2004; Brunk, 2001; Zehr, 1990). They tend, in fact: (1) to describe crime as the breach of a given (social, political, legal) order, rather than a personal and interpersonal violation; (2) to conceive punishment as the legal consequence foreseen by such order in order to 'reconstruct' its validity or

to personally deal with conflict in a constructive way. Modern 'myths' developed within the narrations of authors such as Thomas Hobbes, John Locke, Samuel Pufendorf, Jean Jacques Rousseau, commonly tended to describe a (hypothetical or real) state of nature as an unbearable and unsustainable situation which required an artificial regulation in order to prevent conflict exercising its most destructive outcomes. Such an artificial 'body' (let's think of Hobbes' Leviathan, for instance) was, namely, the state, originated by a social contract by which each individual renounces, to some extent, its natural condition in order to obtain a certain set of guarantees, including individual rights and freedoms. As a result, the only social order which was conceived as able to prevent and resolve conflict was the one artificially granted (Locke), or even created (Hobbes, Rousseau) by the state. For historical considerations about the relationship between the modern idea(l) of state and criminal justice, see also Lenman and Parker, 1979; Cavalla, 1979; Berman, 1983; Zehr, 1990; Bianchi, 2004.

effectiveness; and (3) to delegate such process to a monopolistic actor, such as the state (see Zehr, 1990; Cavalla, 1979; 2000; Brunk, 2001). State and *status quo* tended, in other terms, to coincide, and were intended in a way that opposed the individual to the given order, so that the 'conflict' was to be seen as a contrast between the individual and such pre-determined order.

If this reconstruction, albeit very schematic, is able to catch some core-ideas of the modern approach to criminal justice, and to show some aspects of the legal conceptions that underlie such perspective, it should not be surprising that they are in deep friction with some core-themes of the restorative understanding of justice (and, as I would like to show, also of the idea of law that such understanding seems to call for).

Such frictions can probably be summed up thus: (1) while modernity is characterised by a mainly individualistic and utilitarian approach, RJ pays deep attention to 'relational textures'; (2) while one of the modern worldview's main features is the tendency to outline an abstract, rationalistic, geometrical, standardised conception of (natural, societal, political, legal) order, RJ attempts to envision an experience-based, context-sensitive and open-to-complexity idea of legal order; (3) while one of the products of the modern conception of law is a norm-centred and formal vision, in which the legal order is a hierarchically organised system of norms, placed within the pyramid of the state's articulations and enforced by the sanctions that the state can dispose of as a monopolistic actor, RJ tends instead to conceive a horizontal, relational and context-sensitive idea of legal regulation (see Reggio, 2013).[14]

The criticism developed, in the last decades, within the post-modern reflection has helped in many ways to acknowledge some of the most evident weaknesses and failures of many of those ideas, letting conceptions emerge that, on the contrary, emphasise factors like complexity, inter-relatedness, risk assessment (see Pelikan, 2007). Such development is consistent also with the evolution of the contemporary legal practice (see Minda, 1995; Montanari, 2005; Moro and Sarra, 2012). This does not mean, however, that the contemporary legal theory and practice have abandoned a norm-centred approach. Also in the latter context, the risk of leaving the above-mentioned 'human dimension' peripheral to legal practice is quite tangible, despite being apparent in other dimensions and through other manifestations (see Mazzuccato, 2010; Blad, 2013; Walgrave, 2013; Wright, 2013).

Post-modern critical theories can, in any case, helpfully de-construct modern myths and illusions, as George Pavlich has brilliantly pointed out in his connection between a Derridean approach and RJ (see Pavlich, 2006; 2007). Those approaches might turn to be rather problematic when

[14] On post-modernity and its openness to complexity, see Bauman, 1993 and 2000, and, in relation to RJ, Pelikan, 2007; Pavlich, 2007.

it comes to (philosophically) sustaining alternative proposals (see Pavlich, 2007: 616). There is a justified doubt that the innovative strength of RJ can be adequately consolidated while remaining inside the 'unsustainable lightness' of the post-modern way of thinking.[15] This suspicion is due to post-modernism's aversion towards global thinking and to its resistance to discourses that may appear foundational (that is, those that ground their proposals on a set of values or on a type of knowledge argued to be preferable to others).[16]

Especially when the deconstructive force of post-modern argumentations falls into a full-fledged sceptical relativism, it is easy to enter some sort of vicious triangle, which risks taking away the ground from any discourse.[17] Going back to our biblical metaphor, if we remain within such an attitude, we might easily find ourselves willing to escape from the Pharaoh's pyramidal order, yet unable to get through 'the desert', stuck in a never-ending exodus from modern dreams, nightmares and illusions, and incapable even of glancing towards (truly) alternative destinations.

III. A DIFFERENT PATH: VICO'S DISCARDED IMAGE

Now that we can critically outline and experience the outcomes (and the many failures) of modernity, as well as the many 'dead-ends' that post-modern approaches seem to lead to, it might be interesting go back at the 'parting of the way', when the modern mentality became dominant. There we can confront the perspective of a thinker like Giambattista Vico (1668–1744), who had emerged as a critical voice in that peculiar moment of Western culture.[18]

Vico consciously undertook a circumstantial critique of the Baroque and early Enlightenment modern philosophy (see Bellofiore, 1954; Lilla, 1993; Galeazzi, 1993; Voegelin, 1998; against Caporali, 1996). In the meanwhile,

[15] Post-modernity encompasses a general 'disillusionment' with the idea of enduring, non-renounceable concepts: short-term, low-range solutions are preferred to wide and extended projects, and this is visible also in the legal world. The post-modern *milieu* is characterised by a highly relativistic attitude, most especially in the sector of ethics. See Lyotard, 1984; Bauman, 1993; Derrida and Defourmantelle, 2000, and critically, Brown, 1988; Connor, 1989; Cavalla, 1990; Williams, 1996; Habermas, 2003; Slob, 2002; Vendemiati, 2007.

[16] This shows a contrast with some of restorative justice's main characteristics, as I pointed out in an earlier writing: see Reggio, 2013: 321.

[17] According to Slob, sceptical relativism 'digs its own grave'. In order to make its point, it must claim that *its* conclusion is not culturally relative. 'Applying the theory of self-referentiality, its validity only extends to the select subculture of Western academic anthropologists and supporting friends'(Slob, 2002: 51). See also Schrag, 1992 and Vendemiati, 2007.

[18] Such an attitude clearly emerges, for instance, in his work *De Nostri Temporis Studiorum Ratione* (written in 1709) dedicated to a comparison between the modern and the 'ancient' method of studies, where the author explores the limits and potentials of both these approaches: see Vico, 1709.

he also developed a personal approach in dialogue both with the tradition of classical humanism and with some of the main issues of his time (see Ambrosetti, 1982; Battistini, 2004; Reggio, 2012). His criticism can be briefly schematised around four main themes which represented pure characteristics of the mainstream perspective of his contemporaries, especially within the theories of Natural Law: (1) the rationalistic and reductionist attitude of the modern approach to knowledge; (2) the individualistic anthropological concept; (3) the abstract idea of law and justice; (4) the (consequent) state-centred vision stemming from those premises.

Vico's (1710) critique of the modern approach to knowledge targets its rationalistic character, which tends to shadow the structural limitedness of human knowledge in favour of a 'blind faith' in the reason's capability of reaching stable knowledge: instead, 'human knowledge is like human beings themselves, limited and imperfect' (1710: 197).

Vico criticises also the modern tendency to narrow the concept of rationality to those types of knowledge characterised by (or imitating) a scientific form (ie forms of reasoning based on a hypothetical-deductive structure and aiming at high levels of certainty).[19] He argues that a reduction of knowledge to a 'Cartesian' model compresses rationality into an abstract frame, which turns out to be inadequate to the complexity of reality (see Mootz, 2009: 13–16). Human beings are characterised by emotions, feelings, fantasy, and different types of rationality.[20] This appears most especially in those fields which we would now categorise as human sciences, which cannot be effectively managed through 'geometrical demonstrations'.[21]

In modern political and legal philosophy, rationalism is strongly bound to an individualistic anthropological conception, that leads us to consider human beings naturally incapable of sociable life, and therefore the origin of society and law stems from an artificial creative act.

According to Vico, history itself belies that hypothesis: since we have memory of it, in fact, humanity has been living within a societal frame

[19] In his dissertation *De Nostri Temporis Studiorum Ratione* (1709) Vico criticises the privilege accorded to the deductive (science-based) structure of reasoning, and especially to the claim of developing systems where conclusions are deduced from axiomatic premises, from which they descend '*more geometrico*'. See also Verene, 2008: 1107–30. On the origins of this geometrical-mathematical idea of order in the modern *Weltanschauung*, see Manzin, 2008.

[20] As Mootz observes, Vico reminds us that 'the critical method undermines the cultivation of common sense, which subtends both practical judgement and eloquence, thereby restricting knowledge to an arid and abstract intellectualism' (Mootz, 2009: 13).

[21] The defence that Vico undertook in favour of disciplines such as dialectics, rhetoric, history and poetry, as well as virtues belonging to humanistic education, such as prudence, eloquence and wisdom, targets a problem which can be characterised as both theoretical and practical: a reason narrowed to a Cartesian model is both abstract and inadequate to human reality. As Vico puts it, to adopt that view would imply, sooner or later, ending up 'caught in the web of contingency' (Vico, 1709: 133).

(see Vico, 1744: VIII *axiom*).[22] Human beings are structured as social agents and so they have always behaved (see Vico, 1719: ch XLV).

Rooted in the classical tradition, Vico sustains the idea of a natural 'relationality' of human beings, which he strongly connects to the idea of natural law, intended not as a predetermined or fully determinable set of rules but as the natural (ie 'originary') co-implication between law and society.

The bi-univocal connection between the relational predisposition of human beings and the regulatory role of law shows that law should not be (solely) intended as heteronomous, as an act of sovereignty.[23] The presence of commands and sanctions is accessory to the coercive element of law, which is neither the one and only manifestation of law, nor its ultimate justification. Law, according to Vico, is one of the most important expressions of people's attitude to be and live in a society, and to regulate, protect and cultivate a relationship of mutuality within such a framework.[24] Law is therefore bound to the need of granting, fostering and protecting (*dominium, libertas, tutela*) peaceful relations among people.[25]

Along this argumentative line 'relationship' and 'mutuality' act both as *principle* and *limit* of law itself: therefore, laws cannot have a fully open and disposable meaning.[26] Indeed, they ought to be evaluated in light of their capability to protect and foster relations of mutuality and equity among people.[27]

According to Vico, the most important 'institutions' of humankind appear all to express a practised dimension of relationality (Vico, 1744: IV, II).[28]

[22] Therefore the idea of a natural, pre-societal, condition of human beings (which can be found in many Natural Law theories, from Grotius to Locke, with a strong accent in Hobbes and Rousseau), would be just hypothetical and, most importantly, lacking in historical evidence.

[23] An interesting comparison between Vico and Hobbes can be found in Zanetti, 2011.

[24] Such view can be confirmed also by the consideration which Vico dedicated to the theme of punishment in his *De Uno*. See, for a critical analysis, Reggio, 2004.

[25] Granting, fostering and protecting human relationality are the three dimensions of the legal sphere: *dominium, libertas* and *tutela*. A rather old but still precious study of this aspect of Vico's philosophy can be found in Capograssi, 1925: 437–51.

[26] Nevertheless, this does not mean that nature's law expresses a fully clear and developed set of rules, which are to be 'translated' into practice: nature's law embodies principles (*neminem laedere, honeste vivere, suum cuique tribuere*) whose practical application remains intrinsically problematic and therefore requires a constant and common research.

[27] Vico's vision of law never allows it to fall into an absolutist scheme: authority, he reminds us, 'can never be opposed to the reason. Therefore, those would not be laws, but legal monsters'. See Vico, 1719: ch LXXXIII (my translation).

[28] Vico recurred to some sort of mythological narration to explain, in the *New Science*, his view about the origin of society. Without reviewing such narrative in details, it is possible to show how Vico's story was focused on the (re)discovery of human finitude, emerging from a practised experience of human limitedness (an overwhelming natural event, like a lightning strike), which generated a feeling of *pudor* (shame). Such a feeling does not lead to a closure, but evolves and turns into a peculiar type of shame (which Vico calls *pudor*) which plays a propulsive role both in promoting an ethical and theoretical breakthrough (*virtus ethica, virtus dianoetica* are both the positive result of *pudor*). *Virtus ethica* generates both ethics and the law.

Moreover, these institutions are granted by norms and, in the meanwhile, are able to produce rules themselves.[29]

This does not mean that Vico adopts a naïve vision of humankind, since he points out that there is always the possibility, at any point of human experience, that dialogue and mutuality be denied in favour of the language of violence and abuse of power.[30] When human reason is unable to recognise its condition of limitedness, it loses the perception of the reciprocity that binds each human being in sharing a common humanity, with the result of treating the 'other' as an object, as several dark pages of history seem to confirm, also in recent times.[31]

While the modern conception considers limitation in a negative way (as a restriction that naturally human beings would not accept, but which can be justified for pragmatic purposes), Vico considers limitation also as a motor, because acknowledging its presence leads to a higher consciousness of our self.[32]

Being human is characterised by a double dimension: the perception of limitedness and the perception of an inherent reciprocity in being limited. Such reciprocity requires guarantees and rules in order to be enhanced, protected and restored if violated, and this is the domain (and the frontier as well) of the legal world.[33] Law, in this idea, is 'eternal but runs in time': eternal in its idea, but historical in its manifestations (see also Vico, 1744: IV). It has therefore a double character: it reveals some lasting and universal(isable) principles, but is also 'living' and contextual(isable), through history (see Bellofiore, 1954; Ambrosetti, 1982; Galeazzi, 1993).

Laws, as historical manifestations, are in fact a human product and therefore informed by the understanding of those who concretely conceive and apply them (see Capograssi, 1925; Marzano Parisoli, 2000).

There is a problematic tension between the ideals that law seeks to embody and pursue (justice, equity, mutuality) and the possibility of concretely

[29] While in his earlier, legal-philosophical writings (*De Uno, De Constantia,* 1719–1721, published together in the *Universal Right*), such a theme emerges mainly from his reflections on the problem of nature's law, Vico confirms this view also when he moves towards a broader study of human institutions in his most famous work, *The New Science* (1725; 1744).

[30] Such a 'shift to barbarity' can have different faces: it might assume the form of a loss of rational capability or, on the other hand, the development of a (supposed-to-be) self-sufficient rationality. Eric Voegelin read Vico's reflections on this point as a critique of the modern 'hubris of self-salvation', as a mirror of a fallaciously optimistic attitude towards the ability of humankind to know and produce stable forms of 'order'. See Voegelin, 1998.

[31] Rises and falls (Vico refers to the remarkable example of the Roman Empire) occur, both as historical evidence and future possibility. Such a reflection clearly appears in the concluding chapters of his *New Science* (1744). See also Galeazzi, 1993.

[32] See, on the concept of limit, Illetterati, 1996 and Moro, 2013.

[33] We can now perhaps better understand why Vico's anthropology is grounded in Augustine's definition of man as a *finitum quo tendit ad infinitum*: a finite who tends to the infinite. A reflection about the nature of man as 'synole' of finitude and infinity had been developed by the Italian philosopher of law, Sergio Cotta. See Cotta, 1991.

adapting these ideals to reality. The 'legal world', therefore, can never be fully identified with the peculiar norms, rules and institutions emerging from each context.[34] Vico's context-sensitivity does not fall into relativism: he strongly defends the presence of values and principles that, although born in a specific context (with a 'bottom-up' process) are common to all humanity, beyond differences (but without any need to ignore differences, either).[35]

The space of law appears wherever there is the need of ruling relations and social organisations: therefore, in the *New Science* Vico argues that human society is organised through a complex web of interacting and complementary institutions, and not only by the state. Moreover, fostering, granting and protecting a safe space for smaller webs of relational structures would act like the state's justification and limit.

By contrasting the modern epistemic and anthropological conceptual premise, Vico sought to undermine the whole construction of the modern political theories, whose focus on a tension between the state and atomised individuals provided strong philosophical justifications to a static and rationalistic idea of social order, granted by legal forms, whose producer and 'owner' would be the state.[36]

Vico's attempt did not succeed, as the history of Western culture preferred the vision that he had so strongly criticised: his perspective remained, therefore, a sort of 'discarded image'.[37] This does not prevent us from rediscovering its soundness: despite the many changes which have occurred in the meantime (of which we must be conscious) such perspective might still have something to say, especially to people who are still searching for a way out of the desert, during the exodus from modernity.

[34] Such an interpretation has been outlined in masterly fashion by Bellofiore, 1954.

[35] This can be also verified with specific reference to the conception of legal methodology outlined by Vico, in which the dynamic and complex concept of *aequitas* plays a vital role. See, for further considerations, 'T Hart, 1982.

[36] See, on the problematic relationship between atomised individuals and the state, Gentile (1983). It is interesting to compare a sentence from Vico's *De Uno* with one from Hobbes' *De Cive*: Vico writes that 'without the Divine Providence in the world there would be nothing but mistake, bestiality, violence, fierceness, blood and dirtiness; and perhaps, or even doubtless, today there would be no humanity left on the wide mass of a horrid and dumb Earth'(*The New Science 1725*, 476, my translation). Hobbes, instead argues that 'Out of this state, every man hath such a Right to all, as yet he can enjoy nothing; in it, each one securely enjoyes his limited Right; Out of it, any man may rightly spoyle, or kill one another; in it, none but one. Out of it we are protected by our own forces; in it, by the power of all. Out of it no man is sure of the fruit of his labours; in it, all men are. Lastly, out of it, there is a Dominion of Passions, war, fear, poverty, slovenliness, solitude, barbarisme, ignorance, cruelty. In it, the Dominion of reason, peace, security, riches, decency, society, elegancy, sciences, and benevolence' (Hobbes, *De Cive*, X, 1). The role that Vico attributes to a provident God belongs, in the Hobbesian view, to the state: the secularisation of God and the absolutisation of the state, as two connected outcomes of modernity, seem to be here fully theorised.

[37] This is the metaphor that I used to describe how Vico's perspective failed to influence the modern debate. See Reggio, 2012.

IV. FROM A DIALOGICAL JUSTICE TO A DIALOGICAL LAW: DRAFTING A PROPOSAL

From our reading of Vico's perspective we can, first of all, criticise the idea of a fixed, static and norm-centred legal order, in favour of a view in which the legal order appears as a dynamic, open and contextual system (see Moro, 1996; 2013). The openness of such order depends on its relational character and origin: law is meant to enable relationships, and therefore is structurally participatory.

Shrinking law within a heteronomous, artificial construction, granted by the possibility of coercion, risks falling into the sceptical option of identifying the legal order with the product of a power. Be it legalised, be it limited by checks and balances, by internal or external safeguards, such close connection between law and power shadows the relational structure of law.

We can, nevertheless, reinterpret also the notion of power in relational terms, where mutual empowerment and recognition act both as source and limit of the power's legitimacy, and also as legitimating factor for the cases in which the legal order is called to intervene, in order to enforce its safeguards when mutuality and relationship have been violated.

It might be not an accidental circumstance that a remarkable Dutch interpreter of Vico, August 't Hart, has interpreted the concept of the Rule of Law in a relational way. As we learn from John R Blad, the Rule of Law can be viewed as a structure:

> in which power would be divided between participants who acknowledge each other reciprocally and wherein law would function in the first place as the structure constituting the relation between the participants in power. Law is then not a pure instrument of the exercise of power, but is understood as a pattern of relations ... expressing a comprehensive structural equilibrium that allows limitation and diffusion of the exercise of power. ('T Hart, 2004: 210, transl. in Blad, 2013: 216)

The division of such power, and the legal safeguards that might result from it, can be viewed as 'spheres' of autonomy in which, as Walgrave puts it, drawing from Braithwaite and Pettit's notion of 'dominion', 'the rights and freedoms of the individual citizen end where the rights and freedoms of the other citizen begin' (Walgrave, 2013: 352). Despite its usefulness, such notion tends to make us fall once again into an individualistic approach (to see rights and freedoms as individually granted within a certain sphere), and, most of all, to obscure the fact that such sphere is not an artificial 'privilege' that the legal framework 'generates' and concedes to its citizens. Such idea recalls some sort of territorial vision of law, meant as a tool for tracing 'borderlines' between individuals: the sphere of autonomy granted within the dominion seems to derive its origin, legitimacy and effectiveness from legal or political sources (ie from a certain 'power'), leaving aside the relational character that rights and freedoms should rather have.

We can try, nevertheless, to see these borders in a different way, as 'thresholds' stemming from an originary, structural reciprocity that binds human beings. It is only when the 'other' is not an 'alien' but a 'reciprocal' (reflecting also traces of my own humanity) that I can see his/her own rights and freedoms as mirror images of mine. Respecting such safeguards equals to respecting mine. In this view, law is there to enable, foster and protect reciprocity and is structurally oriented to respecting such mutuality: it is not a superstructure, at least when it does not pretend or claim to act 'above' or even 'despite' the interpersonal reciprocity which alone justifies, in my view, the possibility of 'arming' law with coercive measures.

Limitedness is not only an individual or interpersonal human category but belongs also to the legal order, binding it to a never-exhausted process of re-discussion and justification through credible and well-argued reasons.

This does not mean that legal safeguards, rights and freedoms have to fall into a sort of undetermined and undeterminable world. It means, more precisely, that:

> The right state of human affairs, the moral well-being of the world can never be guaranteed simply through structures alone, however good they are. Such structures are not only important, but necessary; yet they cannot and must not marginalize human freedom. Even the best structures function only when the community is animated by convictions capable of motivating people to assent freely to the social order. Freedom requires conviction; conviction does not exist on its own, but must always be gained anew by the community. (Ratzinger, 2007: 24)

As I have proposed in a recent writing, the above described human limitedness, intended also as indigence of truth, has a structurally open and relational character:

> no human being can be silenced or set free from asking and providing reasons; and no-one, in fact, is provided with definitive reasons or arguments for claiming that another human life is meaningless and therefore able to be treated as though it was an object. Indigence requires from each person a constant attitude to dialogue and it means that all human beings are reciprocal to each other and mutually involved as subjects entitled to ask questions and offer answers. Denying this dialogical principle embodies both a contradiction (denying the condition of indigence) and an act of violence. (Reggio, 2013: 332)

In the above-mentioned writing, I tried to offer a few philosophical coordinates for rethinking criminal justice in favour of a restorative-oriented shift, through what I called a 'dialogical approach'.[38] Such argumentative

[38] According to the dialogical principle: (1) crime is always and first of all a harm to people and relationships, not only the breach of a legal order; (2) punishment cannot be reduced to a mere application of legal norms; (3) the legal order is called to react without violating the dialogical principle, that acts both as a limit and as a legitimation for 'the reaction to crime'.

If violence is a sort of denial of dialogue, a self-absolutised behaviour, treating someone as an object, then also the reaction to crime cannot imitate violence: it must instead try to react

path aimed to show that there are some philosophical and ethical reasons for sustaining the preference for a participatory and restorative approach to criminal justice, in which the reaction to crime is viewed first as an open question requiring dialogue, confrontation, argumentation and never pre-determined answers.

In facing the legal debate, such a proposal requires a further step, that is: to rethink the idea of law itself, and to set it free from the de-humanising superstructures of a bureaucratic, technocratic idea of legal order, which disempowers human beings and relationships. This ought to happen, nevertheless, without abandoning the task of protecting such persons and their relational activities from those attacks that undermine human reciprocity, resulting in violent and never-legitimate self-absolutisations.

Trying also to actualise some views taken from Vico's perspective, I wish to imagine a law operating for relationships, within relationships, stemming from relationships and remaining open to relational and contextual realisations.

I am suggesting we take the challenge of moving towards a 'dialogical law', which implies, in the first place, rethinking regulation as an always refine-able way for promoting dialogue and relations of mutuality; a relational concept of responsibility; the possibility of enabling self-regulation, limiting coercion and, when it is required and possible, orienting in a restorative way.

It is not possible, here, to trace in a more defined way the characteristics of such an approach, as it shows, for the moment, as a glimmering vision, waiting for the debate and confrontation with other scholars to be discussed, refined, and more precisely drawn.

I will try to summarise some of its possible implications:

Dialogical law:

(a) implies a minimalistic idea of the legal order, where law is meant to be dynamic, flexible, mediatory and only subsidiarily coercive;
(b) considers law as a regulation meant first of all to enable relationships of reciprocity;
(c) implies a participatory model of regulation;
(d) favours bottom-up, contextual regulations stemming from a correct dialogue. Such approaches must be preferred to imposed, standardised solutions (acting as a second option, or even as last resort);

by enabling a renewed mutual respect and a dialogical reciprocity, that begins when: (a) the offender is asked to provide reasons and take responsibility (de-absolutised); (b) the victim is re-empowered and enabled to receive information, care, possibility of dialogue; (c) the legal system is challenged to help find the 'best solution' to the case, taking account of the rights, values and needs that are at stake when crime happens).

(e) justifies (orients and limits) public intervention in order to rebalance power imbalances, to address violations of dialogue and mutuality and to help restore them to the maximum possible extent;
(f) approaches the issue of resolving or transforming conflict with an 'ADR-friendly' view, in which ADR does not mean 'alternative' but 'appropriate' dispute resolution. According to the principle of subsidiarity, autonomous, informal and consensual solutions should be preferred to standardised and imposed solutions, when originating from a process that enables an actual reciprocity, based on mutual respect. In the sector of criminal justice, such approach is oriented to rethinking the whole system in a restorative-oriented way (in the sense of Walgrave's proposal of a 'restorative criminal justice');
(g) sustains an idea of 'appropriate legal regulation', thereby trying to avoid a predominantly technocratic and bureaucratic approach to law and to its administration. It encourages, instead, participative and inclusive forms of legal regulation, meant to be context-sensitive and able, to the maximum extent possible, to synthesise different interests and needs at stake.

V. AN IMAGE: MOSES AND THE BROKEN TABLES

Is this glimmering vision a kind of utopia? Does it risk treating law too badly and exposing us to the risk of 'throwing the baby out with the bathwater'?

Let us return to our metaphorical image of Hebrew people crossing the desert after leaving the oppressive, 'pyramidal', order of the Pharaoh (see Ost, 2004; Drai, 1992; Jacobson, 1990). In the desert, the liberating God had explained, through 'ten discourses', that freedom can easily be lost if we misunderstand or forget the conditions that enable and protect it from deviation. The God who first refused to be named had given examples of conducts which throw human beings back into slavery: idolatry makes someone a slave to constructed items; not respecting the Sabbath makes someone a slave of work; homicide makes someone a slave of damages that can never be properly repaired; theft, as well as desiring someone else's goods, makes that person a slave to desires and greed, and so on.

But the people needed these very high examples to be somehow 'fixed' and this is why Moses had to walk upon the mountain and receive the law from God. According to the biblical narration, while the prophet remained far away from the encampment for quite a long time, his people, in need of certainties and reassurance, fabricated a golden idol.

In our common knowledge of biblical sources we tend to forget what happened to the tablets of the law when Moses discovered that his people were adoring an idol. He broke the tablets. The idol was destroyed, but the tablets as well, and the issue needed to be treated in a different, more dialogical way: Moses planted a tent and there he stipulated with God a Covenant, which originated the Law.

The image is powerful: the idea of 'fixing' the legal order like 'words printed in stone' expresses a desire and aspiration of certainty and reassurance, as the golden idol did. The true Law, the one emerging from the Covenant, requires instead understanding and dialogue, an 'alliance with transcendence' which may also mean that the legal order must remain open to Transcendence, and also to its transcendence. Human limitedness implies that from time to time we plant a tent and discuss in order to make alliances which create a correct relationship; it also requires that we acknowledge the structural limitedness of the answers that we come up with during our history.

This is why we should not be afraid of breaking old tablets—which should never be treated as idols—and try to understand the conditions, even at a legal level, which enable us to maintain our freedom, and the consciousness of our being limited and relational.

This is why:

> every generation has the task of engaging anew in the arduous search for the right way to order human affairs; this task is never simply completed. Yet every generation must also make its own contribution to establishing convincing structures of freedom and of good, which can help the following generation as a guideline for the proper use of human freedom. (Ratzinger, 2007: 25)

REFERENCES

Aertsen, I, Daems, T and Robert, L (eds) (2006) *Institutionalizing Restorative Justice* (Cullompton, Willan Publishing).

Ambrosetti, G (1982) 'Idea ed esperienza del diritto in Vico' in E Riverso (ed), *Leggere Vico* (Milan, Spirali).

Arendt, H (1958), *Vita Activa: The Human Condition* (Chicago, IL, University of Chicago Press).

Battistini, A (2004) *Vico tra antichi e moderni* (Bologna, Il Mulino).

Bauman, Z (1993) *Postmodern Ethics* (Malden/Oxford/Carlton, Blackwell).

—— (2000) *Liquid Modernity* (Cambridge, Polity Press).

Beck, U (1992) *Risk Society: Towards a New Modernity* (London, Sage).

Bellofiore, L (1954) *La dottrina del diritto naturale in G.B. Vico* (Milan, Giuffré).

Berman, HJ (1983) *Law and Revolution: The Formation of Western Legal Tradition* (Cambridge, Cambridge University Press).

Bianchi, H (2004), *Justice as a Sanctuary: Towards a Non-Punitive System of Crime Control* (Bloomington, IN, Indiana University Press).

Blad, J (2013) 'Civilization of Criminal Justice: Restorative Justice Amongst Other Strategies' in D Cornwell, J Blad and M Wright (eds), *Civilising Criminal Justice: A Restorative Agenda for Penal Reform* (Hook, Waterside Press) 209–54.

Bošnjak, M (2007) 'Some Thoughts about the Relationship Between Restorative Justice and the Law' in R Mackay, M Bošnjak, J Deklerck, C Pelikan, B van Stokkom and M Wright (eds), *Images of Restorative Justice Theory* (Frankfurt am Main, Verlag für Polizeiwissenschaft) 93–111.

Braithwaite, J (2003) 'Principles of Restorative Justice' in A von Hirsch, J Roberts, A Bottoms, J Roach and M Schiff (eds), *Restorative Justice and Criminal Justice: Competing or Reconcilable Paradigms?* (Oxford/Portland, OR, Hart) 1–20.

Brown, HI (1988) *Rationality* (London/New York, Routledge).

Brunk, CG (2001) 'Restorative Justice and the Philosophical Theories of Criminal Punishment' in ML Hadley (ed), *The Spiritual Roots of Restorative Justice* (Albany, NJ, State University of New York Press) 31–56.

Buber, M (1947) *Dialogisches Leben* (Zurich, Gregor Müller).

Capograssi, G (1925) 'Dominio, libertà, tutela nel De Uno' 3, III *Rivista Internazionale di Filosofia del Diritto* 437.

Caporali, R (1996) 'Vico: quale modernità?' 1 *Rivista di Filosofia* 357.

Cavalla, F (1979) *La pena come problema: per un superamento della concezione razionalistica della difesa sociale* (Padova, Cedam).

—— (1990), 'Sul fondamento delle norme etiche' in E Berti (ed), *Problemi di etica: fondazione, norme, orientamenti* (Padova, Gregoriana (Lanza Foundation) 142–202).

—— (2000) 'La pena come riparazione. Oltre la concezione liberale dello stato: per una teoria radicale della pena' in F Cavalla and F Todescan (eds), *Pena e riparazione* (Padova, Cedam) 1–109.

—— (2011) *Alle origini del diritto al tramonto della legge* (Naples, Jovene).

Cavalla, F (ed) (1996) *Cultura moderna ed interpretazione classica* (Padova, Cedam).

—— (2007) *Retorica processo verità* (Milan, FrancoAngeli).

Christie, N (1977) 'Conflicts as Property' in 17 *British Journal of Criminology* 1.

Connor, S (1989) *Postmodernist Culture: An Introduction to the Theories of the Contemporary* (Oxford, Oxford University Press).

Cotta, S (1991) *Il diritto nell'esperienza. Linee di ontofenomenologia del diritto* (Milan, Giuffrè).

Cragg, W (1992) *The Practice of Punishment: Towards a Theory of Restorative Justice* (London/New York, Routledge).

Crawford, A (2002) 'The State, Community and Restorative Justice: Heresy, Nostalgia and Butterfly Collecting' in L Walgrave (ed), *Restorative Justice and the Law*. Cullompton, Willan Publishing, 2006).

Derrida, J and Defourmantelle, A (2000) *On Hospitality* (Stanford, CA, Stanford University Press).

Draï, R (1992) *La sortie d'Egipte. L'invention de la liberté* (Paris, Fayard).

Eser, A (2007) 'The Nature and Rationale of Punishment' 28(6) *Cardozo Law Review* 427.

Gallie, WB (1964) 'Essentially Contested Concepts' in WB Gallie, *Philosophy and the Historical Understanding* (London, Chatto & Windus) 157–91.

Galeazzi, U (1993) *Ermeneutica e Storia in Vico. Morale, diritto e società nella 'Scienza Nuova'* (Rome/L'Aquila, Japadre).

Gentile, F (1983) *Intelligenza politica e ragion di stato* (Milan, Giuffrè).

Habermas, J (2003) *Truth and Justification* (Cambridge, MA, Harvard University Press).

Hartmann, A (2007) 'Restorative Justice and the Law' in R Mackay, M Bošnjak, J Deklerck, C Pelikan, B van Stokkom and M Wright (eds), *Images of Restorative Justice Theory* (Frankfurt am Main, Verlag für Polizeiwissenschaft) 129–50.
Illetterati, L (1996) *Figure del limite. Esperienze e forme della finitezza* (Trento, Verifiche).
Jacobson, A.J (1990) 'The Idolatry of Rules: Writing Law According to Moses, with reference to Other Jurisprudences' 11 *Cardozo Law Review*, 1083.
Johnstone, G and Van Ness, D (2007) 'The Meaning of Restorative Justice' in G Johnstone and D Van Ness (eds), *Handbook of Restorative Justice* (Cullompton, Willan Publishing) 5–23.
Lederach, JP (2005) *The Moral Imagination: The Art and Soul of Building Peace* (Oxford, Oxford University Press).
Lenman, B and Parker, G (1979) 'The State, the Community and Criminal Law in Early Modern Europe' in R Gattrel, B Lenman and G Parker (eds), *Crime and the Law: The Social History of Western Europe since 1500* (London, Europe).
Lilla, M (1993) *G.B. Vico, the Making of an Anti-Modern* (Cambridge, MA, Harvard University Press).
Lyotard, JF (1984) *The Post-Modern Condition: A Report on Knowledge* (Minneapolis, MN, University of Minnesota Press).
Mackay, RE (2007) 'Law as Peacemaking: Beyond the Concept of Restorative Justice' in R Mackay, M Bošnjak, J Deklerck, C Pelikan, B van Stokkom and M Wright (eds), *Images of Restorative Justice Theory* (Frankfurt am Main, Verlag für Polizeiwissenschaft) 112–28.
Mannozzi, G (2003) *La giustizia senza spada. Uno studio comparato su giustizia riparativa e mediazione penale* (Milan, Giuffrè).
Manzin, M (2008) *Ordo Juris. La nascita del pensiero sistematico* (Milan, FrancoAngeli).
Marshall, C (2001) *Beyond Retribution: A New Testament Vision for Justice, Crime and Punishment* (Sydney/Auckland, Erdmans Publishing).
Marzano Parisoli, M (2000) 'Lo ius naturale gentium in Vico: la fondazione metafisica del diritto universale' *Rivista internazionale di Filosofia del Diritto* 59.
Mazzucato, C (2010) 'Appunti per una teoria 'dignitosa' del diritto penale a partire dalla restorative justice' in *Dignità e ditítto: prospettive interdisciplinari* (Tricase, Libellula) 99–168.
McCold, P (2000) 'Towards a Holistic Vision of Restorative Justice: A Reply to the Maximalist Approach' 3 *Contemporary Justice Review* 357.
Minda, G (1995) *Postmodern Legal Movements: Law and Jurisprudence at Century's End* (New York, New York University Press).
Montanari, B (ed) (2005) *La possibilità impazzita. Esodo dalla modernità* (Turin, Giappichelli).
Mootz, FJ (2009) 'Vico and Imagination: An Ingenious Approach to Educating Lawyers with Semiotic Sensibility' 22 *International Journal of Semiotic and Law* 11.
Moro, P (1996) 'L'essenza della legge: saggio sul minosse platonico' in F Cavalla (ed), *Cultura moderna e interpretazione classica* (Padova, Cedam) 113–68.
—— (2013) 'Libertà indisponibile. Un percorso critico' in F Zanuso and S Fuselli (eds), *Custodire il Fuoco* (Milan, FrancoAngeli) 121–64.
Moro, P and Sarra, C (eds) (2012) *Positività e giurisprudenza. Teoria e prassi nella formazione giudiziale del diritto* (Milan, FrancoAngeli).

Ost, F (1999) *Du Sinaï au Champ-de-Mars. L'autre et le même au fondement du droit* (Brussels, Lessius).
—— (2004) *Raconter la loi. Aux sources de l'imaginaire juridique* (Paris, Odile Jacob).
Pavlich, G (2006) *Governing Paradoxes of Restorative Justice* (London, Glass House Press).
—— (2007) 'Ethics, Universal Principles and Restorative Justice' in G Johnstone and DW Van Ness (eds), *Handbook of Restorative Justice* (Cullompton, Willan Publishing) 615–27.
Pelikan, C (2007) 'The Place of Restorative Justice in Society: Making Sense of Developments in Time and Space' in R Mackay, M Bošnjak, J Deklerck, C Pelikan, B van Stokkom and M Wright (eds), *Images of Restorative Justice Theory* (Frankfurt am Main, Verlag für Polizeiwissenschaft) 35–55.
Ratzinger, J (2007) *Benedikt XVI: Spe Salvi, Encyclical Letter* (Vatican City, LEV).
Reggio, F (2004) 'Una riflessione sui concetti vichiani di "pena" e "penitenza"' in F Zanuso and S Fuselli (eds), *Ripensare la pena* (Padova, Cedam) 253–95.
—— (2010) *Giustizia dialogica. luci e ombre della restorative justice* (Milan, FrancoAngeli).
—— (2012) 'A "Discarded Image": Rediscovering Vico's Lesson as a Topical Heritage for the Contemporary Reflection on Law and Justice' 1 *l'Ircocervo* 1.
—— (2013) 'Dialogical Justice: Philosophical Coordinates for Rethinking the Reaction to Crime in a Restorative Way' in J Blad, D Cornwell and M Wright (eds), *Civilising Criminal Justice: A Restorative Agenda for Penal Reform* (Hook, Waterside Press) 315–45.
Roche, D (2001) 'The Evolving Definition of Restorative Justice' 4 *Contemporary Justice Review* 341.
Schrag, CO (1992) *The Resources of Rationality: A Response to the Postmodern Turn* (Bloomington, IN, Indiana University Press).
Slob, W (2002) *Dialogical Rhetoric: An Essay on Truth and Normativity After Postmodernism* (Dordrecht, Kluwer).
'T Hart, A (1982) 'La metodologia giuridica vichiana' (XII–XIII) *Bollettino del centro di Studi Vichiani*.
—— (2004) *Openbaar ministerie in rechtshandhaving* (Arnhem, Gouda Quint).
Van Ness, DW (2002) 'Creating Restorative Justice Systems' in L Walgrave (ed), *Restorative Justice and the Law* (Cullompton, Willan Publishing).
Vendemiati, A (2007) *Universalismo e relativismo nell'etica contemporanea* (Genova, Marietti).
Verene, DP (2008) 'Vichian Moral Philosophy: Prudence as Jurisprudence' 83 *Chicago-Kent Law Review* 1107.
Vico, GB (1709) *De nostri temporis studiorum ratione* [*On the Study Methods of Our Time*] (E Gianturco (trans), Ithaca, NY, Cornell University Press, 1990).
—— (1710) *De antiquissima italorum sapientia* [*On the Most Ancient Wisdom of the Italians*] (LM Palmer (trans), Ithaca, NY, Cornell University Press, 1988).
—— (1719) *De Uno: On the One Principle and One End of Universal Law* in (2003) 21 *New Vico Studies* (John D Schaeffer (trans)).
—— (1721) *Il Diritto Universale* [*Universal Right*] (GA Pinton and M Diehl (trans), Amsterdam/Atlanta, GA, Rodopi, 2000).

—— (1744) *La Scienza Nuova* [*The New Science of Giambattista Vico*] (TG Bergin and MH Fisch (trans), Ithaca, NY, Cornell University Press, 1968).
Voegelin E (1998) 'Revolution and The New Science' in B Cooper (ed), *History of Political Ideas*, vol VI (Columbia, LO, University of Missouri Press).
Walgrave, L (1999) 'La justice restaurative: à la recherché d'une theorie et d'un programme' XXXII(1) *Criminologie* 559.
—— (2000) 'How Pure Can a Maximalist Approach to Restorative Justice Remain? Or Can a Purist Model of Restorative Justice Become Maximalist?' 3 *Contemporary Justice Review* 415.
—— (2002a) 'From Community to Dominion: In Search for Social Values for Restorative Justice' in E Weitekamp and HJ Kerner (eds), *Restorative Justice: Theoretical Foundations* (Cullompton/Portland, OR, Willan Publishing).
—— (2002b) *Restorative Justice and the Law* (Cullompton, Willan Publishing).
—— (2006) *Restorative Justice, Self-interest and Responsible Citizenship* (Cullompton, Willan Publishing).
—— (2007) 'Integrating Criminal Justice and Restorative Justice' in G Johnstone and D Van Ness (eds), *Handbook of Restorative Justice* (Cullompton, Willan Publishing) 559–79.
—— (2008) *Restorative Justice, Self Interest and Responsible Citizenship* (Cullompton, Willan Publishing).
—— (2013) 'From Civilising Punishment to Civilising Criminal Justice: From Punishment to Restoration' in J Blad, D Cornwell and M Wright (eds), *Civilising Criminal Justice: A Restorative Agenda for Penal Reform* (Hook, Waterside Press) 347–77.
Wiesnet, E (1980) *Die verratene Versoehnung. Zum Verhaeltins von Christentum und Strafe* (Duesseldorf, Patmos).
Williams, M (1996) *Unnatural Doubts: Epistemological Realism and the Basis of Scepticism* (Princeton, NJ Princeton University Press).
Wright, M (2007) 'Punishment and Restorative Justice: An Ethical Comparison' in R Mackay, M Bošnjak, J Deklerck, C Pelikan, B van Stokkom and M Wright (eds), *Images of Restorative Justice Theory* (Frankfurt am Main, Verlag für Polizeiwissenschaft) 168–84.
—— (2013) 'Could a Restorative System of Justice be More Civilised than a Punitive One?' in D Cornwell, J Blad and M Wright (eds), Civilising Criminal Justice: A Restorative Agenda for Penal Reform (Hook, Waterside Press) 381–408.
Wright, M and Zernova, M (2007) 'Alternative Visions of Restorative Justice' in G Johnstone and D Van Ness (eds), *Handbook of Restorative Justice* (Cullompton, Willan Publishing) 91–108.
Zanetti, G (2011) *Vico eversivo* (Bologna, Il Mulino).
Zanuso, F (1993) *Conflitto e controllo sociale nel pensiero politico-giuridico moderno* (Padova, Cleup).
—— (2009) 'Les avantages de la justice réparatrice et la sagesse du tribunal de l'Héliée' in S Tzitzis (ed), *Déviance et délinquances. Approches psycho-sociales et pénales* (Paris, Dalloz) 331–57.
Zanuso F (ed) (2013) *Custodire il Fuoco* (Milan, Franco Angeli).
Zanuso, F and Fuselli, S (eds) (2004) *Ripensare la pena. Teorie e problemi nella riflessione moderna* (Padova, Cedam).

Zanuso, F and Reggio, F (eds) (2014) *Per una nuova giustizia possibile. Un progetto per la città* (Naples, ESI).
Zehr, H (1990) *Changing Lenses: A New Focus on Crime and Justice* (Scottsdale, AZ, Herald Press).
—— (2002) *The Little Book of Restorative Justice* (Intercourse, PA, Good Books).
Zehr, H and Toews, B (eds) (2004) *Critical Issues in Restorative Justice* (Monsey, NY, Criminal Justice Press).

16

Control Society, Sovereign Victim Culture and Restorative Justice

RONNIE LIPPENS

INTRODUCTION

EU MEMBER STATES were required to comply with EU Directive 2012/29/EU of 25 October 2012 by 16 November 2015. The Directive 'establishes minimum standards on the rights, support and protection of victims of crime'. One element in the Directive is, for our purposes here, worth closer reading, ie the uses of restorative justice in the Directive's 'minimum standards for victims' policy. In the Preamble, the tone is set when it states that:

> restorative justice services, including for example victim-offender mediation, family group conferencing and sentencing circles, can be of great benefit to the victim, but require safeguards to prevent secondary and repeat victimisation, intimidation and retaliation.

Restorative justice 'services' (not: restorative justice) are things that 'can be' of 'great benefit' to 'the victim' (not: communities, relationships, etc). The Guidance Document (December 2013) clarifies this by stating that 'the core objective of this Directive is to deal with victims' needs in an *individual manner*' (orginal emphasis). Member States 'should ensure that the national criminal justice system recognises the victim as an *individual* with *individual* needs' (original emphasis). Article 12 of the Directive focuses on the 'safeguarding' of 'the victim'. 'Restorative justice services' are to be 'used only if they are in the interest of the victim', and if they are based on 'the victim's free and informed consent, which may be withdrawn at any time'. In Article 19, 'Member States' are urged to 'establish the necessary conditions to enable avoidance of contact between victims and their family members, where necessary, and the offender within premises where criminal proceedings are conducted'. They shall also 'ensure that new court premises have separate waiting areas for victims'.

An image of victimhood seems to be emerging from the text. 'The victim' is one, and all victim. An atomically separate entity, unattached to webs of relationships, 'the victim' moves through a world of resources and 'services', and engages with those out of his or her own 'free will', and in his or her own 'interest'. The world ('services' and other resources) has to *proactively* (a word used in the Guidance Document) provide 'the victim' with support and safeguarding measures which 'the victim' may then responsively, and instrumentally, decide to mobilise, use or consume in his or her atomically own 'interest'. Clad in 'individual' rights, 'the victim' chooses to make contact with the world as he, or she, thinks fit.

An attempt will be made here to stituate this image—and indeed the whole imaginary that it evokes—within the context of what could be called a new form of life which, it could be argued, emerged and gradually crystallised in the wake of the Second World War. In this new form of life (which we will call the 'control society') notions such as sovereignty, control, ambivalence, responsiveness and consumption take centre stage. All these aspects of the new form of life called the 'control society' have, in the course of all those post-war decades, generated a pervasive 'sovereign victim culture' which now threatens to undermine the conditions of possibility for anything like *transformative* restorative justice to take shape. In what follows, then, an argument will be made about the conditions of possibility and impossibility of restorative justice in late modern, consumerist, non-communicative 'control societies'.

In a nutshell, the argument goes like this: in the wake of the Second World War a new form of life emerged which, at its heart, was (and continues to be) built around a very deep desire for personal sovereign 'control' over one's life conditions, and which captured, or indeed, gradually flooded the imaginary in what we would call Western democracies. In this form of life a number of events (eg the gradual emergence of practices such as restorative justice) became possible. Over time, though, this form of life has spawned its own parody, ie what we now call the 'consumer society'. The sense of ambivalence that is generated in both, and that underpins what could be called 'sovereign victim culture', is now, well into the twenty-first century, if not threatening, then slowly undermining the conditions of possibility of restorative justice. The argument concludes by stating that we could do worse than thinking through this issue (see also Lippens, 2015a; 2015b; and 2016).

In what follows, 13 theses will be introduced sequentially. The chapter ends with a few cautious concluding remarks.

THESIS 1

At least some of the conditions of possibility for anything like restorative justice to have emerged at all can arguably be located in the experience of the Second World War. That experience engendered a very deep distrust, in broad swathes of Western populations, not just of authoritarianism, but of authority as such. This went hand in hand with a sharp decline in the willingness of many to submit to foundational reasoning and thinking. This sharp distrust of authority and foundationalism was expressed first in philosophy (in existentialism in particular, with its emphasis on life as *choice*), in literature and in the arts. Anyone who has read Albert Camus' 1949 play *Les Justes*, for example (to mention just one of the crucially important texts of the immediate post-war era) could not have missed, in that play, this deep sense of unease about absolute convictions and foundations. That time, and not 1968, it could be argued, was when the anti-foundationalist mood of the later twentieth century can be traced back to. In a way, May 1968 represented a *relapse* into foundationalism. The notion that there is, on the one hand, an utterly corrupt Centre that has to be fought from an innocently pure, alternative Periphery, for example, is itself very much stuck in foundationalist reason. Books such as Mathiesen's *The Politics of Abolition* (1974), it should be reminded, were still, well into the 1970s, very much focused on this notion of the pure alternative.

The distrust of foundations and of authority formed a little kernel at first. It expanded throughout the post-war decades and gradually managed to pervade late modern culture. So much so, one could argue, that this little kernel, slowly radiating outward, came to form the heart of a newly emerging form of life which itself became the more dominant form of life in late modern culture.

THESIS 2

For our purposes here we define a form of life as a collection of ways of seeing, thinking and speaking about the world. It is, so to speak, a way of life in constant formation and dissipation. A form of life cuts across class, gender or any other social division. It is a way of life and a way of looking at and thinking about the world that is, in a particular historical and cultural constellation, widely shared. At the heart of the form of life that gradually emerged from the ruins of the Second World War, one could recognise a widely shared desire for (if your inclinations are towards vitalism, then you'd prefer this term), or will (if your sympathies are with existentialism or related perspectives then you'd probably choose this word) to absolute personal sovereignty. Of course, such a desire, or will, could never be anything else than paradoxical, and therefore imaginary, indeed illusory. Indeed, anyone who desires, or *wills* to be absolutely sovereign will soon find that they are inescapably dependent not just on their very desire or will, but on all that conditions that desire and will as well, and on all that conditions the desired for, or willed, impossible outcome, ie absolute sovereignty. It does not really take a philosopher of Georges Bataille's stature to see this.

It may be noted in passing that there might not be a lot of coincidence in the fact that Bataille was seriously preoccupied, during those post-war years, with the notion of sovereignty in his posthumously published book *La Souveraineté* (written in 1954).

A lot could be said about this desire for, or will to absolute sovereignty. At this point, though, one may suffice by saying that this desire, or will, increasingly implied a refusal to sacrifice. The aspiring sovereign is no longer willing to sacrifice anything to grand schemes that promise a better future. He or she is no longer willing to sacrifice anything to the future. The aspiring sovereign's time is now. It is the present. Not tomorrow, but *now* is the time.

In traditional modernity the heart of the predominant form of life operated according to a particular 'logic' which roughly went as follows: *if all else fails, then submit and sacrifice to foundation*. In the newly emerged predominant post-war form of life the operational 'logic' that circulates at its very heart goes like this: *if all else fails, then refute all foundation*. This has become the new fall-back default position in many an aspiring sovereign's imaginary.

It could now, of course, also be argued that the very possibility for something like restorative justice to emerge at all ultimately finds its roots (at least some of them) in the anti-foundational mood of the post-war era. The move away from the static foundationalism embedded in the law, and in the authoritarian workings of what used to be called the criminal justice *system*, could not have happened on the scale that it did without the crystallisation of that little kernel at the heart of the form of life described above.

THESIS 3

The desire for, or will to absolute sovereignty (however paradoxical, however imaginary, and however illusory this desire or this will, of course) is all about control. The form of life that has crystallised around this desire, or this will, one could call the 'control society'. The phrase 'control society' has been used by philosophers such as Gilles Deleuze before. In his short paper 'Postcript on Control Societies' (the paper was actually a review of Foucault's later work) Deleuze (1995) contrasted the 'control society' with the 'disciplinary society'. Deleuze agrees with Foucault that the disciplinary society is on the wane. At the operative heart of disciplinary societies one finds 'precepts', ie 'order words' that function to form, order, align or otherwise make productive territories and populations. Control societies operate in a much more fluid manner. They generate outcomes ('products') in situations that are operated by 'passwords'. 'Passwords' no longer regulate territories and populations. They merely regulate situations by accepting, ignoring or rejecting particular qualities in 'dividuals' (individuals, in control societies, are no longer in-dividual) according to situationally specific exigencies. Control societies operate through the fluid modulation of situations and passwords (Deleuze, 1995: 179–81). In this contribution we use the phrase 'control society' in a slightly different context (although, of course, we are aware of the possible connections with Deleuze's use of it). Here 'control society' is the location where aspriring absolute sovereigns refuse to allow themselves (and indeed: their selves as well) to be captured by anything that even vaguely resembles foundation. Their desire for, or will to absolute control rests on their imaginary freedom from all capture by anything supposedly foundational.

THESIS 4

One of the manifestations of this desire for, or will to absolute control is the aspiring sovereign's unrelenting flight from law and code. Bataille (1954, 1957) would have said: a flight from all *functionality*. This is a flight from *all law*, and *all code*. And that includes social, gender, and even biological codes (as to the latter, think of physical appearance and plastic surgery, or gender genotype and transgender corrections). The aspiring sovereign's desire for absolute control is not necessarily exercised in attempts to order and structure the world. More often than not the aspiring sovereign exercises control by merely, though unrelentingly, evading all attempts at ordering or structuring his or her life conditions. It is, above all, during such evasions, indeed during this unrelenting flight from all law, from all code, from all foundation, that the aspiring sovereign believes he or she is exercising and even achieving control (however paradoxical, however imaginary, however illusory this belief). Think of Jackson Pollock's signature 'drip' paintings which he started to paint almost immediately after the Second World War. Pollock, who had some difficulty articulating and communicating his thoughts (this is not too irrelevant a comment, as we shall see), claimed that his frantic paint dripping movements were actually all about control, and indeed, even about controlling the sheer laws of physics (more on this is to be read in Lippens, 2011).

THESIS 5

On the road to (paradoxical, imaginary, illusory) control, to *absolute* control, the aspiring sovereign acquires a deep sense of ambivalence. Nothing is sacred, nothing is foundational. Anything stumbled upon on his or her evasive flight can potentially be of use to the aspiring absolute sovereign. Anything could potentially be usefully deployed in the aspiring sovereign's many possible *life strategies* (to evoke Zygmunt Bauman's work here, eg 1993 and 1995). But equally so: nothing is worth sticking to. It all depends.

On the roads to absolute sovereignty all and everything suddenly acquires an ambivalent sheen. This, one could argue, is one of the reasons why, as Bauman (1991) has explored, late modernity, or indeed 'post-modernity' as the phrase went at the time of Bauman's writing, is the point in history when it became clear that ambivalence is ineradicable and here to stay. All attempts at eradicating ambivalence only lead to the production of more ambivalence.

And to add to this one might be able to say that there may not be too much of a coincidence in the fact that theorists and practitioners of restorative justice such as John Braithwaite (2002) tend to put a premium on flexibility and *responsiveness* in issues of regulation and justice. To be utterly and completely, absolutely *responsive* is actually also what the aspiring sovereign desires, or wills. To be *absolutely* responsive means to be able to make full and complete use of all potentially available resources at any time and anywhere, and to do so without any restrictions and without having to face or take account of the consequences of earlier choices and actions. This is about the desire, and will, to eat the cake, and have it at the same time. Aspiring sovereigns, who notice ambivalence everywhere, reserve themselves the right to mobilise it as responsively as they possibly can.

We note in passing that we are still discussing a particular fall-back, or default 'logic' at the heart of a particular form of life here. In actual reality, life is of course much more complicated or 'messy' than this. Not just is it the case that the form of life under consideration here ('control society') is not the only one in late modern culture. It may be the predominant one (as is argued here) but it certainly is not the only one. Furthermore, forms of life never are pure or monolithic. They emerge and then again dissipate in processes of hybridisation with other forms of life. And to make things incurably more complicated than this, the basic fall-back operational 'logics' that work at the heart of a form of life never completely or fully pervade a particular historical era or culture. Life always is a lot more complex and varied than we are able to grasp. With this caveat in mind we should now be able to proceed with the argument.

THESIS 6

The form of life of aspiring sovereigns in search of absolute control has, in the course of the decades, spawned its own parody. From about the 1960s onwards a pervasive consumer culture grew out of an already established consumer economy. A little later, authors began to write about the 'consumer *society*'. There is, of course again, much that could be said about consumer societies. For our purposes here, it may suffice to say that the very deep code of *seduction* (to evoke Bauman again, 1993: 139) that is so typical of consumer cultures (the latter thrive on the former; the former is the fuel that burns in the latter's engines) did manage, roughly by the mid-1960s, to capture and overcode the aspiring sovereigns' desires. It happened quite unobtrusively, without the aspiring sovereigns actually noticing it. Wading through streams of consumer items, making one consumer choice after another, selecting and abandoning lifestyles, collecting and dismantling identities and selves, the now consumer-sovereign still thinks that he or she is exercising sovereign control. The consumer-sovereign still thinks that he or she is on their way to sovereignty. It is at this point that a pervasive consumer culture such as ours comes into its own. Seduced to achieve control (or the illusion thereof) the aspiring sovereign consumes what he takes for the world, ie commodity-image. Consuming and digesting the world, the aspiring sovereign believes he or she is actually exercising sovereign control. Indeed, is he or she not *eating* the world? Is he or she not making the world their own? The opposite, however, is more likely to be the actual case: the aspiring sovereign is created by the consumer world in its commodity-image. This is the deeper dimension that underpins much in Bauman's notion of 'seduction'. The seductive 'logic' in consumer cultures is so strong that the formal characteristics of its operations ('choice', 'selection', and so on), which are very similar to genuine sovereign operations (eg 'transformation', 'creation', etc), quite easily provide the eager consumer-sovereigns with an illusion of control. But it is just an illusion.

THESIS 7

The illusion of sovereignty in consumer culture masks the consumer-sovereign's submission to the law and code that are embedded in image and commodity. This is a thesis that was developed quite thoroughly, already in 1967, by authors such as Guy Debord. In his *La Société du Spectacle,* Debord painted a picture of consumer societies which we would now recognise effortlessly. The endless flood of consumer commodity and consumer images that flows before consumers' eyes, and twirls around their wading feet, wave after wave, does not just have a mesmerising effect on them. It also separates them from each other, and makes genuine communication (genuine communication is communication that is aimed at transformation, or change) obsolete. In productive cultures, which are, almost by definition, transformative, collaboration and cooperation and therefore genuine communication, are necessary. The productive agent needs to know what his or her collaborator thinks if they are to achieve their set goals. Communication is necessary. In consumer cultures, though, none of this holds. Consuming one does alone. Genuine, ie *transformative* communication is, in consumer cultures, no longer necessary. Mere chatter (the chatter of image-obsessed consumers discussing and comparing their lifestyle choices) will suffice.

Separation and non-communication have a certain sovereign feel about them, though. Why would a sovereign wish to be in close proximity with others, and depend on them? Why indeed? Why would a sovereign wish to communicate with others? To achieve what, exactly? Change? Future? But the sovereign moment is now, not tomorrow. It is now. It is the present instant!

As said, most consumer-sovereigns are largely unaware of the subtle ways in which the seductive operational code of consumer culture has actually taken over, and indeed over-coded their sovereign will and desire. They are unaware of the fact that they have actually submitted themselves (a very un-sovereign thing to do) to a very forceful, very pervasive code, ie the one that commands 'Consume and Be!'.

THESIS 8

The submission to the law and the code of a pervasive, hard to resist consumer culture, which provides the aspiring sovereign with an illusion of control, leads to a reactive attitude, is no longer aimed at transformative change, and is therefore non-communicative. Why indeed would the aspiring sovereign, and the consumer-sovereign in particular, want to transform the world? Why transform others in the process? Why transform his or her own self? Aspiring sovereigns are likely to decline any involvement in any of the above. To aim to transform others, to aim to transform life or the world, or their own self, would mean that they are somehow dependent on this transformation. Aspiring sovereigns do not want to be dependent on anything. The world, others, and their own selves should not be transformed. There is no need for that. They should just be controlled, or managed. Or evaded; evasion being, as we have seen, the act of sovereign control *par excellence*. Consumer-sovereigns in particular abhor being tied onto necessity. Things, life, the world, others in it, and selves do not need to be transformed. One should just consume them. Both the aspiring 'genuine' sovereigns and the consumer-sovereigns agree on at least one thing: there is no need for real, genuine, transformative communication because there is no longer any need for real, genuine change.

THESIS 9

With sovereign aspiration come ever-widening images and definitions of 'victimhood'. On the road to absolute sovereignty, the aspiring sovereign tends to perceive ever-more hindrances and blocks. The tiniest of specks on the road to absolute sovereignty could, at least potentially, present an unbearable and therefore 'criminal' problem or issue. The aspiring sovereign's travels on the road to absolute sovereignty are, potentially, those of an eternal 'victim'. The aspiring sovereign's capacity for 'victimhood' is immense. He or she discovers 'victimhood' everywhere. Everywhere the aspiring sovereign goes he or she may suddenly notice, or experience 'victimisation' by forces or by processes that are deemed a threat to their consumerist 'quality of life'. A whole plethora of behaviours, events or 'forces', actual or potential, real or imagined, have come to fall under the remit of 'victimhood'; 'anti-social behaviour', for example, or all kinds of unwanted 'risky behaviours' that harbour the potential to cause 'harm'. Didier Fassin and Richard Rechtman (2009) have shown how, in late modernity, and quite globally so, a victim culture, or indeed a pervasive 'empire of trauma', has gradually grown out of desires to claim 'traumatic' victimhood and compensation or 'justice'. In the process, all manner of 'traumatising' forces are accused. Aspiring sovereigns can even fall victim to the over-protective zeal of a 'nanny' state that is always looking to regain its long lost legitimacy by offering support to 'victims' anyway. By the turn of the twenty-first century, this process was largely complete, prompting authors such as Gabe Mythen (2007) to ask the question, 'are we', culturally speaking, 'all victims now'?

THESIS 10

The aspiring sovereign—always a potential victim ready to accuse—no longer unconditionally accepts anything that has a whiff of law, code or principle about it. He or she is no longer willing to submit to anyone or anything. The aspiring sovereign is even unwilling to accept a fixed subject position, and reserves the right to change his or her life trajectory and corresponding subject positions at whim. The aspiring sovereign is no longer prepared to accept a privileged vantage point amongst the very many which he or she decides to take up in the course of their life. To do so would be to submit to a fixed code. But if this is the case then the world and anything in it suddenly appear, as we have already mentioned above, as so many instances of ambivalence. Yesterday's threat is today's useful resource. Yesterday's enemies are today's allies. Today's opportunity could tomorrow be seen as a risk which needs to be blocked off with all the precautionary zeal one is able to muster. But this means that the aspiring sovereign's accusing 'victimhood' finger can, potentially, be raised from anywhere, and be pointed in any direction imaginable.

At almost every point in the aspiring sovereign's life trajectory, he or she has to face ambivalence. Very often this leads to agony, and the totality of the decisions taken by the aspiring sovereign may present a picture which in a bygone age would have been called 'inconsistent', or 'incoherent'. But the aspiring sovereign no longer minds. He or she no longer cares about the law, code or principle that commands: 'Thou Shallt be Coherent and Consistent'.

THESIS 11

Eternal victim, the aspiring sovereign who, more often than not in a consumerist age is also a consumer-sovereign, is eager to instrumentally consume resources (again: paradoxically so) even if those come in the form of 'support' or 'help'. The aspiring sovereign may not be able to hide, during restorative justice conferences, for example, a certain quantum of instrumental consumer 'logic' in his or her interventions. Whether he or she is officially labelled 'the offender' or 'the victim' in such proceedings is largely irrelevant here: all aspiring consumer-sovereigns, indeed all aspiring sovereigns as such, are 'victims' in so far as that label, for them, represents a resource that can and should be mobilised if the situation so requires. This consumer logic goes as follows: What can I gain from this event, either financially, emotionally, or indeed, 'image'-wise? Or: How can I deal with this situation as responsively as possible? One day the aspiring sovereign, for example, may decide to endorse a restorative justice initiative if it suits him or her (perhaps they heard the words 'victim' and 'reparation' uttered in one and the same breath) whilst simultaneously also rejecting it when someone suddendly mentions 'community building' and 'community relations'. 'Community' is among the last things on the aspiring sovereign's wish list.

THESIS 12

The impulse to engage in creative and communicative transformation, on the other hand, does not come naturally to such aspiring sovereigns. This development in late modern culture (ie the gradually expanding reluctance to engage in communicative, transformative action) is now threatening to become part of the conditions of impossibility of restorative justice. Admittedly, the restorative justice movement is a large and hybrid collection of rationales, strategies, tactics and practices. But much in that collection is not just about the mere 'restoration' of relations and orders. Transformation (or change) is, in many, if not most restorative justice initiatives, one of the aims and goals, albeit often quite implicitly stated. Community relations, however defined, for example, should not just be 'restored'. They should, if at all possible, be transformed so as to eg make future conflicts or confrontations a little less likely. At least, that is the often unspoken hope on which many restorative justice activities float. It is precisely this element in restorative justice that has now come under serious threat. In an age of aspiring sovereigns (consumer-sovereigns in particular) who are eager to exercise absolute control (however paradoxical, however imaginary, and however illusory this control) over their life conditions through the strategic, tactical and instrumental calculation or 'management' of ambivalence and opportunity, the willingness to engage in transformative communication, or in collaborative projects as such, is slowly ebbing away. This is something which the restorative justice movement may wish to consider.

It is, of course, possible to object that this reluctance to engage in transformative and thus genuine communication has not captured—not yet, that is—all of contemporary culture. That is of course true. No form of life could ever completely colonise a particular age or culture. The new post-war 'logic' that emerged as a little kernel in the wake of the Second World War and that holds 'if all else fails, refute *all* foundation' has not reached (not yet, at any rate) every single mind, body and capillary (to evoke Foucault here). Many are still willing to submit to the certainty of foundation whenever they believe the situation calls for it. It could, of course, also be the case now that such submissions are in turn, in late modern culture at least, nothing but the result of strategic or tactical or instrumental calculation. Be that as it may, though, one should admit that the 'control society' of aspiring sovereigns is not, and could never be, totally monolithic. But to the extent that it has pervaded contemporary culture, restorative justice theorists and practitioners alike could do worse than take account of it. It pays to recall here the work done by researchers such as Steve Hall and colleagues (eg 2005) who have been able to trace a terrifyingly cold instrumentalism in populations living in deprivation, and said to have 'no hope, no future, and no fear'.

THESIS 13

The challenge for the restorative justice movement now becomes to think through forms of restorative justice that, on the one hand, connect onto late modern sovereign aspiration and desire for control, but that also, on the other hand, engender transformative communication. The notion of 'sovereignty as control over emergence' may help us to think such forms.

There are many ways in which sovereignty can be conceptualised but if defined as 'control over emergence' the notion implies that sovereignty ultimately rests on creation. One could never attain sovereignty if one was not creative. One only achieves sovereignty (or at least, a sense of sovereignty) and sovereign control in the very act of creation itself, that is, in the act of bringing *newness* into the world. This also means then that sovereignty could never be total, or absolute. The act of creation requires one to engage with the world, and in that very engagement the sheer possibility of absolute sovereignty simply evaporates.

Restorative justice initiatives may wish to think about including elements that unleash the creative potential of the parties involved. This would tap into the desire for, or will to sovereign control, which has now percolated downwards, or radiated outward, throughout late modern culture. But creation also implies engagement with the world and with others. It presupposes cooperation and collaboration, and therefore also communication. Genuine communication.

It is very hard, though, to devise restorative justice initiatives where such creativity could be envisaged, and we should therefore not get our hopes up too quickly. Not just because restorative justice tends to operate within legal and normative frameworks (which, almost by definition, stifle creativity) but also, and perhaps more importantly, because aspiring sovereigns won't easily allow themselves to be herded into collaborative projects. Many would much rather simply say, in a somewhat precautionary vein (there is little coincidence in the fact that late modern culture is also a precautionary culture): 'I don't need any of this. I'm not prepared to sacrifice anything. I don't need future. My time is now'.

A dose of healthy pessimism, then, is warranted. And yet, the artists, writers and philosophers of the immediate post-war era can advise us here. In his book on what he calls the *modern rebellion* of post-war authors such as Albert Camus, Jeffrey Isaac (1992) analyses how those writers made a compelling case for small-scale experiments in living, and in living together, to replace the life-crushing law and code embedded in grand schemes and big, self-righteous utopian visions. Theirs was a politics of care, or care-ful-ness, if you wish. Its anti-foundationalism allowed for creative experiment and care-full cooperation. Camus (1942) knew, however, that such experiments tend to drag themselves, in a Sisyphus kind of way, not just from disappointment to disappointment, but also from hope to hope.

CONCLUSION

The image of consumer-sovereign victimhood projected by EU Directive 2012/29/EU (however partial our reading of this projection may have been, of course) is, one could argue, worthy of note. The point that has been made above is that this image may be able to tell us something about a new form of life that crystallised in the wake of the Second World War. This form of life has a desire for, or will to absolute sovereignty at its heart. This desire, and this will refute all foundation. We readily admit that it may not always be very easy to discern manifestations of this extreme anti-foundationalist form of life. Everyday life goes on. People go about their business. Many are prepared to sacrifice this or that to this or that supposed 'foundation'. Many don't think twice about submitting to law, code, rule or norm. That is understood. The point that was made in this chapter, however, is that much in everyday late modern culture is now underpinned by a shift in the basic operational 'logic' of the predominant form of life in that culture. This logic (which is at heart a logic of *sovereign control*) now goes like this: *if all else fails, then refute all foundation. If all else fails* … This 'logic' has now become the *default* position in late modernity's predominant form of life. It only operates when *all else fails* and so it allows for 'normal' non-sovereign everyday life to go on. But to the extent that the restorative justice movement is about transformative communication (rather than mere 'restoration') it may wish to think through the implications of this 'logic' which has, imperceptibly at first, but gradually and steadily pervaded much in late modern life, and which threatens to become part of restorative justice's conditions of impossibility.

ACKNOWLEDGEMENTS

The author thanks Ivo Aertsen and Brunilda Pali at the Universiteit Leuven in Belgium for prompting him to think about the issues mentioned in this chapter. He also thanks all participants in the 'Critical Restorative Justice' workshop (Universiteit Leuven, 15–17 October 2014) for their incisive but constructive comments following the presentation on which this short chapter is based. Special thanks go to John Blad, George Pavlich, Christa Pelikan, Mario Ragazzi, Leo Van Garsse and Lode Walgrave.

REFERENCES

Bataille, G (1954) *La Souveraineté* (Paris, Lignes, 2nd edn 2012).
—— (1957) *L'Erotisme* (Paris, Les Editions de Minuit, 1960).
Bauman, Z (1991) *Modernity and Ambivalence* (Cambridge, Polity).
—— (1993) *Postmodern Ethics* (Oxford, Blackwell).
—— (1995) *Life in Fragments* (Oxford, Blackwell).
Braithwaite, J (2002) *Restorative Justice and Responsive Regulation* (Oxford, Oxford University Press).
Camus, A (1942) *Le Mythe de Sisyphe* (Paris, Les Editions Gallimard).
—— (1949) *Les Justes* (Paris, Les Editions Gallimard).
Debord, G (1967) *La Société du Spectacle* (Paris, Buchet-Chastel).
Deleuze, G (1995) 'Postscript on Control Societies' in G Deleuze, *Negotiations* (New York, Columbia University Press).
Fassin, D and Rechtman, R (2009) *The Empire of Trauma* (Princeton, NJ, Princeton University Press).
Hall, S, Winlow S and Ancrum, C (2005) 'Radgies, Gangstas, and Mugs: Imaginary Criminal Identities in the Twilight of the Pseudo-Pacification Process' 1 *Social Justice* 100.
Isaac, J (1992) *Arendt, Camus and Modern Rebellion* (New Haven, CT, Yale University Press).
Lippens, R (2011) 'Jackson Pollock's Flight from Law and Code: Theses on Responsive Choice and the Dawn of Control Society' 24(1) *International Journal for the Semiotics of Law* 117.
—— (2015a) 'Ambivalent Sovereigns and Restorative Justice' 1 *Critical Criminology* 125.

—— (2015b) 'Absolutely Sovereign Victims: Rethinking the Victim Movement' 42(1) *Social Justice* 19.
—— (2016) 'Sovereign Minds, Bodies and Victim Culture' in D Spencer and S Walklate (eds), *New Perspectives in Victimology* (Lexington, KY, Rowman & Littlefield).
Mathiesen, Th (1974) *The Politics of Abolition* (London, Martin Robertson).
Mythen, G (2007) 'Cultural Victimology: Are We All Victims Now?' in S Walklate (ed), *Handbook of Victims and Victimology* (London, Routledge, 2011).

17

Promised Communities and Unrestored Justice

GEORGE PAVLICH

I. INTRODUCTION

WHATEVER THEIR DIFFERENCES, proponents of restorative and community justice typically champion resilient, local communities. Many urge parties in conflict to embrace initiatives to cultivate robust communities (see, eg Johnstone's 2013 synopsis). Others emphasise 'community-level' responses designed to prevent, police and sanction criminal harms (Clear and Karp, 1999). All prize communities capable of resisting crime or conflict, offsetting the state's emphasis on law, bureaucracy and punitive criminal justice (eg Elliott, 2009; Johnstone, 2011; Kurki, 2000; Walgrave, 2002; Wenzel *et al*, 2008; Zehr, 2005; Zehr and Toews, 2004; Zernova, 2007). But such unquestioning pursuits for community should be treated with caution because they are potentially dangerous.

One illustrative case—say, South African apartheid policies—indicates how resolute calls for community can be hazardous (Pavlich, 2014). Early apartheid architects viewed separated communities as central to progress for conflicted colonial societies. Geoffrey Cronjé (1937) argued that individuals required 'like-minded' communities to thrive because they fostered interactions with 'characters' at the same levels of personality and social advancement (see Pavlich, 2014). The racism and state violence required to engineer such 'fixed' communities highlights the severe danger. Cronjé's brand of 'deterministic sociology,' for instance, absurdly boiled all social problems down to this: 'blood mixing' or miscegenation. His apartheid 'solution' was to separate racial communities from one another and to encourage individual participation within these. Of course, this is not to suggest that apartheid's brutal outcomes are fated for all who back community; but the latter are always premised on exclusion. There is no universal community; rather communities arise from bordering fortifications that enforce them materially.

While we cannot escape imagining how to live with other people—since our changing relations with others define our historical identities—we need not conceptualise being with others through fixed, idealised notions of community. It is, for instance, possible to conceive of relations between people without setting up exclusionary ideals and universally judging what communities must look like to achieve justice, social progress, advancement, and so on. One could, to put it differently, conceive of communities historically without declaring, restoring or developing absolute versions thereof. In seeking to do precisely that, I will stand on the shoulders of those who have untangled complex webs: the uncertainty of modern communities (Bauman, 2000; 2001); the threat of exclusionary communities (Derrida, 1995; 1997); the always incomplete, or unavowable, sense of community (Blanchot, 1988); or, the perils of mobilising an 'operative' community, whether of communist or liberal communitarian ilk (Nancy, 1991; 2000a; and see generally Devisch, 2012; Morin, 2012: ch 3). I shall mostly, however, reference Esposito's (2010; 2013) recent work (eg *Communitas*).

But how might one approach community critically? In what follows, I outline a critical genre that seeks to be more *dissociative* than *judgmental* (see Pavlich, 2013). It is also intended to be expressly more evocative than definitive. This genre allows us to speak of community as neither completely fixed nor open; to that end, I offer six working proposals on how to approach 'being with' as a definable but endlessly fluid promise of how to live with others. The chapter concludes by looking at what each proposal means for community and restorative justice practically.

II. SETTING A CRITICAL COURSE: WHICH GENRE OF CRITIQUE?

When conceptualising ideal communities, restorative movements often rely on other fields, such as communitarianism (see Devisch, 2012), republican political theory (Braithwaite, 1989; 2002), MacIntyre's (2007) virtue ethics, or Habermas (1990) on normative agreement. Their visions of collective justice variously evoke community as: a product of active individual participation (Walgrave, 2008); the means to achieve common ethical ends (Seymour, Stuart and Pavelka, 2013; Zehr, 2002; 2005); a place to achieve democratic responses to crime (Clear, Hamilton and Cadora, 2011; Clear and Karp, 1999; Elliott, 2009; Seymour, Stuart and Pavelka, 2013); and a way to thwart individual isolation (Bazemore and Schiff 2001; Clear and Karp 1999; Johnstone, 2011; Johnstone and Van Ness, 2007; Karp, 1998). All champion robust, harmonious and consensual communities to avoid the damaging conflict *and* coercions of criminal justice (Elliott, 2009; Johnstone, 2011; Johnstone and Van Ness, 2007; Strang and Braithwaite, 2001; Woolford and Ratner, 2008; Zehr and Toews, 2004).

Whatever else, these approaches adopt a simple, if implicit, critical grammar: define criteria of an ideal community; depict a specific context; and then judge context against criteria to proclaim measures for attaining the ideal. The purported promise of such judgemental critical genres is to realise ideal communities devoid of conflict, crime, alienation, etc; but implementing that ideal inescapably generates an excluded underbelly—those folks deemed not to meet its strictures (Pavlich, 2013). As discussed, there are significant dangers with such thinking, and I therefore propose a different genre of critique, one that persistently tries to open limits erected around forms of being. Specifically, this genre works not by way of criteria-based judgement, but through techniques that 'negotiate' dissociations from familiar limits of collective existence (Pavlich, 2001b; 2013). Interpreting Derrida (2002; 1998; 1988), one might say that dissociative critique views the appearance of a fixed community as possible only through fortifications that try to arrest the fluidity of language (usually by more or less violent means, or the threat thereof). This is precisely why dissociative critiques work by constantly unravelling the limits of changing systems of differentiation, such as those contextual claims to fix 'community' as some or other ideal being. By emphasising *dissociation* over *judgement*, this approach to critique recognises meaning's basic fluidity, instability, and heterogeneity—the closure/opening, differentiation/deferral—through which meanings of community are historically enunciated. It negotiates openings out of (the dissociation of) prevailing limits, suggesting an always provisional approach to specific notions of 'community'.

If dissociative genres of critique thus avoid nostalgic quests for an ideal, authentic or pure community, they also take efforts to retrieve fixed communities as 'supplements' to earlier sign constellations (Derrida, 1998: 141 ff). This predicament is chronic: there can be no authentic recovery, and no restoration of past communities. Such attempts always involve supplementary patterns of deferral to *create* new meanings, adding to, rather than restoring or recovering, what is purportedly essential to them. Indeed, the very attempt to judge the essence of a community ideal is misplaced because it assumes in advance the *a priori* existence of a fixed being. Pursuing genres of critique that do not judge based on idealised criteria may allow us to drive open what is said to be closed, and to name the governmental processes that erect and sustain such closures. By so emphasising the exigencies of any 'community', one guards against the potential devastations of those who offer their contextual visions as obligatory.

III. DISSOCIATIVE CRITICAL GENRES AND REIMAGINING 'COMMUNITY'

But where does this leave us: does it mean that we should dispense with community as a concept? Perhaps, but only if one insists on imposing fixed definitions, ideals, onto community as if necessary. Yet, if approached as the fluid patterns that momentarily form around our 'being with' in context, 'community' may be understood very differently. Perhaps one might even emphasise, as does Esposito (2010), the indeterminate lack that enables such changing forms of the communal:

> It is this nothing held in common that is the world that joins us in the condition of exposure to the most unyielding absence of meaning and simultaneously to that opening to a meaning that still remains unthought. (Esposito, 2010: 149)

From this vantage, community could be understood as the shifting conditions in which 'we' find ourselves (Nancy, 2000a). This does not require one to ask what 'it' is, or 'whether we should claim this or that community'; but rather 'how' we might understand our communal relations as 'distracted, wandering without direction, without goal, without destination' (Nancy, 2000b: 111). Not clinging to a fixed ideal of community that purports to direct us absolutely towards social progress should be recognised for the freedom it offers us: a freedom whose outcomes cannot be determined with certainty, but for which we are always responsible. Calculating the ultimately unconditional justice of historical communities in response to wrongdoing is precisely one instance of that basic responsibility; facing the latter without illusions of assured certainty is another. It too signals the importance of engaging a politics of wrongdoing through open collective practices.

If one does not assume a fixed or universal community, then the analytical task of addressing our being-in-common emphasises moving historical relations that signal 'being with', or becoming (Esposito, 2010; Nancy, 2000a). My discussion below outlines six closely related proposals for how we might conceive of community openly, without assuming a fixed or unchanging essence. The argument works off a sense of community as involving fluid and historical closures (*genus*), but that are permanently overwhelmed by an indeterminate openness (*hetero*)—perhaps a historical heterogeneity.

A. Community as Verb, as Becoming ...

When understood as continually on the way (a becoming rather than a fixed being), 'being with' appears more as a verb than noun. 'Community' surfaces through changing patterns of differentiation in particular circumstances; it helps participants envisage their contextual being with others. Though never fixed, community is equally never a simple dispersal. Rather a sense of community appears through heterogeneous discourses that differentiate how to be with others here and now. The 'with' is primordial precisely because we are always already *with* others, born into pre-existing relations that shape meaning horizons as we learn a language with its historical patterns of deferral, including what to understand by the term 'community', or indeed the historically designated 'I', 'me' or 'self'. Since the verb community evades essential or universal capture, it cannot provide shelter. It continuously exposes those it defines to an incalculable indeterminacy. Through this, we experience the fundamental and unalterable freedom to which we, in common, are abandoned. If nothing else, this highlights the importance of grappling with the moving traces and patterns of deferral—the becoming—through which particular formulations of community emerge.

B. Community as the Relations Between the One and the All

One may need to reimagine the 'individual-community' dichotomy ascribed to local collective patterns. Communities are not determined amalgams of pre-existing individuals, nor are they absolute, self-contained social facts. Rather, communities take local form in liminal and changing *relations between the one and the all.* On this front, Esposito (2010) aptly notes that:

> This means simply that community isn't an entity, nor is it a collection of subjects, but rather is the relation that makes them no longer individual subjects because it closes them off from their identity with a line, which traversing them, alters them: it is the 'with', the 'between', and the threshold where they meet in a point of contact that brings them into relation with others to the degree which separates them from themselves. (Esposito, 2010: 139)

From this vantage, community may be approached as a dynamic movement of the relations *between* the individual subjects it recursively posits. As moving thresholds, communal relations form beyond individuality; but they sustain historical versions of individuality. In this sense, community always surpasses historically conceived individuals. The communal is by definition permanently removed from, or transcendent with respect to, both the 'I' and the 'me'. It is a moving relational placeholder through which the 'I', 'me' or 'self' is fashioned, but remains detached from such singularities. The liminal threshold here is a relational one that appears *between* historically enunciated versions of the one and the many. Such relations embrace every newborn's arrival into the 'world', and contour the communal.

C. 'I' Experience Community as a Loss, Dissociation

Directly related to the previous point, relations of a moving community are experienced by the 'I' or 'me' as a loss, a lack—something not yet fulfilled. Perhaps this explains the unending communitarian quest to define, restore, or even develop new communities. Regardless, as a transcendent relation, community permanently recedes mirage-like, into the sands of future relations, beyond the borders of contextually defined individuals. It is, to quote Esposito (2010), 'the break, the trauma, the lacuna after which we originate' (Esposito, 2010: 8). For this reason, community is always experienced by (historically generated) individuals as absence, as something never quite to hand. It is experienced, that is, as a moment of dissolution where images of an individual dissolve into a collective abyss; the point at which the singular subject voids into moving collective relations.

Community is thus not a being but a lack; and moreover, a lack that permanently transcends specific individuals. As such, it cannot be appropriated by individual subjects, and is experienced by them at the limits of their historical experience. From Bataille's work, Esposito retrieves an idea that the 'I' is always contoured by, and exposed to, a death-like abyss: the limits of its contingent being. This exposure is glimpsed through liminal moments of 'not-being-ourselves', or 'our-being-other-from-ourselves' while at the same time it is our 'being-other-from-the-other' (Esposito, 2010: 122). Such experiences are possible at moments where a stable sense of self is dissolved, where relations form. Experiencing community as loss indicates a permanent exposure to uncertainty, dissolution and transformation—to absence, to what is not there. Thus, community cannot be considered a warm, comforting or embracing whole that shields us from foreign worlds beyond. On the contrary, the experience of community as lack perpetually exposes 'me' to disquieting moments of disassociation where any comforts provided by the individuality we imagine ourselves to be are momentarily dispersed. One might then say:

> communitas is utterly incapable of prolonging the effects of commonality, of association ... and of communion. It doesn't keep us warm, and it doesn't protect us; on the contrary, it exposes us to the most extreme of risks: that of losing, along with our individuality, the borders that guarantee it's inviolability with respect to the other; of suddenly falling into the nothing of the thing. (Esposito, 2010: 140)

D. Community Shapes the Individuals It Obliges

Fourthly, even if experienced as a loss or lack, the community shapes fundamentally the individuals it obliges. As a relational absence, a trace, it draws out specific individuals from birth. 'I' constantly experience the pull of communal relations; and that very attraction shapes the changing historical forms of my individuality. This tug is unyielding and experienced as obligation; it generates a duty of responding—specific kinds of individuals surface historically through particular responses. In other words, transcendent communal relations extract historical forms of 'the individual' through obligations that border and define subjects through their replies. The etymology of the word 'community', though various, may signal the force, bordering and fortification required to sustain particular visions of community, as implied by the Latin '*municeps*' and '*com*' or with (Pavlich, 2001a). However, Esposito also notes another dimension of its etymology: '*com*' (with) and '*munus*' (obligation) suggest that 'being with' is fundamentally about obligation, about asymmetrical communal demands and individual gift-giving. For him, such obligations are perpetual and amorphous rather than absolute and set. This obligation is a never-ending, insatiable, lack that draws responses from, and thereby creates, individuals. As he puts it, community appears to a historically shaped 'me' as a void:

> in the limit experiences that distance us from ourselves, that distance us from being the masters of our own existence. Yet these experiences are nothing other than the anthropological effect (or the subjective dimension) of the void of being that gives rise to them. (Esposito, 2010: 147)

The obligations of community thus compel a constant, if amorphous, gift-giving out of which specific images of givers emerge. The binding pull of community is endless and unquenchable, prompting responses from specific individuals. Such obligation exposes subjects to what is beyond current self-definitions, and their contingent responses produce historical forms of individuality. 'I' am then propelled by the obligations of being with others in context; 'I' experience these compulsions as a lack or obligation that is never satisfied—a debt never repaid. Even with attempts to immunise specific versions of individuals from community (via, for instance, human rights, liberal politics) or the community from individuals (communism), the indeterminate 'being with' remains. It is precisely within ongoing interactions between subjects, and liminal spaces that dissolve borders of individuality, that coterminous obligations draw subjects outside of historical limits of subjectivity and into an 'immense devastation' of present meanings. At such moments, then, we find traces of community:

> the community isn't anything else except the border and the point of transit between this immense devastation of meaning and the necessity that every singularity, every event, every fragment of existence makes sense in itself. (Esposito, 2010: 149)

E. The Indeterminate Individual as a 'Series of Alterations'

One might ponder how historical 'individuals' emerge as perpetual responses to a communal lack. Is this 'I', 'self' or 'me' a product of the communal obligations that draw 'me' to the limits of my being? As one commentator puts it:

> Munus takes me outside the bonds of my proper subjectivity and leads me through a series of alterations, rendering me otherwise than a coherent, bonded self. (Hole, 2013: 111)

If so, then the historical individual is a contingent outcome of a series of alterations. It is the moving, constant exposure to a lack that obligates responses by calling for duties that define subjects in context. Individuals thus appear through repeated deferrals; historical versions of individuality are constantly shaped by the inducements of an amorphous communal duty. As Esposito puts it, 'wanting to be everything, the subject is at the mercy of a nothing not produced by him but to which he submits' (Esposito, 2010: 130). This subject is both autonomous and dependent, and can place itself at its limits, being not quite immanent, and not quite transcendent. As such, individuals are constituted through ongoing flows of deferred communality:

> the community isn't joined to an addition but to a subtraction of subjectivity, by which I mean that its members are no longer identical with themselves but are constitutively exposed to a propensity that forces them to open their own individual boundaries in order to appear as what is 'outside' themselves … If the subject of community is no longer the 'same', it will by necessity be an 'other'; not another subject but a chain of alterations that cannot ever be fixed in a new identity. (Esposito, 2010: 138)

In short, the individual, like the figurative nomad, may then be considered as a 'chain of alterations' without fixed identity, permanently responding to unfulfilled obligations, a pervasive lack that contours the horizons beyond particular identities.

F. Addressing Community as Law

Considered as a transcendent lack that obligates and so perpetually draws responses that generate historical individuals, a community's limits are never set in stone. But then how might one address this community? Esposito (2010: ch 3) extracts a helpful allegory from Kant's understanding of law (and indeed the law of the categorical imperative) as always transcendent. Put simply, law is always before the persons that it obligates: it is there before birth, remains a presence for unfolding lives, and persists after our deaths. Laws cannot be possessed or fully calculated by the 'I', or actualised as a fully-fledged object without yielding its transcendental quality. It is thus not actualisable; it is a shifting heterogeneity, simultaneously decisive in particular instances but always receptive to promises of what lies beyond (Fitzpatrick, 2001; Golder and Fitzpatrick, 2009). In this sense while law must determine in particular instances, it cannot thereby sacrifice its transcendental responsibility to the infinite promise of justice that is never synonymous with finite, particular determinations.

It is, as with Kafka's parables, always before us, but it can never fully be appropriated or even entered. This is a token of law whose heterogeneity moves between closure and opening out to a response that is beyond, and yet structures, the present decision. Here one glimpses the close relationship between law and community: 'It's the law and not the will that is at the origin of community, so much so that one could even say that the community is identical to law' (Esposito, 2010: 64). As such, one might say that community and its heterogeneous modulations remain responsive (Fitzpatrick, 2001) to infinite promises (of justice or solidarity) at the same time as being historically determinative (through law or obligation, Derrida, 2000). Law understood as a form of indeterminacy and community as an obliging lack draws individuals out into historical identities: but both law and community are transcendental and so can never be fully appropriated. They are precisely the remainders when subjectivity is subtracted.

These six proposals for approaching community through dissociative (rather than judgemental) grammars of critique may seem abstracted. They are, but then again considerations that call for different approaches are perhaps inexorably so, especially within the self-reflective terrain that is here scanned. Regardless, many might ponder what such reimagining of community could possibly mean for practitioners of community or restorative justice. This legitimate concern will occupy the remainder of the chapter as it draws out the practical implications of each proposal.

IV. UNRESTORED JUSTICE AS PRACTICE

First, and working through the proposals in the same sequence, if community is conceived as a verb rather than a noun, then its movement defies attempts to recover, restore or develop static visions. Dynamic communities are always in flux, and so work against programmes that claim to judge, entrench or serve a frozen grouping. While restorative justice programmes may be expected to frame tactical and strategic aims, they should be careful not to hypostatise historical community relations; for example, by positing today's version of a 'strong community' as a necessary solution to criminal reoffending (Kurki, 2000). Such assertions gloss over moving relations between people that produce historical visions of wrongdoing or conflict. If the overall aim is to move beyond relations enunciated as wrongdoing, then community and restorative justice measures could be seen as augers for change, redirecting relations that bring participants to events of wrongdoing and conflict in the first place.

Community and restorative justice programmes (eg victim/offender mediations) that demand responsibilities solely from individual identities associated with wrongdoing today (eg offender, victim) need to be mindful of inadvertently shoring up problematic identities, or affirming a restoration of the communal relations that enabled them to emerge. Some have indicated the transformative potential for justice practices, calling for changes at thresholds of limit (identity) formation (eg Cunneen, 2010; Woolford and

Ratner, 2008). Such a transformative approach could, for instance, engage social thresholds that: define wrongdoing in the first place (are the acts at hand appropriately governed as crime, conflict or are there economic, gender, race inequalities that also need to be addressed?); accuse an individual wrongdoer (when broader relational structures might be more apt sites of focus); and define offenders/victims in fixed terms. Threshold politics of this sort will likely be broad and multilayered (see Woolford and Ratner, 2008); it might involve critical forms of mediation or negotiation as ways to dissociate the limits of relations that buttressed forms of wrongdoing. Rather than a 'justice' that simply seeks agreements between 'individuals' to restore or develop fixed communities, one may work with concepts of hospitality, as per Derrida (2000). The allegory of hospitality and the negotiations between historically possible visions of the limited welcome issued by host to guest could help to frame transformative justice carried out at the relational thresholds of context (Pavlich, 2001a).

Secondly, if not simply a collection of *a priori* individuals, or a fixed social fact, community might be approached as a relational remainder that constantly generates both. Community and restorative justice would target neither fixed individuals nor predefined communities; rather it would mark the moving *relations* between (and that create) subjects and collections. By focusing on these relations per se, community and restorative justice movements need not approach wrongdoing as the domain of determinate individuals (whether offenders, victims or mediators), or clear-cut communities (or a perceived lack thereof). Rather, dissociative community justice techniques might explore the relations that draw subjects out as particular individuals and deposit visions of fixed collectives. What sorts of communal responsibilities have brought subjects to the current situation? How might community justice open these relations out to different horizons, and new ways of being together? What relational dynamics might be attended to not simply through individual change, but by changing the very forms of obligation and response that create particular circumstances?

These sorts of questions suggest a political engagement with the relations behind specific kinds of individuals and communities. Again, referring to an allegory of hospitality, one might explore relations between host and guest as a paradigm for targeting diffuse and complex relations at thresholds that, through the responsibilities they require, and the responses offered thereto, shape both individuals and the local gatherings. This focus implies political approaches aiming to forge new and different relational complexes out of conflicted relations variously framed as wrongdoing (Blagg, 2005; 2008; Capeheart and Milovanovic, 2007; Chapman, 2012; Cunneen, 2010; Morris, 2000; Woolford and Ratner, 2008). Again, the target would be a critical engagement with the *relations* that: define specific forms of wrongdoing (Meyer, 2010); enable the conditions from which subjects respond as wrongdoers; frame subjects to be considered as the wronged; and generate and sustain attendant identities for both individuals and communities in context. To be sure, the political work required here would interrogate local historical closures, but this does not require that the host yield mastery over spaces of hospitality. Calculations of justice must be made, and promises sent forth—we cannot avoid this. However, infinite promises of justice remain inestimable from finite horizons, requiring analytic diffidence and an avid commitment to keeping any particular reckonings from posing as necessary or absolute (Derrida, 1992). The prospects for critical dissociation should thus always be protected within community and restorative justice initiatives—therein lies a vital escape from totalitarian closure.

Thirdly, as Esposito notes, to comprehend what it is to be fully immersed in, and constituted by, relations with others requires individual subjects to lose (part of) familiar identities because community by definition appears where historical formulations of individuality end. Consequently, the 'community' is less a source of comfort for the subjects and more an experience of loss: a moment where familiar individual identifications of a past self are exposed to new relations with others (eg in restorative justice programmes). Negotiating the transformation of familiar self-identifications accompanying enunciations of wrongdoing, community and restorative justice initiatives will expressly work with such loss when moving from familiar (and problematic) relational orders to unfamiliar relations with attendant (new?) forms of subjectivity. Such dispositions are central rather than peripheral to how subjects identify within, and eventually respond to, situations of wrongdoing. Community and restorative justice initiatives might here conceive of themselves as forming at relational thresholds to negotiate and open up limits that somehow have led to wrongdoing.

The practical implication is that community initiatives need not shore up familiar or fixed identities around wrongdoing; instead, they could develop techniques that recognise what is involved with processes that transform self-identities, and develop alternate relational channels for new responsibilities and ways to be with others in future. Negotiating departures from familiar identities, their dissociation, is very much part of this terrain—a sort of nomadism that never settles. In this quest, community and restorative justice operations could cultivate political technologies to help local participants negotiate the loss of familiar individual identities (offender, victim, witness, etc) and to 'be with' in ways that are not destructive, injurious or harmful. Placed at thresholds where individual identities dissolve into relations with others, justice techniques need not presume either absolute individuals or communities, but could instead direct themselves to changing the relational patterns that create both. To be sure, such initiatives may provide little comfort for those seeking total solutions right now; but they do emphasise finding ways to transcend relations that nurture injustice, wrongdoing and so on (Aertsen, 2008). The use of dissociative critique to enable new forms of life implies an ability to examine existing visions of harm or wrongdoing, and an understanding of community as a relational complex that generates both individual and images of specific collectives.

Fourthly, if communality comprises insatiable obligations of 'being with' that relationally draw out specific sorts of individuality, then justice practices, whether restorative or community, issue communal obligations of their own. For example, mediation practices require, expect and encourage many things from participants at the start of sessions. What obligatory pulls or appeals do specific restorative justice methods and practices deploy? What kind of individual borders do they thereby promote? What sort of gift-giving does this justice require of its participants, and what kind of gift-givers does its justice presume? What sorts of responsibilities and duties does it cultivate, and what kinds of identities are so induced? By attending to these questions, practitioners of community and restorative justice can articulate the *munus* (obligation) of their interventions. Here, community justice might be enlisted to develop a politics that renders its forms of obligation and responsibility open to scrutiny. Foucault's (2014) lectures that outline how different juridical forms rely on particular kinds of avowal and truth telling provide a way to conceptualise this issue. Since community justice initiatives require avowals of truth about events from participants differently from criminal justice processes, we might focus on the kinds of truth-telling practices community and restorative justice technologies require. How do these shape new kinds of subjects, subjections, responsibilities and communal forms? In sum, a basic question to be asked of all community and restorative justice practices is this: how might the processes, obligations and required avowals foster transformations that dissociate rather than entrench the relations that have brought subjects to the circumstances at issue?

Fifthly, if the individual is not an *a priori* identity but a series of alterations (emerging from obligations created by relations with others), then the target of community justice cannot be a static individual (say, criminal, offender, or even victim, accuser or judge). Indeed, community and restorative justice initiatives focused on defining (fixing) subjects as criminals—or requiring offenders to define themselves as offenders in order to accept responsibility for past actions—tend to imitate the state's criminal justice that requires such identities to incapacitate, punish or deter individuals (Pavlich, 2005). Equally, but from another vantage, when victim-offender reconciliation efforts seek to empower victims as victims (contra the definition), their emphasis on bringing out an empowered form of a disempowered identity seems fated from the outset. While it is important to locate obligations and recognise the emotional feelings of those involved, it is important to avoid reifying identities of wrongdoing, wrongdoer and victim. Doing so tends to buttress problematic relations and identities. Of course, this is not in any way to deny or ignore the injuries, harms or responsibilities that attend to given instances of wrongdoing. On the contrary, it is an attempt to confront and transform the complex patterns of communal obligation, relation, responsibility and associated forms of individuality that spawn instances of wrongdoing and injustice. And then it is to find dissociative paths that enable new ways of being with, or new responsibilities and forms of life for all concerned.

Here, community and restorative justice techniques might again assume a transformative guise; but now with a focus on political technologies directed to communal relations behind subjective forms that lead to wrongdoing. Various practical technologies could be beneficial here, including Meyer's call to conceive of communal justice as involving mercy, thus working through the potential responsibilities attendant upon disgraced identities rather than judging guilt and demanding vengeance or punishment for expiation (Meyer, 2010). That is, consequential social transformation may depend on mercy to enable new subjective forms. Practitioners might also find value in returning to Braithwaite's classic idea of 'reintegrative shaming' in specific contexts, with the proviso that one rescind the individual focus by emphasising relational obligations that contour dissociations of particular identities (Braithwaite, 1989). In general, there may be considerable value in seeking inclusive forms of governance without yielding to the vacuous idea that injustice, harm and wrongdoing ought simply to be endured. Community and restorative justice movements may here pursue techniques that take advantage of the openness inherent in a community, striving towards transformed contexts that work with situated (though democratically) conceived versions of wrongdoing.

Finally, if community and law share a transcendental relationship with respect to subjects, one might say that legal obligation and community duty are not as distinct as some protagonists of restorative justice might suggest (Zehr, 2005). Indeed there is some imitation involved, as suggested by the 'imitor paradox' which I described in a previous text (Pavlich, 2005), and that is signalled variously by other analysts (Aertsen, 2008; Walgrave, 2002; Wenzel *et al*, 2008). Here, there may be good reason to understand community justice not as a simple alternative to criminal justice but to recognise common structural configurations that issue obligations to subjects who stand before them, requiring responses that shape specific individuals in the service of collective orders. Their respective calibrations of justice may at times be different, one disavowing coercion as far as possible, the other centred on monopolising the violence of legitimate force for state forms of vengeance. However, in many instances (especially where their practices focus on crime, criminal individuals, offenders and victims) proffering justice in the name of a community order may be common to both. If either community or criminal justice is enlisted to offer determinate, finite calculations of what is never fully calculable, then the margins for an alternative, may be transformative, justice remain slim.

Perhaps one might recognise that the incalculable promises of any justice, whether state or communal, draw us to relational complexes whose voids ultimately propel an indeterminate 'being with' others. Justice can strive to sustain or variously transform the complexes at hand. From such possibilities, one glimpses both the freedom and responsibility to which human life is providentially exiled, but without certainty on how to face common futures. Perhaps justice, in whatever form, might seek to embrace rather than deny such indeterminacy, structuring the processes that bear its name in ways that lean out—without end—to the infinite promise of an incalculable justice that is paradoxically calculated within limited meaning horizons.

V. CONCLUSION

To reiterate, this chapter has traversed an ambitious analytical journey deliberately more evocative than definitive. It has examined ideas of community through dissociative (rather than judgemental) genres of critique before drawing on Esposito's work to frame six proposals for approaching community as an open relational matter arising from moving instances of 'being with'. Finally, from these proposals, it has extracted practical possibilities for community and restorative justice initiatives. Much further work is, of course, required to translate the practical consequences of a dissociative approach to community; but perhaps reviewing specific cases is the next step to fleshing out the bony skeleton sketched above. At least, the previous discussion has worked with the benefit of hindsight, and urged incalculable promises of community justice to rescind the pretence of final, deterministic solutions to communal matters. It has called upon the field to confront a deeply disturbing existential complex: being condemned to freedom means that certainties are not within our grasp. No guarantees and no final solutions can forever point us towards perfect communal arrangements. At the same time, in the aftermath of wrongdoing, there is no escape from responding to a perpetual question, 'whereto from here?' Our responses to this question recursively create the very beings that we, often imperceptibly, become.

REFERENCES

Aertsen, I (2008) 'Racak, Mahane Yehuda and Nyabyondo: Restorative Justice Between the Formal and the Informal' in I Aertsen, J Arsovska, H Rohne, M Valiñas and K Vanspauwen (eds), *Restoring Justice After Large-Scale Violent Conflicts: Kosovo, DR Congo and the Israeli-Palestinian Case* (Cullompton, Willan) 413–43.

Bauman, Z (2000) *Modernity and the Holocaust* (Ithaca, NY, Cornell University Press).

—— (2001) *Community: Seeking Safety in an Insecure World* (Cambridge, Polity).

Bazemore, S, Schiff, G and Schiff, M (2001) *Restorative Community Justice: Repairing Harm and Transforming Communities* (Cincinnati, OH, Anderson Publishing).
Blagg, H (2005) *A New Way of Doing Justice Business?: Community Justice Mechanisms and Sustainable Governance in Western Australia*, Background Paper (Perth, Law Reform Commission of Western Australia).
—— (2008) *Crime, Aboriginality and the Decolonisation of Justice* (Annandale, VA, Hawkins Press).
Blanchot, M (1988) *The Unavowable Community* (Barrytown, NY, Station Hill Press).
Braithwaite, J (1989) *Crime, Shame, and Reintegration* (New York, Cambridge University Press).
—— (2002) *Restorative Justice and Responsive Regulation* (New York, Oxford University Press).
Capeheart, L and Milovanovic, D (2007) *Social Justice: Theories, Issues, and Movements* (New Brunswick, NJ, Rutgers University Press).
Chapman, T (2012) 'Justice in Transition: Community Restorative Justice in Northern Ireland' 14(4) *Punishment and Society* 497.
Clear, TR, Hamilton, JR and Cadora, E (2011) *Community Justice* (New York, Routledge).
Clear, TR and Karp, DR (1999) *The Community Justice Ideal: Preventing Crime and Achieving Justice* (Boulder, CO, Westview Press).
Comack, E (2012) *Racialized Policing: Aboriginal People's Encounters with the Police* (Halifax: Fernwood Pub).
Cronjé, G (1937) 'Die Deterministiese Standpunt in die Sosiologie' (Pretoria, University of Pretoria).
Cunneen, C (2010) 'Justice in Transition: Community Restorative Justice in Northern Ireland' 43(2) *Australian and New Zealand Journal of Criminology*, 376.
Derrida, J (1988) *Limited Inc* (Evanston, IN, Northwestern University Press).
—— (1992) 'Force of Law: The "Mystical Foundation of Authority"' in D Cornell, M Rodenfeld and DG Carlson (eds), *Deconstruction and the Possibility of Justice* (New York, Routledge).
—— (1995) *Points …: Interviews, 1974–1994* (Stanford, CA, Stanford University Press).
—— (1997) *Politics of Friendship* (New York, Verso).
—— (1998) *Of Grammatology* (Baltimore, MD, Johns Hopkins University Press).
—— (2000) *Of Hospitality* (Stanford, CA, Stanford University Press).
—— (2002) *Positions* (New York, Continuum).
Devisch, I (2012) *Jean-Luc Nancy and the Question of Community* (New York, Continuum).
Elliott, L (2009) 'A Geometry of Its Own: Restorative Justice, Relationships and Community in Democracy' in JI Ross (ed), *Cutting the Edge* (Edison, NJ, Transaction Publishers).
Esposito, R (2010) *Communitas: The Origin and Destiny of Community* (Stanford, CA, Stanford University Press).
—— (2013) *Terms of the Political: Community, Immunity, Biopolitics* (New York, Fordham University Press).
Fitzpatrick, P (2001) *Modernism and the Grounds of Law* (Cambridge, Cambridge University Press).

Foucault, M (2014) *Wrong-doing, Truth-Telling, the Function of Avowal in Justice* (Chicago, IL, University of Chicago Press).
Golder, B and Fitzpatrick, P (2009) *Foucault's Law* (New York, Routledge).
Habermas, J (1990) *Moral Consciousness and Communicative Action* (Cambridge, MA, MIT Press).
Hole, K (2013) 'The Ethic of Community: Nancy, Blanchot, Esposito' 18(3) *Angelaki* 103.
Johnstone, G (2011) *Restorative Justice: Ideas, Values, Debates* (New York, Routledge).
—— (2013) *A Restorative Justice Reader* (New York, Routledge).
Johnstone, G and Van Ness, DW (2007) *Handbook of Restorative Justice* (Cullompton, Willan).
Karp, DR (1998) *Community Justice: An Emerging Field* (Lanham, MD, Rowman & Littlefield).
Kurki, L (2000) 'Restorative and Community Justice in the United States' 27 *Crime and Justice* 235.
MacIntyre, AC (2007) *After Virtue: A Study in Moral Theory* (Notre Dame, IN, University of Notre Dame Press).
Meyer, L (2010) *The Justice of Mercy* (Ann Arbor, MI, University of Michigan Press).
Morin, M (2012) *Jean-luc Nancy* (London, Polity Press).
Morris, R (2000) *Stories of Transformative Justice* (Toronto, Canadian Scholars' Press).
Nancy, J (1991) *The Inoperative Community* (Minneapolis, MN, University of Minnesota Press).
—— (2000a) *Being Singular Plural* (Stanford, CA, Stanford University Press).
—— (2000b) *The Speculative Remark* (Stanford, CA Stanford University Press).
Pavlich, G (2000) *Critique and Radical Discourses on Crime* (Aldershot, Ashgate).
—— (2001a) 'The Force of Community' in H Strang and J Braithwaite (eds), *Restorative Justice and Civil Society* (Cambridge, Cambridge University Press).
—— (2001b) 'Sociological Promises: Departures or Negotiating Dissociation' in L Simmons and H Worth (eds), *Derrida Downunder* (Palmeston North, Dunmore Press)— (2005) *Governing Paradoxes of Restorative Justice* (London, GlassHouse Press).
—— (2013) 'Dissociative Grammar and Constitutional Critique?' in K van Marle and S Motha (eds), *Genres of Critique: Law, Aesthetics and Liminality* (Stellenbosch, Sun Press).
—— (2014) 'Adminsitrative Sociology and Apartheid' 46(3) *Acta Academica* 153.
Seymour, AM, Stuart, BD and Pavelka, S (2013) *The Legacy of Community Justice* (Vernon, CT, J Charlton).
Strang, H and Braithwaite, J (eds) (2001) *Restorative Justice and Civil Society* (Cambridge, Cambridge University Press).
Tönnies, F (1988) *Community and Society* (New Brunswick, NJ, Transaction Books).
Walgrave, L (2002) *Restorative Justice and the Law* (Cullompton, Willan).
—— (2008) *Restorative Justice, Self-Interest and Responsible Citizenship* (Cullompton, Willan).
Wenzel, M, Okimoto, TG, Feather, NT and Platow, MJ (2008) 'Retributive and Restorative Justice' 32(5) *Law and Human Behavior* 375.

Wetzell, RF (2000) *Inventing the Criminal: A History of German Criminology* (London, University of North Carolina Press).
Woolford, AJ and Ratner, R (2008) *Informal Reckonings: Conflict Resolution in Mediation, Restorative Justice, and Reparations* (New York, Routledge-Cavendish).
Zehr, H (2002) *The Little Book of Restorative Justice* (Intercourse, PA, Good Books).
—— (2005) *Changing Lenses: A New Focus for Crime and Justice* (Scottdale, NY, Herald Press).
Zehr, H and Toews, B (2004) *Critical Issues in Restorative Justice* (Cullompton, Willan).
Zernova, M (2007) 'Restorative Justice: Ideals and Realities' in *International and Comparative Criminal Justice* (Aldershot, Ashgate).

18

*A Radical in Disguise: Judith Shklar's Victimology and Restorative Justice**

ANTONY PEMBERTON AND PAULINE GM AARTEN

I. INTRODUCTION

FORTY YEARS AGO it was safe to say that the victim was the forgotten party of the criminal justice system (Groenhuijsen, 2014). In theories of criminal justice, in public debate, in the guidelines underlying day-to-day practice, victims barely figured. Following their report to the police, victims often felt neglected, alienated, and even revictimised. The latter is known as secondary victimisation and describes the extent to which victims felt that the reaction of the criminal justice actors mimicked the act from which they sought refuge with the police, prosecution and magistrates (Williams, 1984).

Nevertheless in earnest, given the level of interest from policy, practice and academia in the current day and age, this is no longer the case. Within various national jurisdictions the interest in victims has been steadily increasing, with the efforts of the European Union culminating in the Victims Directive of 2012 (EU Directive 2012/29/EU) (eg Pemberton and Groenhuijsen, 2012; Groenhuijsen, 2014). The Victims Directive is testament to the importance the EU places on the rights, protection and support of victims of crime within our criminal justice processes. In the Communication of the European Commission, optimism and ambition jockey for first place. There is an earnest belief that putting the provisions of the Directive in place will have a real tangible effect on the experience of victims of crime across Europe. In this way, the Directive is hoped to improve the lived experience of 90 million people across Europe, who annually fall victim to various forms of criminal behaviour.

* Work on this chapter was supported by a Veni-grant (451-13-019) from the Dutch Science Foundation (NWO) for the first author.

But while laudable ambitions are one thing, and the seemingly unending stream of policy seminars, working groups, projects, exchange venues for best practices, are another, the victimological reality with criminal justice is still not very much different from what it was 40 years ago (eg Biffi *et al*, 2016). Reporting and attrition rates (Daly and Bonhours, 2010), satisfaction with proceedings (Laxminarayan *et al*, 2013), and secondary victimisation (Kunst *et al*, 2014) all confirm that the criminal justice system is something between a large burden and a minor boon for victims of crime (Pemberton, 2014). Some find some solace, support or perhaps even some emotional benefit; others still feel the experience of secondary victimisation most keenly.

It is time to consider the possibility that the experience of victimisation is fundamentally at odds with features of criminal justice systems (eg Pemberton, 2015; Pemberton, 2016a). Piece-meal reform of the system, tinkering with its edges, while the core remains intact, will not overcome the significant mismatch between victims and criminal justice. That it is not to say that we need to argue for a full-scale overhaul of the criminal justice process, but it does mean that at a certain point we should acknowledge the limitations of criminal justice in achieving the kind of blanket and large-scale benefits to which the European Union and other international bodies aspire (eg Pemberton and Letschert, 2016).

Of course, saying that there is a mismatch between victim experience and criminal justice processes in a volume about restorative justice is hardly the most daring statement. It has been a staple of the restorative justice literature that we need to change the lenses of the way we view crime, away from the pain game and the blame game played by the criminal justice process, toward a response that makes restoring people, relationships and communities its focal point (Zehr, 1990). In doing so, we might need to jettison the concept of crime in its entirety, and seek to retrieve the 'conflict' between victim and offender from the state and its minions. These conflicts are our property, as the late Norwegian criminologist Nils Christie would have had it (eg Christie, 1977). And following this, our also dearly departed fellow countryman Louk Hulsman would have abolished the whole of the criminal justice process (see Hulsman, 1986).

But although much of what we want to consider in this article might resonate with the restorative justice (RJ) literature, we believe that RJ does not fully represent the victimological perspective. To make our case, we return to one of the most important thinkers about the subject and experience of victimology, even though she is not always recognised as such (see also Pemberton, 2015). And what is also not fully recognised is the extent to which her views are radical, not only about the way we shape our institutions in response to crime, but also about the way we should try to understand the subject of injustice and the manner in which we go about increasing our knowledge of this experience and the effects of our responses to it.

II. JUDITH SHKLAR AND THE ASYMMETRY OF JUSTICE AND INJUSTICE

Judith Shklar, a professor of government at Harvard until her death in 1992, was a radical in disguise. Two of the publications that bookended her career are particularly important to our current argument: *Legalism* from 1964 and *The Faces of Injustice* from 1990 still repay careful study. Shklar's unique analysis of injustice includes the role of radical choices, such as revenge and forgiveness, and context-dependence in the manner in which injustice is experienced and the consequences this has for the bearing of justice processes on the experience of injustice. These are all of key importance to the understanding of victimology and its wake of restorative justice as well.

A. The 'Normal' Account of Injustice

Central is the way Shklar understands injustice (Shklar, 1990). She points out that most normative and political theories do not spend much time thinking about the nature of injustice. Injustice is normally conceptualised, in line with its etymology, as a lack of justice. A typical example of what she means she finds in the work of John Stuart Mill:

> Normal accounts do begin, as John Stuart Mill's typically does with the thought that justice, like many other moral notions is best defined by its opposite. He then goes on to tell us in a very few sentences what injustice involves. It needs the violation of good laws, the breaking of promises, the refusal to recognize valid claims, to reward positive merit and to punish crimes and finally be partial in deciding controversies. With that he leaves the subject having in fact only shown that it is unjust to break the rules of normal justice. In this procedure he was by no means unique, but that does not mean that it is a wholly satisfactory one. (Mill, 1871: 18–19)

In doing so, injustice is understood as one dimension with justice, with injustice and justice as opposite poles. In a similar vein, justice is the countervailing force against injustices. This also means that undoing injustice and doing justice are inseparable, they are the same activity. Given the centrality of the experience of injustice, of wrongfulness to victimisation (eg Pemberton, 2014), it provides justice with a self-evident and primary role in the aftermath of victimisation. Indeed, any attempt to weigh the demands of justice against other ends is viewed as injustices in themselves (Pemberton and Letschert, 2016). It also positions justice—being the counterforce to injustice—as unquestionably the right thing to do.

We will add one more point here: Shklar (1964) argues that the opaque beneficence of justice gives the opportunity to connect it to other values or goals, like economic justice, social justice or political justice. And if we may add, to start preparing a point we will make later, restorative justice.

However, as Shklar argues, there is good reason to question whether this easy marriage of these pairs of terms obscures the extent to which they can be at odds with each other.

B. The Face of Injustice

Indeed, when Shklar takes her own advice, and looks at injustice first and more in depth, it takes her in a very different direction (Shklar, 1990). The phenomenological experience of injustice is emotional, embodied, particular, idiosyncratic, rooted in a particular context. Coming to terms with it requires sense-making, and this sense-making occurs through narrative explanations (eg Pemberton, Aarten and Mulder, forthcoming). Victimisation creates a narrative rupture in the victim's life story (see Pemberton Aarten and Mulder, forthcoming; Crossley, 2000), and the experience of injustice and the way we make sense intimately involves the way we understand ourselves, the manner in which the past before the injustice occurred, and how it is connected to our present and future (Crossley, 2000; McAdams, 1993). Janoff-Bulman (1992) framed the consequences of victimisation as *Shattered Assumptions* and we find that the most central of these shattered assumptions are the ones relating to our identity, our sense of self, the manner in which we experience ourselves continuously over time and continuous with the wider social context. This sense of continuity of self throughout time and with others is maintained by our life stories (McAdams, 2013; Hammack and Pilecki, 2012), the unfolding narrative that is a central component of our identity.

And the reaction to injustice is similarly idiosyncratic and storied (Pemberton, 2015; Pemberton, Aarten and Mulder, 2017). People construct a story about their experience, but this does not stop with the victimisation itself, what happens in reaction to the victimisation is part of the same unfolding narrative. It retrospectively alters the memory, narrative and experience of victimisation. This is true for the responses of third parties, including those involved with the justice process and the victim's social surroundings, but also of the victim him or herself.

Indeed, in this narrative the actions and the choices of the victim him- or herself are key. They are *radical choices* in the terms of the Russian-English theorist Isaiah Berlin, because they defy principles, often necessitate striking a balance between two incommensurable and incompatible values, and can provide a complete overhaul of the situation of the victim (Berlin, 1997a; 1997b). These are choices and actions that are connected to the victim's own identity, his or her own imagination and interpretation of the situation. They cannot be (fully) understood in abstract, and rely on a full-blown, thick, first person understanding of the reality of victimisation experience. As we will clarify below, this bears similarity to the imaginative, open-ended, creative and context-dependent activity of playing (eg Schechner, 1988; Sutton-Smith, 2001; Graeber, 2015).

C. Revenge and Forgiveness

Perhaps this is most clearly evidenced by the experience and action of revenge. As Shklar explains:

> Even if legal justice must to some degree at least satisfy the vengeful urges of the injured and their friends, it cannot succeed consistently. Revenge is not detached, impersonal, proportionate or rule-bound. And it is because of its disorderly nature that as Bacon thought the law must weed it out'. (Shklar, 1990: 93)

The disorderly nature lies in the personal imagination and creative choices of the avenger in a given situation; in his or her actions attempting to undo the previous injustice, however futile this might turn out to be (French, 2001; Miller, 2006). That revenge is 'a dish best served cold' concerns the importance of surprise, of emergence, of unpredictability in revenge. Revenge fantasies sprout from the imagination of the avenger, while their narration entails a complete understanding of the circumstances of the victimising event, with descriptions of the victim and the victimiser.

An abstract, rule-bound revenge fantasy is hard to fathom. The repeated view that there *need be no generality in revenge* is often taken to mean that an avenger would act differently if the same circumstances repeated themselves (see famously Nozick, 1981; see also Zaibert, 2006). However, the only way to achieve the generality that the law requires lies in abstracting from the particular circumstances at hand: it is this abstraction that is already incompatible with revenge. There is no generality in revenge, due to revenge's nature as a fully context-dependent activity (on the importance of context-dependence, see Flyvbjerg, 2001).

Revenge can have radical implications for the relationship of between avenger and former victimiser (Pemberton, 2015). Upon success, the tables can be fully turned. Cycles of revenge are born in this possibility, and this is also the well from which much of the danger for social stability springs. The interest of society in quelling the desire for revenge is located here. The to and fro of vengeful actions imperils the order of society.

Revenge is normally seen as antithetical to restorative justice, which makes this perhaps a difficult subject in this volume, but similar remarks could be made about the experience of forgiveness. We find forgiveness—more so than recovery—to serve as a counterpoint to the experience of victimisation by injustice. It concerns releasing the negative feelings, eg anger, resentment, hatred and contempt (Richards, 1988) caused by the wrongfulness of victimisation (see also Arendt, 1958), while the erstwhile victimiser cannot make a claim to deserve this release, for instance that by making good whatever damage was done to the victim. Forgiveness acquires additional meaning in the situations where full recovery/ full repair is difficult to achieve or even impossible (Duff, 2003). In cases of homicide, but also in rape or even infidelity, any reparatory (or retributive) action cannot, in any real sense, undo what has happened. The victim of homicide cannot be returned to life, the rape victim cannot become un-raped, and the perpetrator of infidelity cannot retrospectively become faithful. The victim in these cases will always have a ground for resentment. The only manner in which the victimisation/ crime can be disconnected from the current state of affairs will need to include forgiveness.

The choice to forgive has similar radical implications for the situation of the victimiser and victim. The former is released from the debt to the victim, as the latter has wiped the slate clean (Allais, 2008). The latter changes his or perspective on what happened. Where victimisation maintains a link between the past event, and the present and future, forgiveness entails situating wrongdoing in the past. 'The past shall not be forgotten, but it will be the past' (Govier, 2012: 26; Walker 2006). In this sense, it serves as an endpoint to the narrative of victimisation, the only way in which the victimisation experience can resume to have purchase on the present, is by the wrongful deed being un-forgiven anew.

The importance of radical choice in the seemingly opposite experiences of revenge and forgiveness and their equally radical consequences for the experiences of victims and victimisers illustrates that these are general and even ontological features of the experience of injustice (Pemberton, 2015). These narratives unfold in an idiosyncratic and context-dependent fashion. Acts of will on the part of the victim can result in altering, transforming or fully overhauling the situation.

D. Asymmetry of Injustice and Justice

But they also contain much that it is not covered in the way we conceive of justice. As Shklar (1964; 1990) observes, theories and processes of justice emphasise countering arbitrariness and ensuring predictability. They are universal, impartial, impersonal and rational. Their focus is well-oiled social functioning in general, sometimes to the detriment of the requirements and necessities of the particular situation. Here justice is both wider and narrower than responding to injustice, as it looks only to what is relevant for their main social aim, not to all that matters about misfortune and injustice (see also Tessman, 2014).

Of course, these are important ends, but the issue here is that this also means that pursuing the ends of justice is not the same activity as undoing injustice. That crucial insight from Shklar's work counters most normal understanding of the relationship between justice and injustice: rather than opposing ends of the same dimension, they are two asymmetric dimensions. And although doing justice might often overlap with the business of undoing injustice, these ends might also conflict. Nowhere is this more explicit than in the business of international criminal justice: we are increasingly sceptical of the manner in which the 'international community' sees fit to spend billions of euros on trying a few offenders in the Hague, while those suffering from these atrocities languish without recourse to necessary help and support (Pemberton and Letschert, 2016). That is a choice motivated by justice, but is not experienced as such by anyone in close vicinity of these crimes. Justice may be done, but injustice remains, and might even be compounded by the failure of justice to engage with this lingering injustice.

The analysis of revenge also draws our attention to what came first. First was the experience of injustice, and attempts to undo injustice, and as a means to absorb some of this impetus, but also to counter the wild nature of revenge, systems of justice were developed. Here we return to considering the *playfulness* of revenge, and juxtapose this against the *game-like nature of law.* Although games and play are often used interchangeably David Graeber (2015: 159) showed that games have the following features:

> First they are clearly bounded in time and space, and thereby framed off from ordinary life. There is a field, a board, a starting pistol, a finish line. Within that time space, certain people are designated as players. There are also rules, which define precisely what those players can and cannot do. Finally there is always some clear idea of the stakes of what players have to do to win the game. And critically: that's all there is. Any place, person, action, that falls outside that framework is extraneous; it doesn't matter; it's not part of the frame.

Playing instead is an imaginative enterprise that fundamentally contains freedom and arbitrariness (see Pemberton, 2015). Where games have a clear beginning and end, and have clear boundaries to indicate what and who does and does not belong to it, in play all these things are ambiguous: play may seep into other activities, has porous borders, if any, and does not (have to) make explicit who is and who is not part of it. Where games are an attempt to confine, restrict or even rule out the possibilities for play, play can and often will generate new games. Systems of justice are games, drawing upon the purpose of the playful drive to undo injustice that preceded it initially, but qualitatively changing this experience, by setting rules, boundaries, goals, defining participants, and generally trying to contain the imagination and creativity of individuals confronted with the experience of injustice.

But playfulness as a creative, transformative, and sometimes destructive force cannot be fully contained. The imagination of play continuously challenges the rules imposed upon play by games, while each individual instance of playing can also give rise to new games. The radical experience of injustice therefore goes beyond the individual: it is personally radical in the choices people make to come to terms with their experience, but politically radical in the unique material it contains to question systems of justice. As Shklar explains:

> The normal model of justice continues to have severe difficulties in coming to terms with victims. It limits itself to matching their situation against rules, which is inadequate as a way of recognizing victims.

And:

> Victimhood has an irreducibly subjective component that the normal model of justice cannot easily absorb. If I am the victim of disappointed expectations, who is to say that I am or am not justified in holding them? (Shklar, 1990: 37)

Merely asserting that our rules, procedures, norms and modes of thinking can present answers to these questions is mistaken (Pemberton and Letschert, 2016). Mistaken first in that our values cannot avoid involving contradictions and conflicts in themselves, and secondly, in that it assumes a stability in perspective that does not, has not and cannot exist. Much necessary change in our institutions, and the acknowledgement of the inevitable limits of the capabilities of our social institutions is located in victimological experience. Change agents, both positive and negative, often derive the impetus for their actions, and the moral stance that justifies their position, from a core of victimisation (see also Gamson, 1992). That is as true for Mandela as it is for Milosevic. As Shklar found in any case:

> Those who believe themselves to be at the receiving end of social evils have a distinctive perspective and a detailed and thick view of social evils that political theories ignore at their peril.

III. JUDITH SHKLAR AND RESTORATIVE JUSTICE

Returning to the topic of this volume, restorative justice. We find four issues derived from the previous discussion to be pertinent and in need of further elaboration. First, there is the possibility of juxtaposing restoration and justice; secondly, the view of justice as a political choice, rather than a matter of reason; thirdly, the limits of the experience of injustice in achieving restoration; and finally, the importance of considering the radical qualities in the experience of injustice in the manner in which we understand restorative justice.

A. Restoration Versus Justice

To reiterate, Shklar reveals the experience of injustice to be prior to justice, and undoing injustice and doing justice to be two different dimensions. This is something that we believe has a good deal of connection to restorative justice thinking (see also Pemberton, 2016b). The focus of undoing injustice is the reality of the situation following crime: not adherence to some abstract, transcendental set of rules laid down in legislation. That is something that is endorsed in restorative justice as well. We might consider restoration to be similar to or focused on undoing injustice.

But if we do, so we should be alive to the extent to which Shklar's work shows that undoing injustice and doing justice can contradict each other. Like other words to which 'justice' is often attached (social justice, economic justice, political justice), the ease with which this association is made serves to mask this contradiction. Restoration and justice are in themselves both virtuous ends, but the reality of many cases is that they cannot be pursued together. Only in aspirational language do restoration and justice exist without getting in each other's way. But the focus of restorative justice thinking is not on aspiration in abstract, but steadfastly on the reality of harm, conflict and injustice in the experience of real-life conflicts. The marriage of restoration with justice then stands in the way of fully unlocking the transformational potential in restorative processes. Restorative processes come into their own when they are fully context dependent: the essence of justice always contains elements that run counter to this.

This is not only a theoretical point: it is a recurring feature of the development of restorative processes, that it is difficult to contain them in legal frameworks (Cleven, Lens and Pemberton, 2015). Each choice made at the level of the law, or provisions in international legal instruments as to the structure, position, requirements of restorative processes, ends up hampering practice in individual cases, in a way that runs counter to restorative purposes. The straightjacket of law is regularly a poor fit for the attempts to achieve restorative ends.

This is not to say we should not attempt to develop such frameworks. A core argument that Shklar made in *Legalism* is that the law, for all its shortcomings, is often the best we can do. But it does restrict the extent to which legal structures can accommodate restorative practices, while the reality of restorative practices will continuously offer a vantage point from which to criticise the definitions and choices made in the legal framework.

B. Justice as a Political Choice

This is connected to a second point. Justice is normally argued from rational and universal arguments. It appears to speak with a universal voice of reason (Bandes, 1996; Pemberton, 2016a). But work in the field of law and emotions (Bandes, 1996) and of storytelling in politics (Polletta, 2006) already shows that this narrative of universality and reason is a particular rhetorical device designed to disarm competing narratives, rather than a true reflection of fact. In similar vein, Shklar's analysis suggests that prioritising doing justice over undoing injustice is a choice, and a politically motivated choice at that. It privileges the interests of certain factions of and certain interests in society over others. The fact that it maintains the pretence of being above politics, of not being muddied by the machinations of political expediency, should not fool us. The choice to do justice as a means to counter injustice occurs under the *circumstances of* politics, and is always open to political criticism and debate (Waldron, 1999).

A prominent place from which to do so is victimological. The experience of injustice supplies the material to criticise, rethink and transform the processes and mechanisms by which we seek to do justice. It should act as a continuous reminder that our processes and institutions might be the result of our best efforts, but they are inherently limited and they are by no means infallible. Shklar's disguised radicalism calls upon us to be perpetually alive to the fact that the reality of our best laid plans for conceiving justice is that people bearing the brunt of life's most brutal features will often have good cause to consider them part of the problem, rather than part of the solution. In her *Liberalism of Fear* she makes this explicit (Shklar, 1998; see also Williams, 2005).

For all their flexibility, this applies to restorative processes no less than formal criminal procedures. Once restorative processes become too wedded to sets of abstract principles, the danger emerges that these principles will be used to overrule the reality of lived experience. Even where considerable empirical evidence underlies these notions, what works in theory or in general cannot and should not be submitted as a knock-down argument against their failure in a concrete case. Contexts and individual experiences of victimisation are too varied and the resulting desires, needs and pursuits too divergent. In addition, all too rigid structuring of RJ processes should be resisted. Some of our dearest colleagues might have an earnest belief that they are working towards 'real justice', but should be brought to understand that their extensive prescriptions bar the flexibility needed to deal with 'real injustice'.

C. Face of Injustice and Restoration

Starting from the reality of injustice not only offers the position to question whether justice is the best way of countering injustice, but also suggests the inherent limits of any social institution in achieving this aim. We are wont to quote Hannah Arendt's observation following the Second World War, that 'the enormity of evil' exploded the limits of the law, which can be generalised in two ways. It is not only the law that is limited, but all social institutions, and the limits of these institutions are reached at lower levels of evil than the enormity of the Holocaust (Pemberton and Letschert, 2016).

Facing up to the reality of injustice entails acknowledging that there is often not much others and/ or victims themselves can do to counter the harm, suffering and injustice they were forced to experience.

It is in part a reflection of the psychological law that 'bad is stronger than good' (Baumeister *et al*, 2001). One bad experience can have an impact that years of good experiences before and after this event fail to achieve. Losing a loved one to murder or the experience of violation of rape can unravel a lifetime of beneficial and wholesome experiences (eg Brison, 2002). In turn the extent to which our reaction to injustice amounts to restoration in any real sense of the word is always open to question. Often any expectation that this is possible is already tantamount to wishful thinking, and our aspirations that restoration can be achieved might stand in the way of our admission that it cannot.

Some of the most important victimological issues arise at this juncture. Undoing injustice and doing justice can be relatively easily reconciled when we can within reason foresee what would be involved in doing the former. A stolen bike can be replaced, an apology can repair trust when the harm was not intended, and community service is suitable for the juvenile vandal. Beyond this, offering general prescriptions is a decidedly hazardous affair. What might help one co-victim of homicide is tantamount to adding insult to injury for another. Whether others can attempt to do anything beyond steering clear of making a bad situation worse often remains to be seen. And the extent to which justice processes contribute to reducing injustice or add another layer of injustice to victim experience is similarly unpredictable. Perhaps the most general statement that can be made at this point is that our attempts to undo injustice are best undertaken without the expectation of large miraculous improvement breathing down their neck (eg Pemberton, 2015; 2016a). Uncovering what can and should nevertheless be done in these situations, even with the acknowledgement that any effort is likely to fail, is what victimologists should take as their Prime Directive.

D. Radical Victimology

Shklar's deep insights into injustice finally have important implications for the manner in which academic research into victims' experiences should be pursued (Pemberton, 2015; Green and Pemberton, 2017). Victimology should embrace fully the importance of the particular, the idiosyncratic, the context-dependent, the narrative, the moral and the historical if it is to be relevant to victim experience. Nobody is raped, beaten, oppressed or murdered in abstract: the essence of experiencing this first-hand lies in the impossibility of escaping into abstraction. Any attempt at abstracting, or at generalisation in victimology needs to proceed under the awareness that abstraction and generalisation can run counter to the reality of victimisation. The victimological subject will often not allow universalisation and will defy general laws, and the victimologist needs to fully understand the perspective (s)he draws from ethics and philosophy.

This is where the radical nature of the victimology that can be drawn from Judith Shklar's work comes fully into its own. It not only presents a challenge to our current institutions trying to counter injustice, our normative frameworks underlying them, but to the very way in which we understand our subject. It is part of the project that one of us called 'Victimology with a Hammer', that is located in an earnest attempt to peer into the abyss of suffering, and see where this will lead us, without hiding behind abstraction and unwarranted aspiration: to harness our pain so it turns toward life, rather than away from it.

This radical victimology necessitates a more humble stance of academia. Rather than pretending to know more than the 'subjects' of study, victimology should aim to know better what their individual experience actually entails. Rather than seeking to distance itself from the reality of victims' lived experience in an attempt to create abstract, general and even paradigmatic knowledge, victimology should be fully immersed in it. Rather than imposing methodological standards that seek academic rigour in their allusion to objectivity, victimology should fully recognise the futility and impossibility of value-freedom in its research domain and acknowledge the normative frameworks with which this comes equipped.

Restorative processes offer the promise of opening up exactly the type of space needed to explore the new vistas of this radical victimology. To capitalise on this potential they should, however, steer clear of the pretensions of an all too epistemological social science (eg Flyvbjerg, 2001). Restorative processes are co- or even self-produced by their participants, which makes each individual mediation or conference a unique experience, and this idiosyncrasy is strengthened by the 'double hermeneutic' (Giddens, 1984) of victims' (and offenders') interpretation of this process, and a researcher's subsequent understanding of what this interpretation entails.

IV. FINAL REMARKS

It is clear from this chapter that we think the work of Judith Shklar, our radical in disguise, can greatly contribute to our understanding of the experience of victims in justice processes. Her key point of the asymmetry of undoing injustice and doing justice reveals that the distance between victim experience (located in the former) and criminal law (the latter) cannot be fully overcome. Justice might be rooted in the desire to undo injustice, but also attempts to contain this desire, while introducing values that can lead doing justice and undoing injustice to be at odds with each other.

This is not an argument against justice per se, but it does introduce the material to critically scrutinise our justice processes on the basis of the individual lived victimological experience. Moreover, if we consider restoration to be focused on undoing injustice, Shklar's work questions the wisdom of unreflectively associating it with the concept of justice, as is the case in the phrase 'restorative justice'. Indeed, the criticism that her work levels against the formal criminal justice procedure can also be applied to any practice that would prioritise rule-bound, abstract principles over lived experience. To be clear, this criticism is not that such law-like approaches should be abandoned outright, but that we should own up to their limitations and their existence as a function of (political) choice, rather than of (universal) reason.

This means that Shklar can provide further ammunition in favour of restorative practices, but also serves as a word of caution for their development. Restorative practices are not immune to the adoption of the type of principles that can create rather than counter injustice in concrete cases. The marriage of restoration and justice can serve to hide that achieving the latter does not mean that the former has been accomplished. Moreover, if restorative practices, as we think they should, focus on the concrete case over the abstract rule, they should steer clear of the type of aspirational thinking, language and goals that can only be achieved within such abstractions. Realistic efforts to counter the messy, complex and sometimes outright dire personal experience of victimisation might pale in comparison to these lofty aspirations. But the veneer of the latter wears thin quickly, and the only manner to preserve them entails averting our gaze from victimological reality.

The past 40 years have, then, taken victims from being forgotten to being misunderstood. Hopefully our radical victimology can contribute to correcting this assessment in the next 40 years. Unlocking the potential of restorative practices is a main vessel to this end.

REFERENCES

Allen, J (2001) 'The Place of Negative Morality in Political Theory' 29(3) *Political Theory* 337.

Allais, L (2008) 'Wiping the Slate Clean: The Heart of Forgiveness' 36(1) *Philosophy and Public Affairs* 33.

Arendt, H (1958) *The Human Condition* Chicago, IL, University of Chicago Press).

Bandes, SA (1996) 'Empathy, Narrative, and Victim Impact Statements' 63 *University of Chicago Law Review* 361.

Baumeister, RF, Bratslavsky, E, Finkenauer, C and Vohs, KD (2001) 'Bad is Stronger Than Good' 5 *Review of General Psychology* 323.

Berlin, I (1997a) 'The Concept of Scientific History' in H Hardy and R Hausheer (eds), *The Proper Study of Mankind: An Anthology of Essays* (London, Vintage).

—— (1997b) 'The Pursuit of the Ideal' in H Hardy and R Hausheer (eds), *The Proper Study of Mankind: An Anthology of Essays* (London, Vintage).
Biffi, E *et al* (2016) *Implementing Victim Oriented Reform in Europe*, IVOR Report (Lisbon, APAV).
Brison, SJ (2002) *Aftermath: Violence and the Remaking of Self* (Princeton, NJ, Princeton University Press).
Christie, N (1977) 'Conflicts as Property' 17 *British Journal of Criminology* 1.
Cleven, I, Lens, KME and Pemberton, A (2015) *De rol van herstelbemiddeling in het strafrecht* (Tilburg, Prismaprint).
Crossley, ML (2000) 'Narrative Psychology, Trauma and the Study of Self/Identity' 10(4) *Theory and Psychology* 527–546.
Daly, K and Bonhours, B (2010) 'Rape and Attrition in the Legal Process: A Comparative Analysis of Five Countries' 39 *Criminal Justice, A Review of Research* 565.
Duff, RA (2003) 'Restoration and Retribution' in: A Von Hirsch *et al* (eds), *Restorative and Criminal Justice: Competing or Reconcilable Paradigms* (Oxford, Hart Publishing) 43–60.
Flyvbjerg, B (2001) *Making Social Science Matter: Why Social Inquiry Fails and How It Can Succeed Again* (Cambridge, Cambridge University Press).
French, P (2001) *The Virtues of Vengeance* (Lawrence, KS, University of Kansas Press).
Gamson, W (1992) *Talking Politics* (Cambridge, Cambridge University Press).
Giddens, A (1984) *The Constitution of Society* (Berkeley, CA, University of California Press).
Govier, T (2012) 'Public Forgiveness: A Modest Defense' in B Van Stokkom, N Doorn and P Van Tongeren (eds), *Public Forgiveness in Post-Conflict Contexts* (Antwerp, Intersentia) 25–36.
Graeber, D (2015) *The Utopia of Rules: On Technology, Stupidity and the Secret Joys of Bureaucracy* (London/New York, Melville House).
Green, S and Pemberton, A (2017) 'The Impact of Crime: Victimisation, Harm and Resilience' in S Walklate (ed), *Handbook of Victims and Victimology*, 2nd edn (Oxford, Routledge).
Groenhuijsen, MS (2014) 'The Development of International Policy in Relation to Victims of Crime' 20(1) *International Review of Victimology* 31-.
Hammack, PL and Pilecki, A (2012) 'Narrative as a Root Metaphor from Political Psychology' 33(1) *Political Psychology* 75.
Hulsman, LHC (1986) 'Critical Criminology and the Concept of Crime' 10(1) Crime, Law and Social Change 63.
Janoff-Bulman, R (1992) *Shattered Assumptions: Towards a New Psychology of Trauma* (New York, Free Press).
Kunst, M, Popelier, L and Varekamp, E (2014) 'Victim Satisfaction with the Criminal Justice System and Emotional Recovery: A Systematic and Critical Review of the Literature' 16(3) *Trauma, Violence and Abuse* 336.
Laxminarayan, M, Bosmans, M, Porter, R and Sosa, L (2013) 'Victim Satisfaction with Criminal Justice: A Systematic Review' 8 *Victims and Offenders* 119.
McAdams, DP (1993) *The Stories We Live By: Personal Myths and the Making of the Self* (New York, Guilford Press).

—— (2013) 'The Psychological Self as Actor, Agent, and Author' 8(3) *Perspectives on Psychological Science* 272-.
Mill, JS (1871) *Utilitarianism* (London, Longmans).
Miller, W (2006) *An Eye for an Eye* (Cambridge, Cambridge University Press).
Nozick, R (1981) *Philosophical Explanations* (Cambridge, MA, Harvard University Press).
Pemberton, A (2014) 'Respecting Victims of Crime: Key Distinctions in a Theory of Victim's Rights' in I Vanfraechem, A Pemberton, and FN Ndahinda (eds), *Justice for Victims: Perspectives on Rights, Transition and Reconciliation* (Oxford, Routledge).
—— (2015) *Victimology with a Hammer: The Challenge of Victimology*, Inaugural Lecture Tilburg University (Tilburg, Prismaprint).
—— (2016a) 'Empathy for Victims in Criminal Justice: Revisiting Susan Bandes in Victimology' in H Conway and J Stannard (eds), *Emotional Dynamics of Law and Legal Discourse* (Oxford, Hart Publishing).
—— (2016b) 'Dangerous Victimology: My Lessons Learned from Nils Christie' 19(2) *Temida, Serbian Journal of Victimology* 257.
Pemberton, A, Aarten, PGM and Mulder, E (2017) 'Beyond Restoration, Retribution and Retributive Justice: The Big Two in Victims' Perspectives on Justice' *Psychology, Crime and Law*, available at http://dx.doi.org/10.1080/1068316X.2017.1298760.
—— (forthcoming) *Narrative Psychology and Victimology: Towards a Narrative Victimology* (Manuscript under review).
Pemberton, A and Groenhuijsen, MS (2012) 'Developing Victims' Rights Within the European Union: Past, Present, Future' in H Morosawa, J Dussich and G Kirchhoff (eds), *Victimology and Human Security: New Horizons* (Nijmegen, Wolf Legal Publishers) 535–59.
Pemberton, A and Letschert, RM (2016) 'Justice as the Art of Muddling Through: The Importance of *Nyaya* in the Aftermath of International Crimes' in C Brants and S Karstedt (eds), *Engagement, Legitimacy, Contestation: Transitional Justice and its Public Spheres* (Oxford, Hart Publishing).
Polletta, F (2006) *It was Like a Fever: Storytelling in Protest and Politics* (Chicago, IL, University of Chicago Press).
Richards, N (1988) 'Forgiveness' 99(1) *Ethics* 77.
Schechner, R (1988) 'Playing' 1(1) *Play and Culture* 3.
Shklar, J (1964) *Legalism: Law, Morals and Political Trials* (Cambridge, MA, Harvard University Press, 2nd edn 1986).
—— (1990) *The Faces of Injustice* (New Haven, CT, Yale University Press).
—— (1998) 'The Liberalism of Fear' in J Shklar, *Political Thinkers and Political Thought* (Chicago, IL, University of Chicago Press).
Sutton-Smith, B (2001) *The Ambiguity of Play* (Cambridge, MA, Harvard University Press).
Tessman, L (2014) *Moral Failure* (Oxford, Oxford University Press).
Waldron, J (1999) *Law and Disagreement* (Oxford, Oxford University Press).
Walker, MU (2006) *Moral Repair: Reconstructing Moral Relations After Wrongdoing* (Cambridge, Cambridge University Press).

Williams, B (2005) 'In the Beginning There was the Deed' in B Williams, *In the Beginning There was the Deed: Realism and Moralism in Political Argument* (Princeton, NJ, Princeton University Press).
Williams, JE (1984) 'Secondary Victimization: Confronting Public Attitudes About Rape' 9 *Victimology* 66.
Zaibert, L (2006) 'Punishment and Revenge' 25 *Law and Philosophy* 81.
Zehr, H (1990) *Changing Lenses: A New Focus for Crime and Justice* Harrisonburg, VA, Herald Press).

Index